CREATING WOMEN: AN INTERDISCIPLINARY ANTHOLOGY OF READINGS ON WOMEN IN WESTERN CULTURE

VOLUME TWO
RENAISSANCE TO THE PRESENT

Edited by Jean Gould Bryant
Florida State University

Linda Bennett Elder
Valdosta State University

PEARSON

Prentice
Hall

Upper Saddle River, NJ 07458

Library of Congress Cataloging-in-Publication Data

Creating women : an anthology of readings on women in Western culture /
[edited by] Jean Gould Bryant, Linda Bennett Elder.-- 1st ed.
    p. cm.
  Includes bibliographical references and index.
   ISBN 0-13-759622-7 (v. 1) -- ISBN 0-13-759630-8 (v. 2)
   1. Women--History.   2. Women--History--Sources.   I. Bryant, Jean Gould.
II. Elder, Linda Bennett.

HQ1121.C67 2005
3054'09--dc22   2003056544

VP, Editorial Director: Charlyce Jones Owen
Executive Editor: Charles Cavaliere
Associate Editor: Emsal Hasan
Editorial Assistant: Shannon Corliss
Executive Marketing Manager: Heather Shelstaad
Senior Marketing Assistant: Jennifer Bryant
Managing Editor: Joanne Riker
Production Editor: Jan H. Schwartz
Permissions Supervisor: Ron Fox

Permissions Researcher: Melinda Alexander
Manufacturing Buyer: Tricia Kenny
Cover Design: Bruce Kenselaar
Photo Researcher: Julie Tesser
Manager, Print Production: Michelle Gardner
Composition: PineTree Composition, Inc.
Printer/Binder: R.R. Donnelley
Cover Printer: Phoenix Color Corporation

Credits and acknowledgments borrowed from other sources and reproduced, with permission, in this textbook appear on appropriate page within text.

Pearson Education LTD.
Pearson Education Singapore, Pte. Ltd
Pearson Education, Canada, Ltd
Pearson Education–Japan
Pearson Education Australia PTY, Limited
Pearson Education North Asia Ltd
Pearson Education de Mexico, S.A. de C.V.
Pearson Education Malaysia, Pte. Ltd

10 9 8 7 6 5 4 3 2 1
0-13-759630-8

We dedicate this book to our husbands Jerry and Bob,
our children Steven, John, Martha, and Peter,
and to the creative women—past, present, and future—
who enrich our world.

Contents

Preface

Our goal in writing this two-volume work is to provide students and instructors with a more comprehensive understanding a part of the history of humankind than has previously been available to the non-specialist. As the title suggests, these volumes document the significant part women have played in the development of Western civilization, from the Upper Paleolithic era (we begin ca. 35,000 B.C.E.) to the present. We have brought together a varied collection of primary source materials including archeological artifacts, images, and texts that reveal women's participation in all aspects of human culture, religion, the visual and performing arts, literature, philosophy, and public affairs.

We deliberately chose our title, *Creating Women,* because, in addition to its obvious reference to *creative* women, it reflects another important dimension of Western civilization: The ways in which societal notions of gender (masculine/feminine) and gender roles have in essence "created" and/or "constructed" women. A significant consequence of this social construction is that women's experiences and opportunities have often differed in significant ways from those of men. Together, the documents tell much about Western notions of sex differences and how and why "the woman question" continues to be among the most persistent controversies in Western thought and discourse.

Creating Women, like many other new texts, evolved from the need for reading materials for a new course. In 1985, a team of Florida State University faculty and graduate students from history, dance, theater, music, English, classics, religion, humanities, and art history received a university grant to develop an introductory course for women's studies that would also fulfill part of the university's liberal studies requirements. Jean Gould Bryant, director of the women's studies program, led that project and Linda Bennett Elder was a member of the development team from its inception.

The decision to develop an interdisciplinary humanities course was prompted by several considerations. We wanted a course to complement an existing humanities sequence that introduced students to the traditional canon of cultural developments of Western civilization but made few references to women's contributions. We also sought to fill curriculum gaps in classics, music, art history, theater, and European history and to provide a catalyst for the creation of courses on women and gender across the arts and sciences. We hoped as well to create incentives for faculty to include information related to women's accomplishments and experiences within existing courses. The course, Women in Western Culture: Images and Realities, was a vital addition to our women's studies curriculum that had previously focused almost exclusively on the Western world since the seventeenth century, with heavy emphasis on contemporary American society.

In 1986, as now, there were a few discipline-specific texts and anthologies of secondary articles and primary source readings, but no interdisciplinary text or anthology concerning women existed and no anthology spanned the entire history of Western civilization. As we proceeded to refine Women in Western Culture, we recognized not only the need for an interdisciplinary reader, but also a unique situation for developing such a text. Since 1986, we have used a variety of readings, audio-visual resources, and lecture material in our respective courses on women in Western humanities. We have also explored different configurations of chronology and course themes suggested by the critiques, questions and responses of our students, and our mutual assessments. We discovered, for example, that although many contemporary feminist scholars ignore religion, religion is one of the most prevalent markers of women's participation in culture from prehistory through the medieval period, and it remained a critical factor through the nineteenth century. Over time we integrated the discrete multidisciplinary pieces of our examination of women into a coherent truly interdisciplinary course that highlighted major themes and patterns that emerged across disciplines and centuries.

The results have been exciting for us and for our students. We discovered that examining women's cultural achievements and struggles provides an innovative framework for discussing women's legal, socioeconomic, religious, and/or political status in different times and places. We found that the multidisciplinary approach ensures that each student will discover some individuals whose life/work matches her or his personal interests or career aspirations and may indeed discover new role models or cultural icons for inspiration. We also learned that bringing women and their voices to the forefront sometimes radically changed our understanding of certain periods of Western civilization and often introduced provocative new cultural forms, alternative visions of society and its institutions, and challenging critiques of values, ideas, and societal arrangements that many have regarded as "fixed" Western cultural traditions.

Creating Women is the product of an extended period of living with the material, adding to it and reconfiguring it in response to input from our students and colleagues. Both volumes integrate insights from an abundance of new scholarship that has enriched women's history in all fields over the last three decades. We believe that the interdisciplinary approach we have taken in these volumes and the expansive time-span that we have elected to cover will generate spirited discussion. Our approach will also add significantly to the reader's understanding of women and gender in Western civilization, thereby providing a more complete and realistic picture of the history of humankind.

CREATING WOMEN: STRUCTURE

Each volume consists of three parts with five chapters in each.

Volume one encompasses women and culture from prehistory through the middle ages:

Part I: **Women in Prehistory and the Ancient Near East**

Part II: **Women in the Mediterranean and Greco-Roman World**

Part III: **Women in the Roman Empire, Early Christianity, Late Antiquity, and the Middle Ages**

Volume Two encompasses women and culture from the Renaissance to the present:

Part I: **Women in Early Modern Europe**

Part II: **Women and Culture, 1750–1920**

Part III: **Women and Culture in the Twentieth Century**

CREATING WOMEN: FEATURES

- The narrative, biographical vignettes, and document introductions place women and their achievements within the broader social-political context in which they lived and worked.

- Introductory narrative helps guide students' analysis of material and facilitates class discussion.

- Maps, charts, and narrative link women and their achievements with more familiar events and personages in Western civilization and also illustrate significant clusters of female creativity.

- Selected bibliographies facilitate student projects and enable instructors to enrich classes with audiovisual material.

ACKNOWLEDGMENTS

A work of this scope and magnitude is never a solitary effort and we are deeply indebted to the many individuals and institutions that made these two volumes possible. A 1985 grant from Florida State University underwrote the initial research for the interdisciplinary humanities course that was the genesis of these two volumes. The team of faculty and graduate students that developed the course, including, among others, Ellen Burns, Cynthia Hahn, and Catherine Schuler, introduced us to many of the women who appear in the pages that follow. In recent years, team members Nancy De Grummond, Tricia Young, and Karen Laughlin provided sage advice as we were selecting documents and writing these volumes. Our students have also shaped our work. Their questions, perceptive observations, and excitement when introduced to many of the women and documents that appear in these pages influenced our selections and introductory material. Lisa Beverly, Leah Cassorla, Cameron Cooper, Douglas and Berkay Grove, Tina Ports, Jan Richardson, and Maggie Willman provided invaluable assistance with the time-consuming mechanical details involved in tracking down documents, transcribing interviews and micro-materials, and obtaining permissions.

Creating Women would not have been possible without the scholarship of the women and men who recovered the works and lives of many who appear in the pages that follow and who placed women's history on a solid foundation. We are particularly grateful to those scholars who granted permission to include excerpts of their work in these volumes and who encouraged us, made suggestions, and shared our excitement about bringing the works of women who they had restored to history to a wider audience. Numerous archivists and publishers helped us locate elusive documents and obtain permissions. We are also indebted to the women who gave generously of their time to grant us interviews.

This book would not have been possible without the support of the History editors at Prentice Hall who believed in this project when we submitted our initial proposal and assisted us in its early stages: Sally Constable, Charlyce Jones Owen, and Todd Armstrong. During the arduous process of bringing these volumes to print, we have been blessed with the support and guidance of Charles Cavaliere, Executive Editor for History; Emsal Hasan, Associate Editor for History; Joanne Riker, Managing Editor for Production; Mirella Signoretto, Artist; Martha Williams, Copyeditor; Sharon Gonzales, Proofreader; and above all, our Production Editor, Jan Schwartz. The final product owes much to their patience and editorial assistance.

Finally, we thank our friends, colleagues, and relatives whose support and interest in this project sustained us through many years as we struggled to bring it to fruition. We are eternally grateful to Karen Laughlin, Dean of Undergraduate Studies at Florida State University, who interrupted an incredibly full schedule to give the entire manuscript a perceptive critique that helped us refine the book. Special thanks are due Gerald Bryant and Valerie Jean Conner who helped proof the final copy.

Introduction

As half of the human race, women have always been "making" history, yet their part in building Western civilization has been largely invisible. Until very recently, in fact, school and college courses and texts in the humanities, social and natural sciences, and the arts rarely mentioned women. Generations of students studied the activities, achievements, and ideas of men without realizing that the story was incomplete.

Why were women missing from our books and curriculum? And was their absence important? In the mid-1960s and early 1970s when some students and scholars began to question the invisibility of women, they met with widespread surprise that the question had even been raised. Women, the explanation went, were missing because they had not shaped major historical events and they had contributed little of significance to culture. Their lives revolved around the details of domestic routines and family concerns, whereas men dealt with matters of public import. There were, certainly, some exceptions, but those women were so rare and so exceptional that their visibility simply underscored the general rule.

To many of the scholars who began their professional careers in the 1970s, such explanations seemed highly suspect. This new generation included many women who owed their careers to the women's movement which had forced the removal of barriers that had long restricted women's access to graduate programs, academic positions, and male-dominated professions in Europe and North America. (In North America, it also included minorities who had benefited from the expanding Civil Rights movement.) These female scholars suspected that the real reason women were missing related to perspectives and assumptions of the male scholars who wrote and taught history. They also knew that women's (and minorities') historical invisibility had provided a rationale for their exclusion from an entire range of leadership positions, professions, and creative endeavors. The absence of a "female" Beethoven, Leonardo da Vinci, Shakespeare, Aristotle, or Einstein, for example was often cited as proof that women were incapable of producing great works.

WHAT IS HISTORY?

Not surprisingly, many challenged the traditional claims of scholarly objectivity and joined others in questioning the idea that written history was an accurate, complete record of events. History is not some abstract "Truth"; rather it is only what is recorded, interpreted, written, and disseminated as "history." It is the product of persons who have the education and resources to "write" history. It reflects their judgments regarding what and who is important, and the concerns of society as they experience it. History also reflects the interests of those who support its writing and dissemination. Until very recently, the "written history" of Western civilization has been almost exclusively *androcentric* or male-centered and *ethnocentric*. That is, it has been written and supported by men of the privileged class and has reflected their experiences and values.

REDISCOVERING AND RECREATING WOMEN'S HISTORY

Knowing this, the new scholars concluded that women's history needed to be told. Like their male colleagues and predecessors, these academic women drew on their life experiences and personal interests as well as the concerns and values of their generation and culture as they selected topics of inquiry and framed the questions that guided their research and teaching.

Scholars dedicated to research on women's history found evidence of talented women who were highly respected during their lifetimes. Proof of women's cultural contributions consisted of art, music, and literary works by women and a wide variety of artifacts discovered or re-analyzed by historians, archeologists, and anthropologists. Evidence was also abundant in records of male contemporaries who corresponded with women or wrote about them and their work. Early "histories," in fact, turned out to be important sources of information about women's activities, as did well-known texts by men whose works comprised the canon of Western civilization. As more scholars joined the search and documents became more widely accessible (in translations, microform, and databases for manuscript collections), it became evident that the "exceptional" women in Western culture were not such anomalies after all.

PATTERNS AND THEMES IN WOMEN'S HISTORY

The evidence gathered in the last three and a half decades has revealed some intriguing patterns. Clusters of creative women or women who fostered cultural developments, for example, turned up in unexpected places. Some time periods, geographical locations, and/or societies known for significant male achievements seemed to produce few women of note. In contrast, evidence of significant female creativity and leadership often appeared in times and geographical places not commonly thought of as culturally vibrant.

References to prominent women often disappeared from the historical record and their works vanished. Sometimes a once-famous woman was forgotten, then rediscovered as much as a century or more later, only to disappear from history again until her more recent "recovery" in the late twentieth century. Occasionally, when a woman's work was rediscovered, it was attributed to a male contemporary while she remained invisible. Experts sometimes pronounced work signed by a woman as a plagiarism or a fraud perpetrated by the discoverer. Typically, however, creative women were omitted from the historical record on the grounds that their works were inferior to the works of men or failed to address topics of "universal" concern.

We also find that, despite their virtual absence from the historical record as creators and artists, women were quite visible as subjects or objects of male attention through much of Western history. Women appear in the dramas, literature, art, songs, legal codes, and religious and philosophical treatises written by men far more frequently than they appear in person as performers or creators of these cultural artifacts. In many documents, men seem preoccupied with a need to define the differences between men and women. They focus on women's physical attributes, mental and moral limitations, and their societal roles. Indeed, the "woman question" has been a persistent theme in male discourse throughout Western history.

Finally, although men and women shared much in common, it is evident that their life experiences, perspectives, and creative contributions often differed, sometimes dramatically. Women's creative endeavors frequently addressed different topics, gave a different slant to a popular theme, used a different language style, or exhibited a different vision of the world. Women often pursued their creative work and exercised leadership within a very different context than men. Women also relied upon different support systems and created separate institutions and networks. Even as they perpetuated and supported existing societal values and structures, women often voiced discontent and disagreement with prevailing standards. In both direct and indirect ways, they challenged male depictions of women and restrictions on women's lives and opportunities. Through their work, many also sought to discover and tell their own history.

GENDER AS A PRIMARY COMPONENT OF SOCIAL ORGANIZATION

The patterns summarized in the preceding section reveal the centrality of a more fundamental pattern in Western civilization: the role of gender as a major element of social organization and determinant of human experience. One of the major contributions of the new scholarship of the last 30 or more years has been to advance our understanding of the complex ways in which gender (intersecting with social class, ethnicity, race, and religion) shapes human experiences and serves as a central organizing principle in human culture.

Gender is a social construct. It is how a particular group or culture defines the roles of males and females based on their biological sex. Gender roles vary from culture to culture and also vary over time within cultures. Particular circumstances and societal needs may bring temporary changes in how gender is constructed, as when women fill male jobs during wartime. The rigidity of gender roles and definitions of gender may also fluctuate from time to time. Wrenching societal changes often produce pressure for rigid adherence to prescribed gender roles, whereas prosperity and security permit more flexible roles.

The social construction of gender roles and ideology does not necessarily mandate a particular gender structure. Some societies or organizations construct a complementary system of gender where, though the duties of men and women might differ, all are regarded as of equal importance. Others, in contrast, construct a hierarchical social order in which one sex is deemed innately inferior to the other and the roles and activities of the dominant sex are naturally believed to be more important. Gender-based power relationships may also undergo periodic changes within a given society.

In *Creating Women,* as the title suggests, we examine women's contributions to Western civilization from prehistory to the present through primary sources. Focusing primarily on the cultural aspects of Western civilization, the anthology documents the roles and achievements of women in religion, art, music, drama, dance, discourse, and literature and their impact on Western cultural traditions as patrons and leaders. Equally important, we also examine the ways in which Western societies "created" or shaped women by their definitions of womanhood and prescribed gender roles.

In selecting the documents for the anthology, we have sought to include a broad sampling of the rich evidence that demonstrates women's varied and significant contributions to culture. We have also included selections that illustrate the complex relationships between men and women that affected female creativity: their friendships, partnerships, and collaborations; familial ties; and rivalries and conflicts. In addition, we have included some of the works by men that were instrumental in creating and perpetuating images of women and gender ideology that inhibited female creativity and women's full participation in society throughout much of Western civilization. Above all, we have selected documents that bring women's voices to life. Through the documents we learn about female experiences, what women thought about their work, their creative processes, their dreams, self doubts, and frustrations. We learn how they negotiated their multiple social roles, as well as their class, race, ethnic, religious, and gender identities, and how they defined and created their own institutions and support systems. We also learn how women themselves often helped perpetuate traditional notions of gender. Finally, we learn much about women's resistance, as we see how some women challenged societal barriers and developed a feminist critique of Western patriarchal values and a vision of a new and more inclusive society.

We hope that you will share the excitement we felt as we discovered the fascinating women who appear in the pages that follow – that you, too, will be moved by their lives, their struggles, and their work, and be inspired by their courage and achievements to follow your own dreams, however impossible they might seem to be. It is our dream that you, in turn, will tell others about these women and strive, as so many of them did, to ensure that the work of our foremothers is passed on to the generations to come. Perhaps you will rediscover others yet unheralded and restore them to their rightful place in human history!

VOLUME TWO

Volume Two is divided into three parts and covers a chronological time frame that extends from ca. 1450 C.E. to the present. Each of the three parts in Volume Two and each chapter is preceded by an introduction to place its reading selections in historical and cultural context. Chapters and reading selections are organized thematically, within a broad chronological framework.

In this time period, we find a veritable explosion of creative work by women in all fields of culture. We have more cultural artifacts—compositions, art work, literary texts—by women and more personal documents by and about women, such as correspondence, interviews, and media reports. As a result, in preparing this volume, we were faced with the pleasant but extremely difficult task of having to select a representative sample from a huge array of rich sources by women. We were blessed, however, with an abundance of biographical and autobiographical information on many that sheds more light on the factors that facilitated and hindered female creativity, and tells much about the aspirations, social views, and philosophy of individual women. Documents in this volume, particularly in Part II, "Women and Culture, 1750–1920," and Part III, "Women and Culture in the Twentieth Century," are also drawn from a broad cross section of women that reflects the increased educational and occupational options available to women of all classes and ethnic/racial groups. The documents also reflect the continuing expansion of print media. Finally, the geographical scope of Volume Two, particularly in Parts II and III, extends beyond Western Europe. Here, however, (unlike Volume One which focused heavily on the Mediterranean Basin) it extends westward, reflecting on the gradual emergence of the United States as a vibrant cultural center within the Atlantic community.

In preparing our introductions and selecting the women and documents for inclusion, we have aimed to provide a broad sampling of the rich variety of creative work by women of all classes and regions and to illustrate the variety of perspectives and viewpoints women brought to their work. We have also chosen documents that bring the women alive, that convey their personalities, their "philosophies" of art and life, and their varied personal and professional relationships. Many of the selections shed light both on the ways gender, as well as class, race, and ethnicity, shaped their lives and work and on their various strategies for dealing with these dynamics.

Part I, "Women in Early Modern Europe," encompasses the time frame from ca. 1450 to ca. 1750. The five chapters in Part I examine women's experiences and cultural participation during the Renaissance, the Reformation and Counter Reformation, and the Baroque Era.

Part II covers the period from the mid-eighteenth century to 1920. Its first chapter, Chapter 6, "Age of the Enlightenment and Revolutions," focuses on female creativity in the context of the Enlightenment and the political revolutions of the late eighteenth century. Chapters 7 through 10, "The Victorian Ideal: Writers and Musicians," "The Victorian Ideal: The Performing and Visual Arts," "Challenging

Orthodoxy: Women and Religion in America," and "The 'New Woman' and the Performing Arts," concentrate on women's cultural contributions between 1800 and 1920.

Part III covers women and culture in the twentieth century. The first two chapters include documents drawn chiefly from the first half of the century. The final three chapters focus on themes and patterns of female creativity since the 1970s.

WOMEN IN EARLY MODERN EUROPE

CULTURAL MARKERS	DATE	PEOPLE/EVENTS	CONTRIBUTION
Italian High Renaissance	1488	Laura Cereta (Brescia, It.)	Humanist
	1490	Antonia Pulci (Florence, It.)	1st woman to publish a play
Northern Renaissance	1490-1539	**Isabella d'Este (Mantua, It.)**	Patron and ruler
Reformation begins	1517	Martin Luther (Germany)	*95 Theses*
	1523	Argula von Grumbach (Germany)	*Letter to Frederick the Wise*
	1525	Katherine von Bora (Germany)	marries Luther; Protestant
	1528	Baldesare Castiglione (Italy)	*Book of the Courtier*
	1531-1534	Maria Cazalla (Spain)	Inquisition examinations
	1534	Henry VIII (Tudor) (England)	Heads Church of England
	1536	John Calvin (Switzerland)	*Institutes of Christian Religion*
	1538	Vittoria Colonna (Italy)	1st volume of poetry published
	1540s	Gaspara Stampa (Venice)	Poet and musician
Council of Trent	1555	Louise Labé (Lyon, France)	Poems: *Debate of Folly and Love*
English *Querelle des femmes*	1550s	Katharina Schutz Zell (Strasbourg)	Protestant lay reformer
	1553-1558	**Mary I**	**Rules England**
	1558	Elizabeth Young (England)	Inquisition examinations
	1556-1596	**Philip II**	**Rules Spain**
	1558-1603	**Elizabeth I**	**Rules England**
	1559	Elizabeth I	Religious Settlement
		Marguerite of Navarre (Navarre)	*Heptameron*
	1559-1579	Sofonisba Anguissola (Italy)	Artist at court of Philip II, Spain
	1560s	Jeanne d'Albret (Navarre)	Defender of Huguenots
Counter Reformation	1563-1580	Teresa of Avila (Spain)	Founds 17 convents across Spain
	1570s	Veronica Franco (Venice, Italy)	Poet and courtesan
	1576	Isabella Andreini (Italy)	*Commedia dell'arte* acting debut
	1580s	*Concerto delle donne* (No. Italy)	Women's vocal ensemble
	1589	Jane Anger (England)	*Protection for Women*
	1594	Sara Lopez (England)	*Petition to Elizabeth I*
	1603-1629	**James I (Stuart)**	**Rules England**

WOMEN IN EARLY MODERN EUROPE

CULTURAL MARKERS	DATE	PEOPLE/EVENTS	CONTRIBUTION
Northern Renaissance			
English *Querelle des femmes*			
Counter Reformation			
	1613	Elizabeth Cary (England)	*Tragedy of Mariam*
Baroque style emerges (music/art)	1618	Francesca Caccini (Florence, It.)	*Il Primo Libro* (composer/singer)
	1625	Artemisia Gentileschi (Italy)	*Judith and Her Maidservant* (Art)
	1629-1649	**Charles I (Stuart)**	**Rules England**
	1640	Tattlewell and Hit-him-home (England)	*Women's sharp revenge*
	1641	Anna M. van Schurman (Holland)	Essay on women's education
	1643-1715	**Louis XIV, King of France**	**Rules France: 1666-1715**
	1648	French Royal Academy founded	Controls art
	1649-1660	**Cromwell and Puritans**	**Rule England**
	1650	Anne Bradstreet (Mass. Bay)	*The Tenth Muse* (Poetry volume)
	1654	Barbara Strozzi (Venice, Italy)	*Cantatas,* vol. 3 published
	1660-1685	**Stuart Restoration: Charles II**	**Rules England**
	1662	Margaret Cavendish (England)	Volume of plays published
	1670	Aphra Behn (England)	*The Forc'd Marriage,* her 1st play
	1673	Anna M. van Schurman (Holland)	*Eukleria*
	1673-1715	Elizabeth Jacquet de la Guerre	(France) Composer/harpsichordist
	1685-1688	**James II**	**Rules England**
Enlightenment and Scientific Revolution Begin	**1688**	**Glorious Revolution**	**William and Mary rule England**
	1691	Sor Juana de la Cruz (Mexico)	*La Respuesta*
	1713	Anne Finch (England)	Poetry published anonymously
Rococo style begins	**1715**	**Louis XV**	**Rules France**
	1720	Rosalba Carriera (Italy)	*Louis XV as a Boy* (portrait)
	1721	Marie Sallé (France)	Prima ballerina, Paris opera debut
	1726	Marie Camargo (France)	Prima ballerina, Paris opera debut

WOMEN AND CULTURE, 1750–1920

CULTURAL MARKERS	DATE	PEOPLE/EVENTS	CONTRIBUTION
Enlightenment	1715-1774	**Louis XV**	**Rules France**
Neoclassical style	1762	Jean Jacques Rousseau	*Émile*
	1769	British Royal Academy founded	
		Angelica Kauffmann (Switzerland)	A founder of Br. Royal Academy
Romanticism	1774	Mother Ann Lee (England/America)	Leads Shakers to New York
	1774-1792	**Louis XVI (Marie Antoinette)**	**Rules France**
	1775-1783	**American Revolution**	
	1787	Elisabeth Vigée-Lebrun (France)	*Marie Antoinette with Her Children*
	1789-1799	**French Revolution**	
	1790	Judith Sargent Murray (U.S.)	*On the Equality of the Sexes*
	1791	Olympe de Gouges (France)	*The Rights of Woman*
	1792	Mary Wollstonecraft (England)	*Vindication of the Rights of Woman*
	1793	Louis XVI, Marie Antoinette, and Olympe de Gouges (France)	Guillotined by Jacobins
	1804-1815	**Napoleonic Era**	
	1807	Germaine de Staël (France)	*Corinna*
	1818	Mary Shelley (England)	*Frankenstein*
	1819	Jarena Lee (U.S.)	AME preacher
	1821	Lucretia Coffin Mott (U.S.)	Quaker minister
Victorian Ideal	1830	*Second Great Awakening* begins	Religious fervor in U.S.; new sects
	1830s	Actresses appear in breeches roles	
	1832	George Sand (France)	*Indiana*
		Marie Taglione (Italy)	Premiers *La Sylphide* ballet
	1838	Clara Schumann (Germany)	Concert debut
	1840s	African Methodist Episcopal (U.S.)	(AME) Women's Bible Bands
	1845	Phoebe Palmer (U.S.)	*The Way of Holiness*
		Ellen Gould White (U.S.)	Seventh-Day Adventist founder
		Charlotte Cushman (U.S.)	London theater debut
	1846	Fanny Mendelssohn Hensel (Germany)	Publishes her compositions
		Frances Harper (U.S.)	Prints 2nd volume of poetry

WOMEN AND CULTURE, 1750–1920

CULTURAL MARKERS	DATE	PEOPLE/EVENTS	CONTRIBUTION
Neoclassical style			
Romanticism			
Victorian Ideal			
	1855	Rosa Bonheur (France)	*The Horse Fair*
	1859	Harriet Hosmer (U.S.)	*Zenobia in Chains*
	1861-1865	**U.S. Civil War**	
	1865-1870	**Reconstruction Era**	
Realism	1867	Edmonia Lewis (U.S.)	*Forever Free*
Impressionism	1871	Vienna Lady Orchestra	New York City concert
	1875	Mary Cassatt (U.S.)	Paris Impressionist exhibition
	1878	Clara Schuman (Germany)	Last concert
	1875-1879	Mary Baker Eddy (U.S.)	Founds Christian Science church
	1880s-90s	Virginia Broughton (U.S.)	Black Baptist women's Bible bands
Modern Dance	1892	Loie Fuller (U.S.)	Paris dance debut
Art Nouveau	**1893**	**Chicago World's Fair**	(World Columbian Exhibition)
		Mary Cassatt (U.S.)	*Modern Woman* mural
		Hannah Solomon (U.S.)	National Council of Jewish Women
	1895	Elizabeth Cady Stanton (U.S.)	*Woman's Bible*
	1898	Marie Curie (France)	Discovers radium
	1904	Anna White (U.S.)	*Shakerism: Its Meaning & Message*
Avant-Garde	1907	Elizabeth Robins (U.S.)	*The Convert*
styles	1909	Cicely Hamilton (England)	*Pageant of Great Women*
	1911	Edith Craig (England)	Founds *Pioneer Players*
	1914-1918	**World War I**	
	1915	Ruth St. Denis and Ted Shawn (U.S.)	*Denishawn Dance School*
	1917	**Russian Revolution**	
	1923	Charlotte Perkins Gilman (U.S.)	*His Religion and Hers*
	1927	Isadora Duncan (U.S.)	*My Life*

WOMEN AND CULTURE IN THE 20th CENTURY

CULTURAL MARKERS	DATE	PEOPLE/EVENTS	CONTRIBUTION
Expressionism	1890s	Käthe Kollwitz (Germany)	*Revolt of the Weavers* prints
	1911	Ethel Smyth (England)	*March of the Women*
	1914-1918	**World War I**	
Abstraction (sculpture)	1917	Georgia O'Keeffe (U.S.)	Exhibition at 291 Gallery
Avant-garde	**1920-1935**	**Harlem Renaissance (U.S.)**	
Surrealism	1927	Martha Graham (U.S.)	*Martha Graham Dance Company*
	1928	Barbara Hepworth (England)	First sculpture exhibition
	1929	Virginia Woolf (U.S.)	*A Room of One's Own*
	1929-1940	**Great Depression**	
	1933	**Nazis to power in Germany**	
	1934	Antonio Brico (U.S.)	Founds New York Women's Symphony
	1937	Zora Neale Hurston (U.S.)	*Their Eyes Were Watching God*
	1938	Women Musician's Union (U.S.)	Protests discrimination, New York City
	1939	Frida Kahlo (Mexico)	*Las Dos Fridos*
	1939-1945	**World War II**	
Existentialist and Modernist movements	**1945**	**U.S. drops atomic bombs**	**Japan surrenders**
		United Nations established	
		Margaret Bourke-White (U.S.)	*The Living Dead of Buchenwald*
	1946	Simone de Beauvoir (France)	*The Second Sex*
	1948	**India-Pakistan partition**	
	1950-1953	**Korean War**	
	1950	Maria Tallchief (U.S.)	Premiers *Firebird* ballet
	1955-1970s	**U.S. Civil Rights Movement**	
	1961-1973	**U.S. in Vietnam War**	
	1964	Barbara Hepworth (England)	*Single Form* at UN building
	1966	**New Feminist Movement**	**Revival of Feminism**
Feminist Art and Theater movements	1975	Christiane Rochefort (France)	*Are Women Writers Still Monsters?*
	1974-1979	Judy Chicago (U.S.)	*The Dinner Party*

WOMEN AND CULTURE IN THE 20th CENTURY

CULTURAL MARKERS	DATE	PEOPLE/EVENTS	CONTRIBUTION
Abstraction **Feminist Art and Theater** **movements**			
	1977-1981	Katherine Hoover (U.S.)	Women's Music Festivals
	1976-1985	Women's Experimental Theatre	*The Daughters Cycle* play
	1982	Maya Lin (U.S.)	*Vietnam Veterans' Memorial*
Post Modernism and **Post Colonialism**	1983	Ellen Taaffe Zwilich (U.S.)	Pulitzer Prize in Music
		Susannah Heschel (U.S.)	*On Being a Jewish Feminist*
	1984	Elisabeth Schüssler Fiorenza (U.S.)	*In Memory of Her*
		Jawole Zollar (U.S.)	*Urban Bush Women* dance company
	1985	Guerrilla Girls (U.S.)	Fight sexism and racism in arts
	1987	Wilhelmina Holladay (U.S.)	National Museum of Women in Arts
	1988	Toni Morrison (U.S.)	*Beloved* wins Pulitzer Prize
		Rosemary Radford Ruether (U.S.)	*Women-Church*
	1989	Carter Heyward (U.S.)	*Touching Our Strength*
	1990	Martha Graham (U.S.)	*Maple Leaf Rag* – her 191st dance
	1990s	Amalia Mesa-Bains (U.S.)	*Venus Envy, Chs. I, II, III*
	1992, 1994	Deepa Mehta (Canada/India)	*Young Indiana Jones* – 2 episodes
	1993	Toni Morrison (U.S.)	Nobel Prize for Literature
		Rita Gross (U.S.)	*Buddhism after Patriarchy*
		Ada María Isasi-Díaz (U.S.)	*La Palabra de Dios Nosotras*
	1996	Sheila Ortiz Taylor (U.S.)	*Imaginary Parents*
	1997	Anna Lelkes (Austria)	Member of Vienna Philharmonic
	2000	Savitri Bess (U.S.)	*Path of the Mother*
	2001	Riffat Hassan (U.S.)	"Wearing the Hijjab Today"

WOMEN IN EARLY MODERN EUROPE

Part I examines women's contributions to culture in early modern Europe from around 1450 to 1750. Most of the documents in this part reflect the views and experiences of women from a narrow strata of society: members of the nobility who had access to education and the benefits of social and political connections. We do find some, however, by or about women from other sectors of society, which suggests that opportunities were expanding for nonelite women as well.

We begin our story in Chapter 1, "The Italian Renaissance," with an examination of women and the Italian Renaissance. The first text comes from an extremely influential book that established the model of the "Renaissance lady"—an ideal to which all European women of noble rank or pretensions were expected to conform. Subsequent documents illustrate how this model served both to foster and to inhibit female creativity, cultural participation, and leadership. Texts introduce Italian women who made important contributions to Western culture as patrons, artists, writers, musicians, and actresses. Some readings also highlight the achievements of pioneers who successfully made the transition from talented amateur to professional artist, actress, or musician, and thus became important role models for subsequent generations of aspiring women.

Chapter 2, "The Age of Religious Ferment," focuses on women's experiences in the context of the religious ferment that began during the Renaissance with the Protestant Reformation or Revolt and continued well into the Baroque Era with the Catholic Counter Reformation and the emergence of a variety of distinct Protestant sects. Some texts in this chapter show how male Protestant leaders sought to redefine the societal and religious roles of women and describe women's participation in the expanding Protestant revolution. Others delineate Catholic women's responses to Protestantism and their efforts to reform Catholicism from within. Documents also reveal efforts of both Catholic and Protestant women to combat patriarchal and misogynist trends and to carve out significant roles for their sex within their respective faiths.

In Chapter 3, "The Northern Renaissance," we examine women's participation in the Renaissance in northern Europe, focusing in particular on the English Renaissance. Texts demonstrate the spread of humanist ideas about women and the Renaissance lady model from Italy to northern Europe. We also learn more about the role of women, particularly royal women, as patrons and disseminators of culture, often across national borders. We focus first on two French women from very different social strata. The next section of documents examines Elizabeth I of England as a model Renaissance lady and patron of culture. This section also shows how secular and religious ideas of the Renaissance and Reformation affected a woman who assumed the throne. Other documents attest to women's interest in the theater despite its masculine character. The chapter closes with selections from some of the first works by English women written in response to misogynist male writers who were debating the "woman question" among themselves in Renaissance England.

The last two chapters in Part I include a variety of documents that attest to the increasing evidence of creative women during the Baroque Era (ca.1600–ca.1750). Chapter 4, "Artists, Musicians, and Performers in the Baroque Era," documents the lives, work, and cultural impact of some women artists, musicians, and performers from Italy to northern Europe and illuminates the factors that facilitated and inhibited female creativity in particular places, contexts, and times. Chapter 5, "Writers and Intellectuals in the Baroque Era," examines the works of women writers and intellectuals, with particular attention to their critiques of societal images of women and their responses to the gender barriers they confronted.

A number of themes and patterns in women's experiences emerge in Part I. Creative women become increasingly visible in many fields as we move from the Renaissance to the end of the Baroque Era. We also find increasing numbers of professional women and small but growing numbers of nonelite "middle-class" women in their ranks by the eighteenth century. Evidence of women's increasing visibility as contributors to culture, however, is not uniform throughout Europe at any particular time. Instead, we find clusters in certain places and times of women in particular fields (e.g., musicians in Italy) and different specialties within artistic fields. These clusters remind us of the importance of examining cultural developments and women's achievements in their particular contexts. The documents also reveal that male support and collaboration are important factors in the development and recognition of female talent.

The readings in Part I also attest to the resilience of established gender ideology and gender roles in Western civilization. Although the Renaissance and the religious ferment produced by the Protestant Reformation precipitated discussions about education and the roles of men and women among other topics, in the end the notions of woman's nature and place in society changed very little from what had been set forth in classical and biblical texts and Western legal codes.

On the other hand, however, we begin to see an awakening of gender consciousness in the works of many creative women. In particular, the "woman question" or debate over the nature of woman and her proper roles became a prominent and continuing theme during this time period. And, by the seventeenth century, we find women beginning to participate in this debate and to speak out in defense of their sex as the French writer Christine de Pizan had first done in the 1400s.

Chapter 1

The Italian Renaissance

The Renaissance is rightfully seen as one of the high points of Western civilization, a golden age of culture. Renaissance Italy produced an incredible cluster of artistic geniuses and an outpouring of art, sculpture, architecture, literature, scholarship, and music. In 1977, however, historian Joan Kelly-Gadol challenged conventional views of the era when she asked: "Did women have a Renaissance?" Using four criteria—the regulation of female sexuality, women's political and economic roles, women's cultural roles, and ideology about women—she concluded that women as a group did not have a renaissance. In fact, she argued, they experienced a contraction of opportunities relative both to men of their class and to medieval women. Women are conspicuous by their absence from the lengthy lists of the great artists, architects, musicians, mercantile leaders, scholars, and writers of the period. Where women do appear their numbers are minuscule compared with men in that field; the "exceptional" woman is the norm. Moreover, these exceptional women tend to emerge in the late Renaissance, indicating that a renaissance for women occurred in what is often seen as the post-Renaissance era (Kelly-Gadol 1977, 139–63).

The developments that fostered cultural creativity in Italy, namely, the emergence of an early capitalist economy, rise of consolidated states, and evolution of a post-feudal modern social structure, reduced women's economic and political options. Women were excluded from the guilds that trained male artists and produced valued textiles, from the universities and cathedral schools that trained musicians and scholars, and from the mercantile houses and banks that replaced family home-based businesses.

As their traditional household economic functions declined, women of the nobility and mercantile families acquired passive economic roles. Clothed in expensive dresses and precious jewels, their bodies became showcases, "portable dowries," used to display the wealth and status of husbands and fathers. More importantly, they once again served as pawns in the marriage game, used to cement political and business alliances and increase the power and wealth of both father and husband. Ultimately, reproduction was their primary economic function. Upper-class Italian women usually married at 16 or 17, though many brides were 13, and some as young as 10. They were betrothed at 4 or 5. Their husbands were in their thirties. Northern European women, in contrast, generally wed at 25 or 26. (Harriman 1995, 184-85) On average, elite Italian women bore three more children than northern women

With so much value placed on marriage and reproduction, female sexuality was carefully regulated. Noble women were not to appear in public or travel unchaperoned. Their homes were built around inner courtyards to prevent interaction with street life. The ultimate symbol of sexual control was a new wardrobe item, the chastity belt. Renaissance marital and reproductive patterns, insistence on female chastity and strict separation of the sexes into two spheres, the public world of men and the private world of women, mirrored the social-sexual patterns of classical Athens and Rome. Reverence for classical culture also shaped Renaissance ideology about women and gender. Humanists revived classical theories that saw the two sexes as fundamentally different, and women as innately inferior. In particular, they saw the intellectual woman as departing from her true sexual nature, abandoning both her reproductive function and female chastity.

The Renaissance, however, also brought some positive changes for Italian women that led to a significant increase in female creativity and a women's renaissance in the seventeenth century. Despite their debt to classical philosophers, Italian humanists believed in the value of education for girls as well as boys. The sophisticated rulers in Renaissance Italy required that both ladies and gentlemen of the court be educated. Nearly all the women discussed in this chapter were educated according to the principles of humanism and the courtly lady ideal. As a result, their unexpected talents and intellectual or creative interests were discovered.

The outburst of human creativity that marks the Italian Renaissance occurred in large part because no single political entity was the dominant cultural center. Instead, the princely courts of Ferrara, Mantua, Urbino, and Milan, the city-state of Florence, the Republic of Venice, the kingdom of Naples, and the papacy in Rome vied for pre-eminence. Their rivalries and alliances were cultural as well as political and military. Creativity and innovation flourished as they competed for cultural superiority, each seeking to attract the best artists, musicians, architects, and scholars, and to build the most impressive monuments and cultural collections. Talented women in diverse fields had more opportunities to emerge in this decentralized competitive environment than elsewhere.

As we examine the lives and work of the women who appear in this chapter, we find clusters of talented, well-educated women in certain ruling families and at certain courts. One or several generations of such women emerged from the d'Este family of Ferrara, the Gonzaga family of Mantua, the Montefeltro family of Urbino, and the Medici family of Florence. Intermarriages among the d'Este, Gonzaga, and Montefeltro families created an interlocking network that made all three courts vibrant cultural centers in which women played significant roles throughout the Renaissance.

Talented women from outside the nobility or elite mercantile class flourished in the cosmopolitan republic of Venice. There, however, the intellectual and artistic centers were salons or *ridotti,* located in private residences, where the mercantile elite mingled with students, scholars, artists, visiting nobility, and *courtesans.* Courtesans emerged in Rome and Venice, as Italian high society copied Greek culture. Like the *hetairae* of classical Athens and the Hellenistic world, they were talented, educated women who served men sexually but also provided intellectual companionship and entertainment. Some were musicians and poets, and some established salons. They enjoyed the respect of the Venetian elite and often earned enough to live relatively independent lives.

Convents continued to be important centers of female education and creativity in Italy, as they had been throughout the Middle Ages in much of Europe. In the sixteenth century, the majority of unmarried women of the Italian nobility lived in convents. Convents were well endowed from the dowries families paid to commit their daughters and offered training in a variety of fields.

THE RENAISSANCE LADY: THE IDEAL AND TWO EXEMPLARS

Baldesar Castiglione (1478–1529)

Baldesar Castiglione is best known as the author of *The Book of the Courtier,* a best-selling handbook for the training and behavior of men and ladies of the courts of Europe. The chapter in which he describes the ideal lady of the court was an important contribution to the hundreds of treatises about women that circulated during the Renaissance. In many respects, his description reflects prevalent notions of women, but his views of women's potential and their courtly roles were somewhat more enlightened than those of many other writers. The book played a key part in shaping the education of women of the nobility and merchant classes and ultimately widening the options of Italian women.

Castiglione was born into a noble family near Mantua and received a humanist education. After serving the duke of Milan, in 1500 he began his career as a soldier-diplomat with the Gonzaga family. From 1504 to 1516, he served at the court of Urbino and then returned to Mantua in the service of Francesco Gonzaga and Isabella d'Este. In 1524, he became papal ambassador to Spain and ended his career as bishop of Avila.

He wrote the *Courtier* in 1516 but published it in 1528. The book recounts an evening at the Urbino court of the duke of Montefeltro, when a group that regularly met for conversation, presided over by Duchess Elisabetta Gonzaga, decided to play a game in which the men took turns describing the perfect court gentleman or *courtier.* The ideal courtier, all agreed, must be loyal to his prince, a courageous soldier, a scholar, a diplomat, and a gentleman. He must be familiar with the classics, languages, music, art, dance, and literature. He must be honorable with women, and a charming conversationalist. He was a man of action, able to serve his prince in many capacities beyond the court and to enrich court life. In sum, he was the humanist's ideal: a virtuous, well-educated "whole person."

Duchess Elisabetta then suggested they create a model lady of the court or *donna di palazzo.* Her qualities are set forth in the third chapter or book of Castiglione's work. As you read the excerpt that follows, identify the most important qualities a lady of the court should possess and the extent to which her qualities and behavior should differ from those of a *courtier.*

THE RENAISSANCE LADY FROM *THE BOOK OF THE COURTIER**

> Then the Magnifico, turning to [the Duchess], said: "Since it is your pleasure, Madam, . . . I will speak of this excellent Lady as I would have her to be; . . . And, though signor Gasparo has said that the same rules which serve for the Courtier serve also for the Lady, I am of a different opinion; for although some qualities are common to both and are as necessary for a man as for a woman, there are yet others that befit a woman more than a man, and others that befit a man and to which a woman ought to be a complete stranger. I say this of bodily exercises; but above all I think that in her ways, manners, words, gestures, and bearing, a woman ought to be very unlike a man; for just as he must show a certain solid and sturdy manliness, so it is seemly for a woman to have a soft and delicate tenderness, with an air of womanly sweetness in her every movement, which, in her going and staying, and in whatever she says, shall always make her appear the woman without any resemblance to a man.

*Excerpts from Baldesar Castiglione, *The Book of the Courtier, Book 3.* Trans. Leonard Eckstein Opdycke (New York: Scribner, 1903), pp. 174–76, 179–80.

. . . And I do think that beauty is more necessary to her than to the Courtier, for truly that woman lacks much who lacks beauty. Also she must be more circumspect, and more careful not to give occasion for evil being said of her. . . .

[I]n my opinion, in a Lady who lives at court a certain pleasing affability is becoming above all else. . . . "

". . . I think there is none here who does not recognize that, as for bodily exercises, it is not seemly for a woman to handle weapons, ride, play tennis, wrestle, and do many other things that are suited to men." . . .

Messer Cesare Gonzaga added: ". . . I have seen women play tennis, handle weapons, ride, hunt, and engage in nearly all the exercises that a cavalier can."

The Magnifico replied: "Since I may fashion this Lady as I please, not only would I not have her engage in such robust and strenuous manly exercises, but even those that are becoming to a woman I would have her practice in a measured way and with that gentle delicacy that we have said befits her; and so when she dances, I should not wish to see her make movements that are too energetic and violent; nor, when she sings or plays, use those loud and oft repeated diminutions that show more skill than sweetness; likewise the musical instruments that she plays ought in my opinion to be appropriate to this intent. Consider what an ungainly thing it would be to see a woman playing drums, fifes, trumpets, or other like instruments; and this because their harshness hides and removes that suave gentleness which so adorns a woman in her every act. Hence, when she starts to dance or to make music of any kind, she ought to begin by letting herself be urged a little, and with a certain shyness bespeaking a noble shame that is the opposite of effrontery.

. . . I wish this Lady to have knowledge of letters, of music, of painting, and know how to dance and how to be festive, adding a discreet modesty and the giving of a good impression of herself to those other things that have been required of the Courtier. And so, in her talk, her laughter, her play, her jesting, in short in everything, she will be most graceful and will converse appropriately with every person in whose company she may happen to be, using witticisms and pleasantries that are becoming to her." . . .

Isabella d'Este (1474–1539): Model Renaissance Lady

Isabella d'Este is arguably one of greatest women of her age and one of the most important patrons of the Renaissance. She corresponded with nearly every important figure in literature and the arts of her day. More than 2,000 letters from her correspondence have survived. Under her leadership and patronage, the city-state of Mantua became one of the major cultural centers of Italy and the Renaissance. She was also widely respected for the political and diplomatic skills she exhibited while governing during her husband's lengthy absences and in the early years of her son's reign. Indeed, Castiglione cited her as one of several women who epitomized his ideal.

Isabella was the oldest child of Ercole d'Este (1431–1505), the duke of Ferrara, and the well-educated, politically astute Leonora d'Aragona. She grew up in a stimulating environment, for Ferrara, thanks to both her parents, was a center of the arts and learning. At the age of 6, she was betrothed to the Marchese Gian Francesco II Gonzaga (1466–1519) of Mantua. Her marriage on February 12, 1490, at the age of 16, cemented a political and cultural alliance between the two adjoining states. She and Francesco had six children, five of whom survived. Their oldest son, Federigo (1500–1540) became duke of Mantua, and another, Ercole (1505–1563), became a cardinal in the church, thanks in part to

Isabella's efforts. Her firstborn, Leonora (1493–1550), was married to the duke of Urbino, while her second daughter was pledged to the monastic Order of Poor Clares at birth. These marital and religious links enhanced the influence of the d'Este and Gonzaga houses.

Her education typified that prescribed for a courtly lady (*donna di palazzo*). In addition to instruction in the "feminine arts," she received a solid humanist education, however she quickly progressed beyond the level of learning intended for women. She had a special talent for languages and was reportedly "able to speak Latin better than any women of her age" (Ady 1903, 9). Her musical training was unusually extensive, thanks to the musicians her father brought to Ferrara. She and her sister were known as fine singers and talented lute and clavichord players.

Music remained one of Isabella's lifelong passions. In Mantua, she continued her own musical education as time permitted but devoted most of her energies to building a musical establishment that would rival in quality and size that of her father's court. She increased the number of musicians, particularly fine vocalists, and even sent her musicians to other cities for further study. The Gonzaga court soon became the most important musical center in Italy and enjoyed an international reputation. Mantuan singers, composers, and instrumentalists were highly sought after by other courts. Isabella and Francesco commissioned new forms of music by Italian composers and sought Italian poetry to have set to that music. In so doing, they fostered the development of both Italian poetry and secular music and helped shift their countrymen's preferences from French *chansons* to indigenous Italian music.

Significantly, Italian musicians rather than foreigners benefited from their patronage. Marchetto Cara, their most prized musician and director of the Gonzaga chapel between 1494 and 1525, became one of Italy's most famous secular singers and one of the most prolific and highly regarded of Italy's first generation of secular composers. The couple also supported composer Bartolomeo Tromboncino. In fact, in 1499, to prolong his career, Isabella urged her husband to grant clemency to Tromboncino after he murdered his wife. Isabella and Francesco also employed two women as court musicians: Cara's wife, Giovanna Moreschi, and Paula Poccino. (Prizer 1980, 12, 42–43, 58) They are among the first known female court musicians.

The reading that follows focuses on Isabella's role as a patron. The letter reveals her interest in the welfare of the Gonzaga musicians.*

Isabella to Cardinal Luigi d'Aragona, 13 January 1519

> *My most reverend and illustrious Monsignore:*
>
> I have not sent sooner your most reverend and illustrious Lordship the song on that thing [verse] that you sent me many days ago to have done, because it was not finished earlier. Your Lordship may well know that these excellent musicians need time to compose, correct, and write down their compositions. However, if I am tardy, [please] deign to pardon me, understanding the cause. Now I am sending it enclosed here. Our Marchetto [Cara] says that, if he succeeds in pleasing your most reverend and illustrious Lordship, he himself will be most pleased. If it were otherwise, however, he would offer to do it again differently. He and I should like to be informed of your receipt of this song, and also if you are satisfied.

*Letter from William F. Prizer, *Courtly Pastimes: The Frottole of Marchetto Cara* (Ann Arbor, Michigan: UMI Research Press, 1980), p. 40. Copyright © 1980, by William Flaville Prizer. By permission of William Flaville Prizer.

Over a 50-year period, d'Este amassed a superb collection of antiques, maps, art, books, manuscripts, and some of the finest musical instruments in Europe. From 1496 until his death in Mantua in 1517, Lorenzo da Pavia, the most famous instrument maker of his day, crafted organs, lutes, and viols to her specifications and helped her acquire many of her treasures. Among these were the exquisite editions of classics she had him acquire from Aldo Manuzio of Venice. Her patronage was an important stimulus to the growth of printing. It also drew craftsmen and artists such as sculptor Cristoforo and painters Mantegna, Raphael, and Leonardo da Vinci to Mantua.

LORENZO DA PAVIA TO ISABELLA, 26 JULY 1501*

Most illustrious Madonna,

I saw by your last letter that you wished me to send you the three books, Virgil, Petrarch, and Ovid, in parchment, and so I went at once to the house of Maestro Aldo, who prints these books in a small form and in the finest italic type that you ever saw. . . . At present only Virgil is to be had in parchment, so I send it to you herewith. The Petrarch is not yet finished. . . . M. Aldo has promised me to choose a copy for you leaf by leaf, so that yours shall be the finest of all, and the said Maestro will do this all the more gladly because he has been helped in his work by M. Pietro Bembo, who is most devoted to Your Signoria. . . . As soon as it is finished I will send it to you, as they wish yours to be the first that appears, and . . . feel sure the work will obtain a great success since Your Excellency will have had the first copy. . . . Your Highness may trust me to do my utmost. I mean you to have something as rare and incomparable as Your Most Excellent Highness herself. And nothing in the world pleases me more than to obey your orders, remembering the kindness which you have ever shown me. . . .

Sofonisba Anguissola (1532–1625): Renaissance Artist

Sofonisba Anguissola was a pioneering role model for women artists and an inspiration for other women as well. She was the first prominent woman artist of the Renaissance, and the first woman artist for whom a significant body of work is known. Her financial success was an important example for other women who dreamed of careers in art and music. Anguissola advanced several new directions in art. She was one of the earliest artists to paint on canvas, an experimental medium that required meticulous preparation. She also became known for her self-portraits at a time when the self-portrait was still a new art form. In addition, she created a new type of portrait that depicted her subjects in action or informal poses rather than the conventional, stiff formal poses.

Anguissola was the oldest of seven children born to Amilcare and Blanca Anguissola, members of the minor nobility of Cremona. Her parents provided their six daughters with the education appropriate for an aristocratic lady, and the girls displayed such talent in painting, music, and letters that they became known as child prodigies. Amilcare sent Sofonisba and her sister Elena to train with a Cremonese artist, Bernardino Campi (1522–1591), when Sofonisba was 14. In 1554, Amilcare sent Sofonisba to Rome for further training. While in Rome, she worked under the guidance of Michelangelo, Italy's most important artist. His praise of her drawing of a smiling girl with a crying boy pinched by a crayfish was an important impetus to her career. Her reputation spread after copies of the drawing began to circulate.

*From Ady, *Isabella d'Este, Marchioness of Mantua,* vol II, pp. 21–23.

Between 1555 and 1559, Anguissola lived in Cremona and painted primarily self-portraits and members of her family. In becoming a specialist in portraiture, she turned the liability of her sex into an asset. Women were not permitted to study the male nude or to work in a shop with male artists. By doing family and self-portraits and working essentially within her family home, she did not violate standards of propriety. More importantly, her intimate knowledge of her siblings, servants, and parents, and their ease with her when she was painting probably enabled her to develop her trademark of animated portraits that captured the personalities of her subjects.

In 1559, Sofonisba went to Spain at the invitation of Philip II to enter the service of his new queen, Isabel de Valois. She remained at Philip's court for 20 years, but she was not listed among those employed in the king's household and was not called a court painter. Instead, her official title was *dama* or lady-in-waiting to the queen. She was one of several hundred members of the queen's household and was paid by the queen. (Perlingieri 1992, 121) In reality, she served multiple roles as the court painter to both the queen and king and as the queen's lady-in-waiting, companion, and teacher. Philip II selected Anguissola at the recommendation of his emissary, the duke of Alba, who recognized her talent but also thought she would be an excellent companion for the queen who was only 13. Although Anguissola was then 27, her father had the sole legal authority to accept the king's offer of employment.

Anguissola's court position placed her in an unusually comfortable financial position. Other artists, including Michelangelo and Titian, struggled to get payment from delinquent patrons. In contrast, her living expenses, including servants, were paid by the queen. In addition, she received wages, gifts, and payment for paintings in the form of money, gold, expensive textiles, and jewels from both the queen and king. When Queen Isabel died from a miscarriage in 1568, the king kept Anguissola on as court painter and governess "in charge of the infanta," two-year-old Isabella Clara Eugenia. He also established a generous dowry for Anguissola, who, as an unmarried woman, was legally his ward. In 1570, he selected a Sicilian of noble Spanish lineage as husband for the 38-year-old artist and arranged and paid for their lavish wedding the following year. Anguissola and her husband began married life in Sicily, but in 1572, they returned to Spain at Philip's request and she resumed her court functions. Sofonisba also received a lifetime pension from the king. After her husband's death in 1579, she returned to Italy, but her ties with the king and especially with his eldest daughter, Isabella Clara Eugenia, remained strong until his death in 1598.

The three documents that follow illustrate different facets of Anguissola's life and career at the Spanish court. The two letters she exchanged with the pope attest to her ability to convey her subject's personality in the portraits she painted of Spanish royalty as well as her portraits of family members.*

LETTER FROM SOFONISBA ANGUISSOLA TO POPE PIUS IV, 16 SEPTEMBER 1561

Holy Father,

I have learned from your Nuncio that you desired a portrait of my royal mistress by my hand. I considered it a singular favour to be allowed to serve your Holiness, and I asked Her Majesty's permission, which was readily granted, seeing the paternal affection which your Holiness displays to her. I have taken the opportunity of

*Letters from Giorgio Vasari, *The Lives of the Painters, Sculptors and Architects in Four Volumes,* vol. III, trans. A. B. Hinds, ed. William Gaunt. Everyman's Library (London: J. M. Dent; New York: Dutton, 1927), pp. 319–20.

sending it by this knight. It will be a great pleasure to me if I have gratified your Holiness's wish, but I must add that, if the brush could represent the beauties of the queen's soul to your eyes, they would be marvellous. However, I have used the utmost diligence to present what art can show, to tell your Holiness the truth. And so I humbly kiss your most holy feet. Madrid, September 16, 1561.

LETTER FROM POPE PIUS IV TO ANGUISSOLA, FROM ROME, 15 OCTOBER 1561

We have received the portrait of our dear daughter, the Queen of Spain, which you have sent. It has given us the utmost satisfaction both for the person represented, whom we love like a father for the piety and good qualities of her mind, and because it is well and diligently executed by your hand. We thank you and assure you that we shall treasure it among our choicest possessions, and commend your marvelous talent which is the least among your numerous qualities. And so we send you our benediction. May God save you.

DOCUMENT ESTABLISHING SOFONISBA'S DOWRY, ISSUED BY PHILIP II*

Whereas we hold in high esteem the fine manner in which you, Sofonisba Anguissola, served the most serene Queen Dona Isabel, my very dear and beloved wife (may she rest in glory), and were a lady of her private service, and in satisfaction and reward of your residence, cares of your office, and such related matters which you held on the staff of her household and for which she bequeathed for you in her will and for whatever responsibility and obligation in which the forementioned most serene Queen and we may be to you. For this cause, we have had and now do have consideration to grant you with this document 3,000 ducados which are worth 125,000 maravedis, as capital benefice to your dowry and marriage, which comes to, above and beyond others, a sum of 250,000 maravedis which we have ordered in your name through our account to Melchior de Heirera, our general treasurer, on the date of this document, in fulfillment of the two sums of 375,000 maravedis. Therefore, by this document we promise and assure you, the aforementioned Sofonisba Anguissola, that once it had been made clear to us by faith and sufficient testimony that you have married and taken all vows according to Holy Mother Church, and for whose effect are promised to you the aforementioned 3,000 ducados, we will have them delivered to you so that the payment may be made to you openly and in due form. I desire from you still another favor: residence in any of our royal estates in Castile or in some place equivalent. Should I die before your marriage or taking of vows, which in any of these cases may cause stoppage of payment, so that you may be certain and assured of all stipulated above, I

*From Perlingieri, *Sofonisba Anguissola: The First Great Woman Artist of the Renaissance*, p. 152. By permission of Ilya Sandra Perlingieri.

order you to present this document, signed by our hand and countersigned by our secretary below. Dated in Madrid, 6 August 1569.

WOMEN HUMANISTS AND POETS

A growing number of women writers emerged in Italy in the fifteenth and sixteenth centuries. Thirty were humanist scholars; more were poets. These women were trained by tutors and studied and wrote in the privacy of their homes. If they became serious scholars and writers however, they often experienced difficulties. Because few women shared their interests, they had to gain acceptance in male intellectual and literary circles. This was particularly difficult for women humanists. Male humanists taught and encouraged some bright young women, but when these "prodigies" reached puberty, their tutors expected them to assume the proper roles of a lady and marry or retire to a convent. Under such social pressure, ambitions often withered. While they pursued their studies, however, female humanists wrote Latin letters and demonstrated their mastery of all the literary forms and most areas of scholarship male humanists prized.

Literary women were more accepted than scholars, but they too sometimes met with disapproval if they participated in public literary discourse or were published. And they faced another challenge: the enduring legacy of the great humanist poet Petrarch (1304–1374). All Italian writers were judged by their ability to emulate his writing. Petrarchan poetry, like the courtly love, romance, and troubadour songs of the medieval period, was a male art form that reflected the views and experiences of men. While women could master the meter or structure of the Petrarchan sonnet, they could not convincingly emulate its core essence: the anguish, desire, and anticipation a man felt toward his unattainable female love object. It was difficult in this genre for a woman to find or express her own voice or to draw on her own experiences.

The readings that follow illustrate the achievements of some of Italy's learned women. They also reveal the kinds of pressures intellectual women experienced, how each woman responded to societal expectations or criticisms, and the support networks that sustained them.

Laura Cereta (1469–1499): Humanist

Cereta, the eldest child of a noble family in Brescia, was another talented prodigy. After two years of convent education, she returned home where her father taught her mathematics, Latin, and some Greek. She embarked on serious studies, determined, as she stated in the prologue to her published letters, to achieve fame and immortality through her writing. At 15, she married a Brescian businessman who was equally supportive of her studies. Within 18 months she was a childless widow. She overcame her grief by resuming her studies and letter writing, encouraged by two circles of intellectuals who regularly gathered for discussions.

Her writing took the form of Latin letters on many subjects including mathematics, history, and moral philosophy. Five dealt with women and learning. All were written between July 1485 and March 1488, when she was between 16 and 18 years old. She published her letters in 1488. Although praised by some, Cereta was viciously attacked by both men and women. One accused her of plagiarizing books by learned men. Others claimed her father had written the letters. She never wrote again. Her father's death in 1488 perhaps led her to accept the advice of a Dominican friar who urged her to seek religious humility instead of intellectual fame.

The letter that follows was one of five she wrote on women and learning in which she articulated the most spirited and direct defenses of women's intellect voiced since Christine de Pizan's *Book of the*

City of Ladies was published in 1405 (see Volume One, Chapter 15, "Medieval Culture: The Secular Context"). Bibulus Sempronius is probably a fictitious person.

EXCERPTS FROM LETTER TO BIBULUS SEMPRONIUS, 13 JANUARY 1488*

My ears are wearied by your carping. You brashly and publicly not merely wonder but indeed lament that I am said to possess as fine a mind as nature ever bestowed upon the most learned man. You seem to think that so learned a woman has scarcely before been seen in the world. You are wrong on both counts, Sempronius, and have clearly strayed from the path of truth and disseminate falsehood. . . .

You pretend to admire me as a female prodigy, but there lurks sugared deceit in your adulation. You wait perpetually in ambush to entrap my lovely sex, and overcome by your hatred seek to trample me underfoot and dash me to the earth. . . .

I would have been silent, believe me, if that savage old enmity of yours had attacked me alone. . . . But I cannot tolerate your having attacked my entire sex. For this reason my thirsty soul seeks revenge, my sleeping pen is aroused to literary struggle, raging anger stirs mental passions long chained by silence. With just cause I am moved to demonstrate how great a reputation for learning and virtue women have won by their inborn excellence, manifested in every age of knowledge, the [purveyor] of honor. Certain, indeed, and legitimate is our possession of this inheritance, come to us from a long eternity of ages past. . . . [She cites many women who prove her point, such as prophets Sappho, Zenobia, Cornelia, and contemporaries such as Isotta Nogarola.]

All of history is full of these examples. Thus your nasty words are refuted by these arguments, which compel you to concede that nature imparts equally to all the same freedom to learn. . . .

I have been praised too much; showing your contempt for women, you pretend that I alone am admirable because of the good fortune of my intellect. But I, compared to other women who have won splendid renown, am but a little mousling. You disguise your envy in dissimulation, but cloak yourself in apologetic words in vain. The lie buried, the truth, dear to God, always emerges. You stumble half-blind with envy on a wrongful path that leads you from your manhood, from your duty, from God. Who, do you think, will be surprised, Bibulus, if the stricken heart of an angry girl, whom your mindless scorn has painfully wounded, will after this more violently assault your bitter words? Do you suppose, O most contemptible man on earth, that I think myself sprung [like Athena] from the head of Jove? I am a school girl, possessed of the sleeping embers of an ordinary mind. Indeed I am too hurt, and my mind, offended, too swayed by passions, sighs, tormenting itself, conscious of the obligation to defend my sex. For absolutely everything—that which is within us and that which is without—is made weak by association with my sex.

*From Margaret L. King and Albert Rabil, Jr., eds. *Her Immaculate Hand: Selected Works by and about the Women Humanists of Quattrocento Italy,* vol. 20 of Medieval and Renaissance Texts and Studies Series (Binghamton, NY: Center for Medieval and Early Renaissance Studies, State University of New York at Binghamton, 1983), pp. 81–84. Copyright © Center for Medieval and Early Renaissance Studies. By Permission.

I, therefore, who have always prized virtue, having put my private concerns aside, will polish and weary my pen against chatterboxes swelled with false glory. Trained in the arts, I shall block the paths of ambush. And I shall endeavor, by avenging arms, to sweep away the abusive infamies of noisemakers with which some disreputable and impudent men furiously, violently, and nastily rave against a woman and a republic worthy of reverence.

Vittoria Colonna (1492–1547): Poet

Vittoria Colonna enjoyed an international reputation in her own time and for centuries remained the most famous Italian woman writer. She was a model Renaissance lady, known for her virtue and piety as well as her poetry and intellect. She wrote approximately 400 poems but allowed none to be published before 1535. The first volume of her poetry appeared in 1538, followed by over 20 editions of her works in the remaining years of the sixteenth century.

Colonna received an education worthy of her social status. Her father was from one of Rome's leading families, and her mother was a Montefeltro, the rulers of Urbino. At 17, she was married to a Spanish nobleman from Naples to whom she had been betrothed at age three. As an officer in the army of Charles V, he was rarely home. The childless Colonna found stimulation in a circle of intellectuals and artists who gathered at her home. Despite her husband's absences and infidelities, Colonna glorified him in poems written after his death in 1525 from battle wounds.

At 35, the widow Colonna returned to Rome and took up residence in the convent of San Silvestro. She traveled widely, had frequent visitors, and again presided over a circle of literary men, artists, and Catholic reformers. Her correspondents and admirers included the gifted Frenchwoman Marguerite Navarre and Isabella d'Este who, with her son Federigo, gave Colonna a gift of a Madonna painting by da Vinci. Probably no one was closer to Colonna than Michelangelo, as evidenced in the poetry, letters, and drawings they exchanged. He was at her side when she died in February 1547.

Colonna's early poems were love lyrics (*rime amorose*) dedicated to her deceased husband. Her later work consisted of sacred poems (*rime spirituali*). Her poetry became more mystical after 1542 when she and friends were investigated by the Inquisition for their unconventional theology and reformist ideas. "Aspiration" is typical of her *rime spirituali*.*

ASPIRATION

If I have conquered self, by Heaven's
    strength,
'Gainst carnal reason and the senses
    striven,
With mind renewed and purged, I rise
    at length
Above the world and its false faith to
    heaven.

My thoughts, no longer now depressed
    and vain,
Upon the wings of faith and hope shall
    rise,
Nor sink into this vale of tears again,
But find true peace and courage in the
    skies.

*Poem from Rossiter Johnson and Dora Knowlton Ranous, eds., *An Anthology of Italian Authors from Cavalcanti to Fogazzaro (1270–1907) with Biographical Sketches,* Literature of Italy, 1265–1907 Series (New York: The National Alumni, 1907), p. 80.

I fix my eye still on the better way;
I see the promise of the Eternal Day.
Yet still my trembling steps fall erringly.
To choose the right-hand path I must
    incline—
That sacred passage toward the life
    divine;
And yet I fear that life may ne'er be
    mine.

Gaspara Stampa (1523?–1554): Poet

Gaspara Stampa, called by some the "Italian Sappho," is one of Italy's most important women writers and is regarded as the "most significant and singular female voice" of the Italian Renaissance (Johnson and Ranous 1907, 96; Bassanese 1994, 404, 406). She was born between 1520 and 1525 in Padua. Her father was a wealthy jeweler who gave his three children musical training and a classical education. After his death around 1531, her mother, Cecilia, moved the three children to Venice and hired tutors to continue their education. Cecilia turned their home into a *ridotto* (salon) that attracted a mix of musicians, intellectuals, nobles, students, and artists typical of cosmopolitan Venice. The *ridotto* gave Stampa an alternative to life in a convent or the seclusion at home expected of a married or unmarried respectable woman. Contemporaries praised her poetry, her intellect, and the musical talent she and her sister shared. Some think that both Stampa daughters were probably courtesans.

Stampa was accepted in at least one of the intellectual academies in Venice where she participated in discussions and shared her poetry with male writers, artists, and nobility. Only three of her sonnets were printed before her death, but her sister and an editor published over 300 of her poems shortly after she died. Stampa had a passionate love affair with Count Collaltino di Collalto whose descendants republished her poetry in 1738. He is the subject of much of her early love poetry. As this poem illustrates, she subtly departed from the Petrarchan model as she sought to present a woman's experiences of the joy and pain of love.*

She Dictates Her Own Epitaph

Weep, O ye women! Set Love weeping
    too,
  For that he weeps not, he that
      wounded me;
  Soon shall my weary soul departed
      be
From this tormented body which he
    knew.
And if some gentle charity would do
    Aught to fulfil a last request of mine,
    When I am lying dead within the
        shrine,
  Write this sad history of my grief in
      view:

"Because she loved much and was little
    loved
  She lived and died in pain; she rests
      in peace,
Most faithful lover that was ever proved.
    Pray, passer-by, for her repose and
        ease.
Learn her life's lesson: how a heart
    unmoved,
  A fickle heart, to love she could not
      cease."

*Poems from Johnson and Ranous, eds. *An Anthology of Italian Authors*, p. 98.

Veronica Franco (1546–1591): Poet

Venetian-born poet and courtesan Veronica Franco was the daughter of a merchant from a family of noble rank. Her mother reportedly introduced her to prostitution and served as her procuress. By her twenties, Franco had clients from Venice's wealthiest families. She frequented one of the most famous salons in Venice and cultivated contacts with many prominent political, literary, and artistic figures. Henry III of France chose her to entertain him when he passed through Venice, and she later sent him some of her sonnets. As a successful courtesan, she was able to live in luxury and was free to participate in Venetian cultural circles in ways that few other women of her time could do. She apparently quit her profession around 1580 and engaged in pious works. Some think that she founded a refuge house for prostitutes. While her reputation as a courtesan tended to overshadow her importance as a poet, she wanted to be taken seriously as a writer. She published a volume of over four dozen letters, as well as a volume of poetry that consisted largely of her own work. She also edited a volume of sonnets by others in which she included nine of her own poems. Unlike other women's poems, some of hers are quite frank sexually and show pride in her skill as a courtesan. The following selection is a revealing letter to a friend who was grooming her daughter to be a courtesan. It reflects some of her concerns about women's societal status that also appear in her poetry.*

A WARNING TO A MOTHER CONSIDERING TURNING HER DAUGHTER INTO A COURTESAN

The fact that you go around complaining that I'm no longer willing for you to come to my house to see me, loving you as well as I do, bothers me less than the fact that I have a good reason for it. . . . I would like to respond to you in this letter, making a last attempt to dissuade you from your evil intent, . . .

You know how often I've begged and warned you to protect her virginity. And since this world is so full of dangers and so uncertain, and the houses of poor mothers are never safe from the amorous maneuvers of lustful young men, I showed you how to shelter her from danger and to help her by teaching her about life in such a way that you can marry her decently. I offered you all the help I could to assure that she'd be accepted into the Casa delle Zitelle,** and I also promised you, if you took her there, to help you with all the means at my disposal, as well. At first you thanked me and seemed to be listening to me and to be well disposed toward my affectionate offer. Together we agreed on what needed to be done so that she'd be accepted there, and we were about to carry out our plan when you underwent I don't know what change of heart. . . . All at once, you let her show up with curls dangling around her brow and down her neck, with bare breasts spilling out of her dress, with a high, uncovered forehead, and every other embellishment people use to make their merchandise measure up to the competition. . . . [and] you led people to believe that she has little concern for her honor through the gossip and scandal you . . . provoked.

*Excerpts from Veronica Franco, *Poems and Selected Letters*, eds. and trans. Ann Rosalind Jones and Margaret F. Rosenthal, The Other Voice in Early Modern Europe Series, Margaret L. King and Albert Rabil, Jr., series eds. (Chicago: University of Chicago Press, 1998), pp. 37–40. Copyright © 1998 by The University of Chicago. Reprinted by permission of The University of Chicago Press.

**A charitable institution for poor girls designed to preserve their chastity and thus their chance for marriage.

Now, finally, I wanted to be sure to write you these lines, urging you again to beware of what you're doing and not to slaughter in one stroke your soul and your reputation, along with your daughter's—who, considered from the purely carnal point of view, is really not very beautiful . . . and has so little grace and wit in conversation that you'll break her neck expecting her to do well in the courtesan's profession, which is hard enough to succeed in even if a woman has beauty, style, good judgment, and proficiency in many skills. . . .

I'll add that even if fate should be completely favorable and kind to her, this is a life that always turns out to be a misery. It's a most wretched thing, contrary to human reason, to subject one's body and labor to a slavery terrifying even to think of. To make oneself prey to so many men, at the risk of being stripped, robbed, even killed, . . . along with so many other dangers of injury and dreadful contagious diseases; to eat with another's mouth, sleep with another's eyes, move according to another's will, obviously rushing toward the shipwreck of your mind and your body—what greater misery? What wealth, what luxuries, what delights can outweigh all this? Believe me, among all the world's calamities, this is the worst. . . .

. . . Don't allow the flesh of your wretched daughter not only to be cut into pieces and sold but you yourself to become her butcher. Consider the likely outcome; and if you want to observe other cases, look at what's happened and happens every day to the multitude of women in this occupation. . . .

As for me, besides the promises I've already made you, which I have every intention of keeping, ask me to do anything I can and I'll be ready immediately to help you in any way possible—as I now beg you . . . to avoid this dire possibility before it's too late. For once you've thrown the stone into the water, you'll find it very hard to get it out again. . . . May Our Lord save you from your obvious intention to ruin and corrupt what you created from your own flesh and blood. However much I could say to you, I'd still have more to say on this subject. So I'll go no further but leave you to think carefully before you come to any decision.

FROM NOBLE AMATEURS TO PROFESSIONAL PERFORMERS: WOMEN IN THEATER AND MUSIC

The Revival of Italian Drama: Theater at Court and Popular Theater

Isabella d'Este's father, the duke of Ferrara, revived Italian drama in 1486 when he inaugurated performances of the comedies of Roman playwrights Terence and Plautus with his courtiers serving as amateur actors. The performances grew more lavish, with music, tableaux, and dancing added during *intermezzi* (intermissions). After Isabella and her sister appeared, it became acceptable for noblewomen to participate in court performances.

Meanwhile, popular theater began to emerge. Actors in these all-male, often bawdy comedies did not perform in scripted plays; rather, they developed a theater of improvisation. As they spontaneously interacted following a general plot line, they created lasting character types. As early as 1545, professional acting companies emerged in northern Italy. In 1564, a company comprised of six actors and one actress signed a performance contract. Soon, the companies or *commedia dell'arte* (theater by professionals) required at least four women and six or seven men for the standard roles that had evolved. Female characters included two servants and two *innamorate* (ladies in love or ladies beloved).

Isabella Andreini (1562–1604) and the Commedia dell'Arte

Isabella Andreini changed the image of women on stage and helped make professional women accepted in the theater and subsequently in music as well. Her admirers and patrons included Vicenzo Gonzaga (who served as godfather for one of her daughters), the d'Este and Medici families, the king and queen of France, an archbishop, a cardinal, and many poets, scholars, dukes, and princes.

She was born in Padua to a Venetian family named Canali and somehow received the broad education given a lady courtier. She made her theater debut in 1576 at the age of 14, playing a *prima donna innamorata* (first lady in love) with the Gelosi company. In 1578, she married her leading man and the director of the Gelosi troupe, Francesco Andreini (1548–1624). Despite a career that took the company to Bavaria and Austria, all over northern Italy, and four times to France, the couple had seven children. She died in 1604 in Lyon, France, from a miscarriage she suffered as the company was returning to Italy after performing for several months in Paris for Henry IV and Queen Marie de' Medici.

Her talent was legendary. She could dance, and was an accomplished singer and lute player. Other actors called her "the greatest comic actress the profession has ever known" (Dersofi 1994, 23). Her characterization of the *prima donna innamorata* was so popular it became a stock role in the *commedia,* named, after her, the "Isabella character." Her "Isabella" was loving and virtuous, yet also an outspoken, lively heroine, whether appearing as lucky Isabella, Isabella the prankster, or jealous Isabella. Her most famous role, *La Pazzia di Isabella* (Isabella's madness), showcased her diverse talents as she roamed the stage switching among several languages, dialects, and characterizations. Her mad scenes became a permanent part of theatrical and operatic traditions. (Dersofi 1994, 22–23)

Andreini elevated acting to a respectable profession for women because she had an impeccable reputation. Her personal behavior and her efforts to elevate theater and eliminate its more bawdy elements solidified her image as a *donna di salda virtu* (woman of solid virtue). She enhanced her reputation as a model of piety by committing four daughters and a son to monastic life. Andreini also won acclaim as a writer. She wrote a pastoral play, *Mirtilla* (1588), and over 300 poems that were published in one volume, *Rime,* in 1601. She had the rare honor for a woman of being admitted to an academy and her election to the Academy of the *Intenti* in Pavia was celebrated throughout Italy.

The letter that follows illustrates the importance she placed on her reputation as a virtuous woman. For some reason she had fallen out of favor with Duke Vicenzo di Gonzaga, and in this document she tries to repair the damage. Her concern about her own reputation mirrored a general concern about woman's honor that was a frequent theme in her letters.

LETTER TO DUKE VICENZO DI GONZAGA OF MANTUA, FROM BOLOGNA, 27 NOVEMBER 1598*

> A wrong which might fall upon us because of our shortcoming would be most easy to bear, but it is intolerable that this one has fallen upon us through no fault of our own: this injustice is especially intolerable and most seriously displeasing to me because I see, my Most Serene Lord, that I have fallen out of the grace of your Most Serene Highness, whose grace I esteem as much as life itself, not through my own fault but through that of others. But having given this, and having conceded as well that it is to my enemy's advantage that I might be considered guilty of an offense

---

*From D'Ancona, Alessandro, *Origini del teatro italiano* (*Origins of the Italian Theater*), *libri tre con due appendici sulla rappresentazione drammatica del contado toscano e sul teatro mantovano nel sec. XVI,* 2d. ed. rev. vol. II (Torino: E. Loescher, 1891), p. 521. Trans. Chris Harris.

against your Highest Lordship, might you not remember though, your grace, my Benign Lord, that princes are nothing more than earthly gods, and since it's not allowed only of the gods to put aside disdain or anger against mortal things, so might you be forgiving, my earthly Lord, of having been angry or offended by me, your most infinite servant, because it is truly a character of the great souls to soon forget offense. Whether this has happened through my foolishness or through others' fraudulent offense, it pleases me to believe that your Highest Lordship might both be placated and might condemn the offense to oblivion, so that I am completely forgiven and so that I and all my world will be secure, and that at a time pleasing to your Highest Lordship I will be recalled to your most desired service. With utmost affection I pray again to God that he grant to your highness, to your most serene wife and children, greater happiness.

Your most humble servant, Isabella Andreini

The Emergence of Professional Female Musicians

By the early Renaissance, music, except in convents, had become a masculine field. Male musicians and composers were trained in cathedral schools for boys, universities, and church choirs, and only men could pursue a profession in these institutions or at the courts of the nobility. By 1600, however, women could pursue a career in music as an alternative to marriage or life in a convent. What changed Italian attitudes toward women musicians?

The most important step in the emergence of professional women musicians occurred in Ferrara. In 1580–81, Duke Alfonso of Ferrara (grandson of Isabella d'Este's brother) and his wife created a unique madrigal group of three talented women. In 1583, a fourth woman was added. Like Sofonisba Anguissola, the women were brought to court as ladies-in-waiting for the duchess. In reality, however, they were court musicians. They were daughters of minor nobility, court poets/musicians, and wealthy merchants. The women were paid handsomely, with housing, an annual salary, and, if single, a dowry. They performed in the *musica secreta,* or intimate concerts, for the family and guests, but their fame spread quickly as visitors praised the *concerto delle donne* (group of singing ladies) of Ferrara. Between 1584 and 1590, *concerti di donne* were established in Florence, Mantua, and Rome. By 1589, some courts had begun to bring talented girls of lower classes to court where they were trained specifically to become professional court musicians. The excerpts from *The Madrigal at Ferrara* that follow illustrate the central role music played at Duke Alfonso's court.* Urbani was the Florentine ambassador to Ferrara and Alessandro Striggio was a Mantuan composer.

Urbani Dispatch to Grand Duke Francesco I de' Medici, 26 June 1581

Cardinal Madruccio was entertained on the day of his arrival with the usual music of the ladies, which takes place every day without fail. The Duke is so inclined to and absorbed in this thing that he appears to have placed there not only all his delight but also the sum total of his attention. One can give him no greater pleasure than by appreciating and praising his ladies, who are constantly studying new inventions.

*From Newcomb, Anthony, THE MADRIGAL AT FERRARA, 1579–1597. Vol. I, pp. 24, 55. Copyright © 1980 by Princeton University Press. Reprinted by Permission of Princeton University Press.

ALESSANDRO STRIGGIO TO GRAND DUKE FRANCESCO I DE' MEDICI, 29 JULY 1584

Here the Duke of Ferrara wants to hear my bass lyre every day and was rather pleased with Sandrino. And then he favored me by allowing me to hear for two hours without break his *concerto di donne,* which is truly extraordinary. Those ladies sing excellently; both when singing in their *concerto* [from memory] and when singing at sight from part books they are secure. The Duke favored me continually by showing me written out all the pieces that they sing by memory, with all the diminutions that they do.

THEATER AND MUSIC IN ITALIAN CONVENTS

Women in many convents enjoyed a rich cultural environment that was enhanced by the supportive atmosphere of their female subculture and by periodic visits of outsiders. Not surprisingly, nuns constituted the largest group of women writers in sixteenth-century Italy (Weaver 1986, 173). Drama had long been a part of convent life. In fact, Hrotswitha of Gandersheim (c. 935–1001), author of six Latin plays, was the first European playwright since the Romans, and Abbess Hildegard of Bingen (1098–1179) wrote the first play set to music. Their works were performed in their convents (see Volume One, Chapter 14, "Medieval Culture: The Religious Context"). Convents also regularly celebrated special days with dramatic productions. Convent theater in Renaissance Italy drew upon this rich tradition but was also shaped by trends in the secular world.

Antonia Pulci (1452–1501)

Playwright Antonia Pulci was the daughter of a Florentine banker. She received a broad classical education typical of that provided sons and daughters of Florentine merchants. In 1470, she was married at 18 to Bernardo Pulci. Both wrote poetry and plays, and they collaborated on sacred dramas that were performed and published in Florence. When Bernardo died in 1487, Pulci resisted her brother's demands that she remarry and chose instead to live as a *pinzochera,* or uncloistered Augustinian sister.

Pinzochere were middle- and working-class women who chose a religious life but lived at home or in informal communities with other women instead of inside a convent. They lived a life of piety, did charitable work, and often worked as midwives and healers. More importantly, they were independent of both male family members and male religious superiors. The *pinzochere* were the Italian counterpart of the Beguines of northern Europe whom the Church charged with heresy and suppressed in the thirteenth century (see Volume One, Chapter 14). These independent female communities thrived in fifteenth-century Italy. Around 1500, Pulci founded a new religious order, the Order of Santa Maria della Misericordia. She funded her order and its charitable works with her dowry (which reverted to her after her husband's death) and with income from her plays (Cook and Cook 1996, 18).

Antonia Pulci contributed to the growth of convent theater by writing five plays, each of which called for elaborate costuming and staging. The plays were performed for convent and lay audiences and helped increase the popularity of convent drama among the public. Her plays were printed in 1490, and woodcuts depicting some of the performances were also produced (Cook and Cook 1996, 35).

More importantly, she was among the first women in Renaissance Europe to write in a "feminist voice." In her plays, women were the strongest characters: intelligent, active, goal-oriented, and stable.

They grappled with the issues and challenges she and all women confronted in their daily lives, such as dependency on men, legal and social subordination, marriage and children, and sexual pressures. She also portrayed women finding means of empowerment and alternative ways of living their lives through women's communities.

This play opens with the emperor rewarding one of his barons by giving him the noblewoman Domitilla as his wife. Initially, she welcomes her bridegroom. Her Christian servants, however, who had promised her deceased mother they would care for her and rear her in their faith, are horrified that she will marry a pagan. Thus, they try to convince her that a religious life is a better choice for her than marriage.

THE PLAY OF SAINT (FLAVIA) DOMITILLA*

[DOMITILLA RESPONDS TO HER SERVANTS]

What greater sweetness could be, I don't
    know,
Than having a husband worthy to be
    yours
And sharing with him the flower of his
    youth,
Young and rich and with a courteous
    wit,

Thereafter children, who in your old age
Will be your life's support, its staff; and
    who
Can cease to value certainties? Who
    would
Exchange them for uncertainties to
    come?

[ONE OF THE SERVANTS ANSWERS]

You, Domitilla, have placed your every
    trust
In the pomp of this false world, which
    will,
Just like a flower, pass and not endure,

And where you seek, peace never can be
    found, . . .
[Her servants urge her to reconsider, ar-
    guing a woman can only find hap-
    piness and peace by committing
    herself to God.]

[DOMITILLA RESPONDS]

What is more difficult than to despise
The riches of this present life and not
Desire to taste the pleasures manifold
Of human splendor, great nobility,
So one can want, at last, another life
That one gains for oneself with torment
    and

With harshness, fasting, and with
    discipline?
These your doctrines—who can
    understand?

*Excerpts from *The Play of Saint (Flavia) Domitilla,* in Antonia Pulci, *Florentine Drama for Convent and Festival. Seven Sacred Plays,* trans. James Wyatt Cook, eds. James Wyatt Cook and Barbara Collier Cook. The Other Voice in Early Modern Europe Series, Margaret L. King and Albert Rabil, Jr., eds. (Chicago: University of Chicago Press, 1996), pp. 78–82. Copyright © 1996 by The University of Chicago Press. Reprinted by permission of The University of Chicago Press.

[ONE OF THE SERVANTS REPLIES]

When you have been united with your
    spouse,
The title of virginity you'll lose,
And whether he will kindly be to you
Is hidden from you, for one's often
    blithe,
But knows not why; always, to know
    about
The future is unsure, and so one weighs
These outcomes: you today a maiden's
    gown
Wear, then you'll be a woman and a
    wife,
   And you, who could not even
    entertain
The very notion that your virginal
Nobility might be defiled, would to
A pagan base submit and bend yourself
To every pleasure of his, transform your
    life,

Your habits, and your manners, and
    your style,
His every vile commandment would
    perform
So that his appetite might sated be.
   All these husbands put their best foot
    forward:
When their lady is engaged to them
How humble, then, they wish to seem,
    and mild
At least until they've led her to their
    home.
However, secrets like those you can't
    know
If you have not first spent some time
    with him
You will be filled with fear and full of
    doubt.
Be sure you think about such outcomes
    well.

[DOMITILLA SAYS]

My mother suffered, as I well recall,
So many torments throughout all her
    life;
Because of her husband's jealousy alone
Bore very great distress; and if I were
To think that I would follow such a
    path,

The garments of the world I'd never
    don,
Though I don't think my spouse
    Aurelian
Would act like this because he is so kind.

[ONE OF THE SERVANTS CONTINUES]

That which I tell you often comes to
    pass,
Lo, some keep mistresses or concubines,
And some their ladies batter painfully,
Torment them with harsh discipline so
    cruel;
Many scornful outbursts, too, they bear;
One needs to think through all things to
    their end
About the pangs of childbirth and the
    woes
So grievous when the children are
    brought forth.

   Sometimes, as well, when coming
    forth, a child
Will be born dumb, deformed, or sense-
    less, whence
The mother will experience great grief,
For one who's born blind by the world is
    scorned;
Consider now if you'd have great regret
For ever having borne a child like these.
Sometimes the children, too, when they
    are born,
May be the causes of their mothers'
    deaths. . . .

[DOMITILLA IS WON OVER AND SAYS]

Truly I seem to feel my heart unfold,
Such power have your words, and what within
I feel I can't tell you, but I'm much grieved
I took a spouse because I wish

To serve Christ Jesus and his holy law
Be one who wants to flee the world and each
Vain thought—yet I desire to go away
From my intended spouse, Aurelian.
But how may I flee from his hands?

[SHE REALIZES SHE CAN DEPEND ON GOD FOR PROTECTION, AND MAKES HER DECISION.]

Arrange for me to take the veil at once
And to be consecrated to my Spouse
Eternal who entirely has inflamed
Me with his love, for his delights and peace
Most high, behold me present here, prepared
To serve my lord, compassionate and just,
Thou who has opened me and seized my heart

Oh, make me constant in thy tender love.
[The rest of the drama unfolds in a powerful series of scenes that depict the struggle between Christians and non-Christians, as the emperor and her betrothed try to force Domitilla to recant and marry. She remains firm, and the play ends with her burned at the stake, but gaining eternal glory.]

Convent Music

A few convents offered some of the finest musical training available in Europe. The convent of San Vito in Ferrara was the most famous musical convent in the second half of the sixteenth century, renowned for its singers and its extraordinary range of instrumentalists. Courtier Hercole Bottrigari, who visited San Vito in the 1570s and 1580s, described what he heard in the dialogue that follows. Note the gender assumptions that surface in the dialogue.

THE CHOIR OF CONVENT SAN VITO, 1594*

[Alemanno Benelli tells Gratioso Desiderio he has heard] . . . musical concerts into which all sorts and diverse kinds of instruments enter in the highest degree of perfection which human and earthly imperfection can achieve. [Gratioso is puzzled by hints the musicians might be women.]

Gr. These are women, indeed?

Al. They are indubitably women; and when you watch them come in . . . to the place where a long table has been prepared, at one end of which is found a large clavicembalo, you would see them enter one by one, quietly bringing their instruments, either stringed or wind. . . . Finally the Maestra of the concert sits down at one end of the table and with a long, slender and well-polished wand . . . , and when all the

*From Hercole Bottrigari, *Il Desiderio, or Concerning the Playing Together of Various Musical Instruments.* Musicological Studies and Documents Series, no. 9, pt. 1–2 (Rome: American Institute of Musicology, 1962), pp. 57–59. Copyright © 1962 by Armen Carapetyan. By permission of the American Institute of Musicology.

other sisters clearly are ready, gives them without noise several signs to begin, and then continues by beating the measure of the time which they must obey in singing and playing. . . .

[Al. identifies the musicians as nuns at the convent of San Vito in Ferrara.]

Gr. . . . But what about the particulars of their learning to sing, and even more, to play instruments, particularly those of wind, which it is almost impossible to learn without maestri. Being women they cannot easily manipulate Cornetti and Trombones, which are the most difficult of musical instruments.

Al. Those instruments are nearly always used doubled in the music which they play ordinarily on all the Feast days of the year. And they play them with such grace, and with such a nice manner, and such sonorous and just intonation of the notes that even people who are esteemed most excellent in the profession confess that it is incredible to anyone who does not actually see and hear it. And their passage work is not of the kind that is chopped up, furious, and continuous, such that it spoils and distorts the principal air, which the skillful composer worked ingeniously to give to the *cantilena*; but at times and in certain places there are such light, vivacious embellishments that they enhance the music and give it the greatest spirit.

Gr. I am stupefied; I am truly amazed. But, after all, who instructed them in the beginning? It must be necessary if one wishes to maintain, if not to increase the bright splendor of musical concerts, that there be someone who looks after it, and is intelligent and expert enough to instruct, so that it may be done so carefully and dextrously.

Al. That same nun who is the director of the concerto is also Maestra of all the beginners both in singing and in playing; and with such decorum and gravity of bearing has she always proceeded . . . in this office that her equals . . . are glad to acknowledge her and esteem her for their superior, loving and obeying her, fearing and honoring her completely.

Gr. She must have a rare and noble intellect to direct and instruct in the profession of music those other honest and learned persons, . . .

SUGGESTED READINGS

Parker, Rozsika. *The Subversive Stitch: Embroidery and the Making of the Feminine.* New York: Routledge, 1989.

Wiesner, Merry E. *Women and Gender in Early Modern Europe.* Cambridge: Cambridge University Press, 1993.

Art

Ferino-Pagden, Sylvia and Maria Kusche. *Sofonisba Anguissola: A Renaissance Woman.* Washington, D.C.: The National Museum of Women in the Arts, 1995.

Patrons

Lawrence, Cynthia, ed. *Women and Art in Early Modern Europe: Patrons, Collectors, and Connoisseurs.* University Park: Pennsylvania State University Press, 1997.

Prizer, William. "Isabella d'Este and Lucrezia Borgia as Patrons of Music: The Frottola at Mantua and Ferrara." *Journal of the American Musicological Society.* 38, no. 1, (Spring, 1985), 1–33.

Humanists and Poets

Bassanese, Fiora. *Gaspara Stampa.* Boston: Twayne, 1982.

Lawner, Lynne. *Lives of the Courtesans: Portraits of the Renaissance.* New York: Rizzoli, 1987.

Rabil, Albert. *Laura Cereta, Quattrocento Humanist.* Binghamton, NY: Center for Medieval and Early Renaissance Studies, 1981.

Rosenthal, Margaret. *The Honest Courtesan: Veronica Franco, Citizen and Writer in Sixteenth-Century Venice.* Chicago: University of Chicago Press, 1992.

Music

Brown, Howard Mayer. "Women Singers and Women's Songs in Fifteenth-Century Italy." In *Women Making Music: The Western Art Tradition, 1150–1950.* Jane Bowers and Judith Tick, eds. Urbana & Chicago: University of Illinois Press, 1987. [Hereafter cited as *Women Making Music.* Bowers and Tick, 1987.]

Map 1–1   Renaissance Italy

Chapter 2

The Age of Religious Ferment

The religious reformations in Europe in the sixteenth century were a response to transitions and transformations in the social and political sphere that had been emerging for well over a century. As we have seen in previous chapters, Europe was experiencing the breakdown of the feudal system, decentralization, and the rise of nation states.

Seeds for reform in the religious sphere, expressed in both the Protestant and Catholic reformations had been germinating since the Renaissance in Italy. Although essential differences defined both reform movements, elements of humanist thought were common to each. As humanist ideas formulated in Italy were disseminated in the north, we find significant influences that became integral to the Protestant impetus.

We discuss first the Protestant Reformation and the influence of humanist thought that, in the religious context, was characterized by the *new learning*. This new learning was grounded in the rediscovery of philosophy from ancient Greece and Rome, writings of the early Church fathers, and scholarship that insisted on reading sacred texts, for oneself, in the original Hebrew, Greek, or Latin. With the advent of the printing press it became equally significant to make such texts available in the vernacular. Antischolasticism was also common to both humanists and Protestant reformers, specifically as regards an overemphasis on *dialectic,* the dualistic concept of the contradiction of opposites as in a thesis and antithesis. Both recognized the Scholastics' dualistic theological persuasion as functioning for control among the masses and in the Church.

Humanists and Protestant reformers saw monastic life as making a distinction between elitist forms of religion and the ordinary life of Christians in the world. Both Protestants and humanists were interested in the priority of interior religious experience with a de-emphasis on external expressions such as visual arts, architecture, statuary, ornate vestments, and opulent liturgical celebrations.

Three major differences between humanists and Protestant reformers include humanist's *universalism* in its religious orientation as seen, for example in Erasmus' love of Origen, who said that "all the world will be saved," rather than in Luther's "One Way." Humanists, embracing the notion of human perfectibility, also held that it is possible to *teach* goodness, ethics, and the search for the Good. Reformers held fast to the idea that all humans are "in sin" and that God's Grace alone was sufficient for salvation. Humanists were more inclusive and optimistic, while reformers were more exclusive and pessimistic.

In the present chapter we proceed with the understanding that yet a different interpretive framework among Renaissance humanists produced Machiavelli. His classic work *The Prince* declared that among the aristocracy where the *end* (Greek *telos,* consequence) is preservation and extension of one's rule and peace for the common person; the *means* can consist of whatever is expedient. This aspect of humanism, and its interest in the centrality of human agency, was not necessarily concerned at all with religion for the sake of religion. The political agendas of aristocrats and an emerging wealthy middle class who were embroiled in strategies to secure or obtain and maintain their desired status are interwoven throughout the entire period of the reformations. Political ambitions among aristocrats that extended from the popes and clerical hierarchy to major and minor players among the nobility became an integral feature of struggles for Catholic and Protestant reforms. The quest for equal treatment and fairness among the poor also became a significant feature of the struggle. Agendas such as those suggested above influenced everything from the social organization of religious fellowships to doctrinal considerations among Protestant and Catholic reformers. By the sixteenth century the principal families in the Italian nobility discussed in Chapter 1 wed their daughters and widows to families in Germany, Poland, Sweden, Denmark, Norway, and the Netherlands. Powerful Italian families were thus integrally woven into the political machinations of the Reformation in the north. As we proceed there will be brief references to some of the more influential *dramatis personae.*

Principal components of Protestant reform are characterized by the break with the *imperial authority of Rome.* Political agendas, warfare, and bloodshed that achieved such autonomy are, tragically, also part of the Protestant legacy. Transfer of ecclesiastical and spiritual authority to local geographical districts and the local parish churches became a primary feature of reform. Protestants were agreed that no professional intermediaries were needed for the laity, that all members of the Church could receive both bread *and* wine at Holy Communion, and that all Christians have a religious calling, not just priests and monastics.

Among Protestants, this anti-monastic position resulted in a major focus on the family as central to living out the Gospel *in the world.* The patriarchal family unit took on a new significance, replacing monastic life as *the* ideal model for Christian community. Convents were raided and hundreds of medieval religious compounds were destroyed. Male and female Protestants proselytized the nuns and monks. Such invasions into the cloisters were often horrifying. Among nuns who did decide to join the reform, marriages were arranged, often immediately after the nuns left their convents. Women who had recently emerged from convents were seen as excellent "matches" for monks who had left their monasteries. The decision making about whom would wed whom sometimes took place in the midst of a village square only hours or days following the women's arrival in that village.

For Protestant male clerics and scholars who sought theological reform, the new theologies were liberating. Yet, these same males determined an *ideal* for women that robbed women of their autonomy outside the home. *Virtue,* so defined, again mirrored the oppressive ideal for Roman matrons of antiquity that persists as an integral aspect of the patriarchal paradigm. A good woman must be bound to the private sphere.

The Catholic Reformation was characterized predominately by an aggressive momentum to re-establish and re-enforce, ever more resolutely, the primacy and authority of the *Church of Rome.* Means to this end were varied and many proceeded from the writings of humanists such as Erasmus of Rotterdam (1466–1536) who had sought Church reform from within the institution. Reforms from within included the founding of universities such as the University of Alcala in Spain, Corpus Christi University at Oxford, and the College de France in Paris, where humanist principles of biblical scholarship flourished. Among new monastic communities there was a more intentional interaction between monks and nuns increasingly referred to as *Brothers and Sisters* and the laity. The Society of Jesus, founded by the Spaniard Ignatius of Loyola (1539), excelled in scholarship and made its impact in re-conquering much of Europe for the Church. The Jesuits also established foundations abroad to bring Christianity throughout the known world.

Greater emphasis on the interior life of prayer, contemplation, and return to simplicity of life were exemplified by Teresa of Avila (1515–1582), who became one of two female Doctors of the Church. John of the Cross, the revered mystic and spiritual teacher, shared in Teresa's vision and was a signifi-cant voice in her reform of the Carmelite Order.

A resurgence of the Inquisition and the physical torment and psychological anguish of its victims are unspeakably horrendous aspects of the battle for hegemony by the Roman Church. Positive initia-tives toward reform took place on a variety of fronts that culminated in the Council of Trent which convened on three occasions between 1545 and 1563. Principle issues addressed by the Council in-cluded primacy of the papacy, the ritual of the Mass, dogma concerning transubstantiation, and assur-ance of a more effective ecclesiastical government.

Catholic women in religious orders continued to find greater agency and autonomy in the Church than all but a relatively few of their Protestant sisters. The lives of Catholic women outside religious or-ders continued much as before. As proliferation and expansion of monastic orders outside of Europe and the British Isles increased, opportunities for women in religious orders to pioneer such efforts began to increase as well. In Volume One, Chapter 14, "Medieval Culture: The Religious Context," we read that legends of St. Ursula and her 10,000 Virgins were a particularly favorite theme in liturgical celebrations composed by Hildegard of Bingen. In centuries following the reformations thousands of the Sisters of the Order of St. Ursula were pioneers in bringing Christianity to newly discovered terri-tories around the world.

WOMEN IN THE PROTESTANT REFORMATION

Whereas two of the earliest leaders of religious reform were John Wycliffe (d.1384) and John Huss (d.1415), it was almost a century after Huss that Martin Luther (1483–1546) tacked his 95 Theses for Re-form on the door of the church at Wittenberg in late October of 1517. Prevalent names associated with Protestant reform tend to be males and include Philip Melancthon in the German states, John Calvin pre-dominately in Geneva, Ulrich Zwingli in Zurich, and Martin Bucer in Strasbourg, among many others.

Political realities of the period played a major role in the social organization of Protestant churches. The major centers on the continent where the early impetus to reform was most pronounced included the German states, Holland, Austria, Switzerland, and France. In England Henry VIII broke away from Rome in 1534. As queen from 1558 to 1603, his daughter Elizabeth I facilitated the masterful balance between Protestant and Catholic concerns that characterize the Anglican Church. Puritans broke away from the Church of England in the seventeenth century as did the Church of Scotland which adopted a Calvinist ethos as Presbyterians. Numerous sectarian communities of men and women emerged, in-cluding the Anabaptists, Quakers, Huguenots, and Moravians, among others. Luther's theology was adopted throughout the German states and eventually spread to Scandinavia, Hungary, and Switzer-land. Calvinism was exported to France, the Netherlands, Scotland, and elsewhere.

The influence of Protestant reform on the interpretation of gender and women in Europe and in European colonies is more disappointing than encouraging. The emphasis on family meant that the *ideal woman* was relegated to the private sphere: to the home as wife and mother. Opportunities for education were a positive feature of reform as were the designation of the marriage contract to the status of a civil document and the greater opportunities for women to obtain divorce under certain conditions.

Over time, however, the frail status of women's autonomy declined even further. As practices became policies, and policies became laws, the legal systems deprived women of property rights to the extent that they were effectively chattels of their husbands. Despite the fact that many women managed both enormous estates and small farms when their menfolk were away at war, neither the farms nor the children bred to help farm them, were *theirs*.

During the initial years that Protestant reform was expanding, however, we discover anew a pattern that characteristically emerges in periods of significant social change, namely, a flourishing among women as notable contributors to culture. Despite assertions to the contrary in Eurocentric and androcentric sources, many women did, in the early years of the Reformation, assume notable roles as patrons, teachers, evangelists, providers of sanctuary, preachers, writers of tracts and letters, and martyrs for the cause. Names of some of these women include not only those who left the Catholic Church, but women who did not leave and were agents of change from within the institution. Many women whose reformist persuasions influenced the thought of clerics, monastics, and members of the laity were suspect by the Inquisition and vulnerable to martyrdom. A representative list of women who were active in religious reform includes: Katherine von Bora Luther, Ursula of Munsterberg, Wibrandis Rosenblatt, Elizabeth of Brandenburg (late in her life), Catherine Melancthon, and Anna Zwingli from the German States. From France we note Marguerite of Navarre, who is discussed in the following chapter, Jeanne d'Albret, Charlotte de Bourbon, and Louise de Coligny. From the powerful Bresgna family in Italy, Isabella Bresgna came north to live as a Protestant. In Scotland, Elizabeth Bowes and her daughter Marjory Knox and Anne Locke were avowed Protestants. In Denmark, Isabel, the queen of Christian II was a devoted Lutheran, as was Queen Dorothea, queen of Christian III, and Anna Hardenberg, who also became Queen of Denmark for a brief time. In Poland, Jadwige Gnoinskiej founded the Rakovians, an egalitarian Christian community, in 1567, in which women as well as men were preachers. The majority of women in the Protestant Reformation whose legacies are recorded were members of the nobility. Several royal and aristocratic women in the north were members of aristocratic families in Italy whose marriages served to expand, geographically, the family dynasties.

Selections by Martin Luther and John Calvin that follow provide a sense of the prevailing ideas among male leaders about gender in the Protestant Reformation.

Martin Luther (1483–1546)

Martin Luther looms larger in tradition than many other reformers because of the particular part that he played in precipitating events that required the Church to respond. Numerous excellent biographies are available that explore the complex life of Martin Luther and his considerable contributions to the Reformation. His wife Katherine von Bora Luther (1499–1552) was born into a family whose status as *nobility* was no longer defined by wealth. She went to a Benedictine convent school from the age of five and was professed as a nun after her sixteenth birthday. When a group of Protestants entered her convent to proselytize, Katherine was one of a group of eleven nuns who left the convent to join the reform. As was customary, the women were paired with males at the soonest possible opportunity. When neither of two men selected for Katherine worked out, it was decided that she would marry Martin Luther. Luther had great admiration for his "Katy," who, over time, managed the ever-expanding Luther household, gardens, animals, guest quarters, hospice, the six children that she bore him, and all elements of hospitality for the never-ending stream of theologians, students, guests, and family who dined at the Luthers' table.

The *Table-Talk* is a favorite source for candid, humorous insights into the "lived" theology of Martin Luther. When at table with Katherine he praises her, teases her, and clearly acknowledges his delight in her and his clear preference for married life above celibacy. Yet, as the short excerpt from his sermon on Genesis demonstrates, Luther's theology of gender left a great deal to be desired. Note the extent to which he is wedded to the second creation story in Genesis chapter 2 and its story of Adam and Eve rather than the Genesis chapter 1 account wherein the two human beings are equal in the sight of God. Note, as well, the extent to which the female is understood to exist in order to be in the service of the male.

LECTURE ON "GENESIS"*

The Lord God also said: It is not good that man is alone; I shall make him a help which should be before him.

We have the church established by the Word and a distinct form of worship. There was no need of civil government, since nature was unimpaired and without sin. Now also the household is set up. For God makes a husband of lonely Adam and joins him to a wife, who was needed to bring about the increase of the human race. Just as we pointed out above in connection with the creation of man that Adam was created in accordance with a well-considered counsel, so here, too, we perceive that Eve is being created according to a definite plan. Thus here once more Moses points out that man is a unique creature and that he is suited to be a partaker of divinity and of immortality. For man is a more excellent creature than heaven and earth and everything that is in them.

But Moses wanted to point out in a special way that the other part of humanity, the woman, was created by a unique counsel of God in order to show that this sex, too, is suited for the kind of life which Adam was expecting and that this sex was to be useful for procreation. Hence it follows that if the woman had not been deceived by the serpent and had not sinned, she would have been the equal of Adam in all respects. For the punishment, that she is now subjected to the man, was imposed on her after sin and because of sin, just as the other hardships and dangers were: travail, pain, and countless other vexations. Therefore Eve was not like the woman of today; her state was far better and more excellent, and she was in no respect inferior to Adam, whether you count the qualities of the body or those of the mind. . . .

. . . So the woman was a helper for Adam; for he was unable to procreate alone, just as the woman was also unable to procreate alone. Moreover, these are the highest praises of sex, that the male is the father in procreation, but the woman is the mother in procreation and the helper of her husband. When we look back to the state of innocence, procreation, too, was better, more delightful, and more sacred in countless ways.

John Calvin (1509–1564)

Among Protestant reformers, John Calvin was the most familiar with humanist thought. Calvin was a brilliant man who, when he first encountered the literature of the Reformation, wished nothing so much as to devote himself to quiet, contemplation, and thoughtful reading of the emerging literature.

*From Martin Luther, "Lectures on Genesis," *Luther's Works,* trans. and ed. Theodore G. Tappert, vol.1 (Philadelphia: Fortress Press, 1967), pp. 115, 118.

Such was not to be the case. John Calvin became one of the most significant Protestant theologians, a preacher, teacher, founder, and spiritual architect of a model for Christian community.

Calvin, like most other reformers had female patrons who were dedicated to reform as expressed in his theology and as *lived out* in theocratic Christian communities such as Geneva. Myriad biographic works on John Calvin abound in the literature and can be consulted for further information on this significant contributor to the success of the Protestant reform movement. The following brief selection articulates the Calvinist notion of a "woman's place."

EXCERPT FROM *THE INSTITUTES**

THE INSTITUTES II.VIII.41

Man has been created in this condition that he may not lead a solitary life, but may enjoy a helper joined to himself [cf. Gen. 2:18]; then by the curse of sin he has been still more subjected to this necessity. Therefore, the Lord sufficiently provided for us in this matter when he established marriage, the fellowship of which, begun on his authority, he also sanctified by his blessing. From this it is clear that any other union apart from marriage is accursed in his sight; and that the companionship of marriage has been ordained as a necessary remedy to keep us from plunging into unbridled lust. Let us not delude ourselves, then, when we hear that outside marriage man cannot cohabit with a woman without God's curse. . . .

Argula von Grumbach (1492–ca.1568)

Born in 1492, Argula von Stauff lived at the castle in the village of Eherenfelt throughout her childhood. Her family, members of the Bavarian nobility, were known to be refined and were recognized and admired for their defense of religious tolerance. The von Stauff family was a religious family who had a keen interest in politics and who placed a premium on excellence in education. Argula's confidence, as an adult, in skillfully addressing the confluence of religion and politics had its genesis in her familiarity with the topics from her family environment as well as teenage years at the court of the politically astute and deeply spiritual Queen Kunigunde.

Following the tendency of women in the north to marry later than women in the Mediterranean, Argula's first marriage, to the wealthy Frederich von Grumbach, was consummated in 1521. In their nine years of marriage before he died they had three sons and a daughter. Argula was intentional about the education of her children. Although reared as a Roman Catholic, Argula became a Protestant and was among the earliest female writers in the Protestant Reformation. The reformers who most influenced her own theology were the Lutherans at Wittenberg and she insured that her son Georges studied there. Her two remaining sons studied at Ingolstadt with respected reformers and her daughter Apollonia matriculated at Nuremberg. Argula managed the expenses incurred in financing the children's education as well as her own activities nurturing friendships focused on mutual interest in Reformation theologies.

Argula von Grumbach penned and published at least eight pamphlets and wrote numerous letters and poems. Argula spoke out in defense of the rights of Bavarian women and against violence and sexual promiscuities of husbands. Confident in her position as a laywoman skilled in

*John Calvin, *The Institutes of the Christian Religion,* ed. John T. McNeil, trans. Ford L. Battles, 2 vols. The Library of Christian Classics Series (Philadelphia: Westminster Press, 1960), II.VIII.41, vol.1, p. 407.

comprehension of the Bible and its relevance to society, Argula was effective in challenging the Court and the Church. Catholic sympathizers reviled Argula but Protestants championed her courage and dedication.

Frederick the Wise was the Elector to the Imperial Diet or *Reichstad* and was the principal supporter of the reform movement among the electors. Argula's letter to Frederick, encouraging him and exhorting him, has the tone of a spiritual counselor. Such intimate counsel from a woman to a man of Frederick's importance is, in this time, extraordinary! Argula's confidence in the message she brings and in herself as messenger is grounded in her profound faith.

LETTER TO FREDERICK THE WISE*

May the grace and peace of God be with your Electoral Grace forever—this is my heartfelt wish. Most gracious prince and lord, I could not refrain from writing to your Electoral Grace, for I am delighted at the prospect of the Reichstag which has been summoned. I trust that God Almighty may direct the proceedings and bestow grace, wisdom and strength on all who participate in it so that the word of God may again be preached to the poor; so that there can be an end to its deplorable proscription by those pagan princes who have forcible deprived the poor of it, and who are now persecuting and crucifying Christ anew.

May your Electoral Grace with the help of God stand firm by this certain word of God. For this is how it must be. We must always be ready to proclaim God publicly, as Matthew 10 states. It is my hope and prayer to God that your Electoral Grace will persist in the firm intention he has already shown, giving God the honour, and that your Electoral Grace may be of good cheer, and face up to them with Christian confidence. God says in Isaiah 51: 'I myself will comfort you. Who are you to fear mere mortals. . . ' They will be powerless, as we see in Isaiah 28 and Psalm 11: 'I will bring salvation to the people, so they can resist [their oppressors] confidently.' We already see this salvation, God be praised, and have all the might on our side.

Your Electoral Grace, let them storm and rage all they like; they are powerless. The rock will crush them and cast them to the ground; it will be trap for them. But for those who believe, there will be the resurrection and the precious stone of great worth, as it says in I Peter 2: 'I will lay in Zion a stone which is chosen and precious, to be the capstone, and whoever believes in him will not be put to shame. . . ' But they will be put to shame. One can see how foolish and misled they are, for they can neither speak nor write anything at all.

May your Electoral Grace pay no heed at all when they grind their teeth against Christ; for all power has been taken from them. As Psalm 139 says: 'They have sharpened their tongues like serpents' but their antics are as harmless as the arrows children use for their games. In the same way Isaiah 8 declares: 'You may gather your forces, you peoples; but you will be defeated; give ear, all nations: you may arm yourselves, but you will be defeated; you may gird yourselves for battle, but you will be defeated. Plan a campaign; it will be torn to shreds. Spout forth your opinion, it will come to nought. For God is with us.'

May your Electoral Grace consider how much power God deigned to grant them before, when they still had their full authority, and made them like gods. How

*From Peter Matheson, ed., *Argula von Grumbach: A Woman's Voice in the Reformation* (Edinburgh, UK: T and T Clark, 1995), pp. 132–34. By permission of T and T Clark Publishers.

much more now when God puts them under the feet of women, since they despise their authority! Therefore may your Electoral Grace speak to them from the word of God, let him stand defiantly before them with its power behind him, for your Electoral Grace can see the pot is already boiling, as Jeremiah 1 says. And faced by God in the middle of the night they are powerless to extinguish it.

I spoke last night with Duke Johann, too. I would also gladly have spoken much more with some of the other rulers, if people had been there to listen. God willing, I would not be afraid to meet them face to face when they wanted and as often as they pleased. God grant that Your Electoral Grace may be of good cheer, remembering thankfully that by God's providence our salvation has been preached from your Electoral Grace's land and under his protection, so that Christ is once again taught and known. May the blessing of God Almighty be with your Electoral Grace now and for evermore. Amen. Tuesday after St. Andrew's day, in the year of our Lord 1523.

Your Electoral Grace's humble servant

Argula von Grumbach, née von Stauff.

Katharina Schütz Zell (1498–1562)

A female reformer, Church-Mother, theologian, and follower of the Gospel, Katharina Schütz Zell is perhaps the most widely known woman in the Reformation who was a laywoman, from the artisan class, in a major urban center. Born in Strasbourg in 1498, her religious instruction during childhood and adolescence was shaped by late-Medieval piety. Conversion in her early twenties heralded Katharina's vocation as a *confessional* Protestant.

Her husband Matthew Zell (1477–1548) was engaged as a minister in the reform movement and, until his death, the two of them worked together as a powerful contingent. Following his death in January 1548, Katharina was totally devoted to the reform movement. Although Katharina's education included neither humanist training nor Latin, she was very articulate and wrote extensively from 1524 to 1558. Her writings included devotional meditations, religious instruction, polemical theology, apologetics, sermons, and the call for civil reform. She defined herself as a lay reformer who stood between the pulpit and the pew. She spoke to and for the gathered community from within the midst of the community. Elsie Ann McKee, Schütz Zell's biographer, suggests that perhaps her greatest significance resided in the picture she gives us of what a laywoman from the artisan class could know and say with authority. Her doctrinal theology addresses issues of religious authority and her theological positions focus on a practical theology of worship, devotion, and ethical piety. After the death of her husband, Katharina embodied The Church Mother Militant. She became a fisher of people and a mother to the poor and refugees.

Autobiographical Notes on Her Calling*

> . . . *when I was young all the parish priests and those related to the church loved and feared me. Therefore also my devout husband Matthew Zell, at the time and beginning of his preaching of the Gospel, sought me for his wedded companion.*

*From McKee, ed., *Katharina Schütz Zell. Vol. 1—The Life and Thought of a Sixteenth-Century Reformer* (Leiden, Boston, Koln: Brill, 1999), pp. 427, 428, 449.

To him I also have been a faithful assistance in his office and household management, to the honor of Christ, Who also will give witness to this before all believers and unbelievers on the great day of His judgment, when all will be revealed. (That is) that I have not acted according to the measure of a woman but have done faithfully and simply according to the measure of the gift which God through His Spirit has given to me, with great joy and work day and night; with all good will I have given my body, strength, honor, and goods for you, dear Strasbourg, and made them a footstool for you. For my devout husband was also very heartily glad to allow this, and he also loved me for it, and often permitted there to be something lacking in his own physical and household needs because of my absence, and gladly sent me as gift to the community, and also at his death commended me to continue such activity, not with a command but with a friendly request. That I also hope I have faithfully followed. . . . So up till now, besides bearing my (own) great crosses and severe illnesses, I have gladly served many with counsel and act, according to my resources (as much as God has bestowed on me), as I was also obligated before God to do, and as my husband commended to me at his end, which behest I have gladly followed, since I know that it is godly and came out of God's behest . . . .

Since I was ten years old I have been a church mother, a supporter of pulpit and school; I have loved all the clergy, visited many, and had conversations with them—not about dances, worldly pleasures, riches, or carnival, but about the kingdom of God. Therefore also my father, mother, friends, and citizens and also many clergy whom I have much questioned, have held me in high love, honor, and fear. Since however my distress about the kingdom of heaven grew great, and in all my hard works, worship, and great pain of body, from all the clergy I could not find or achieve any comfort or certainty of the love and grace of God, I became weak and sick to death in soul and body (Lk. 7:2, Phil. 2:27), and it was with me as with the poor little woman in the Gospel (Mk. 5:25–34) who spent all her property and strength with doctors, but lost yet more. When, however, she heard of Christ and came to Him, then she was helped by Him. So it was for me also and many afflicted hearts, who along with me were in great distress—many honorable old women and virgins who sought out my society and were glad to be my companions. There we stood in such anxiety and worry about the grace of God, but in all our many works, practices, and sacraments of that same church we could never find any peace. Then God had mercy on us and many people, He awakened and sent out by tongue and writings the dear and now blessed Dr. Martin Luther, who described the Lord Jesus Christ for me and others in such a lovely way that I thought I had been drawn up out of the depths of the earth, yes, out of grim bitter hell, into the sweet lovely kingdom of heaven. So that I thought of the word which the Lord Christ said to Peter: "I will make you a fisher of people and henceforth you shall catch people" (Lk. 5:10). And I have striven day and night that I might grasp the way of the truth of God (which is Christ the Son of God, Jn. 14:6); what distress I have drawn upon myself because I have learned to know and helped to confess the Gospel here, that I commit to God . . . .

I went into the homes of the poor and the rich, supporting those afflicted with plague and death with all love, faithfulness, and compassion; I visited and comforted the afflicted and those suffering in dungeon, prison, and death, and always thought of the wise man's proverb: "It is better to go into a house of mourning than into a house of joy" (Eccl. 7:2). I have also—God be praised— taught much in those places, and affirm before God that I have done more work, of body and tongue, than any assistant or chaplain of the church; I have watched and run, night and day, and many times I have neither eaten nor slept for two or three days. Therefore also my devout husband (whom this so well pleased) only called me his assistant minister, even though I also never stood in the pulpit, nor did I need to do so for my work.

Elizabeth I, Rex (r. 1558–1603)

Because Elizabeth I of England is discussed in considerable detail in the following chapter, this astute politician and great protector of reform in England is not discussed at length in this chapter. Upon the death of her Catholic half-sister, Queen Mary I (Tudor), daughter of Catherine of Aragon, Elizabeth assumed the throne in 1558 amid dreadful persecution of Protestants. For the next four years Elizabeth directed the approval in Parliament of a religious agreement that in its final expression became the Church of England. The settlement proposed a governance structure based upon the episcopacy, of which she, as queen, was the head. The doctrinal persuasion was a broadly conceived Protestant foundation expressed in the context of traditional Catholic ritual. With the assistance of her principal advisor, Sir William Cecil, Elizabeth was able to put a stop to the bloodshed and restore religious order in England.

Throughout her reign, as history attests, not only was religious order interrupted but Elizabeth was also frequently in mortal danger from dissident Catholics who wished to see her cousin Mary, Queen of Scots, on the English throne. Extremist Protestants, especially the Puritans, proved to be foes who were just as formidable, because of their desire to destroy every trace of anything remotely related to Catholicism. Puritans were especially eager to transform governance structures in the Church that would destroy Elizabeth's hierarchical control. In the end, after 40 years of persistent threats to the religious systems she put in place, Elizabeth's Conventicle Act of 1598 that gave separatists the option of leaving England, being exiled, or executed was adopted.

Jeanne d'Albret (1528–1572)

Roland Bainton tells us that Jeanne d'Albret, the sole daughter of Marguerite of Navarre, is the only sixteenth-century sovereign who put no one to death for religion (Bainton 1973, 43). This distinction represents perseverance and tenacity that characterize commitment to principles Jeanne d'Albret embraced as a Huguenot. The confluence of politics and religion that weighed on her life extracted resolve not witnessed in a lesser person. A first marriage, arranged to form a political alliance in England, was annulled. Her second marriage to Antoine de Bourbon was arranged in order to consolidate territories in the north and south of France. This was a more successful venture, at least until Jeanne, as Queen of Navarre and Duchess of Vendome, with Theodore Beza as her mentor, embraced the reform and gravitated to the doctrinal positions of the Huguenots. Antoine had political motivations that made unmodified Calvinism more attractive. The complexities that besieged the couple from this point included two religions; four families—Guise, Chatillon, Valois, and Bourbon; and six wars. (Bainton 1973, 46–47)

Antoine was won back into the Catholic fold on the promise of lands lost in war. Jeanne broke with Antoine and stood fast as a Huguenot. She was championed among crowds of thousands, and although she disapproved of some actions by the Huguenots, Jeanne assumed administrative duties at Navarre and mended judicial and economic problems. But the social revolution over issues of religion taxed her heavily. In 1562, following a demonstration in which a group of Huguenots melted metal relics from a Catholic Church, Cardinal de Armagnac, who had convinced Antoine to return to his Catholic roots, now wrote an impassioned letter to Jeanne. He said she was being led astray, then appealed to her maternal responsibilities not to deprive her children of their Church and their legacy. Jeanne's response is provided in the following selection. Not long after she refused to succumb to the Cardinal's plea, Jeanne was kidnapped and summoned by the Inquisition (1563). Undeterred, following threats to the stability of her position, Jeanne drafted an edict to advance religious diversity. By 1565 she had returned to her Court, was reunited with her son, and despite offenses and threats by the Roman Catholic Church, Jeanne persisted to advance Huguenot worship and to permit Roman services to continue.

LETTER TO CARDINAL DE ARMAGNAC*

My cousin, I am not unmindful of your services to my parents. As for Pau and Lescar I am following the example of Josiah who destroyed the high places. I am not planting a new religion but restoring an old one. My subjects are not in rebellion against me. I have forced no one with death, imprisonment or condemnation. As for Spain, we differ indeed, but that does not prevent us from being neighbors. And when it comes to France the Edict allows both religions.

Your feeble arguments do not dent my tough skull. I am serving God and He knows how to sustain His cause. On the human level I am ringed about by small principalities providing more security than does the channel for England. I do not believe that I am despoiling my son of his heritage. How much good did it do my husband to defect to Rome? You know the fine crowns that were offered to him and what became of them all when he went against his conscience, as his final confession proves.

I am ashamed of your throwing up to us the excesses on our side. Take the beam out of your own eye. You know who are the seditious through their violation of the Edict of January. I do not condone outrages committed in the name of religion and I would punish the offenders. Our ministers preach nothing but obedience, patience and humility. I, too, will refrain from doctrinal discussion, not because I think we are wrong but because you will not be brought to Mount Zion. As for the works of the Fathers, I recommend them to my ministers. You have abandoned the holy milk of my mother for the honors of Rome and have blinded your understanding.

I know that Scripture is sometimes obscure, but when it comes to the Prince of Darkness you are an example. With regard to the words, "This is my body," you should compare the twenty-second chapter of Luke. If I err I may be excused as a woman for my ignorance, but yours, as a cardinal, is shameful. I follow Beza, Calvin and others only in so far as they follow Scripture. You say they are divided among themselves. So are you. I saw this at Poissy [Where the cardinals of Tournon and Lorraine differed]. You charge that we think Christ has been hidden for twelve or thirteen hundred years. No indeed! We pass no judgment on the dead. I am amazed

---

*From Roland H. Bainton, ed., *Women of the Reformation in France and England* (Minneapolis, MN: Augsburg Publishing House, 1973), pp. 60–61.

that you endorse idolatry to the ruin of your conscience and for your own advancement in the Church.

If you have not committed the sin against the Holy Ghost you have not missed it far. You say our preachers are disturbers. That is just what Ahab said to Elijah. Read 1 Kings chapter 18. You appeal to your authority as the pope's legate. The authority of the pope's legate is not recognized in Béarn. Keep your tears for yourself. Out of charity I might contribute a few. I pray as I have never prayed from the bottom of my heart that you may be brought back to the true fold and the true shepherd and not to a hireling. I pity your human prudence which, with the apostle, I regard as folly before God. I do not know how to sign myself. After you have repented I will sign as your *cousine et amye*.

English Female Martyr Elizabeth Young

From John Foxe's *Acts and Monuments of These Latter and Perilous Dayes* in editions from 1563 and 1570, we get the most thoroughgoing account of the experiences of female English martyrs in the Protestant Reformation. The excerpts that follow consist of 5 of 13 examinations of Elizabeth Young in 1558, at the end of the reign of Mary I. The accounts are abridged by Bainton but give a vivid sense of the candor and spirit of this courageous woman. Young, mother of three children, had gone to Holland to secure books printed in English. She brought these books back to England to sell and for this action she was brought before the examiners. Elizabeth Young was released following the death of Queen Mary.

INQUISITION EXAMINATIONS OF ELIZABETH YOUNG*

SECOND EXAMINATION

Examiner: What are the books you brought from over the sea? I hear you won't swear. If you are stubborn you will be racked by the inch, you traitorly whore and heretic.

Elizabeth: I don't know what it is to swear. As for the books you have impounded them.

Examiner: Yes, and you have sold some of them already. We know every place where you have been. We are not fools.

Elizabeth: No, you are too wise for me.

Examiner: I'll make you tell to whom you sold those books.

Elizabeth: Here is my carcass. Do with it what you will. You cannot take more than my blood.

Then the examiner gave order that Elizabeth should be given bread on one day and water the next.

Elizabeth: If you take away my meat I hope God will take away my hunger.

*From Roland H. Bainton, ed., *Women of the Reformation in France and England* (Minneapolis, MN: Augsburg Publishing House, 1973), pp. 217, 218, 19.

THIRD EXAMINATION

Examiner: Give me the names of those in exile on the continent or you will be racked. Elizabeth gave no answer.

FOURTH EXAMINATION

She was sent to the bishop of London who told her that the refusal to swear was the mark of an Anabaptist. One present, seeing her courage, bet twenty pounds she was a man.

Elizabeth: I am not a man. I have children.

He was evidently convinced, for he called her a whore.

She was examined as to her belief with respect to the sacrament of the altar and declared:

Elizabeth: I believe in the holy sacrament of Christ's body and blood . . . . When I do receive this sacrament in faith and spirit I do receive Christ.

Examiner: Nothing but spirit and faith, is it? Away with the whore.

She was told that being a woman she should stick to the distaff and spindle and not meddle with Scripture.

SEVENTH EXAMINATION

Examiner: Do you believe that the pope of Rome is the supreme head of the Church?

Elizabeth: No, Christ is the head.

Examiner: Haven't you prayed that God deliver you from the tyranny of the bishop of Rome and all his detestable enormities?

Elizabeth: Yes, I have.

Examiner: Aren't you sorry?

Elizabeth: Not a whit.

NINTH EXAMINATION

Examiner: Are you any wiser than last time?

Elizabeth: I haven't learned much since.

The two women who came to offer surety were asked whether they also "did not smell of the frying pan of heresy?" This they denied. Then why did they come? "Because," said one, "she has three children who are like to die. I got a nurse for one. I'll have to look after her children and that's why I want her out."

The death of Queen Mary brought about her release.

WOMEN IN THE CATHOLIC REFORMATION

There are several ways to approach a discussion on women in the Catholic Reformation. First we should note that until the Council of Trent many women in the royal families and the nobility resisted reform and actively sought to preserve the status quo. There were, nonetheless, numerous women both inside and outside religious orders, especially among the nobility, whose education was grounded in the *new learning* of the humanists. The humanist perspectives provided these women with linguistic skills and intellectual autonomy that extended into their reading and understanding of theological issues. Aristocratic women in Italy and Spain who sought reform, and their sisters and daughters in arranged marriages throughout Europe, tended, with a few notable exceptions, to seek change from within existing ecclesiastic structures. The external changes in the formal living of their lives would, therefore, be minimal. Among Roman Catholic women outside the nobility who sought or hoped for reform within existing structures, some were martyred for their faith by Protestants. Some Catholic women who sought reform within the Roman Church were martyred by the Inquisition.

Family names of notable women in the Italian aristocracy during the Renaissance persisted; among these Guila Gonzaga, Caterina Cibo, Vittoria Colonna, Renee of Ferrara, Bona Sforza, and, of course, Marie de' Medici are the most prominent. In addition to their distinction in the arts and/or politics, each of these women is also remembered for her assertions concerning reform movements. They are included in the discussion of the Catholic Reformation because their loyalty to the ecclesiastic structures of the Roman Church remained important to their religious and spiritual lives.

It is in Spain that perhaps the most dramatic reform within Catholicism occurred. And, not surprisingly, it is in Spain that the Church's most repressive responses to women's spiritual agency and autonomy occurred. Reform here was characterized by a flourishing in humanist scholarship and mystical spirituality. Concurrently a resurgence of the Spanish Inquisition was initiated to investigate and punish infractions, heretical beliefs, and practices. There was special concern to punish those who read prohibited Protestant literature and those who practiced or encouraged so-called *diabolical* spiritual excesses. We recall that the most authentic expression of spiritual authority for the mystic is found in direct experience of the Divine. As was true in Early Christianity belief systems or spiritual practices that recognized spiritual authority outside the clerical hierarchy became suspect and were perceived by the hierarchy as potentially dangerous. Pious men and women throughout Spain were tried, tortured, or executed for their beliefs.

Women from Spain whose religious convictions concerning reform have been preserved include Francesca Hernandez, Marina de Guevara, and Anna Marchocka Teresa of Poland who returned to Spain in 1608. Mystic and teacher Isabel de la Cruz, founder of the *Alumbrados,* was profoundly influential in the development of the Spanish mystical tradition. We have none of Isabel's writings, but Alcaraz, one of her followers, faithfully transmitted many of her precepts concerning the spiritual life. Isabel had a profound understanding of the omnipresence of the Love of God and the indwelling of God in humankind. She was first brought before the Inquisition in 1524, on the word of a former disciple. Isabel de la Cruz was incarcerated, intimidated, and tortured, and in 1529 was executed by the Inquisition.

Teresa of Avila is by far the most celebrated woman in the Catholic Reformation and two selections from the corpus of her writings are included in this chapter. A selection is also included from Maria Cazalla, a far less known mystic of the Catholic Reformation in Spain, who suffered and died for her faith.

Teresa of Avila (1515–1582)

St. Teresa of Avila was a woman whose life as a Christian mystic, teacher of the spiritual life, author, poet, founder, and reformer was honored by the Roman Catholic Church when she was designated one of two female Doctors of the Church. In a manner reminiscent of Hildegard of Bingen in the

Medieval period, Teresa also had influence among members of the political and clerical hierarchy both in Spain and abroad. She was born the daughter of Don Alonzo de Cepeda and Dona Beatriz Ahumada. Her father's family were *conversos* (Jewish families who converted to Catholicism during the purge of 1492 when all Jews and Muslims were banished from Spain). Teresa was one of 13 children and was sensitive to the harshness of her mother's existence from incessant childbearing. Some of Teresa's biographers suggest that witnessing her mother's plight, which eventually caused an early death, had a long-term effect on Teresa's quest for autonomy and a life that did not entail the demands of marriage and child rearing.

Teresa entered the Carmelite convent of the Incarnation in 1536 and was professed the following year. Conventual protocol at Incarnation was rather remiss and many features of monastic life were substantially relaxed. During the next 22 years, although she suffered several instances of illness, Teresa acquired a reputation as the most charming of the nuns. Her ready laughter made her a favorite of visitors to the Convent of the Incarnation. Teresa's spiritual life developed only gradually over these two decades and she describes herself as torn between worldly pleasures and what she owed to God.

In 1554, Teresa experienced what she referred to as a second conversion experience. Her spiritual life was characterized by an increasingly vivid awareness of God's presence. This ever-deepening experience of God is described in great detail in Teresa's autobiography. The rigorous interrogation to which she was subjected by priests and bishops who sought to determine the authenticity of her experience is also recorded in detail. The next significant phase of her extraordinary life began with a remarkable vision, referred to as the *transverberation* of her heart that is depicted so powerfully in the Bernini altarpiece in St. Peters Cathedral, Rome. Teresa wrote that following this piercing of her heart by the Love of Christ, she was wed to Christ in a new and deeper way. Her letters from this period onward often refer to Jesus as her silent partner, guiding and comforting her throughout the myriad holy adventures that characterized the rest of her life. She felt called by God to reform the Carmelite order and return it to the life of simplicity and contemplative prayer that its founders intended.

It is in her work as the founder of the *Discalced* (barefoot) Carmelite Order that we see Teresa blossom into the fullness of her person. Her agency and autonomy and delightful sense of humor are most vividly expressed in her letters and in the *Foundations* where she describes her travels, sometimes by donkey, sometimes by horse-drawn wagons, and sometimes by carriage, as she established new monasteries for women and men throughout Spain. The following selections provide some sense of this remarkable woman whose writings on the spiritual life continue to inspire Christians around the world.

THE CIRCUMSTANCES SURROUNDING THE FOUNDATION OF THE MONASTERY OF ST. JOSEPH IN MEDINA DEL CAMPO*

The circumstances surrounding the foundation of the monastery of St. Joseph in Medina del Campo.

WHILE I WAS HAVING ALL these concerns, the thought came to me to ask help from the Fathers of the Society, for they were well accepted in that place, that is, in Medina. As I have written in my account of the first foundation, they guided my soul for many years. I always feel especially devoted to them because of the great good they did for it. I wrote to the rector in Medina about what our Father General had ordered me to

*From Teresa of Avila, *The Book of Her Foundations* in *The Collected Works of St. Teresa of Avila,* vol. 3, trans. Kieran Kavanaugh, OCD, and Otilio Rodriguez, OCD (Washington D.C: Institute of Carmelite Studies, 1985), pp. 105–13.

do. The rector happened to be the one who had been my confessor for many years, whom I mentioned, although I did not give his name. His name is Baltasar Alvarez, and at present he is provincial. He and the others said they would do what they could about the matter. They thus did a great deal to secure permission from the people and the bishop, for since the monastery is to be founded in poverty, permission is everywhere difficult to obtain. So there was a delay of several days in the negotiations. . . . Well, now that I had the permission, I didn't have a house or a penny to buy one with. Furthermore, how could a poor wanderer like myself get credit for a loan unless the Lord would give it? The Lord provided that a very virtuous young lady, who because of lack of room could not enter St. Joseph's, heard that another house was being founded and came to ask if I would accept her in the new one. She had some money which was very little and not enough to buy a house but enough to rent one and to help with the travel expenses. And so we found one to rent. Without any more support than this and with our Father Chaplain, Julián de Avila, we left Avila. Besides myself, there were two nuns from St. Joseph's and four from the Incarnation, the monastery of the mitigated rule where I stayed before St. Joseph's was founded.

3. When our intention became known in the city, there was much criticism. Some were saying I was crazy; others were hoping for an end to that nonsense. To the bishop—according to what he told me later—the idea seemed very foolish. But he didn't then let me know this; neither did he hinder me, for he loved me much and didn't want to hurt me. My friends said a great deal against the project. But I didn't pay much attention to them. For that which to them seemed doubtful, to me seemed so easy that I couldn't persuade myself that it would fail to be a true success.

Before we left Avila, I wrote to a Father of our order, Fray Antonio de Heredia, asking him to buy me a house, for he was then prior at St. Anne's, the monastery of friars of our order in Medina. He spoke of the matter to a lady who was devoted to him, for she had a house that had completely collapsed except for one room. The house was situated in a fine location. She was so good she promised to sell the house and so they came to an agreement without her asking for any surety or binding force other than his word. If she had asked for any, we would have had no resources. The Lord was arranging everything. This house was so tumble-down that we had rented another to live in while it was being repaired, for there was much to do on it. . . .

6. . . . I desired that we take possession of the house before our intentions be made known, and so we determined to do this at once. Our Father Master Fray Domingo, agreed.

7. We arrived in Medina del Campo on the eve of our Lady's feast in August at twelve midnight. We dismounted at the monastery of St. Anne's so as not to make noise and proceeded to the house on foot. It was by the great mercy of God that we were not struck by any of the bulls being corralled at that hour for the next day's run. We were so engrossed in what we were doing that we didn't pay any attention. However, the Lord, who always takes care of those who seek to serve Him (and indeed, that's what we were trying to do), kept us from being harmed.

8. When we arrived at the house, we entered the courtyard. The walls looked to me to be quite dilapidated, but not as dilapidated as they looked when daylight came. It seems the Lord wanted that blessed Father to be blinded and thus unable to

see that the place was not suitable for the Blessed Sacrament. When we saw the entrance way, it was necessary to clear away the dirt since overhead was nothing but a rustic roof of bare tile. Because the walls were not plastered, the night almost over, and all we had were some blankets—I believe there were three—which for the whole length of the entrance way were nothing, I didn't know what to do. For I saw that the place wasn't suitable for an altar. It pleased the Lord, who wanted the place to be prepared immediately, that the butler of that lady who was the owner had at her house many tapestries belonging to her and a blue damask bed-hanging; and the lady had told him to give us whatever we wanted, for she was very good.

9. When I saw such nice furnishings, I praised the Lord, and so did the others—although we didn't know what to do for nails, nor was it the hour for buying them. We began to look in the walls. Finally, through much effort, a supply was found. With some of the men hanging the tapestries, and we cleaning the floor, we worked so quickly that when dawn came the altar was set up, and the little bell placed in a corridor; and immediately Mass was said. Having Mass was sufficient in order to take possession. But not knowing this, we reserved the Blessed Sacrament, and through some cracks in the door that was in front of us, we attended the Mass, for there was no place else for us to do so.

10. Up to this point I was very happy because for me it is the greatest consolation to see one church more where the Blessed Sacrament is preserved. But my happiness did not last long. For when Mass was finished I went to look a little bit through a window at the courtyard, and I saw that all the walls in some places had fallen to the ground and that many days would be required to repair them. Oh, God help me! When I saw His Majesty placed in the street, at a time so dangerous, on account of those Lutherans, as this time in which we now live, what anguish came to my heart! . . .

14. After eight days had passed, a merchant who lived in a very nice house, told us when he saw our need that we could live on the upper floor of his house and stay there as though in our own. It had a large gilded room that he gave us for a church. And a lady who lived next to the house that we bought, whose name was Doña Elena de Quiroga, a great servant of God, told me she would help so that construction of a chapel for the Blessed Sacrament could be immediately started, and also accommodations made so that we could observe the rule of enclosure. Others gave us many alms for food, but this lady was the one who aided me most.

15. Now with this I began to calm down because we were able to keep strict enclosure, and we began to recite the Hours. The good prior hurried very much with the repair of the house, and he suffered many trials. Nonetheless, the work took two months. But the house was repaired in such a way that we were able to live there in a reasonably good manner for several years. Afterward, our Lord continued bringing about improvements for it. . . .

18. The nuns were gaining esteem in the town and receiving much affection. In my opinion, rightly so, for they were not interested in anything else than how each one could serve our Lord more. In all matters they lived the same way as at St. Joseph's in Avila since the rule and constitutions were the same.

The Lord began to call some women to receive the habit, and the favors He gave them were so great that I was amazed. May He be ever blessed, amen. In order to love, it doesn't seem that He waits for anything else than to be loved.

Maria Cazalla

The fact that Teresa of Avila was twice brought before the Inquisition is, with very few exceptions, eliminated by her numerous biographers. Paradoxically, references to Maria Cazalla are centered specifically in the context of her torture and execution by the Inquisition for apostasy. From 1531 to 1534 Maria was subjected to grueling examination and torture. A few of the areas concerning her intellectual and spiritual religious life about which she was questioned include: Erasmus' critique of scholastic thought and her agreement with certain doctrinal positions of Luther on the lack of the importance of merit. The influence of Isabel de la Cruz on her mystical experiences and the fact that she had preached to conventuals were also areas about which Maria was questioned under torture. The selection below includes horrifying descriptions of the torture to which Maria Cazalla was subjected.

ON THE INQUISITION*

A particularly heinous offense was ascribed to her that, though a *woman,* she had dared to preach. Among others Alcaraz had made this accusation, saying that she was arrogant, presumptuous and inspired by self love. She had preached to conventicles, he said. She replied that no conventicles had met in her house. This left open the possibility that they might have met in some other house.

After compiling the charges and her responses the inquisitors decided to put her to the torture. "Why do you need to torture me?" she asked. "I have told the truth and can say no more."

She was taken to the torture chamber and informed that if she were killed, or maimed or bled, the fault would not be theirs. She was ordered to disrobe. "You do this to a woman? I dread more the affront than the pain." When stripped, she cast down her eyes. The torture took two forms. One consisted in tying cords around the thighs and arms with a belt around the waist from which in front cords went up over the shoulders and down to the belt in the back. Tourniquets dug the cords into the flesh at any point of the body.

The other method was the water torture. The victim was bound to a trestle like a ladder with sharp rungs. The head was lower than the feet. The head was clamped immobile and the mouth pried open. Water then trickled from a jar into mouth and nostrils until the victim was nearly suffocated. Then the water was discharged and the process repeated sometimes until as many as eight jars were emptied.

When Maria was strapped, she said, "Even so was Christ lashed to a column." (A familiar depiction in Christian art though not mentioned in the gospels.) As the executioner was about to apply the pressure she exclaimed, "You are trying to make me lie. Do you believe liars?"

One by one the accusations were read to her and after each the inquisitor said, "Tell the truth." And each time she replied, "I have . . ."

"Have you despised the sacraments? Tell the truth."

"I have told the truth."

---

*From Roland H. Bainton, *Women of the Reformation from Spain to Scandinavia* (Minneapolis, MN: Augsburg Publishing House, 1977), pp. 37, 39.

"Did you conduct conventicles in your house? Tell the truth."

"I have told the truth."

"Did you refuse to genuflect? Tell the truth."

"I have told the truth."

As the tourniquet was tightened, she screamed, "O Thou who suppliest strength in need, I confess Thee, I adore Thee. Give me strength in my trial." To the constant charges to tell the truth, she cried, "Oh, why do you want me to lie? Saint Stephen, Saint Lorenz, Saints Simon and Jude . . . can the innocent confess what has never been done?" Again she was adjured, "Tell the truth."

"I have, I have, I have told the truth."

"Tell the truth."

"To what I have said I hold. O God to Thee alone will I confess."

The inquisitors said, "It's getting late. We might as well stop." Torment was not to be repeated but could be continued in a later session.

In her case there was none. Since her utterances were deemed to have occasioned scandal, the inquisitors, invoking the name of Christ, passed sentence that she should pay a heavy fine, do public penance and be restricted in her movements. She requested that her husband be informed. She had recanted nothing and incriminated no one.

Writings from the Catholic Reformation also survive by and about Katarina Jagellonica of Sweden and Maria of Hungary and Bohemia.

Although numerous Catholic males who threatened Elizabeth I of England were persecuted during her reign, few female figures from the Catholic Reformation in the British Isles were martyred for their beliefs. Catherine of Aragon, first wife of Henry VIII and mother of Mary Tudor, had been an excellent queen, and did keep her head, but was deposed, exiled, and died virtually alone, firm in her faith. When her daughter Mary I became queen of England, Mary's allegiance to the Roman Catholic Church was so intractable and resolute that she was labeled "Bloody Mary" as commentary on her rigorous persecution of Protestants. Probably the most famous Catholic woman to be persecuted in England was Elizabeth's cousin Mary of Scotland. Their strained relationship and Elizabeth's reluctance to execute Mary are the subjects not only of history, but are also retold in biographies of both women, in novels, dramas, films, and television miniseries. A wonderful exercise for the reader entails compiling the numerous films and miniseries on Elizabeth and observing the cultural commentary that is implicit in the transformations of her mythos.

JEWS AND THE ENGLISH REFORMATION

The Jews, about whom little has been said in this chapter, were expelled from England in 1290, on charges of ritual murder. Jewish families who remained became *conversos*. Following the expulsion of Jews from Spain and the Iberian peninsula in 1492, a new *diaspora* occurred throughout other European countries. A few of these Jewish families settled in Elizabethan London. It was understood that many such new "Christian" families were also *Marranos* who continued to practice Judaism in secrecy. The selections included below relate to English Protestant persecutions and exiles of Jews, as well as petitions for Jewish families' permission to *return* to England from the very late sixteenth century into the seventeenth century.

Sara Lopez (1550–159?)

Sara Ames Lopez, a Jewess, petitioned Elizabeth I in 1594 following the execution of Dr. Roderigo Lopez, Elizabeth's physician. Dr. Lopez was executed as a result of Essex's accusations against him concerning a supposed plot to poison Elizabeth. After Lopez was put to death, Sara petitioned Elizabeth to return, to her and her children, Dr. Lopez's confiscated possessions. Travitsky and Prescott note that Elizabeth agreed, but that she kept for herself a ring, given to Dr. Lopez by Phillip of Spain and then given to Elizabeth by Lopez. It is said that she "wore the ring at her waist for the rest of her life" most probably as a sign of her belief in Lopez's innocence. (Travitsky and Prescott 2000, 188)

A Petition to Elizabeth I*

To the Queen's Most Excellent Majesty:

Humbly lamenting, beseecheth your Majesty, for God's sake, to have pitiful consideration of her afflicted and miserable estate, Sara Lopez, the condemned and poor widow of Doctor Lopez:

That where your suppliant (utterly confounded and dismayed with the heavy ruin of her late husband) lieth at this present in woeful agony and extremity of sickness, utterly despairing the recovery of her former health and strength and rather expecting the speedy shortening of her perplexed life through the inward conceit of her present desolation (being the sorrowful mother of five comfortless and distressed children born within your Majesty's realm, three of them being maiden children, and only relying upon your suppliant's hands).

And forasmuch as your poor suppliant and all her poor children are innocent of her said husband's crime and have in no sort (as they hope) offended your highness or the state of this realm, she most humbly beseecheth your highness, for God's sake, that her said husband's offense and the rigor of the punishment thereof may cease and be determined with the infamous loss of his life.

And that your poor suppliant and her children may have the lease of your suppliant's house for their habitation, with her household stuff and such goods and other things as have been taken from her during her husband's first imprisonment, being their whole stay and substance for their relief and succor.

Whereof, pleaseth it your highness to be advertised that one John Gatherne detaineth from your oratrice 50 or 60 pounds due by the licenses of sumac and aniseeds before her husband's imprisonment which he will not restore without my Lord Treasurer's warrant, who referreth your oratrice to sue for your highness' warrant in that behalf, which said license of sumac and aniseed is also taken away from your suppliant.

As also one Mr. Conway hath made stay of certain plate to the value of 100 pounds of her late husband's, remaining in the court, pretending a debt of 30 pounds to be owing him by her husband, whereof your oratrice can make good proof that the same is long since paid and discharged.

---

*"The Petition of Sara Lopez" in Betty S. Travitsky and Anne L. Prescott, eds., *Female and Male Voices in Early Modern England: An Anthology of Renaissance Writing* (New York: Columbia University Press, 2000), pp. 189–190, 191–92.

And whereas it pleased your highness of your princely bounty to vouchsafe the gift of a parsonage to the value of 30 pounds per annum upon Anthony Lopez, one of your suppliant's miserable children, for his maintenance at school and learning, the same is likewise taken from him.

In tender consideration of the premises it may please your most excellent Majesty to stand so gracious sovereign to your miserable suppliant as to redress and cause restitution of the premises to be made unto her according to your highness' special bounty for her and her poor children's succor, who are at this present utterly destitute and forsaken of all friends and comfort and, without such your highness' great mercy and compassion towards them, ready to perish and to be driven to extreme begging and penury.

Whereof, it may please your highness, for God's sake, of your princely clemency towards the poor widow and fatherless, to have tender consideration. And your poor suppliant and her poor children (as duty bindeth) shall daily pray for your highness' long life with increase of continual felicity in this life and in the world to come. Amen.

SUGGESTED READINGS

Ahlgren, Gillian T. W. *Teresa of Avila and the Politics of Sanctity.* Ithaca, NY: Cornell University Press, 1996.

Bainton, Roland H. *Women of the Reformation from Spain to Scandinavia.* Minneapolis, MN: Augsburg Publishing House, 1973.

Bainton. *Women of the Reformation in Germany and Italy.* Minneapolis, MN: Augsburg Publishing House, 1973.

Bryson, David. *Queen Jeanne and the Promised Land: Dynasty, Homeland, Religion, and Violence in Sixteenth-century France.* Leiden; Boston; Koln: Brill, 1999.

Kunze, Bonnelyn Young. *Margaret Fell and the Rise of Quakerism.* Houndmills, Basingstoke, Hampshire, and London: Macmillan, 1994.

Mack, Phyllis. *Visionary Women: Ecstatic Prophecy in Seventeenth-century England.* Berkeley: University of California Press, 1992.

Medwick, Cathleen. *Teresa of Avila: The Progress of a Soul.* New York: Alfred A. Knopf, 1999.

Roelker, Nancy L. *Queen of Navarre: Jeanne d'Albret, 1528-1572.* Cambridge, MA: Belknap Press of Harvard University Press, 1968.

Stuard, Susan Mosher. "Women's Witnessing: A New Departure." In *Witnesses for Change: Quaker Women over Three Centuries.* Edited by Elisabeth Potts Brown and Susan Mosher Stuard. New Brunswick and London: Rutgers University Press, 1989.

Trevett, Christine. *Women and Quakerism in the 17th Century.* York, England: Sessions Book Trust, Ebor Press, 1991.

Wilcox, Catherine M. *Theology and Women's Ministry in Seventeenth-century English Quakerism: Handmaids of the Lord.* Lewiston, NY: E. Mellen Press, 1995.

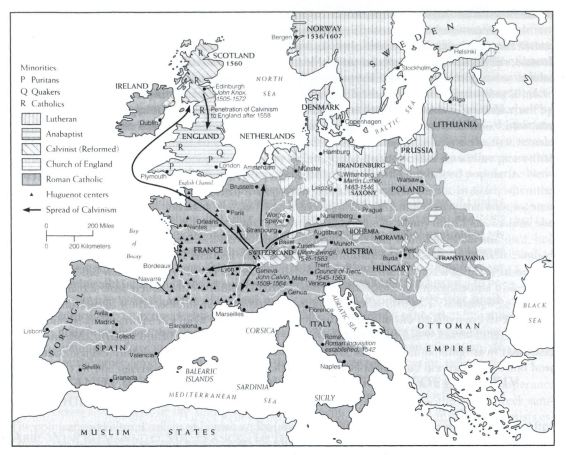

Map 2–1   The Age of Religious Ferment

Chapter 3

The Northern Renaissance

Joan Kelly-Gadol's thesis that women had no renaissance (at least during the Renaissance era) seems to be particularly true of northern Europe (Kelly-Gadol 1977). No women artists, or professional musicians, composers, or actresses, such as we found in Italy, emerged during the Renaissance in northern Europe, although, as we will see, there were a number of well-known women writers and learned women. Political and religious developments in much of northern Europe re-enforced patriarchy and sharply reduced women's economic independence and legal status. The emergence of strong centralized monarchies, particularly in England, France, and Spain, deprived noble women of the autonomy and authority they had often enjoyed during much of the medieval period. Family structure increasingly emulated the hierarchal political system. As we saw in Chapter 2, "The Age of Religious Ferment," Protestant views of marriage as a social and religious imperative, deprived women in Protestant regions of a socially acceptable alternative to marriage and motherhood. The Protestant notion of the male as head of the household also eroded women's autonomy. As these political, religious, and familial ideals were enshrined in law, men acquired control over all property and more freedom to dispose of property as they alone wished. Upon marriage, women ceased to exist as legal beings under the common law of Renaissance England, and became totally subordinate to their husbands. As in Italy, the emergence of a capitalistic economy squeezed women out of jobs and small businesses.

Renaissance ideology, re-enforced by both Catholic and Protestant beliefs, was hostile to the idea of female rule. Though women frequently served as stand-ins for absent husbands or regents for young sons, women rulers were notably absent from Italy and France. Indeed, the Salic law outlawed the accession of a woman to the French throne. The French were so insistent on male rule that when the Valois king Henry III died in 1589 without an heir, leaders bypassed his sister Marguerite and put her husband, Henry, King of Navarre, on the throne as Henry IV, even though he was a member of the rival Bourbon family and a Protestant. His marriage to Marguerite Valois was annulled, and he married a new queen, Marie de' Medici.

In Spain, England, and some smaller kingdoms, however, the desire for political stability and for keeping a family dynasty in power overrode the prevailing prejudice against female rule. As a result, we find a number of women rulers in northern Europe, including two of the most powerful and effective monarchs of the Renaissance, Isabella of Spain and Elizabeth I of England. Women rulers were important patrons of learning and the arts, and some created the political, social, and economic climate in which Renaissance culture could thrive, although, ironically, it remained pre-eminently a male culture. Isabella of Castille (1451–1504) built a large library of religious and secular works and commissioned the first Castilian grammar as she sought to make Spain a major intellectual center.

Women who married rulers in other countries disseminated Renaissance culture across Europe. Catherine of Aragon helped spread humanist ideas in England by bringing Juan de Vives from Spain to serve as tutor to her daughter Mary Tudor and commissioning his treatise on the education of women. Catherine de' Medici (1519–1589), who at 14 married Henry II of France, introduced the dance pageants she had enjoyed in Italy to the French court and became a patron of ballet. In so doing, she helped shift the center of Renaissance dance from Italy to France. She also spread the Italian fashion in cosmetics to northern Europe, notably, white skin, reddish blond hair, pale eyebrows, and a high forehead, along with all the bleaches, dyes, powders, and time-consuming processes necessary to achieve the ideal (Anderson and Zinsser 1988, 20). Isabella Andreini undoubtedly paved the way for actresses in French theater after Henry IV brought the Gelosi company to France to please his bride, Marie de' Medici. Young noble girls spread their tastes in literature and the arts, and their languages as they entered arranged marriages in a new country.

In northern Europe as in Italy, humanist theories of education as well as family interests produced a number of learned women, although women as a group remained educationally disadvantaged relative to men. Humanists Thomas More of England (*Utopia*, 1516), Juan Luis Vives of Spain (*Instruction of a Christian Woman*, 1523), and Desiderius Erasmus of Rotterdam (*Colloquies*, 1519–1533) all thought that females had the intellectual capacity to learn more than most people thought and argued that they, too, should receive a classical education. Like Castiglione, however, they believed that their classical education could differ from that given their brothers. They also agreed that girls should continue to receive training in the feminine skills. Erasmus advanced the new idea that women outside the nobility could also benefit from a rigorous education.

Nevertheless, educational options for girls were much fewer than those for boys. Few noble women received the classical education reformers suggested; most only became literate in the vernacular and learned some music to augment their domestic training. Girls were excluded from schools that prepared boys for universities, and women were excluded from all universities. In England, many elementary schools did not admit girls and, if they did, girls attended for shorter periods of time than boys. Parents often hired tutors only for their sons. The Reformation, as we have seen, had mixed consequences for women's education. Although Protestants placed new emphasis on reading literacy in the vernacular for girls as well as boys, many Protestants saw little need to study Latin, Greek, or the classics. Moreover, the closing or destruction of convents in England and elsewhere eliminated a traditional source of education for daughters of the nobility, the wealthy gentry, and mercantile families.

Gender differences in literacy rates reflect the severity of educational inequities. Between 1580 and 1640, barely ten percent of London's females could write, and only male laborers had a lower writing literacy rate than women as a group. But changes were in process. By the end of that period, an increase in the number of girls' boarding schools in London had brought a dramatic increase in writing literacy from 10 to 48 percent among London women. Reading literacy was higher than writing literacy in Renaissance England, however, as evidenced in the increasing number of books published for women readers. Between 1570 and 1640, nearly one half million volumes intended for women were sold (Henderson and McManus 1985, 88–89, 91). As female literacy became more widespread and printing made literature less expensive, the Renaissance notion of the "ideal lady" spread from the nobility to the growing bourgeois class through a new genre of "conduct books" aimed specifically at these new readers.

Throughout the Renaissance, women continued to be a major subject for male writers as they had been since the earliest literature of Western civilization. In fact, both the volume of literature about women and the intensity of the debate about women's worth increased substantially, continuing a trend that had begun during the Middle Ages. In her study *Doctrine for the Lady of the Renaissance,* Ruth Kelso identified nearly 900 treatises written specifically about the education, behavior, and roles of noble-women between 1400 and 1600 (Kelso 1956). Most were by Italian and French writers. The Reformation added to these works about women as Protestants and Catholics sought to define or redefine the position of women from their particular theological perspectives. As the Renaissance spread to northern Europe and England, the debate about women widened even more as it began to encompass the concerns of the new urban middle class and lower gentry and to reflect the more secular outlook of the modern post-medieval society. Slowly, moreover, new voices began to participate in the debate.

During the Middle Ages, women had become the target of increasing attacks by theologians and secular writers. These attacks generated an increasing number of defenses of the female sex. All the literature about women, however, was written by men. In 1399, a French woman, Christine de Pizan (1363–1430?), entered the fray in response to a particularly misogynist popular romance, *Roman de la Rose,* by Jean de Meun. In her "Letter to the God of Love," Pizan attacked the poet and the negative stereotypes about women that pervaded contemporary literature. Her letter touched off a lengthy debate among prominent male scholars and literary figures. Pizan continued her attack on misogyny in a poem and a book-length defense of women, *The Book of the City of Ladies (Le livre de la cité des dames),* in 1405. Her book was the first full-scale defense of her sex and the first defense of women written by a woman. With her works, Pizan opened a new chapter in the ages-old debate over woman's worth, initiating the modern *querelle des femmes* (debate about the woman question) that would persist into the twenty-first century. (See Volume One, Chapter 15, "Medieval Culture: The Secular Context".)

During the Renaissance other women began to follow Pizan's lead. As we have seen in the previous chapters, some Italian women responded forcefully to misogynists, while some Protestant women defended women's equality in the eyes of God. In this chapter we will meet some French women who entered the debate and we will follow the renewed *querelle des femmes* as it evolved in England.

WOMEN WRITERS OF FRANCE

More women writers emerged in France during the Renaissance than elsewhere in Europe. Marguerite of Navarre and Louise Labé were two of the most important literary women, and, in fact, were regarded as two of the four best French writers of the period. Both were instrumental in fostering the development of French literature and culture, although they did so in quite different contexts. They and other French women writers were quite likely beneficiaries of the legacy left by Pizan, France's first professional woman writer, the first person to mount a comprehensive argument for women's education, and a key figure in the development of French as a literary language.

Marguerite of Navarre (1492–1549)

Marguerite of Navarre was one of the most significant female writers of the sixteenth century, and as a patron of writers and humanists was an important figure in the French Renaissance. She was the sister of Francis I (1494–1547) and the grandmother of Henry IV. Born Marguerite d'Angouleme, she became duchess of Alençon upon her marriage to the duke in 1509 and then queen of Navarre by her second marriage in 1527 to King Henri d'Albret. She is representative of those elite women, such as Isabella d'Este and Elizabeth Tudor, who were trained to be stand-ins for ruling men if necessary. Her education and political skills enabled her to serve occasionally as regent for her brother and to govern Navarre in her husband's absence.

Marguerite, as part of three generations of well-educated and politically astute women centered around the French court, is also an excellent example of what historian Gerda Lerner identified as clusters of learned women that emerged from support networks created for and by women in certain convents, courts, and families. Marguerite and Francis were educated by their mother, Queen Louise of Savoy (1476–1531), in French, Spanish, Italian, and some Latin and Greek. Marguerite of Navarre, in turn, educated Catherine de' Medici, who married Henry II, and after his death, served as regent for her son Charles IX. She also educated her own daughter Jeanne de Navarre and supervised the education of René de France (1528–75), duchess of Ferrara, and of her niece, Marguerite de France (1523–74) who, after her marriage to the duke of Savoy, was known as a scholar and patron of poets (Lerner 1993, 226–29).

Throughout her life, Navarre shaped French culture through her patronage and her reputation as a learned woman. During her first marriage, she made her court of the Duchy of Berry a humanist center of learning. She was also influential in the growth of the University of Bourges. When she became queen of Navarre in 1527, she again made her court a center of Renaissance culture. She presided over a circle of poets, humanist scholars, and artists from diverse backgrounds who brought together courtly and classical Latin traditions and popular vernacular culture. Through her and her intellectual circle, the ideas and works of Dante and Petrarch became known to the French court. She, like other humanists, came to question many Catholic teachings and rituals, and through her studies was somewhat influenced some by Calvin's theology and Lutheran teachings. Thus, despite her husband's objections, she protected humanists and Protestants at her court and reform-minded Catholics from other locales.

Navarre's literary legacy is extensive. Her major works included eight dramas (two moralities, two farces, and four mysteries), verse epistles, rondeaux and songs, and eight long poems on love and sacred and historical topics. Her most famous work is *Heptameron* (Book of Seven Days), on which she was working at the time of her death. Her learned writings earned the "faint praise" male scholars typically gave highly educated women. They were "so excellent 'that you would hardly believe they were done by a woman at all'" (King 1984, 76). Her religious poetry is intensely mystical and reflects the deeply personal ways in which mystics experience the Divine without the intervention of a priestly intermediary or formal church rituals.

Heptameron, Navarre's famous prose work, consists of 72 short stories that range from risqué to spiritual tales. Her work was modeled loosely after Boccaccio's *Decameron.* In fact, she had planned to write her own *Decameron* and was beginning work on the eighth day when she died. The book was published posthumously in two volumes in 1559. Her tales provide witty insights into the elite French society. Some emphasize the virtue and intelligence of women. Others, which describe abuses in the church and monasteries, reflect her interest in church reform. Each story concludes with an epilogue in which she gives her views on current topics.

"FIRST DAY, NOVEL VII" OF THE HEPTAMERON, VOL. I*

Trick put by a mercer of Paris upon an old woman, to conceal his intrigue with her daughter.

There was a mercer in Paris who was enamored of a girl in his neighborhood, or, to speak more properly, who was loved by her, rather than she by him, for he only

---

*From Marguerite, Queen of Navarre, First Day, Novel VII, in Vol. I of *The Heptameron of Margaret, Queen of Navarre*, ed. M. Le Roux de Lincy (Printed for the Bibliophist Library, 1902), pp. 50–53.

pretended to be attached to her in order to conceal another amour with a more exalted object. For her part, she was very willing to be deceived, and loved him so much that she forgot all the usual coyness of her sex. After the mercer had long taken the trouble of going in search of her, he used afterwards to make her come to him wherever he pleased. The mother, who was a respectable woman perceived this, and forbade her daughter ever to speak to the mercer, under pain of being sent to a convent; but the girl, who loved the mercer more than she feared her mother, behaved worse than ever. One day the mercer, finding her alone in a convenient place, began to entertain her on matters that ought not to be discussed before witnesses; but a servant who had seen him come in, ran and told the mother, who hastened to the spot to put an end to the conversation. The daughter hearing her footsteps, said with tears in her eyes, "My love for you will cost me dearly, here comes my mother, and she will now be convinced of what she has always feared." The mercer, without losing his presence of mind, instantly quitted the girl, ran to meet her mother, threw his arms round the old woman's neck, hugged her with all his might, threw her on a little bed, and began to expend upon her all the rage her daughter had excited within him. The poor old woman, quite confounded at being treated in this way, could only exclaim, "What are you about? Are you mad?" But he no more desisted than if she had been the handsomest young girl in the world; and if her screams had not brought the servant men and maids to her assistance, she would have suffered the fate she apprehended so much for her daughter. The servants dragged the good woman by force out of the mercer's hands, without the poor creature ever knowing why she had been so worried. During the scuffle, the daughter escaped to a neighbor's house, where there was a wedding going on; and she and the mercer often afterwards laughed at the expense of the old woman, who never detected their intercourse.

Here you have, ladies, an instance of a man's having been cunning enough to deceive an old woman, and save the honor of a young one. If I were to name the persons, or if you had seen the countenance of the mercer and the surprise of the old woman you must have had very tender consciences to keep from laughing. I have sufficiently proved to you by this example that men are not less ingenious than women in inventing expedients upon the spot; and so, ladies, you need not be afraid of falling into their hands, for, should your own wit fail, you will find theirs ready to screen your honor.

"I own, Hircan," said Longarine, "that the story is comical and the stratagem well invented; but, for all that, it does not follow that the example is one which ought to be imitated by girls. I have no doubt there are plenty whom you would wish to approve of it; but you have too much sense to wish that your wife and your daughter, whose honor is dearer to you than pleasure, should play at such a game. I believe there is no one who would watch them more closely, and put a stop to such doings more promptly, than yourself."

"Upon my conscience," replied Hircan, "if my wife had done the same thing, I should not esteem her the less, providing I knew nothing about it. I don't know if some one has not played as good a trick at my expense, but, fortunately, as I know nothing, I give myself no concern."

"The wicked are always suspicious," said Parlamente; "but happy are they who give no cause for suspicion."

"I can't say I ever saw a fire without some smoke," said Longarine; "but I have certainly seen smoke without any fire. Those who have bad hearts suspect alike where there is mischief and where there is none."

"You have so well supported the cause of ladies unjustly suspected," said Hircan to Longarine, "that I call upon you for your novel. I hope you will not make us weep, as Madame Oisille has done, by too much praise of honest women."

"Since you would have me make you laugh," said Longarine, laughing with all her heart, "it shall not be at the expense of our sex. I will let you see how easy it is to cheat jealous wives who think they are wise enough to cheat their husbands."

Louise Labé (c. 1520–1566)

Louise Labé's background is quite different from that of Marguerite of Navarre. Like Gaspara Stampa and Veronica Franco, she emerged from an artisan and mercantile background. She lived in Lyon, a major commercial and cultural center with strong ties to Italy. Although her father was a rope maker, she received a much better education than was typical of men or women of her class. She was taught music, letters, languages, and art, as well as needlework. But she was also trained in rope making and the use of weapons and was reportedly a renowned horsewoman and archer. Most agree that she participated in jousting tournaments, and some suggest she even fought on horseback, disguised as a man, in a battle against the Spanish. She was also said to have been a courtesan before her marriage, although neither that nor her military exploit have been verified.

After her marriage to a wealthy rope manufacturer 30 years her senior, Labé's home became a center for poets and writers from Lyon and other parts of France. She was one of the few talented French women of the sixteenth century able to establish a literary circle outside of the courts. Her circle provided the same intellectual stimuli and artistic support that Stampa and Franco had found in the Venetian salons. Labé's works include a prose dialogue, *The Debate between Madness and Love* (1555), elegies, and sonnets. She is best known for her frank and sensual love poetry. Some of the poems share the intense joy, pain, and anger she experienced in an adulterous love affair with a man who subsequently abandoned her. In others Labé flaunts social conventions as she asserts her intellectual and sexual independence.

LABÉ'S SONNETS*

SONNET 18

Kiss me again, kiss, kiss me again;
Give me the tastiest you have to give,
Pay me the lovingest you have to spend:
And I'll return you four, hotter than live
    Coals. Oh, are you sad? There! I'll Ease
The pain with ten more kisses, honey-
    sweet.
And so kiss into happy kiss will melt,
We'll pleasantly enjoy each other's selves.

Then double life will to us both ensue:
You also live in me, as I in you.
So do not chide me for this play on
    words
    Or keep me staid and stay-at-home,
      but make me
Go on that journey best of all preferred:
When out of myself, my dearest love,
    you take me.

*From Louise Labé, *Sonnets by Louise Labé,* ed. Peter Sharratt. Copyright © Edinburgh University Press. By permission of Edinburgh University Press. Sonnets 18, and 24 as published in Louise Labé, *Sonnets,* Peter Sharratt, Intro. and commentaries; trans. Graham Dunstan Martin, Edinburgh Bilingual Library series, vol. 7 (Austin: University of Texas, 1972), pp. 37, 43.

SONNET 24

Do not reproach me, ladies, if I've loved
And felt a thousand torches burn my veins,
A thousand griefs, a thousand biting pains.
If all my days to bitter tears dissolved,
Then, ladies, do not denigrate my name.
If I did wrong, the pain and punishment
Are now. Don't file their needles to a point.

Consider: Love is master of the game:
No need of Vulcan to explain your fire,
Nor of Adonis to excuse desire,
But with less cause than mine, far less occasion,
As the whim takes him, idly he can curse
You with a stranger and a stronger passion.
But O take care your suffering's not worse.

Labé also had strong views on the importance of education for women. In the preface to a volume of her complete works published in 1555, she expressed pride in her intellectual accomplishments: "I trained my wits, my body and my mind with a thousand ingenious works" (Thurman 1980, 92). She expounded on her beliefs in the dedication of her book to a noblewoman whom she urged to pursue learning and writing.

DEDICATORY EPISTLE TO MADEMOISELLE CLÉMENCE DE BOURGES, 25 JULY 1555*

The time having come, Mademoiselle, when men's strict laws no longer prevent women from applying themselves to knowledge and study, it seems to me that those who have the opportunity should use this honorable freedom, which our sex has desired so much in the past, to study and show men the wrong they have done us in depriving us of the benefit and honor which might have come to us. And if anyone of us reaches the level where she can put her ideas into writing, she should do so with care, not despising fame, but adorning herself with it rather than with chains, rings and sumptuous clothes; . . . [for] the honor which knowledge brings us will be ours entirely. Neither a thief's cunning, nor an enemy's force, nor the passage of time can take it away from us.

. . . I cannot myself fulfill the wish I have for our sex to see it surpass or equal men, not only in beauty but also in knowledge and virtue. I can only urge virtuous Ladies to raise their minds somewhat above their distaffs and spindles, and strive to have the world understand that although we are not made to command, those who govern and are to be obeyed should not disdain us as partners in both private and public affairs. Besides the reputation that our sex will acquire thereby, we will also contribute to the general good, as men will take greater pains to study the humanities

*From Louise Labé, *Debate of Folly and Love: A New English Translation with the Original French Text*, trans. Anne-Marie Bourbon, vol. 8 of History and Language Series, Maria Edlinger Stoffers, gen. ed. (New York: Peter Lang, 2000), pp. 15, 17, 19. Copyright © Peter Lang Publishing, Inc. By permission.

for fear of being shamefully outstripped by women over whom they have always claimed to be superior in nearly everything. . . .

If there is anything else to be recommended, after fame and honor, the pleasure which the study of literature usually brings should incite every one of us to action. This pleasure is different from most entertainments: when one has enjoyed them for as long as one wants, one can only boast of having passed the time. Study, however, is so personally satisfying that it remains with us much longer. . . . when we happen to put our thoughts into writing, even though afterwards our mind races after a myriad of things and is constantly on the move, yet on going back to our writing, even a long time afterwards, we return to the same point and the same state of mind we were in before. Then our enjoyment is doubled, because we rediscover the pleasure we had in the past, either in the subject matter we were writing about, or in the understanding of the study to which we were then devoted. . . .

And because women do not willingly appear alone in public, I have chosen you to serve as my guide, dedicating this little work to you. I am sending it with no other intention than to assure you of the goodwill I have borne you for a long time, I want to inspire you, so that when you see this crude and clumsy work of mine, you will want to bring to light your own better polished and more refined work.

God keep you in good health. Your humble friend, Louise Labé

WOMEN IN RENAISSANCE ENGLAND

Elizabeth I of England (1533–1603)

Elizabeth Tudor has long been recognized as one of England's greatest rulers and as one of the most important figures in Renaissance Europe. She also stands as one of the pre-eminent female rulers in Western history. During her long reign (1558–1603), England enjoyed peace and prosperity and the English Renaissance reached its peak. Under her leadership, the principle of religious toleration and its legal foundation were established and Protestantism took firm hold in England. She epitomized the humanist ideals for women, and, by her success, remained a constant challenge to the persistent Western belief that a woman was incapable of ruling.

Elizabeth and her half-sister Mary Tudor were beneficiaries of humanist theories of education, and both were trained to rule, should the need arise. Humanist Sir Thomas More was Henry VIII's lord chancellor, and his educational ideas were used as a model for the king's children, while Juan Louis Vives' ideas guided Mary's early education. Between the ages of 11 and 16, Elizabeth was tutored by three leading male scholars. Both girls were also well trained in the traditional feminine skills, including music and embroidery.

Elizabeth's education served her well throughout her life. Her linguistic skills proved extremely useful in diplomacy, and, combined with the breadth of her learning, earned her great respect among both admirers and foes in England and abroad. Her literary and musical skills also provided solace during difficult periods, and a welcome break from affairs of state. She wrote poetry periodically, and throughout her life translated literary works, including Navarre's *Mirror of the Sinful Soul* and works of Petrarch, Plutarch, Horace, Xenophon, Boethius, and a play by Euripides. Scholars have noted that she translated works that reflected her own values and her personal and political concerns. At 65 she translated a history by Sallust that dealt with problems of succession, incompetent leadership, and civil strife, deep concerns of hers as she faced leaving England with no successor. She also translated a selection from Seneca's drama *Hercules Oetaeus* that explored the disloyalty of subjects, specifically male courtiers, to their leaders. It is also a piece in which female speakers praise women for their loyalty. (Cerasano and Wynne-Davies 1996, 8–9)

Equally important was the perhaps overlooked legacy that Elizabeth, the learned queen, left women of her realm. During her long reign, many English families educated their daughters along humanist lines and encouraged them to write poetry, learn languages, and do translations, in the hope they might become accepted as members of her court. She, like other learned public women, helped make a rigorous education for girls more acceptable.

The poem that follows was written by Elizabeth in the nineteenth year of her reign when she was concerned about the return of Catholic Mary, Queen of Scots, to England.

THE DOUBT OF FUTURE FOES, CIRCA 1577*

The doubt of future foes
Exiles my present joy,
And wit me warns to shun such snares
As threaten mine annoy.
　For falsehood now doth flow
And subjects' faith doth ebb,
Which should not be if reason ruled.
Or wisdom weaved the web.
　But clouds of joys untried
Do cloak aspiring minds
Which turn to rage of late repent
By changèd course of winds.
　The top of hope supposed
The root of rue shall be
And fruitless all their grafted guile,
As shortly ye shall see.
　Their dazzled eyes with pride,
Which great ambition blinds,

Shall be unsealed by worthy wights
Whose foresight falsehood finds.
　The daughter of debate
That discord aye doth sow
Shall reap no gain where former rule
Still peace hath taught to know.
　No foreign banished wight
Shall anchor in this port:
Our realm brooks no seditious sects—
Let them elsewhere resort.
　My rusty sword through rest
Shall first his edge employ
To pull their tops that seek such change
Or gape for future joy.
　Vivat Regina ["Long Live the
　　Queen"]

Although the English believed as strongly as other Europeans that women were not fit to rule, they adopted a policy of "strict inheritance" by which the crown would pass to a daughter in the absence of a male heir in order to keep the Tudor dynasty intact and avert civil disorder. Nevertheless, throughout her reign, Elizabeth's gender remained a troublesome issue. The documents that follow illustrate her successes in governing as well as the challenges she repeatedly encountered because she was a woman. Be attentive to the ways her sex affected her authority and the strategies she used to overcome that liability or turn it to her advantage. Also, consider the extent to which she re-enforced or challenged traditional sex roles and images of women.

One of Parliament's first acts in 1559 after Elizabeth's accession to the throne was to petition the queen to marry. Her response, which follows was read to the House of Commons. Parliament and her advisors continued to pressure her to marry in order to bear an heir to the throne. She responded by pretending to consider various suitors and dangling prospects of marriage before potential husbands.

*From Leah S. Marcus, Janet Mueller, and Mary Beth Rose, eds. *Elizabeth I: Collected Works* (Chicago: University of Chicago Press, 2000), pp. 133–4.

In 1566, a frustrated Parliament limited her subsidies to force her to become betrothed. She responded by cutting her expenses, getting loans, and investing in such enterprises as Sir Francis Drake's circumnavigation. Ultimately, she made enough money from his expedition and other investments to ignore Parliament. Throughout her reign, she cultivated her image as Virgin Queen.

ELIZABETH'S RESPONSE TO PARLIAMENT'S PETITION THAT SHE MARRY, 10 FEBRUARY 1559*

As I have good cause, so do I give you all my hearty thanks, for the good zeal and loving care you seem to have, as well towards me, as to the whole state of your country. Your petition, I perceive, consisteth of three parts, and mine answer to the same shall depend of two.

And to the first part, I may say unto you, that from my years of understanding, [since] I first had consideration of myself to be born a servitor of almighty God, I happily chose this kind of life in the which I yet live, which, I assure you, for mine own part, hath hitherto best contented my self and I trust hath been most acceptable to God. . . .

For the other part, the manner of your petition I do well like of and take in good part, because it is simple and containeth no limitation of place or person. If it had been otherwise, I must needs have misliked it very much, and thought it in you a very great presumption, being unfitting and altogether unmeet for you to require them that may command, . . . or to take upon you to draw my love to your liking or frame my will to your fantasies. . . .

Nevertheless, if any of you be in suspect, whensoever it may please God to incline my heart to another kind of life, ye may well assure yourselves my meaning is not to do or determine anything wherewith the realm may or shall have just cause to be discontented. And therefore put that clean out of your heads. For I assure you . . . I will never in that matter conclude anything that shall be prejudicial to the realm, for the weal, good, and safety whereof I will never shun to spend my life. And whomsoever my chance shall be to light upon, I trust . . . he shall be such as shall be as careful for the realm and you as my self.

And albeit it might please almighty God to continue me still in this mind to live out of the state of marriage, yet it is not to be feared but He will so work in my heart and in your wisdoms as good provision by His help may be made in convenient time, whereby the realm shall not remain destitute of an heir that may be a fit governor, and peradventure more beneficial to the realm than such offspring as may come of me. For although I be never so careful of your well-doings, and mind ever so to be, yet may my issue grow out of kind and become, perhaps, ungracious. And in the end this shall be for me sufficient: that a marble stone shall declare, that a queen, having reigned such a time, lived and died a virgin. And here I end, and take your coming unto me in good part, and give unto you all . . . my hearty thanks, more yet for your zeal and good meaning than for your petition.

*Excerpts from Marcus et. al., "Queen Elizabeth's First Speech Before Parliament, February 10, 1559," speech 3, version 1, in *Elizabeth I: Collected Works*, pp. 56–58.

One of the biggest challenges Queen Elizabeth faced was the threatened invasion of England by Spain in 1588. With the Armada approaching, she traveled to her army's encampment at Tilbury and exhorted her troops to defend the country in the speech that follows. Here she cultivates the image of herself as a warrior king. It is significant that she also signed official papers as *Rex* (king) rather than *Regina* (queen). Here, too, she is like some female scholars and literary women who had to see themselves as a man in a woman's body in order to pursue male activities.

THE QUEEN'S SPEECH TO HER ARMY ON THE EVE OF THE SPANISH INVASION, 1588*

My loving People,

We have been persuaded by some that are careful of our safety, to take heed how we commit ourselves to armed multitudes, for fear of treachery; but I assure you, I do not desire to live to distrust my faithful and loving people.

Let tyrants fear; I have always so behaved myself, that, under God, I have placed my chiefest strength and safeguard in the loyal hearts and good will of my subjects, and therefore I am come amongst you, as you see, at this time, not for my recreation and disport, but being resolved in the midst and heat of the battle, to live or die amongst you all, to lay down for my God, and for my kingdoms, and for my people, my honour and my blood, even in the dust.

I know I have the body but of a weak and feeble woman; but I have the heart and stomach of a king, and of a king of England too; and think foul scorn that Parma or Spain, or any prince of Europe should dare to invade the borders of my realm; to which rather than any dishonour shall grow by me, I myself will take up arms, I myself will be your general, judge, and rewarder of every one of your virtues in the field.

I know already, for your forwardness you have deserved rewards and crowns; and we do assure you in the word of a prince, they shall be duly paid you. In the mean time, my lieutenant-general shall be in my stead, than whom never prince commanded a more noble or worthy subject; not doubting but by your obedience to my general, by your concord in the camp, and your valour in the field, we shall shortly have a famous victory over those enemies of my God, of my kingdoms, and of my people.

Women and Renaissance Drama

The Renaissance was a golden age for theater in both Spain and England, yet, like Roman and Greek drama, in both realms it was a quintessential masculine domain. Playwrights were men, theaters were run by men, and all parts, male and female alike, were played by males. Ironically, like Greek drama, the best of Elizabethan and Spanish drama included some superb female characters, but the plays also re-enforced popular stereotypes about women. Elizabethan, particularly Shakespearean, comedies featured elaborate plots with cross-dressing (male characters masquerading as women and vice versa)

*"The Authentic Speech of Queen Elizabeth to her Army encamped at Tilbury, 1588," in *Military Tracts: Tracts during the Reign of Queen Elizabeth,* 2d. ed., rev. and arr. Walter Scott (London: Cadell and W. Davies, 1809–1815), in John Somers, *The Somers Tracts,* Vol. I (New York: AMS Press, 1965), pp. 429–30.

and considerable confusion as to the gender identity of characters. Some scholars have linked this phenomenon to the societal ambivalence created by having a woman as ruler of the nation despite the pervasive belief that women were not fit to govern.

It was impossible, Virginia Woolf contended in her 1929 essay "A Room of One's Own," for Shakespeare's mythical sister to have entered the theater world, written a play, and had it staged in Elizabethan England (Woolf 1929, ch. 3). (See Woolf in Chapter 11, "New Directions in Literature and the Arts.") Strong societal opposition to women's presence on the stage and behind the scenes also extended to women's presence as spectators in the theater. In the late sixteenth and early seventeenth centuries, however, English women began to break down the barriers that excluded their sex from the world of theater. As in Italy, noblewomen participated in court entertainments and, during the reign of King James I, Queen Anne and her ladies performed in a pastoral and in masques or pageants replete with elaborate costumes and blackened faces. Women from the lower classes participated in May Day and popular theatrical celebrations. Moreover, the published diatribes against the evils of theater and admonitions that plays destroyed a woman's morals and even led to prostitution clearly indicate that even respectable women were beginning to attend plays in public theaters. Women also began to enter the financial world of theater. Some served as "gatherers" who collected money from spectators, and several were investors or shareholders in theater companies and play houses (Cerasano and Wynne-Davies 1996, 158–59, 161–63, 169, 174–75).

More importantly, before 1640 several women produced what some have aptly called "closet drama": translating and writing original plays that were intended only to be read or perhaps performed by family members and close friends in their homes. The private nature of their work reveals the conflicting forces that all learned women of the Renaissance era had to reconcile: their desire to pursue their intellectual interests and talents, on the one hand, and their awareness of the societal sanctions that awaited women who entered the public male sphere and broke the rule of silence imposed on respectable women. As a rule, they portrayed female characters in a more positive, sympathetic light than did male playwrights, and they expressed unconventional, decidedly female perspectives on marriage. These women also advanced English theater by their generous patronage.

Elizabeth Tanfield Cary (1585–1639): Playwright

Elizabeth Cary was the first Englishwoman to write a tragedy, *The Tragedy of Mariam* (1602–04); the first to have her play published (*Mariam*, 1613); and the first to write a history play, *The History of the Life, Reign, and Death of Edward II* (c. 1627–28). A devout Catholic, she also wrote hymns to the Virgin, poems about female saints, and religious and moral instructional works for her children. In addition she translated numerous works for publication from French, Spanish, Latin, and Hebrew. Her works won substantial praise from contemporary male writers.

Her challenging, tragic life was revealed in her biography, *The Lady Falkland, Her Life*, written in 1655 by one of her daughters. Cary was an only child with an insatiable hunger for knowledge. Her parents refused to extend her education beyond literacy in English and French, so she taught herself Spanish, Italian, Latin, and Hebrew. When her mother cut off her supply of candles to make her stop reading, she went into debt to secretly buy candles from servants and continued her education. She read widely, from classical authors to Renaissance writers.

She entered an arranged marriage to Sir Henry Cary in 1602. Her husband was away from England until 1606, first as a soldier and then as a prisoner of the Spanish. During that period, she lived under her mother-in-law's strict authority and was forbidden to read. As a result, she wrote. Between 1609 and 1624, the couple had 11 children, but their relationship steadily deteriorated. After 1605, she turned to Catholicism for spiritual support. Her husband, however, was a strict Protestant, and, in

1622, was appointed lord deputy of Ireland. His harsh rule and persecution of the Catholics and her ties with a pro-Catholic group triggered the collapse of their marriage, and he sent her back to England in 1625. When rumors spread that she was planning to convert to Catholicism, he had her confined to her room for six weeks, cut off her allowance, and took her children from her. Despite legal efforts to force her husband to pay for her support, she died impoverished.

The Tragedy of Mariam, written when she was only 17, reflects Cary's Christian faith and her interest in the position of women. Her play differs in interesting ways from the ancient text *Antiquities of the Jews* by Josephus from which she derived her plot and characters. Her story takes place in a single day, while the original covered nearly a year of events. The play opens with Mariam, King Herod's second wife, agonizing over her desire to love the husband she has come to respect, but hating him for his tyrannical rule and for having had her brother and grandfather killed. In Cary's hands she is an innocent wife who dares to speak out against the abuse of power and to offer cogent insights about public events. Josephus, in contrast, portrayed Mariam as a shrew and an adulteress who plotted against Herod. In both versions, Herod's sister, Salome, in concert with his mother, convinces the king that Mariam was trying to poison him, and, despite her protestations of innocence, Mariam is executed. Cary, however, adds some lively scenes in which Mariam and Salome engage in angry exchanges. Both women are more complete and convincing characters than in the traditional versions of the story. Both are struggling to find a degree of autonomy in a patriarchal world.

The scene that follows is entirely of Cary's creation. Salome believes her brother has been killed in battle. While mourning him, she ruminates about her own life: the death (at her bidding) of her first husband, Joseph; her desire to get out of her marriage to Constabarus, who holds highly traditional views about women; and her feelings for Silleus. Why do you think Cary added this scene?

THE TRAGEDY OF MARIAM, THE FAIR QUEEN OF JEWRY, 1613*

ACT I: SCENE 4

Salome: Lives *Salome* to get so base a style

As foote to the proud Mariam? Herods spirit

In happy time for her endured exile,

For did he live she should not miss her merit:

But he is dead: and though he were my Brother,

His death such store of Cinders cannot cast

My Coals of love to quench; for though they smother

The flames a while, yet will they out at last.

Oh blest *Arabia*, in best climate placed,

I by the Fruit will censure of the Tree:

Tis not in vaine thy happy name thou hast,

If all *Arabians* like *Silleus* bee:

Had not my fate been too, too contrary

When I on *Constabarus* first did gaze,

Silleus had been object to mine eye:

Whose lookes and personage must all eyes amaze.

But now ill Fated *Salome,* thy tongue

To *Constabarus* by itself is tied:

And now, except I doe the Hebrew wrong

I cannot be the fair *Arabian* bride:

*From Lady Elizabeth Cary, *The Tragedy of Mariam, 1613,* Malone Society Reprints Series (London: Printed for the Malone Society by H. Hart at the Oxford University Press, 1914), Act I, Scenes 4 and 5, lines 270–352.

What childish lets are these? Why stand I
  now

On honourable points? Tis long ago

Since shame was written on my tainted
  brow:

And certaine tis, that shame is honours
  foe.

Had I upon my reputation stood,

Had I affected an unspotted life,

Josephus veins had still been stuft with
  blood,

And I to him had lived a sober wife.

Then had I never cast an eye of love,

On *Constabarus* now detested face,

Then had I kept my thoughts without
  remove:

And blusht at motion of the least dis-
  grace:

But shame is gone, and honour wiped
  away,

And Impudencie on my forehead sits:

She bids me worke my will without
  delay,

And for my will I will imploy my wits.

He loves, I love; what then can be the
  cause,

Keeps me for being the *Arabians* wife?

Is it the principles of *Moses* laws,

For *Constabarus* still remains in life,

If he to me did beare as Earnest hate,

As I to him, for him there were an case,

A separating bill might free his fate:

From such a yoke that did so much dis-
  please.

Why should such privilege to man be
  given?

Or given to them, why barred from
  women then?

Are men, then we, in greater grace in
  heaven?

Or cannot women hate as well as men?

I'll be the custome-breaker: and beginne

To shew my Sexe the way to freedomes
  door,

And with an offring will I purge my
  sinne,

The lawe was made for none but who
  are poore.

If *Herod* had lived, I might to him accuse

My present Lord. But for the futures
  sake

Then would I tell the King he did refuse

The sons of Baba in his power to take.

But now I must divorce him from my
  bed,

That my *Silleus* may possesse his roome:

Had I not begged his life he had been
  dead,

I curse my tongue the hindrer of his
  doome,

But then my wandring heart to him was
  fast,

Nor did I dreame of change: *Silleus* said

He would be here, and see he comes at
  last

Had I not nam'd him, longer had he
  staid.

Act I, Scene 5 [Enter Silleus]

Silleus: Well found faire *Salome Judeas*
  pride,

Hath thy innated wisdom found the way

To make *Silleus* deeme him deified,

By gaining thee, a more then precious
  prey?

Salome: I have devised the best I can
  devise,

A more imperfect means was never
  found:

But what cares *Salome*, it does suffice

If our endeavours with their end be crown'd.

In this our land we have an ancient use,

Permitted first by our law-givers head:

Who hates his wife, though for no just abuse,

May with a bill divorce her from his bed.

But in this custome women are not free,

Yet, I for once will wrest it, blame not thou

The ill I doe, since what I do is for thee,

Though others blame, *Silleus* should allow.

The Woman Question in England

The *querelle des femmes* (debate about women) began in England during the first half of the sixteenth century when many English translations of continental works about women, including Pizan's *Book of the City of Ladies* (1405) and the treatises on women's education by humanists Erasmus, Castiglione, and Vives, became available. Englishmen joined the debate at mid-century with the publication of *The Schoolhouse of women* that attacked women and a rejoinder by a male defender of the sex. The controversy continued to simmer when first Mary Tudor and then Elizabeth assumed the throne, particularly with the untimely publication of Protestant reformer John Knox's misogynist *First Blast of the Trumpet* in 1558 and the reprinting of *The Schoolhouse* in the 1560s and more rebuttals. This first stage of the English debate reached a climax in the late 1580s and 1590s as increasing numbers of pamphlets appeared. Among these was the first pamphlet on the subject written by an English woman, Jane Anger.

In 1615 a major pamphlet war erupted with the publication of Joseph Swetnam's *The Arraignment of Lewd, idle, froward, and unconstant women* under the pseudonym Thomas tell-Troth. Three women were among the respondents to Swetnam's misogynist tract. By this time, the literary debate about the alleged failings and worth of women was becoming enmeshed with a real-life controversy over clothing. At issue were women who donned masculine-style dress. A series of pamphlets followed that focused on masculinity and femininity. Some attacked women's adoption of "masculine" attire as a hidden attempt to obtain sexual freedom or assume male prerogatives. Others responded by shifting the attack to the "effeminate fop" or by attacking both masculine behavior by women and effeminate behavior by men. Between 1620 and 1640, the debate focused more on such topics as marriage, the double standard, education, and women's roles in history. The English *querelle des femmes* culminated in a final pamphlet war triggered by publication of a series of humorous popular "lectures" on marriage (written by men) in which women lectured other women, mostly about "typical" female faults.

The English Renaissance debate about women is significant for a number of reasons. The printing press (1455) with its ability to turn out numerous cheaper publications, the spread of reading literacy in the vernacular, and the economic decision of printers to fuel interest in the topic by publishing many pamphlets and several editions combined to draw the growing middle class into the debate for the first time. As interest widened, the debate spilled over into poetry, drama, conduct books for the bourgeoisie and gentry, sermons, ballads, and everyday conversations. In turn, the pamphlet wars increasingly reflected bourgeois experiences and daily secular concerns.

Significantly, as attacks on women increased and were disseminated more widely than ever, defenses of women also increased, though they never matched the attacks. Most importantly, for the first time, significant numbers of women began to publish defenses of their sex. As women attacked and sought to counter the negative stereotypes of woman as a sexually insatiable seductress, a domineering shrew, and a vain and extravagant creature, they began to develop a consciousness of women as a distinct class and to lay the foundation for the development of feminist thought.

Jane Anger's *Protection for Women* (1589) is the first known defense of women by a woman in England. The identity of the author is a mystery. Jane Anger is probably a pseudonym, and the author quite likely chose the name because it reflected her feelings about the woman question. Her signature, "Ja: A. Gent," appears on the title page of the tract, suggesting that she was a "gentlewoman" or a woman from the lower gentry. The numerous Latin quotations that appear in the tract indicate that she was one of the relatively few women of her social class who had acquired at least a limited classical education.

JANE ANGER, HER PROTECTION FOR WOMEN (1589)*

To defend them against the Scandalous Reports
of a late Surfeiting Lover
and all other like Venerians
that complain so to be overcloyed
with women's kindness.
    Written by Jane Anger, Gentlewoman 1589 . . .

To all Women in general, and gentle Reader whatsoever.

Fie on the falsehood of men, whose minds go oft amadding, and whose tongues cannot so soon be wagging but straight they fall arailing. Was there ever any so abused, so slandered, so railed upon, or so wickedly handled undeservedly as are we women? Will the Gods permit it, the Goddesses stay their punishing judgments, and we ourselves not pursue their undoings for such devilish practices? . . . Shall Surfeiters rail on our kindness, you stand still and say nought, and shall not Anger stretch the veins of her brains, the strings of her fingers, and the lists of her modesty to answer their Surfeitings? Yes, truly. And herein I conjure all you to aid and assist me in defense of my willingness, which shall make me rest at your commands. Fare you well.

Your friend, Jane Anger

A PROTECTION FOR WOMEN

. . . It is a wonder to see how men can flatter themselves with their own conceits. For let us look, they will straight affirm that we love, and if then *Lust* pricketh them, they will swear that *Love* stingeth us. Which imagination only is sufficient to make them assay the scaling of half a dozen of us in one night, when they will not stick to swear that if they should be denied of their requests, death must needs follow. Is it any marvel, though, they surfeit, when they are so greedy? But is it not pity that any of them should perish, which will be so soon killed with unkindness? Yes, truly. Well, the onset given, if we retire for a vantage, they will straight affirm that they have got the victory. Nay, some of them are so carried away with conceit

*Excerpts from Jane Anger, *Jane Anger, her Protection for Women* . . . (London: Printed by Richard Jones and Thomas Orwin, 1589), reprinted in Katherine Usher Henderson and Barbara F. McManus, eds. *Half Humankind. Contexts and Texts of the Controversy about Women in England, 1540–1640*, (Urbana and Chicago: University of Illinois Press, 1985), pp. 173–74, 183, 187–88.

that, shameless, they will blaze abroad among their companions that they have obtained the love of a woman unto whom they never spoke above once, if that. Are not these forward fellows? You must bear with them, because they dwell far from lying neighbors. . . . Their fawning is but flattery; their faith, falsehood; their fair words, allurements to destruction; and their large promises, tokens of death or of evils worse than death. Their singing is a bait to catch us; and their playings, plagues to torment us. . . .

To the reader of the same, from the author

Though sharp the seed by Anger sowed,
    we all (almost) confess,
And hard his hap we aye account,
    who Anger doth possess,
Yet hapless shall thou (Reader) reap
    such fruit from ANGER'S soil,
As may thee please, and ANGER ease
    from long and weary toil;
Whose pains were took for thy behoof
    to till that cloddy ground,
	Where scarce no place free from disgrace
	    of female Sex was found.
	If aught offend which she doth send,
	    impute it to her mood,
	For ANGER'S rage must that assuage,
	    as well is understood.
	If to delight aught come in sight,
	    then deem it for the best,
	So you your will may well fulfill,
	    and she have her request.

The following selection is from a pamphlet *The women's sharp revenge* (1640) by Mary Tattlewell and Joan Hit-him-home that was written in response to two humorous "lectures" satirizing women, published by John Taylor in 1639. It is also an attack on all the satirical lectures that were so popular in that period. The identities of the authors are unknown.

MARY TATTLEWELL AND JOAN HIT-HIM-HOME, *THE WOMEN'S SHARP REVENGE* (1640)*

The women's sharp revenge
Or an answer to Sir Seldom Sober
that writ those railing Pamphlets called
    the *Juniper* and *Crabtree Lectures*, etc.
Being a sound Reply and a full
    confutation

of those Books, with an Apology
in this case for the defense of us women.

Performed by Mary Tattlewell and Joan
    Hit-him-home, Spinsters, 1640

[After chastising men for not defending women from the attacks by Sir Seldom Sober and others, the authors bring Sober and his "lying lectures" to trial before a jury of women. While finding Sober guilty of heresy and abuse by attributing every evil and weakness to the entire female sex, they go on the attack.]

*Excerpts from Mary Tattle-well and Joane Hit-him-home, *The women's sharpe revenge: Or an answer to Sir Seldome Sober* . . . (J. O[kes] for J. Becket, 1640), as reprinted in Henderson and McManus, eds., *Half Humankind. Contexts and Texts of the Controversy about Women in England, 1540–1640* (Urbana and Chicago: University of Illinois Press, 1985), pp. 306, 313–14, 324–25. Original pamphlet in the Bodleian Library, University of Oxford.

... And this is an argument which we might amplify even from the Original of all History, nay, and would not spare to do it, had we but the benefit of your breeding.

But it hath been the policy of all parents, even from the beginning, to curb us of that benefit by striving to keep us under and to make us men's mere Vassals even unto all posterity. How else comes it to pass that when a Father hath a numerous issue of Sons and Daughters, the sons forsooth they must be first put to the Grammar school, and after perchance sent to the University, and trained up in the Liberal Arts and Sciences, and there (if they prove not Blockheads) they may in time be book-learned? And what do they then? Read the Poets perhaps, ... And in the stead of picking out the best Poets, who have strived to right us, follow the other, who do nothing but rail at us. ...

When we, whom they style by the name of weaker Vessels, though of a more delicate, fine, soft, and more pliant flesh and therefore of a temper most capable of the best Impression, have not that generous and liberal Education, lest we should be made able to vindicate our own injuries, we are set only to the Needle, to prick our fingers, or else to the Wheel to spin a fair thread for our own undoing, or perchance to some more dirty and debased drudgery. If we be taught to read, they then confine us within the compass of our Mother Tongue, and that limit we are not suffered to pass; or if ... we be brought up to Music, to singing, and to dancing, it is not for any benefit that thereby we can engross unto ourselves, but for their own particular ends, the better to please and content their licentious appetites when we come to our maturity and ripeness. And thus if we be weak by Nature, they strive to make us more weak by our Nurture; and if in degree of place low, they strive by their policy to keep us more under. ...

[The authors defend their sex with stories of women's virtue and chastity.]
... Thus good and modest Women have been content to have none or one man (at the most) all their whole lifetime, but men have been so addicted to incontinency that no bounds of Law or reason could restrain them. For ... the wisest that ever reigned, Solomon, had no fewer than three hundred Wives and seven hundred Concubines, and that his Son ... had eighteen Wives and sixty Concubines by whom he begat twenty-eight Sons and threescore Daughters.... [*Tattlewell gives additional examples from Greek history and the Old and New Testaments of women who were models of courage, piety and chastity.*]

Thus have I truly and impartially proved that for Chastity, Charity, Constancy, Magnanimity, Valor, Wisdom, Piety, or any Grace or Virtue whatsoever, women have always been more than equal with men, and that for Luxury, [arrogance], obscenity, profanity, Ebriety, Impiety, and all that may be called bad we do come far short of them. Now we think it meet only to tell them a little of one fault which we are sure they do know already, and that our repetition of it will be no means to Reform it. Yet to show the World that Women have great cause to find fault and be discontented with their odious general vice of Drunkenness, we will relate unto you the delicate, dainty, Foppish, and ridiculous conceits of Sir Seldom Sober, with the most foolish, idle, and sottish tricks and feats of his idle and addlepated followers. ...

SUGGESTED READINGS

Davis, Natalie Zemon, and Arlteet Farage, eds. *A History of Women: Renaissance and Enlightenment Paradoxes.* Cambridge: Belknap Press of Harvard University Press, 1993.

Warnicke, Retha M. *Women of the English Renaissance and Reformation.* Westport, CT: Greenwood Press, 1983.

Rulers

Hopkins, Lisa. *Women Who Would Be Kings: Women Rulers of the Sixteenth Century.* London: Vision Press; New York: St Martin's Press, 1991.

Levin, Carole. *The Heart and Stomach of a King: Elizabeth I and the Politics of Sex and Power.* Philadelphia: University of Pennsylvania Press, 1994.

Liss, Peggy. *Isabel the Queen: Life and Times.* New York: Oxford University Press, 1992.

MacCaffrey, Wallace T. *Elizabeth I.* London and New York: E. Arnold; New York: Oxford University Press, 1994.

Literature

Beilin, Elaine V. *Redeeming Eve: Women Writers of the English Renaissance.* Princeton, NJ: Princeton University Press, 1987.

Benson, Pamela Joseph. *The Invention of the Renaissance Woman: The Challenge of Female Independence in the Literature and Thought of Italy and England.* University Park: Pennsylvania State University Press, 1992.

Cameron, Keith. *Louise Labé: Feminist and Poet of the Renaissance.* Oxford, UK: Berg Publishers, 1990.

Schleiner, Louise. *Tudor and Stuart Women Writers.* Bloomington: Indiana University Press, 1994.

Chapter 4

Artists, Musicians, and Performers in the Baroque Era

In the seventeenth century and early eighteenth century, increasing numbers of women gained recognition for their cultural contributions. We find more references to women artists, musicians, writers, and performers than ever before, and more of women's own works. Unfortunately, the references to women's creative endeavors still vastly outnumber the actual works that have survived. Many worked in private or anonymously because social mores continued to penalize women who "went public" with their work. Equally frustrating, we do not have correspondence or other written documents by some whose works have survived, such as the Flemish and Dutch painters Clara Peeters, Judith Leyster, and Rachel Ruysch, or the prolific Italian composer Isabella Leonarda. Nevertheless, the following pages introduce a range of creative women of this period and shed light on the various factors that facilitated their endeavors and recognition as well as the obstacles they and others faced because of their sex. These women were the beneficiaries of the path-breaking work of the female pioneers of the Renaissance period and of social, economic, and political developments of the era, including the increase of travel and the exchange of cultural trends across Europe. We begin in Italy, where Renaissance culture, the region's numerous political divisions, and the continuing vitality of monastic life provided opportunities for women artists and musicians. The last part of the chapter shifts to France which became Europe's cultural center during the reign of Louis XIV.

WOMEN AND CULTURE IN ITALY

Artemisia Gentileschi (1593–ca. 1653): Baroque Artist

Artemisia Gentileschi is widely recognized as one of the major artists of the Baroque period. Her dramatic use of light and dark and the realism and emotional intensity of her paintings made her one of the most influential painters in the style of Caravaggio, an Italian painter whose use of light and dark contrasts to focus attention on his subject established one trend in Baroque art. Gentileschi was also a path breaker. Instead of portraiture, she specialized in historical, biblical, and mythological stories. Her subjects included many of the women we have met in earlier chapters, particularly in Volume One: Susanna, Bathsheba, Judith, Lucretia, Esther, Cleopatra, Mary Magdalene, and the muse or allegory of painting. These were popular subjects among Renaissance and Baroque artists, but her interpretations were unique. According to Mary Garrard, she portrayed women as "convincing protagonists and courageous heroes, perhaps for the first time in art"(Garrard 1984, 98). Like Christine de Pizan and the Renaissance women writers who used their pens to defend their sex, Gentileschi challenged stereotypical and misogynist images of women through her paintings. Thus, she was the first woman to participate in what might be called the "artistic *querelle des femmes.*" Defying social conventions, she lived a remarkable life as an independent woman and professional artist. During her 40-year career, her patrons included the Medici family, rulers of France, Spain, Austria, and England, and the pope's inner circle. Curiously, however, she was rarely mentioned in histories of art written by her contemporaries and was largely dismissed by art historians until the late twentieth century.

Gentileschi was born in Rome, the only daughter of a prominent artist, Orazio Gentileschi. Her mother died when she was 12. Like most other girls of her class, she had little education, but she received excellent artistic training from her father. Her first known painting, *Susannah and the Elders* (1610) revealed unusual artistic maturity. In 1610–1611, her father arranged for her to receive additional training from a friend, Agostino Tassi, who, after repeated harassment, raped her. When her father learned of the rape, he sued Tassi for economic damages. The trial in 1612 was a painful experience for Gentileschi. Tassi denied the rape, and he and his witnesses falsely testified that she was a promiscuous woman. The court subjected her to two physical examinations to determine whether or not she was a virgin and tortured her with the *sibille* (thumbscrews) to see if her testimony was truthful. The trial ended without a guilty verdict.

In November 1612, Gentileschi married Florentine artist Pietro Antonio de Stiatessi and settled in Florence. Despite bearing four children within six years, she attracted important patrons, thanks in part to her father's links with the Medici family and with the Medici poet Michelangelo Buonarroti the Younger. Buonarroti, the grand nephew of Michelangelo, commissioned several paintings and included her in his cultural circle. In 1616, through the support of Duke Cosimo II, she was the first woman admitted to the Florence Accademia del Disegno. In fact, she was the first of only 13 female artists among the 8,000 to 10,000 male members of the academy from its founding to the mid-eighteenth century (Garrard 1989, 495–96, n. 40). Sadly, she did not achieve financial security. Instead, she was plagued with debts, many of which were secretly incurred by her husband.

In 1620, prompted by health and family problems, she moved to Rome and began her journey as an independent professional. The census of 1624 listed her as head of a household consisting of her daughter Prudenza and two servants (Cropper 1993, 761). This was the most creative period of her life. In addition to works for patrons in Genoa, Venice, and Rome, she collaborated on major church commissions. Two of her most significant works stem from this period: *Self-portrait as the Allegory of Painting* and *Judith and Her Maidservant* (c. 1625), regarded as "one of the great masterpieces of Caravaggesque Baroque" (Garrard 1989, 67).

In August 1630, she moved to Naples, a major art center and the second largest city in Europe. She joined her father at the Stuart court in England in 1638, where she completed private commissions, including ten paintings for Charles I, and collaborated with her father on the ceiling fresco of the Great Hall in the queen's Greenwich house. After her father died in 1639, she returned to Naples, where she worked until her death in early 1653. Her last painting, a *Susannah,* was dated 1652.

In addition to her trial transcript, 28 letters from her correspondence exist. These document her relations with six patrons and friends (including astronomer Galileo) from 1620 to 1651. They also reveal that she provided dowries for Prudenza and a daughter born after 1625 and trained both to be artists. Thirteen of her letters were to Don Antonio Ruffo, her major patron during her Neapolitan period. The following letters highlight some of the challenges artists faced in the competitive art world of the seventeenth century and some of the strategies Gentileschi used to succeed.

LETTERS TO DON ANTONIO RUFFO, 1649*

GENTILESCHI TO DON ANTONIO RUFFO, IN MESSINA. NAPLES,
13 NOVEMBER 1649

My Most Illustrious Sir,

. . . I say to Your Most Illustrious Lordship, with regard to your request that I reduce the price of the paintings that I had quoted, [I can do] a little, but [the price] must be no less than four hundred ducats, and you must send me a deposit as all the other gentlemen do. But I can tell you for certain that the higher the price, the harder I will strive to make a painting that will please Your Most Illustrious Lordship, and that will conform to my taste and yours. Concerning the painting that I have already finished for Your Most Illustrious Lordship, I cannot give it to you for less than I asked, as I have already overextended myself to give the lowest price. . . . Your nephew the Duke thinks that I must hold great affection for Your Most Illustrious Lordship to charge you such a price. I only wish to remind you that there are eight [figures], two dogs, and landscape and water. Your Most Illustrious Lordship will understand that the expense for models is staggering.

I will say no more, except what I have on my mind, that I think Your Most Illustrious Lordship will not suffer any loss with me, and that you will find the spirit of Caesar in this soul of a woman.

And with this, I pay you most humble reverence.

The most humble servant of Your Most Illustrious Lordship,

Artemisia Gentileschi

GENTILESCHI TO DON ANTONIO RUFFO, IN MESSINA. NAPLES,
13 NOVEMBER 1649

My Most Illustrious Sir,

I have received a letter of October 26th, which I deeply appreciated. . . . In it, you tell me about that gentleman who wishes to have some paintings by me, that he would like a Galatea and a Judgment of Paris, and that the Galatea should be different from the one that Your Most Illustrious Lordship owns. There was no need for you to urge me to do this, since . . . never has anyone found in my pictures any repetition of invention, not even of one hand.

As for the fact that this gentleman wishes to know the price before the work is done, believe me, as I am your servant, that I do it most unwillingly, since it is very important to me not to err and thus burden my conscience, which I value more than all the gold in the world. . . . Therefore, I never quote a price for my works until they are done. However, since Your Most Illustrious Lordship wants me to do this, I will do what you command. Tell this gentleman that I want five hundred ducats for both; he can show them to the whole world and, should he find anyone who does not think the paintings are worth two hundred scudi more, I won't ask him to pay me the agreed price. I assure Your Most Illustrious Lordship that these are paintings with nude figures requiring very expensive female models, which is a big headache. When I find good ones they fleece me, and at other times, one must suffer [their] pettiness with the patience of Job.

As for my doing a drawing and sending it, I have made a solemn vow never to send my drawings because people have cheated me. In particular, just today I found . . . that, having done a drawing . . . for the Bishop of St. Gata, he, in order to spend less, commissioned another painter to do the painting using my work. If I were a man, I can't imagine it would have turned out this way, because when the concept has been realized and defined with lights and darks, and established by means of planes, the rest is a trifle. Therefore, it seems to me that this gentleman is very wrong to ask for drawings, ...

The most humble servant of Your Most Illustrious Lordship,

Artemisia Gentileschi

I must caution Your Most Illustrious Lordship that when I ask a price, I don't follow the custom in Naples, where they ask thirty and then give it for four. I am Roman, and therefore I shall act always in the Roman manner.

Women and Music: A Cluster of Female Creativity

"More women emerged as composers in Italy between 1566 and 1700 than in any previous period in Western music history—indeed, than in all of that history taken together." Moreover, women composed in more musical genres and their music reached a wider audience than ever before. This creative surge began when Madalena Casulana, the first woman to publish her compositions, published two books between 1566 and 1570, followed by two more collections in the 1580s. Between 1585 and 1597, three women published madrigals, and a nun published the first collection of sacred polyphonic music by a woman. (Bowers 1987, 116–17) The number of women composers, both secular and religious, increased even more during the seventeenth century. Unfortunately, many whose works were performed never published their compositions.

Despite the achievements of women in this period, their numbers remained minuscule in comparison with the number of male composers, and women generally composed fewer pieces and in fewer genres than men. These differences in productivity reflected the very different social contexts in which women and men lived their lives and the gender barriers that women encountered. In addition to the pervasive assumption that intellect and creativity were masculine traits and the division of society into public and private spheres, women had to overcome beliefs that music was linked with female promiscuity and was incompatible with their domestic roles. A papal edict, issued by Pope Innocent XI, for example, proclaimed that "music is completely injurious to the modesty that is proper for the [female] sex, because they become distracted from the matters and occupations most proper for them" (Bowers 1987, 139). Not surprisingly, women had few job options. Italy's largest institution, the Catholic Church, hired only male singers, instrumentalists, and chapel masters. Even the most progressive courts rarely hired female instrumentalists and none had women in their chapel choir.

The sections that follow reveal the barriers that women, individually and collectively, confronted, and, more importantly, the circumstances and strategies that enabled an unusually large number of women composers to emerge in this period.

Francesca Caccini (1587–c.1630): Medici Composer and Singer

Francesca Caccini or *La Cecchina* as she was called made her singing debut in 1600 at the age of 13 and had gained recognition as a composer by the time she was 18. Over a 20-year period, she wrote secular and sacred songs, music for a sacred play, and at least five dramatic court entertainments. She also composed large-scale carnival entertainments with extensive dance sequences. Two publications of her music have survived: *Il Primo libro delle musiche a una e due voci*, published in 1618, and an opera, *La Liberazione di Ruggiero dall'isola d'Alcina*, published in 1625. Her most important work, *Primo libro*, included 19 sacred and 13 secular solo songs, and 4 duets for soprano and bass, for which she also wrote most of the poems. *Primo libro* was "the most extensive collection of early *monodic* music (accompanied solo songs) by a single composer up to that time." It was also the first collection of sacred *monodies* to be printed. She is also the first woman to have composed an opera. (Neuls-Bates 1982, 55)

Family background, location, and timing were critical factors in Caccini's career. Her parents and her stepmother were singers at the Medici Court in Florence, and her father, Giulio Caccini, was a prominent voice teacher and gifted composer who played an important role in the development of Italian music. Francesca, her brother, and her sister Settimia (also a composer) inherited their parents' talent and received excellent training from their father. Both girls were educated according to the Renaissance lady model to ensure that they would be accepted in the most sophisticated courts.

The Medici court in which she grew up was one of the most cultured courts in Europe. Ferdinando I and Cosimo II were patrons of all the arts, and her father's circle included poets, philosophers, and artists, as well as musicians. The Medici were as interested in new music as they were in the scientific discoveries of their astronomer Galileo. When Caccini began composing, the Medici had 15 paid singers and 13 instrumentalists, plus actors and dancers (Carter 1997, 22). Her father's position in the Medici *camerata* (musical establishment) enabled her talents to be discovered, and her creativity was continually stimulated by her collaboration with superb musicians, actors, poets, dramatists, and dancers.

La Cecchina's reputation as a singer spread rapidly. After her debut, she sang in two of her father's operas and in court performances in Florence and Pisa. Her father molded his talented family into a polished ensemble, and in 1604, Queen Marie de' Medici invited them to Paris where they performed to rave reviews. Henry IV called *La Cecchina* the "best singer ever heard in France," and he and the queen tried without success to persuade the grand duke to allow her to remain at the French court (Silbert 1946, 52). In 1607, Caccini officially entered the employ of the Medici court. She remained the chief "musical ornament" and the "highest paid composer" of the Medici under three successive grand dukes: Ferdinando I, Cosimo II, and Ferdinando II, and during the regency of the duchess (Raney 1987, 22). In 1617, she married another Medici musician, Giovanni Battista Signorini. *La Cecchina* and her husband often performed together and with her father and stepmother. Caccini emulated her father by training a new generation of students *(discepole)*.

The reading that follows is one of the poems that Caccini wrote for the songs in *Il Primo Libro*. The music she composed for this poem to the Virgin Mary expresses in its harmony and melody the feelings the words convey. Her biographer argues that Caccini's *Maria* should rank "with Monteverdi's *Lamento d'Arianna* as one of the most moving and unforgettable examples of early Italian solo song. It is haunting in flavour, descriptive in mood and satisfying in form and content" (Raney 1967, 256).

Maria, dolce Maria from Il Primo Libro*

Mary, sweet Mary
A name so gentle
That whoever pronounces it learns to
    speak from the heart,
Sacred name and holy

That inflames my heart with heavenly
    love.
Mary, never would I know how to sing
Nor my tongue
Draw out from my breast ever

*From Carolyn Raney, "Francesca Caccini, Musician to the Medici, and Her Primo Libro (1618)" (unpublished Ph.D. dissertation, New York University, 1971), p. 169. By permission of Carolyn Raney.

| A more felicitous word than to say Mary. | Tranquil voice that quiets every breath- less agitation, |
| Name that lessens and consoles Every grief. | That makes every heart serene And every spirit light. |

The documents that follow provide glimpses of her relationships with patrons and collaborators and her stature. Angelo Grillo was a poet, abbot of a monastery in Rome, and founder of a famous Academy.

ANGELO GRILLO, LETTER TO FRANCESCA CACCINI, 1612, FROM VENICE*

To Signora Francesca Caccini. Florence. Sent with the following madrigal to that celestial Siren.

A few days ago I sent you three madrigals on the Assumption of the Glorious Queen of the Angels, which perchance made up in weight what they lacked in number. Now I am sending you another [which is] perhaps more tender and yielding in its accents and feeling. I am certain that it will soon hold sway over many hearts and many souls, should it prove suitable to the sweet compulsion and the gentle tyranny of your celestial harmony. May the Blessed Lord listen to it from Heaven, since from Heaven He sent the inspiration to you. Felicitations to you, and also your Father, Mother, and Husband, to whom I send my heartiest greetings.

Most of Caccini's correspondence consists of letters to and from her primary collaborator Michelangelo Buonarroti, who first asked her to compose music for one of his poems when she was 18. In this letter she discusses a *festa,* a dramatic work similar to opera that she and Buonarroti created.

CACCINI TO MICHELANGELO BUONARROTI, 18 DECEMBER 1614, FROM FLORENCE**

My Most Illustrious and Most Honorable Signore

Your Lordship's hasty departure grieved me as much for the need we have of you as for the reason for which you left. Yet the news Your Lordship sends me makes me hope that your nephew will soon be out of danger, may it so please Our Lord.

I am doubly obliged to Your Lordship on account of the verses you sent me for Signora Giralda, for I can imagine the trouble with which you must have composed them, having cause to think of other things than poetry. They arrived most opportunely because, although we have rehearsed my music in the presence of Her Majesty, Madame, and the princesses, the Grand Duke has not yet heard it. However, we daily expect to be commanded, especially as one night we were assembled and ready until three o'clock in the morning, but because of the arrival of an ambassador,

*From Doris Silbert, "Francesca Caccini, Called La Cecchina," *Musical Quarterly* (1946), vol. 32, p. 56. By permission of Oxford University Press.

**Pages 56, 60 from WOMEN IN MUSIC: AN ANTHOLOGY OF SOURCE READINGS FROM THE MIDDLE AGES TO THE PRESENT by Carol Neuls-Bates. Copyright © 1982 by Carol Neuls-Bates. Reprinted by permission of HarperCollins Publishers Inc.

our performance was postponed to another night. This was fortunate because Madame asked why Signora Giralda did not yet sing alone, to which I answered that Your Lordship had not had the time to write your verses because a nephew of yours was in danger of death. I promise Your Lordship that Madame showed such sorrow that she could not have shown more.

Everyone's delight in the *invenzione* [short comic scene] when it was said to be yours and in my prologue and envoi, and, in short, in the music as a whole, I can neither write nor express. Suffice it that I assure you it has been some time since I saw Her Majesty and Madame laugh so heartily. The entire room resounded with loud laughter, and Madame in particular spoke so well of Your Lordship that in truth you could not desire more. I reserve all the particulars to word of mouth; I will only tell you that in a cheerful voice Madame said to Her Majesty and to the entire audience that Your Lordship has no equal and that Your Lordship is able to compose in all styles and to suit yourself to all occasions, either serious or gay, easy or difficult. In short, she showed how delighted she was. As for the ladies, [the singers or *discepole* she trained] they carried themselves well and did themselves great honor.

I do not want to neglect to inform Your Lordship of another particular I had forgotten, that is, that Madame liked the wit of the greedy doctors above all, and she repeated it two or three times. Now that Signora Giralda is singing, the *festa* will be perfect, and it will be ready, it so happens, before the Signor Grand Duke hears it.

I regret that Your Lordship does not think you can be here, but I do not want to fail to advise you to give some thought, if you can, to that little comedy for eleven actors, for we will be precisely that many. Let it be pleasing in its story, humorous, and with varied characters. Although we have not yet fully made up our minds, I have so much in hand that I want to warn you now in order that you not be taken by surprise, but can think about the plot in the meanwhile so that, at need, you will only have to write it out. I pray you, do not speak of this.

Forgive me if I have bothered you too much. May it please God that you return soon with the return of joy and health to your nephew. In closing, I send you my respects. My husband remembers you always, while I pray God for all truly good things for you.

Your Most Illustrious Lordship's Always most ready to serve you.
Francesca Caccini Signorini

I have not made use of those verses Your Lordship sent me for Signora Medicca because Your Lordship's other verses "Non passar tra quelle prode" ("Do not pass through those shores") seemed more appropriate to me. I set them to the tune of "Addio selvaggi monti" ("Farewell wild mountains"), and they fit very well.

Barbara Strozzi (1619–1664?): Venetian Composer and Singer

Barbara Strozzi was a Venetian singer and composer who published seven books of vocal music consisting of over 100 pieces between 1644 and 1664. Her compositions were also published with works by the most important male composers of her day. She was one of the few women known to have composed in the two genres that were popular among seventeenth century male composers: *arias* (solos) and *cantatas* (songs for one or two solo voices in alternating patterns of arias and *recitatives* or narratives sung in speech-like rhythm). In fact, she published more cantatas than any other composer of the century. She earned respect for innovative compositions and her ability to compose music that conveyed the meaning and nuances of her texts. In a letter to a friend, Venetian patrician Giovanni Francesco Loredano, founder of the *Accademia degli Incogniti,* proclaimed: "Had she been born in another era she would certainly either have usurped or enlarged the place of the muses" (Rosand 1978, 253).

Strozzi's background and lifestyle differed from Caccini's in several respects. She grew up in the home of Giulio Strozzi, a prominent Venetian intellectual. She was the daughter of his servant, Isabella Garzoni, and his illegitimate child. Giulio was the founder of several Venetian academies and a poet. He also wrote *libretti* (texts) for every Venetian opera composer from 1630 to 1650. Strozzi nurtured Barbara's talent and used his contacts to advance her career. He had her trained as a composer by some of the city's finest musicians, including Francesco Cavalli (1602–76), the composer of 42 operas. He orchestrated her debut at 16 by having her sing for literati and musicians at his home and encouraged her to compose by writing texts for her first volume of music.

Most importantly, in 1637, he created an academy, the *Accademia degli Unisoni,* to give Barbara an entree into the masculine world of intellectuals and musicians. The *Unisoni* consisted of Venetian cultural leaders who met for intellectual exchanges and shared an interest in music. Most of the *Unisoni* men were also members of the *Accademia degli Incogniti,* a more elite academy that had been a major force in Venetian politics and culture since its founding in 1630. *Incogniti* members were freethinkers who delighted in taking scandalous positions on social issues and church doctrines. Several of them wrote poems for her to set to music, and the *Incogniti* motto appeared on the page she usually reserved for the dedication in her third volume published in 1654.

Strozzi's sex excluded her from the musical positions that were open to men, and Venice had no counterpart to the ducal courts in which Caccini thrived. She apparently supported herself (and paid off her father's debts) by publishing her work. She dedicated her earliest works to persons she hoped would become her patrons or would recommend her to others.

Strozzi, however, was primarily known in Venice as a singer, and, to many, as a woman of questionable morals. Female musicians and intellectuals who frequented the Venetian salons and singers who appeared on the opera stage were widely assumed to be courtesans. Strozzi's family background and her association with the *Unisoni* fueled suspicions naturally aroused by her status as a single woman. Indeed, it is possible that she was a courtesan.

The following excerpts from Strozzi's dedications suggest some of the strategies she and other women utilized as they attempted to carve out professional careers or to publish. Vittoria della Rovere was a well-known supporter of creative women. Strozzi sent *Opus 2* to Ferdinand and Eleanora, famed patrons of Italian musicians, on the eve of their marriage. Anna of Innsbruck was the sister-in-law of Vittoria della Rovere, and Nicolò Sagredo was a patron who Strozzi called her "guardian deity."

STROZZI'S DEDICATIONS*

DEDICATION OF OPUS I (1644) TO VITTORIA DELLA ROVERE, GRAND DUCHESS OF TUSCANY

I must reverently consecrate this first work, which as a woman I publish all too boldly, to the Most August name of Your Highness so that, under an oak of gold it may rest secure against the lightning bolts of slander prepared for it.

*From Ellen Rosand, "Barbara Strozzi, *virtuosissima cantatrice:* The Composer's Voice," *Journal of the American Musicological Society* 31 (1978), pp. 256, 259.

DEDICATION OF OPUS 2 (1651) TO FERDINAND III OF AUSTRIA
AND ELEANORA OF MANTUA

The lowly mine of a woman's poor imagination cannot produce metal to forge those richest golden crowns worthy of august rulers.

DEDICATION OF OPUS 5 (1655) TO ANNA OF INNSBRUCK

. . . and since feminine weaknesses restrain me no more than any indulgence of my sex impels me, on lightest leaves do I fly, in devotion, to bow before you.

PREFACE TO OPUS 7 (1659) DEDICATED TO NICOLÒ SAGREDO

My poor life has been favored and protected with the profuse grace of his excellency. . . . These harmonic notes are the language of the soul and instruments of the heart.

The next selection, *Merci di voi*, can be read as a love song, but perhaps also as an expression of Strozzi's feelings about the challenges and rewards of composing.

MERCE DI VOI (THANKS TO YOU)*

Thanks to you my fortunate star,
I fly among the blessed choirs,
and crowned with everlasting laurels,
perhaps I shall be called the new saffo.
   [Sappho]
The demanding and beautiful task
let be delightful with song, and with the
   cupids,
that uniting their voices, our hearts
will never be untied.

Oh what lovely and sweet harmony
is made by two faithful, loving souls;
that whatever the one wishes, the other
   desires;
that it rejoices at joy and laughs at
   laughter.
They sigh no more, unless that sigh
   should be
from a death that heals and does not
   kill.

Venetian Ospedali-Conservatorios: The First Music Schools for Girls

For nearly 300 years, four Venetian charitable institutions (*ospedali*) nurtured the talent of many girls who lacked family musical connections and the financial means and social status to enter a convent. The *ospedali* (the Pietá, Mendicanti, Incurabili, and Derelitti) were originally orphanages run by nuns who reared infants of both sexes left on their doorsteps or in wall niches. They also took in the illegitimate children of the city's courtesans and accepted girls from mercantile and aristocratic families as boarding students. Barbara Strozzi probably received her early music training as one of these students.

By the seventeenth century, the *ospedali*, now called *ospedali-conservatorios* (orphanage-conservatories), were famous throughout Europe for their music. Their curriculum included rigorous

*Text from *Sonetto proemio dell'opera: Merce di voi.* Deborah Roberts and Massimo De Cillis, trans., booklet, p. 4, accompanying CD *Musica Secreta.* © 1994 Amon Ra Records, England. By permission of Saydisc Records, England.

musical training under some of the finest Italian musicians, such as composer Antonio Vivaldi, who taught violin and was director of instrumental music at the Ospedale della Pietá (Talbot 1999, 49). Talented girls were selected as young as age 3 for the vocal and instrumental ensembles. (Boys were not selected because their voices changed at puberty.)

Some of the music by leading male composers of opera and sacred music was inspired by and written for the superb vocal and instrumental ensembles of these institutions, including half of the sacred music Vivaldi wrote between 1713 and 1719 (Stewart 1999, 11). *Ospedali* alumnae were among the pioneering female opera singers. One of Vivaldi's prize students at Pietá, Anna Girò, had leading roles in several of his operas. Others, such as Maddalena Lombardini Sirmen (b. 1735), a violinist and composer of music for strings and harpsichord, were successful performers and composers.

In the 1770s, Charles Burney, an English music critic and composer, made a "musical tour" of Italy and France. One of the highlights of his trip was a visit to the *ospedali Mendicanti.* His accounts reveal a great deal about the opportunities the *ospedali-conservatorios* offered their female residents and the reputation of these institutions.

BURNEY'S DESCRIPTION OF THE VENETIAN CONSERVATORIES, AUGUST 1770*

[Aug. 5] I had this morning a long visit from Signor Latilla, and procured from him several necessary particulars relative to the present, as well as the past state of Music here. He says the Conservatorios have been established at Venice about 200 years, as hospitals. That at first the girls were only taught canto firmo, and psalmody; . . . but in process of time, they learned to sing in parts, and, at length joined instruments to the Voices. He says that the expense on account of the music is very inconsiderable, there being but 5 or 6 Masters to each of these schools for singing and the several instruments, as the elder girls teach the younger; the *Maestro di Cappella* [chorus master], only composes and directs; . . . and attends all the rehearsals and public performances.

[Aug. 10] This evening, in order to make myself more fully acquainted with the nature of the conservatorios, and to finish my musical enquiries here, I obtained permission to be admitted into the music school of the *Mendicanti . . .* , and was favoured with a concert, which . . . lasted two hours, by the best vocal and instrumental performers of this hospital: it was really curious to *see,* as well as to *hear* every part of this excellent concert, performed by female violins, hautbois, tenors, bases, harpsichords, french-horns, and even double bases. There was a prioress, a person in years, who presided: the first violin was very well played by Antonia Cubli, of Greek extraction; the harpsichord sometimes by Francesca Rossi, *Maestra del coro,* and sometimes by others; these young persons frequently change instruments.

The singing was really excellent in different stiles (sic.); [two of the singers] had very powerful voices, capable of filling a large theatre; these sung *bravura* songs, and capital scenes selected from Italian operas; and [two others] whose voices were more delicate, confined themselves chiefly to pathetic songs, of taste and expression. The whole was very judiciously mixed; no two airs of the same kind followed each other,

*Excerpts from Dr. Charles Burney, *Musical Tours in Europe,* ed. Percy A. Scholes, vol. I (London and New York: Oxford University Press, 1959), pp. 121, 136–37. Reprinted by permission of Oxford University Press.

and there seemed to be great decorum and good discipline observed in every particular; for these admirable performers, who are of different ages, all behaved with great propriety, and seemed to be well educated.

It was here that the two celebrated female performers, . . . Signora Guglielmi, and Signora Maddalena Lombardini Sirmen, who have received such great and just applause in England, had their musical instructions. If I could have staid (sic) a few days longer at Venice, I might have enjoyed the same kind of entertainment at the other three conservatorios, having been tempted to continue there by such an offer from a friend who had interest sufficient to procure me a sight of the *interior discipline* of these admirable musical seminaries; and I declined this obliging offer with the greater reluctance, as there is not in all Italy any establishment of the same kind . . . .

Convent Musicians and Church Restrictions

Over half of the women composers in Italy between 1566 and 1700 were nuns, indicating that monastic life continued to nurture female creativity by giving women access to musical training, opportunities to perform with talented musicians, and time to compose. Yet the most remarkable aspect of the productivity of Italian nuns is that it occurred in spite of persistent efforts by church officials to severely curtail all musical activities in convents. These efforts were part of wide-ranging reforms Catholic leaders had begun to implement in the twelfth century. One key goal was strict enclosure of monastic women. This entailed prohibiting nuns from leaving a convent after they had taken final vows and sharply restricting their contacts with the outside world and secular influences. Other reforms sought to focus nuns' attention on spiritual matters by restricting the types of music they could perform, the instruments they could use, and their participation in musical segments of the worship services within the convents.

The Council of Trent (1545–1563), which was called to address the challenges Protestant reformers posed to Catholicism, addressed these concerns as well as the issues of dogma, church structure, liturgy, and worship practices. The council's final decrees relating to music were a compromise between delegates who wished to eliminate all music from church services and those who sought only to eliminate improper and "lascivious" or "immoral" forms of music that distracted attention from the worship service itself. The council formally ruled that all "profane and worldly forms of music must be excluded permanently from the house of God," but otherwise accepted music as a legitimate part of worship (Hayburn 1979, 28–29). It left it up to provincial church councils and bishops to set and implement specific rules about chanting, singing, and church choirs that were compatible with local customs. The council, however, also adopted the following decree specifically regulating the musical practices of nuns.

COUNCIL OF TRENT DECREE REGULATING FEMALE RELIGIOUS, 20 NOVEMBER 1563*

The Divine Office should be continued by them in high voice and not by professionals hired for that purpose, and they should answer in the Sacrifice of the Mass whatever the choir is accustomed to answer; but they will leave to the Deacon and Subdeacon the office of chanting the Lessons, Epistles, and Gospels.

*From Robert F. Hayburn, *Papal Legislation on Sacred Music: 95 A.D. to 1977 A.D.* (Collegeville, MN: Liturgical Press, 1979), p. 29.

They will abstain from singing either in Choir or elsewhere the socalled "figured" chant.[†]

[†][Polyphonic chant: Two or more parts sung together, but moving in different rhythms.]

In the century and a half after the council adjourned, enforcement of council decrees varied widely as bishops and archbishops exercised their authority to govern according to local customs. Some were zealous in their efforts to enforce strict enclosure of convents and official musical restrictions and even imposed additional limits that they deemed necessary to eliminate "improper" and "lascivious" musical practices. The archbishop of Naples, for example, prohibited secular music in his convents and vigorously enforced a local decree of 1589 that allowed only one instrument, the organ, to be used. In 1658, he placed an *interdict* on the Convent of Santa Croce di Lucca because a man who visited his sisters "brought a lute into the convent parlor" (Bowers 1987, 161, n. 122). Milan's Archbishop Carlo Borromeo, initiated visitations to convents under his authority to uncover violations of his strict enclosure policy and music regulations. In 1571, he ordered punishments for 18 nuns of the Rich Clare house of Sant' Apollinare who had violated his reforms.

PUNISHMENTS ORDERED BY CARLO BORROMEO, 30 MARCH 1571*

Suor Angela Serafina will be deprived of the veil for three months, and will be relieved of her duties as organist, nor can she regain this office for six years. [She will] ask pardon for her offenses each Wednesday for six months, and be deprived of active voice for three months. . . . The large harpsichord should not remain in her room, but somewhere else in the monastery, nor can she play it or any other instrument, nor sing polyphony for three years.

Subsequent visitations to Milanese convents revealed continuing violations and brought new penalties.

ORDERS FOR THE *DESTRUCTION OF VICES AND MAINTENANCE OF VIRTUE* AT THE CONVENT OF MARIA ANNUNCIATA, MILAN, 1622**

1. there was to be no singing or playing in church except in sung masses and in the divine offices of the principal feasts commanded by the Holy Church; . . . If the Madre Abbess permitted such singing or playing, she would be suspended from her office for three months, and those who sang and played would be deprived of the veil and of singing and playing in perpetuity.
2. there was to be no singing or playing in the parlors or at the grates [windows overlooking the outer or public church], either among the nuns or with other people from outside the convent, not even under the pretext of learning or teaching. . . .

*Quoted in Robert L. Kendrick, "Four Views of Milanese Nuns' Music," from *Creative Women in Medieval and Early Modern Italy* edited by Ann E. Matter and John Coakley, p. 326. Copyright © 1994 University of Pennsylvania Press. Reprinted with permission.

**Quoted in Jane Bowers, "The Emergence of Women Composers in Italy, 1566–1700," in *Women Making Music,* edited Jane Bowers and Judith Tick. Illini Books ed. (Urbana and Chicago: University of Illinois Press, 1987), pp.143–44.

Although many convents capitulated to such edicts, some in Rome, Venice, Bologna, Lucca, and Milan were still famous for their music late in the seventeenth century. Those with a strong musical tradition simply ignored the authorities. Inventories revealed, for example, that the Bologna convent of Santa Margherita had clavichords, violins, and trombones, and that one nun owned seven books of vocal and instrumental music, plus "a spinet, a guitar, and a lute," despite the fact that lutes, guitars, violins, and trombones had been banned for several decades (Monson 1994, 305). Nuns were also undoubtedly emboldened by support from families and admirers, such as the Grand Duke of Tuscany who visited several monasteries to hear nun musicians en route to Italy's most famous musical convent, Santa Radegonda in 1664.

ACCOUNT OF COSIMO III DE' MEDICI'S VISIT TO SANTA RADEGONDA, 25 JUNE 1664*

> He went to hear Mass at the Benedictine nuns of Santa Radegonda, nuns noble, rich and skilled, especially in music, in number some 140 . . . they have made such great progress, especially in music, that they have perfected themselves in both instrument playing and in singing like any good *professore* [professional musician].
>
> [After Vespers] at the open door of the monastery, [Cosimo] talked at length with them . . . in the presence of the Abbess, who was also pleased by the idea, the nuns brought out their instruments, and sang *ariette*, lasting more than a good hour.

WOMEN AND CULTURAL CHANGE DURING THE REIGNS OF LOUIS XIV AND LOUIS XV

The political and cultural milieu of France under Louis XIV differed markedly from that of Italy. After Louis XIV (1638–1715) became king in 1643, Cardinal Mazarin, who governed for the child, laid the foundation of his absolutist, divine right government. From 1661 until his death, Louis XIV wielded total cultural as well as economic and political authority in France. Louis XIV was so powerful that in 1682, when he moved his court from Paris to Versailles Palace, those who hoped to curry his favor had to reside at Versailles.

During his reign, France (Paris/Versailles) became the cultural center of Europe, and by 1663, all art in France was brought under the control of the Académie Royale de Peinture et de Sculpture, founded in 1648. The academy dictated what kind of art and architecture and which artists were worthy of royal and, therefore, public support. Versailles (begun in 1669) set architectural standards for the nation and established large-scale history paintings as the highest art form. Portraiture ranked second, followed by genre (scenes of daily life), still-life, and landscape paintings. The academy adopted a policy that only men could be admitted as members. By 1782, it had admitted seven women, but, after each exception, had returned to its original policy. Women were generally denied the official recognition needed to attract patrons and were not allowed to show their work in academy-sponsored salons or to compete for the coveted *prix de Rome* the academy awarded annually to the best artist. Most importantly, *life drawing* classes with nude models were always closed to women, preventing them from gaining the male anatomical knowledge necessary for doing action-packed historical works.

*Quoted in Kendrick, "Four Views of Milanese Nuns' Music," from *Creative Women in Medieval and Early Modern Italy* edited by Ann E. Matter and John Coakley, p. 331. Copyright © 1994 University of Pennsylvania Press. Reprinted with permission.

Likewise, the Académie de Musique Royale, under the governance of the king's minister, Italian-born Jean Baptiste Lully, set the musical standards for the nation. Initially, it too admitted only men to membership. The Royal Opera, as it came to be known, originated in the court ballets initiated by Lully about 1651. The young king frequently danced in the ballets and acquired his nickname, the Sun King, from one of the roles he played. In response to royal demands, court ballet evolved into increasingly lavish theatrical productions and, in the 1670s, to opera. Until his death in 1687, Lully selected the opera performers, composers, and productions.

Elisabeth Jacquet de la Guerre (c. 1664/67–1729): Musician

In this context, the career of Elisabeth Jacquet de la Guerre is revealing. From the moment she dazzled Paris as a child prodigy until her death, she was esteemed by Louis XIV, the French court, other musicians, and the public as a harpsichord virtuoso and versatile composer. Shortly after her death, Louis XV had a medallion struck in her honor, with her profile and the inscription "She competed with [the] greatest musicians for the prize of being best." In 1732, Titon de Tillet, author of the *Parnasse français,* a biographical dictionary of important French citizens, honored Jacquet de la Guerre with an unusually lengthy entry and as one of only four musicians whose portraits appeared in the book. His praise echoed the views of many: " . . . never had a person of her sex had such talents as she for the composition of music, and for the admirable manner in which she performed it at the Harpsichord and on the Organ. . . . " Fifty years after her death, British music historian Sir John Hawkins called Jacquet de la Guerre one of the great musicians in the history of French music. (Boroff 1966, 17, 19, 20)

She was born, it seems, to music. Both her parents were from musical families, and her father was an organist, harpsichordist, and instrument maker. She and her brother Pierre (who became an organist) received superb training from their father. Around age 6, her keyboard artistry captivated Louis XIV, who took her into his court and placed her under the care of the governess of his bastard children. In 1684, she married Marin de la Guerre, son of a respected composer, and settled in Paris where Marin was a church organist. She composed her first theatrical work in 1685, numerous harpsichord works and an opera that was performed in Paris and Strasbourg in 1694, and began writing sonatas. Then tragedy struck. She lost her father in 1702, her only son died at age ten, and she was widowed in 1704.

From 1704 until her retirement in 1717, Jacquet de la Guerre focused on her career. She continued to enjoy royal patronage and to perform at Versailles, but she also inaugurated public harpsichord recitals for which she became famous, and she performed at the public theater. Most of her publications stem from this period and illustrate her versatility as a composer. Her works included theatrical comedy, popular songs, sonatas for violin and harpsichord, secular and religious cantatas, and a ballet. In 1721, her choral work, a *Te Deum,* was performed at a thanksgiving service in the Louvre chapel to celebrate young Louis XV's recovery from smallpox.

Jacquet de la Guerre's career was closely linked with the Sun King, and it reveals aspects of his reign and cultural tastes that are often overlooked. She lived at court when Louis XIV was at the peak of his power, and she enjoyed his support for over 30 years until his death in 1715. She began to compose when Louis XIV was entering a new phase of his life. After the queen's death in 1682, he married his mistress and settled into a more restrained domestic lifestyle. Elaborate theatrical performances gave way to more intimate concerts of chamber music, and, in his twilight years, to religious music. Changing royal tastes opened opportunities for a new generation of musicians, none of whom were members of the Royal Academy. She was the only woman among these composers.

Her career both influenced and reflected other trends in French music in the late seventeenth century. As a pioneer in the development of public recitals, she helped create a public concert system that freed musicians from total dependence on royal or noble patronage. Her participation in public musical theater further broadened the base of support for the arts and artists. Finally, she was among the composers who introduced Italian musical forms, the sonata and cantata, into the French repertoire. Her cantatas were the first to be based on biblical stories, and it is noteworthy that she, like other women artists and writers, selected heroines such as Esther, Rachel, Susanna, and Judith as subjects.

All her published works were dedicated to the king, with the exception of three books of cantatas published after his death that she dedicated to the Elector of Bavaria. Her dedications are significant because one had to have royal permission to dedicate a work to the monarch. Her more famous contemporary, François Couperin, never received that privilege. The following selections illustrate her versatility as a musician. Note also what they reveal about her public reputation, her relationship with the king, and her awareness of women's history. The first document is the earliest known reference to Jacquet de la Guerre. In December 1678, the same Paris monthly paper called her "the marvel of our century" in a report of her performance at a private concert (Boroff 1966, p. 7).

DESCRIPTION OF ELISABETH JACQUET FROM THE *MERCURE GALANT,* JULY 1677*

> For four years a wonder has appeared here. She sings at sight the most difficult music. She accompanies herself, and accompanies others who wish to sing, at the harpsichord, which she plays in a manner which cannot be imitated. She composes pieces, and plays them in all the keys asked of her. I have told you that for four years she has been appearing with these extraordinary qualities, and she still is only ten years old.

Jacquet de la Guerre composed her only ballet to celebrate a French military victory at Mons when she was in her twenties. Unfortunately, the musical score has never been found.

DEDICATION OF *LES JEUX À L'HONNEUR DE LA VICTOIRE* TO LOUIS XIV, 1691**

> When this play was presented to me, I was at once extremely eager to undertake it. Everything having Your Majesty's glory as its end is marvelously exciting; and when the desire to please you is joined to It, what further aim could one have? It is by such a just Incentive that I have always been prompted to work. From the most tender age (this memory will be eternally precious to me), presented to your illustrious court, where I have had the honor to be for several years, I learned, Sire, to consecrate to you all of my waking hours. You deigned at that time to accept the first fruits of my gifts, and it has pleased you to receive several further productions. But these particular marks of my zeal did not suffice for me, and I welcome the happy opportunity to be able to make a public (offering). That is what led me to write this ballet for the theatre. It is not just today, (but earlier) that women have written excellent pieces of

*Quoted in Michel Brenet, "Quatre Femmes musiciennes, I: Mademoiselle Jacquet de la Guerre," *L'Art,* XIV (October 1894), p. 108, reprinted and translated in Edith Boroff, *An Introduction to Elisabeth-Claude Jacquet de la Guerre* (New York: Institute of Mediaeval Music, Ltd., 1966), p. 6. By permission of The Institute of Mediaeval Music, Ltd.

**From "Les Jeux à l'honneur de la victoire," ms.frç. 2217 in Bibliothèque Nationale, quoted in Brenet, "Quatre Femmes musiciennes," pp. 108–09, reprinted and translated in Boroff, *An Introduction to Elisabeth-Claude Jacquet de la Guerre,* pp. 12–13. By permission of The Institute of Mediaeval Music, Ltd.

poetry, which have had great success. But until now, none has tried to set a whole opera to music; and I take this advantage from my enterprise: that the more extraordinary it is, the more it is worthy of you, Sire, and the more it justified the liberty that I take in offering you this work.

Jacquet de la Guerre published her double volume work for harpsichord and for violin and harpsichord shortly after receiving the *Royal Privilege of June 13, 1707,* that granted to "our dear well-loved Elizabeth Jacquet, widow of . . . " permission to publish "Sonatas, Harpsichord Pieces and other music, vocal, as well as instrument, of her composition," for 15 years (Boroff 1966, 113).

DEDICATION OF *PIECES FOR THE HARPSICHORD AND SONATAS FOR THE VIOLIN AND FOR THE HARPSICHORD*, 1707*

TO THE KING / SIRE: I have no longer the merit of a spontaneous homage in offering my works to Your Majesty; a long custom has made it from now on a happy necessity to me. What happiness for me, Sire, if my last work received again from Your Majesty that glorious welcome In which I have enjoyed almost since the cradle, for Sire, permit me to recall it to you, You did not disdain my childhood: You took pleasure In seeing born a talent which I consecrated to you; and You honored me even then with your praises, of which I did not yet know all the worth. My weak talents grew in the following: I have tried, Sire, to merit more and more that approbation which has always meant more than anything else; and I count as the only beautiful Days of my life those when I can give to your Majesty some new testimony of the respectful zeal and the entire devotion with which I am, Sire, of Your Majesty the very humble and very obedient servant, and very faithful subject, Elizabeth Jacquet.

Women on Stage: Ballet

Women first emerged as professional dancers in France during the reign of Louis XIV. Lully introduced ballet to the court in the early 1650s, and, in response to the king's demands, ballet evolved into ever-more lavish theatrical productions, and, in the 1670s, to opera. Lully's operas required elaborate sets and stage machinery, and a large orchestra, chorus, and ballet troupe. To train dancers, Lully established a department of dance in the Royal Academy of Music. At first, the ballet corps consisted only of men, but in 1681, the first ballerina, Mademoiselle La Fontaine, appeared in an opera. She was followed by Mademoiselle Subligny, who also thrilled English audiences when she and several male dancers performed in London.

Lully's successor, Jean Philippe Rameau, took ballet to a new level. In an important treatise on dance, he developed the first written steps and patterns for ballet, or *choreography.* He also added jumps and high leaps, making ballet into a vertical type of dance that differed markedly from Lully's more formal, restrained style of court dancing. By the early eighteenth century French dance enthusiasts were fiercely divided into two camps: the followers of Lully and those of Rameau. The battles (including duels) waged by the two groups fueled popular interest in dance and helped attract large new

---

*From *Pieces for the harpsichord which can be played upon the Violin, Composed by Mademoiselle Dela Guerre and Engraved by H. De Baussen,* reprinted and translated by Boroff in *An Introduction to Elisabeth-Claude Jacquet de la Guerre,* p. 114. By permission of The Institute of Mediaeval Music, Ltd.

audiences from the bourgeoisie as well as the aristocracy at the very time dance, like music in general, was evolving from private courtly entertainments to public theater.

By the early 1700s, the Royal Academy of Music and Dance, as it was then called, had become a public institution that prepared French girls for careers in music and dance. The academy also enabled students to control their own lives, for it granted them the right to live independently of family, husband, or any institution, even if they withdrew shortly after their admission.

As the following selections reveal, access to training, the emergence of public audiences, and the feuding Lully-Rameau followers enabled some dancers to enjoy superstar status as *prima ballerinas* and as innovators who contributed to the further development of ballet. Note the innovations each dancer made and consider how these might have affected audiences and the careers of ballerinas.

Marie Camargo was the prize ballerina of Rameau's followers and the idol of many fans. She was born Marie Anne de Cupis in Brussels in 1710 but used her mother's Spanish name professionally. As a young dancer with the Brussels Opera, she attracted the attention of some noble patrons who sent her to the French Royal Academy where she studied under the leading academy ballerina, Mademoiselle Prévost.

Marie Camargo's Paris Debut, 1726*

> Mlle. Camargo, a dancer from the Brussels Opera, who has not previously been seen here, danced *Les Caractères de la Danse* with all the liveliness and intelligence that could possibly be expected from a young person aged fifteen to sixteen. . . . Her *cabrioles* and *entrechats* were effortless, and although she has still many perfections to acquire before she can venture comparison with her illustrious teacher, she is considered to be one of the most brilliant dancers to be seen, in particular for her sensitive ear for music, her airiness, and her strength.

When Camargo made her debut, female dance costumes were elegant but heavy, multilayered floor-length dresses. Hoop skirts that appeared in 1716 replaced some of the petticoats but still restricted a ballerina's movements. Male dancers wore similar but shorter skirts with tight pants that revealed their footwork and permitted freer movements. Camargo added high-heeled shoes and simplified her costume in order to develop new techniques and movements.

Camargo's Innovations**

> Camargo was the first who ventured to shorten her skirts. This useful invention, which afforded connoisseurs an opportunity of passing judgment upon the lower limbs of a *danseuse*, has since been generally adopted, although, at the time, it promised to occasion a very dangerous schism. [Some] in the pit cried out heresy and scandal, and refused to tolerate the shortened skirts. [Others, however,] maintained that this innovation was more in accordance with the spirt of the primitive

*Excerpt from the *Mercure de France* quoted in Lincoln Kirstein, *Dance. A Short History of Classic Theatrical Dancing.* A Dance Horizons Book (Princeton Book Company, Publishers, 1987), p. 207. By permission of Princeton Book Company, Publishers.

**Excerpt from Grimm's *Correspondance Littéraire* in Kirstein, *Dance. A Short History of Classic Theatrical Dancing,* p. 208. By permission of Princeton Book Company, Publishers.

Church, which objected to *pirouettes* and *gargouillades* being hampered by the length of petticoats.

Camargo's chief rival was Marie Sallé, the favorite ballerina of the Lullists and the royal family. She was also popular with the French public and with English audiences. Born in Paris in 1714 into a lower-class family, Sallé made her debut at the opera in 1721. In 1734, Sallé appeared in a new costume that allowed even more freedom of movement than Camargo's. The occasion was the performance of a new ballet-pantomime created for her and arranged by her, based on the story of Pygmalion. Here she (the statue) responds as Pygmalion begins to dance with her.

Marie Sallé in *Pygmalion*, 1734*

... Pygmalion dances in front of her as if to teach her to dance. She repeats after him the simplest as well as the most difficult and complicated steps; he endeavors to inspire her with the love which he feels and succeeds.

You can imagine ... what the different stages of such an action can become when mimed and danced with the refined and delicate grace of Mlle. Salle. She has dared to appear in this *entrée* without pannier, skirt, or bodice, and with her hair down; she did not wear a single ornament on her head. Apart from her corset and petticoat she wore only a simple dress of muslin draped about her in the manner of a Greek statue.

Rosalba Carriera (1675–1757): Rococo Portrait Artist

We close this chapter as we opened it, with an artist. Like Gentileschi, Rosalba Carriera was Italian, but her life and work reflected the shift of Europe's artistic center from Italy to France and northern Europe, as well as the broader social, political, and cultural changes that emerged at the turn of the century. Carriera was among the most successful women artists of the eighteenth century. Her work influenced many artists of both sexes and helped shape the artistic tastes of a generation of patrons. Her international reputation and success in attracting wealthy patrons from courts across Europe made her a role model for aspiring women painters.

Carriera grew up in Venice, where her father was a minor public official and her mother was a lace maker. As a child she drew lace patterns for her mother, but she did not pursue her mother's craft, perhaps because the demand for Venetian lace was in decline. Instead, she began decorating ivory snuff boxes which she sold to the tourists who flocked to Venice.

By 1703 she had developed two innovations for which she became famous. She invented a technique for painting miniature portraits on ivory, a base that gave the pictures a unique lustrous quality. She also devised techniques for using pastel chalks that gave her portraits an unusual range of textures and subtle, luminous shades of lighting and color that were flattering to her subjects. Portraits and miniatures, it should be recalled, were lower on the scale of art genres than history paintings, and, with flower paintings and still life, were also devalued because they were associated with women painters. With her talent and inventiveness, however, she elevated both art forms, and her miniatures and pastel portraits were widely sought by patrons.

*Excerpt from London correspondent of *Mercure de France,* quoted in Kirstein, *Dance. A Short History of Classic Theatrical Dancing,* p. 209. By permission of Princeton Book Company, Publishers.

Carriera's career also thrived because of the cultural changes in France that followed the death of Louis XIV in 1715. When the court of Louis XV returned to Paris, cultural authority was further decentralized as wealthy aristocrats and commercial elites, seeking art for their elegant homes, replaced the court and académie as arbiters of artistic tastes. One such patron, financier Pierre Crozat, was so impressed with Carriera's portraits on his trip to Venice in 1716 that he invited her to Paris in 1720. She spent a year there as part of a circle of international artists drawn to the city by the promise of large commissions. Her first commission, a lively and flattering, yet realistic painting of the ten-year-old king, made her an instant success. Many, including France's leading artist Antoine Watteau, sought her portraits. Her flattering pastel portraits helped create a new decorative art style known as *rococo* that became quite popular among aristocrats, the commercial elite, and royalty in France and elsewhere. One measure of Carriera's success was her unanimous election to the Académie Royale in October 1720, an honor never before extended to a foreigner. She was, moreover, only the eighth woman admitted since the academy's formation, and the first elected since 1682, the year the academy returned to its original policy of excluding women (Chadwick 1990, 133). Her admission came during a brief period of artistic freedom in France when centralized control of art had weakened.

Carriera returned to Venice in 1721, where she resided with her mother and sisters until the end of her life. She maintained extensive correspondence with her family, former students, and patrons who included England's George III, the king of Poland, and Hapsburg emperor Charles VI. Tragically, she went blind around 1746. The following excerpt is from one of two essays in the collection of her papers. Written in response to a male author's attack on women, it is the first known example of a woman artist's participation in the literary *querelle des femmes*. It reveals her familiarity with the "woman question" and her ideas about gender. Note the strategies she uses to make her case.

CONCERNING FEMININE STUDIES*

... The defense of our gender against so many great intellects who have so strongly attacked it, can appear to be a too complicated task to be undertaken by a woman. This doesn't mean that I am going to admit that we are by nature less able than men for such enterprises and I hope that I'll be able to show plausible reasons before finishing.

But due to men's oppression (especially here in England), there are only very few women, who because of the education of their [minds] or instruction are sufficiently capable of these enterprises. As far as I am concerned, I confess that although there are very few of these women, there may be and there is a great number of women who in their discussions prove more able in the defense of our cause than I, and I am very sorry that due either to their business activities or other occupations or their laziness they are diverted from doing justice to their gender.

Men, through interest or inclination are generally so against us, that we cannot expect any man to be so generous as to stand up and be the champion of our sex,

*From Bernardina Sani, *Rosalba Carriera: Lettere, Diari Frammenti* (Florence: Leo S. Olschki, Editore, 1985). By permission of Bernardina Sani and Casa Editrice Leo S. Olschki. Text as reprinted in *The Voices of Women Artists*, ed. Wendy Slatkin, trans. Nicoletta Tenozzi (Englewood Cliffs, NJ: Prentice Hall, Inc., 1993), pp. 18–19.

against the offenses and oppression of their own sex. Those romantic days are gone and not even one *Don Quixote* is left to help the unfortunate ladies.

It is true that some apology of similar nature was made three or four years ago by one of them; but although his Eugenia might have been grateful to him, in my opinion, the rest of her sex was not very grateful to him. Because, as you noticed, Signora, he took more care in sharpening his satire than in giving strength to his apology.

He plundered a bad loot and he received more blows than he gave and, just like a renegade, he fought under our banner just to have a better opportunity to betray us, but what could you have expected from a Ganymede? an animal who couldn't really praise the spirit of a woman more than the physical body of a man, who compliments us only to show his own good upbringing and manners. He extends the scandal to all women and he believes us sufficiently strong if in the history of 2,000 years he was able to pick a few examples of women famous for their intelligence, wisdom or virtue and men infamous for the opposite. Although I think that the most persistent of our enemies would have saved him this effort, admitting that all epochs produced famous or infamous people of both genders: or they have to abandon all pretence of modesty or reason.

I don't have enough knowledge or inclination to make any use of the book as it was used by Mr. N and I will leave it to the scholars and pedants to dig into the leftovers of Antiquity and to show all the heroes and heroines they can find to provide material for some poor discourse or fill a narrow-minded declaration with meaningful addresses or arguments. I will not enter into any debate if men or women are more intelligent or gifted because of the advantages which men have over us for their education, freedom of speech, and for the varieties of business and social activities. But when some disparity is found between the sexes, this great difference in circumstances must be taken into consideration. I am not going to discuss the superiority of our virtues. I know there are many vicious people and I hope there are a great number of virtuous people of both genders. I can say that whatever vice is found among us, the source usually derives from these differences.

The question I discuss now is whether the time that one sensitive gentle man spends in the company of women could be considered wasted or not?

I put the question in general terms.

SUGGESTED READINGS

Beaumont, Cyril W. *Three French Dancers of the Eighteenth Century: Camargo, Salle, Guimard.* London, C. W. Beaumont, 1934.

Bissell, R. Ward. *Artemisia Gentileschi and the Authority of Art.* University Park: Pennsylvania State University Press, 1999.

Christiansen, Keith and Judith W. Mann. *Orazio and Artemisia Gentileschi.* New York: Metropolitan Museum of Art; New Haven, CT: Yale University Press, 2001.

Sadie, Julie Anne. "*Musiciennes* of the Ancien Régime." In *Women Making Music.* Bowers and Tick, 1987.

Audio Sources

Ars Femina Ensemble, *Non tacete! (I'll not be silent): Music by Women Written before 1800.* Nannerl Recordings, 1991. Compact disc NRARS002.

Bay Area Women's Philharmonic; JoAnn Falletta, conductor. Composers: Martines; Rossi; Duval; Sirmen; Jacquet de la Guerre. *Baroquen Treasures Sound Recording.* Newport Classic, 1990. Compact disc NCD 60102.

Caccini, Francesca. *La liberazione de Ruggiero.* Nannerl Recordings, 1994. Compact disc NR-ARS 003.

De la Guerre, Elisabeth-Claude Jacquet. *Cantates et pieces variees (selections). Cantates bibliques; pieces instrumentales.* Arion, 1986. Two compact discs ARN 26801.

Strozzi, Barbara. *Arie, lamenti e cantate.* Harmonia Mundi, France, 2000. Compact disc HMC 905249.

Strozzi, Barbara. *La virtuosissima cantatrice.* Amon Ra, 1994. Compact disc CD-SAR 61.

Chapter 5

Writers and Intellectuals in the Baroque Era

In the seventeenth century, writers had increasing opportunities to publish their works and reach a wider audience. Concurrently, colonial expansion spread European culture, particularly to the Western Hemisphere. In turn, developments and discoveries in the "New World" fascinated Europeans. The women covered in this chapter reflect these developments. Their lives and works also reflect the religious and political ferment and new intellectual currents, such as the Scientific Revolution, that characterized this period. One feature of this chapter is the range of women's literary and intellectual interests and achievements. Another is that for the first time, we move westward beyond Europe and hear the voices of women in British North America and Spanish Mexico. These writers and intellectuals came from diverse backgrounds and contributed to culture in a variety of genres. Despite their diversity, however, gender shaped their lives and work in similar ways, and all had to come to terms with the reality of their womanhood as they pursued their intellectual and creative interests and personal dreams. As you read, note how each navigates the reality of being a woman and the light each sheds on the "woman question" debate in her work. Consider also how and why some use women's history in their work.

LEARNED WOMEN FROM CONTINENTAL EUROPE AND THE AMERICAS

Anna Maria van Schurman (1607–1678): Learned Woman and Pietist Leader

Anna Maria van Schurman was probably "the most celebrated learned woman of the seventeenth century" (Lerner 1993, 155). Dutch poets called her their "Sappho and their Corneille" (Chadwick 1990, 110). She was also a popular, multitalented amateur artist and a leader in the controversial Pietist movement. Schurman descended from a wealthy noble family of Antwerp that was forced into exile by the duke of Alva after her grandparents' conversion to Calvinism. She was born in Cologne, where her family and other Protestant exiles had settled. In 1615, however, her father, Frederik van Schurman, moved his wife and three children to the Dutch city of Utrecht, where she lived most of her life. His decision was fortuitous, for women enjoyed more legal equality and freedom in Protestant, mercantile Holland than elsewhere in Europe.

Van Schurman's talents were nurtured by her parents. Her mother taught her needlework, and her father sent her to a female engraver for the art training deemed appropriate for girls of her social class.

Although never a professional artist, she attracted a popular following because of her remarkable versatility. She also made a number of significant contributions to Dutch art. She specialized in miniature works and in so-called "minor" art forms that were popular among amateur artists, particularly women: portraits, embroidery, calligraphy, and scissor art (intricate patterns cut from paper). But she distinguished herself by employing a wide range of techniques, some of which women rarely used. She did miniature portraits, drawings, and etchings, working with oil, pencil, pastels, wax, and ivory. She engraved glass, revived and popularized an old technique of carved boxwood portraits, and, in 1640, completed the first known Dutch pastel drawing, a self-portrait. The Utrecht painters' Guild of St. Luke recognized her achievements by granting her honorary membership in 1643.

More importantly, she acquired a broad humanist education. She learned arithmetic, geography, astronomy, and music and acquired writing and speaking knowledge of the major European languages as well as Latin, Greek, Hebrew, Syrian, and Arabic. She also wrote an Ethiopian grammar. Her father encouraged her studies and even urged her to remain single so as not to waste her intellectual talent.

At 14 she caught the attention of some of Europe's leading intellectuals when she wrote a poem in honor of Dutch poet, Jacob Cats. Thus began her extensive correspondence and literary friendships with such male luminaries as Cats, Descartes, and Cardinal Richelieu and with numerous women intellectuals including Bathsua Makin, Queen Christina of Sweden, and Marie de Gournay. By the 1640s she had abandoned her art to focus on writing scholarly treatises, and her fame as a scholar spread. She was the first woman permitted to attend lectures at a Dutch university and was thus an inspiration to educated women in many countries. She remained single, amassed a large library, and pursued her studies and correspondence. Her home became a center for scholars from all over Europe.

At age 60, Schurman abandoned her studies, sold her home and library, and joined a Pietist community led by Jean de Labadie. Labadie was a controversial Reformed (Protestant) minister who was dismissed from his pastoral post because he preached that the "true church" consisted only of regenerate Christians committed to prepare for the imminent coming of God's Kingdom. Pietists believed in the equality of all souls and that one could communicate directly with God. They respected the mystical visions of women as well as men. The movement attracted many German and Dutch women, a number of whom assumed roles as lay preachers and prophets and preached that women would fill a special role in the "second coming." Schurman developed a type of "house church" (home prayer meeting) that gave Pietist women opportunities for religious leadership. Her conversion lent credibility to the movement, particularly to Labadie's sect. She was a member of the community until her death, and through her spiritual autobiography, *Eukleria* (1673), she provided a compelling theological and philosophical defense of Labadism and of her journey to the controversial faith.

Her conversion, she acknowledged, entailed exchanging a comfortable lifestyle for a life of "austerity and external persecution." Many of her contemporaries (and later scholars) were unable to accept her unorthodox religious beliefs. Some who praised her scholarship or art totally ignored her religious ideas; others dismissed and derided her scholarship because she embraced Labadism. Publication of *Eukleria* elicited a huge negative reaction, noted in the following statement by French Carmelite writer Eberti in 1706: "And this crown of the female sex would undoubtedly have been seen by posterity as a shining example of all learned women had she not somewhat tarnished her own lustre and her fame by her reprehensible doctrines" (De Baar and Rang 1996, 6–7).

The two selections that follow illustrate her intellectual range and her powers of persuasion. Both selections are from a collection of her writings.* The first document consists of excerpts from her

*Excerpts from Anna Maria van Schurman, *Whether a Christian Woman Should Be Educated and Other Writings From Her Intellectual Circle,* trans. and ed., Joyce L. Irwin, The Other Voice in Early Modern Europe Series, Margaret L King and Albert Rabil, eds., (Chicago: University of Chicago Press,1998), pp. 26–33, 36–37, 73–77. Copyright © 1998 by The University of Chicago. Reprinted by permission of The University of Chicago Press.

defense of women's right to education. This classic treatise is her most famous work and earned her recognition as one of the most influential feminist voices of early modern Europe. Note the arguments she uses to justify the education of women and consider the extent to which she accepts the notion of inherent differences between men and women.

WHETHER THE STUDY OF LETTERS IS FITTING FOR A CHRISTIAN WOMAN (1641)

Let us apply the following limitations:

First, in respect to the subject, it is presumed that our woman have at least a mediocre ability and not be utterly inept at learning.

Second, we presume that she will be instructed by the necessary means and that the limited wealth of the household does not altogether stand in her way. I introduce this exception because few are fortunate to have parents who either want or are able to educate them themselves, and it is not possible to contract for the work of tutors in this region without expenses.

Third, we presume that the circumstances of her time and fortune are such that it is possible sometimes to be free from any general or special calling, and certainly from the exercises of devotion or from the duties of the household. As follows easily from this, what helps is, in part, in childhood, immunity and freedom from cares and responsibilities and, in part, in a more advanced age, either celibacy or the attendance of servants who usually free wealthy women in large part from domestic duties.

Fourth, the goal of studies is presumed not to be vainglory and show or idle curiosity but rather the general goal of the glory of God and the salvation of one's soul in order that she may also emerge the better and happier and may educate and guide her family (if that duty falls to her) and even be useful to her whole sex, to the extent that that is possible. . . .

I limit *the study of letters* in such manner that I think all honorable disciplines, or the whole circle of liberal arts as it is called, is entirely fitting to a Christian woman (just as it is a proper and universal good or adornment of humanity); but it must be in accordance with the dignity and nature of the science or art and also in accordance with the girl's or woman's capability and fortune so that what is to be learned may follow in its own order, place, and time and be properly connected. First of all, account should be taken of those sciences or arts that have the closest connection with theology and moral virtue, and which primarily serve them. We consider grammar, logic, and rhetoric to be of this sort. Among these first disciplines, however, some expressly identify logic as the key to all sciences.

Then come physics, metaphysics, history, etc., and also knowledge of languages, especially Hebrew and Greek. All of these things are able to move us to easier and fuller knowledge of Sacred Scripture, to say nothing of other authors. Other subjects, namely mathematics (to which music is also assigned), poetry, painting, and similar things, may be pursued as liberal arts, as an excellent adornment or pastime. Finally, we do not especially urge those studies that pertain to the practice of trial law and the military or to the arts of speaking in church, court, and school, as they are less fitting or necessary. Nevertheless, we do not by any means concede that women should be excluded from scholastic or, so to say, theoretical knowledge of those things, least of all from knowledge of the most noble discipline of politics. . . .

Let this then be our thesis: the study of letters is fitting to a Christian woman.

To confirm this we present these arguments . . . :

I. . . . Whoever is instilled by nature with the first principles or the power of the principles of all arts and sciences is suited to study all arts and sciences: [and] women are instilled by nature with these powers or principles. Therefore all arts and sciences are fitting to women. . . .

II. . . . Whoever by nature has a desire for sciences and arts is suited to study sciences and arts: [and] women by nature have a desire for arts and sciences. Therefore . . .

III. . . . Whoever is created by God with a countenance raised and erect toward the heavens is suited for the knowledge and contemplation of lofty and heavenly things. [And] God created woman with a countenance raised and erect toward the heavens. Therefore . . .

IV. . . . Whoever longs greatly for a solid and enduring occupation is suited for the study of letters. [And] woman longs greatly for a solid and enduring occupation. . . .

V. . . . Literary study is fitting for someone who has a more tranquil and free life; [and] women generally enjoy a more tranquil and free life. . . .

VI. . . . Whoever is fit for the study of the principal sciences is also fit for the study of instrumental or auxiliary sciences. [And] the study of the principal sciences is fitting for a Christian woman. . . .

VII. . . . Arts and sciences are fitting for those to whom all virtue in general is fitting. And all virtue in general is fitting to a woman. Therefore . . .

VIII. . . . Whatever perfects and adorns the human mind is fitting to a Christian woman. . . .

IX. . . . Whatever things by their nature contribute to arousing in us greater love and reverence for God are fitting for a Christian woman. . . .

X. . . . Whatever fortifies us against heresies and discloses their traps is fitting for a Christian woman. . . .

XI. . . . Those things which teach prudence without any detriment to reputation and modesty are fitting for a Christian woman. . . .

XII. . . . Whatever leads to true greatness of soul is fitting for a Christian woman. . . .

XIII. . . . Whatever fills the human mind with exceptional and honest delight is fitting for a Christian woman. . . .

XIV. . . . The study of letters is fitting for those whom ignorance . . . is not fitting. [And] ignorance is not fitting for a Christian woman. Therefore . . .

From this we draw the conclusion: women can and ought to be stimulated to embrace this kind of life by the best and strongest arguments, the testimonies of the wise, and finally the examples of illustrious women. This is especially true, however, for those who are better provided than others with leisure and other means and supports for the study of letters. And since it is preferable to imbue the mind with better studies from infancy itself, we think parents themselves should be the first to be urged and seriously admonished concerning their duty.

This selection from *Eukleria,* a title that comes from a Greek word meaning "the right choice," exemplifies the spiritual orientation that marked the second stage of Schurman's life. Note how she explains or justifies her conversion to the controversial beliefs espoused by the Labadists.

EUKLERIA (1673)

CHAPTER ONE: UNIVERSAL AND GENUINE EXPLICATION OF MY PAST AND PRESENT STATE

Everyone is aware from their publications that some renowned men who in the recent past were quite favorably disposed to me now find my new manner of living very displeasing. And no one at this time can be unaware what bitter prejudice and unfair judgment some churchmen hold against the good cause of God for which I have openly declared myself. Therefore, I am glad that this occasion has arisen, on which these outstanding witnesses to the truth and faithful shepherds of our church — Mr. de Labadie, Mr. Yvon, and Mr. DuLignon — have publicly expounded the declaration or defense of their orthodoxy and have opposed the dark missiles of calumny. On this occasion, . . . I will . . . give public testimony to the same celestial truth and piety for the sake of which these men do battle in the company of a few friends and cultivators of truth and piety. By this work I also hope once and for all to explain briefly and candidly to all who love truth and justice the reasons for the remarkable change of my station in life. . . .

I. In the first place, I think that I must explain here that I not only consider the doctrines that these teachers of our church present to the world through this work as well as others to be correct, but I also find that their whole teaching, which they impart to us daily, in public as well as in private, agrees in all ways with Holy Scripture. Further, I see — both in the whole elaboration of divine truths and in the particular articles thereof as well as in the manner of presenting them — so many marks of divine teaching — a great and very pure light, a marvelous ease and simplicity and, as I would say, an ointment-like pleasantness and sweetness, and finally, such an insuperable force — that I could not doubt them, even if I wanted to, any more than I doubt the daylight itself when it envelops and brightens our eyes. Not only am I obliged to assert these things according to the inmost feelings of my heart but also all hearers of this holy teaching who cherish even a spark of the divine light will testify as if with one mouth that they have been touched no less forcibly than sweetly by the pure and simple explanation of that teaching and that they have felt vividly the fiery power of its truth and holiness, like a coal brought by a flying angel from the altar into their hearts, as if they had been touched by some kind of thing recognizable to the external senses. And no wonder, for the more spiritual something is, the more real it is and the more effectively it works.

II. . . . in my whole life I have found no one among mortals who so genuinely and so ardently expressed the spirit and manner of life of the early church or the condition of the first Christians as they have. . . . I do not regret what I have done in the slightest since I hold the true lot of Christians, though despised by others, to be the happiest of all and through the grace of God will hold it to be so into eternity.

III. Since now for some years I have looked with sorrowful eyes at the almost total deflection and defection of Christianity from its origin . . . and since I am left without any hope of its restitution through that common path on which the churchmen of our age walk (most of whom are themselves in need of Reformation), who could fairly blame me for having chosen for myself and joyfully welcomed pastors who are reformed and divinely instructed toward the goal of reforming deformed

Christians? And when the wonderful providence and goodness of God . . . showed me the correct and direct path to the true practice of the original life of the gospel through the singular Mr. Jean de Labadie, who is well practiced in the ways of the Lord and a faithful servant of the Lord, and his partners in grace, who likewise follow in the footprints of Christ, both in teaching and in working and suffering, how could anyone justly reproach me for following them as the best teachers and leaders? Or that I am also supported by the company of many faithful who all with the same mind and zeal look to Jesus the guide and perfecter of our faith, as we strive toward our heavenly homeland . . . ?

IV. Nevertheless, since there are learned and eminent men who consider my old state of life to have been so excellent and admirable that I was not justified to have exchanged it for another except perhaps with the consent of all my friends or even to the applause of the whole literary world (inasmuch as to it I owe the little fame I enjoy), I think I should give here, as I have said, my reasons. . . .

V. As far as that little bit of fame that the learned world has bestowed on me is concerned, I confess that I am greatly indebted to these scholars because through that reputation I have from their good opinion, they have provided me with a great treasure, and they have presented me with ample material for exercising virtue, including renouncing this beautiful ampule of fame and, among other things, dispersing or selling off things that used to be dear to me in order to possess the most precious pearl of the gospel more securely and purely. . . .

Anne Bradstreet (1612–1672): First English Poet of the New World

Anne Bradstreet was America's first published poet, and her book of poems, *The Tenth Muse, Lately Sprung Up in America,* published in London in 1650, was the first English example of New World literature. She is now regarded as one of the best poets of Colonial America, and as having produced some of the most significant writing in the Western world in the mid-seventeenth century (McElrath and Robb 1981, xii, xix). For years, however, her achievements were overshadowed by her prominent male relatives. One literary scholar (1917), for example, spoke of her as a "pleasing figure . . . who was 'fathered and husbanded' respectively by Thomas Dudley and Simon Bradstreet, both in their time governors of Massachusetts," while a historian (1934) made only passing reference to her: "Thomas Dudley, whose daughter afterward became the wife of Governor Bradstreet" (Amore 1982, xii, xv).

Anne was born in 1612 or early 1613 in Northamptonshire, England, the second of six children of clerk Thomas Dudley and Dorothy Yorke, a "gentlewoman." In 1619, the family moved to Sempringham where her father managed the properties of the earl of Lincolnshire. Her father hired tutors to give his children a solid humanist education. They also enjoyed access to the earl's large library. From her poetry it is evident that she studied Greek and Roman literature and history, medieval literature, contemporary history and popular literature, and, of course, the Bible. At the time, probably half of all English women could only sign documents with a mark.

In 1621, Anne met her future husband, Simon Bradstreet, when he came to Lincolnshire to assist her father in managing the earl's estate. Bradstreet, then 20, was a graduate of Cambridge College. They were married in 1628. In 1630, the Bradstreets joined the Dudleys and others in the flotilla of ships that constituted the first wave of the "great Puritan migration" from England to North America. The leaders of this flotilla were members or stockholders of the Massachusetts Bay Company and were financially secure and unusually well educated. They were also bound by their determination to create a "city on a hill"—a model Puritan society that would set an example for "corrupt" England to follow.

Anne Bradstreet was just 18 when she disembarked from the *Arbella* in Salem and began her new life as a pioneer woman. After several moves to nearby communities, she and Simon settled in Ipswich in 1635, where she wrote most of the poetry that appeared in *The Tenth Muse*. Around 1645, they moved to Andover where she spent the remainder of her life. In this frontier colony, Anne bore and reared eight children. As a member of the colony's social and economic elite, she enjoyed an unusually comfortable lifestyle. But she also shouldered family responsibilities when her husband was abroad as the colony's representative to the English court and assumed additional social duties when he served as governor of Massachusetts Bay. All the while, she continued to write, acquire books, and read. A fire that destroyed their Andover house, family treasures, and her library of 800 volumes devastated her.

There was little to distract her from her domestic duties or her writing. As a model Puritan society, Massachusetts Bay permitted few diversions. Theater, dancing, and public concerts were prohibited, and Sundays were devoted to God and church. Independent thinking was frowned upon, particularly if publicly expressed. Two of her contemporaries, Roger Williams and Anne Hutchinson, were banished from the colony in 1638 for expressing unorthodox religious views. Hutchinson's case, in particular, served as a warning of the dangers that awaited any woman who presumed to interpret the Gospel to mixed groups of men and women or publicly disagreed with the clergy. The message must have been particularly clear to Bradstreet, whose father was one of the judges in Hutchinson's trial.

Not surprisingly, Bradstreet presented her first volume of poetry to her father as a gift instead of seeking to have it published. Twenty years later, her brother-in-law, unbeknownst to her, took the collection to England and arranged its publication as *The Tenth Muse, Lately Sprung Up in America* (1650). She subsequently revised the first edition, correcting printing errors and adding new poems; however, her intended second edition was not published until 1678, eight years after her death. Some have argued that she, like so many other women writers, had no desire to publish her poems, but her "Prologue" that follows seems to suggest otherwise.

Her poems, such as "The Prologue," that reflect her knowledge of classical literature, history, and public affairs have often attracted the most attention. More recently, others have argued that her most significant works are her intimate and highly personal domestic poems that reveal seventeenth-century women's daily lives, hopes, and fears. Critics have also expressed disagreement over the language she used in discussing women's place in society. Some have argued that she fully accepted societal definitions of women's roles and duties and contended that her apparent criticisms were simply lighthearted jests. Others, however, detect a sharp critique of the social order and an underlying sense of frustration and anger in many of her poems. As you read the selections from a collection of her poetry that follow, consider which of the critics you think were most correct in their assessment of Bradstreet's views of women and the gender structure of her society, and why.*

THE PROLOGUE

1. To sing of Wars, of Captaines, and of Kings,
Of Cities founded, Common-wealths begun,
For my mean Pen, are too superiour things,
And how they all, or each, their dates have run:
Let Poets, and Historians set these forth,
My obscure Verse, shall not so dim their worth. . . .

*From Anne Bradstreet, *Several Poems,* 2d ed. corrected by the author (Boston: Printed by John Foster, 1678; New Canaan, CT: Readex, 1981–1982), pp. 3–4, 239. Microfiche: Early American Imprints, Series 1, no. 244.

3. From School-boyes tongue, no
Rhethorick we expect,
Nor yet a sweet Consort, from broken
strings,
Nor perfect beauty, where's a maine
defect,
My foolish, broken, blemish'd Muse so
sings;
And this to mend, alas, no Art is able,
'Cause Nature made it so irreparable.
4. Nor can I, like that fluent sweet
tongu'd *Greek*
Who lisp'd at first, speake afterwards
more plaine
By Art, be gladly found what he did
seeke,
A full requitall of his striving paine:
Art can doe much, but this maxime's
most sure,
A weake or wounded braine admits no
cure.
5. I am obnoxious to each carping tongue,
Who sayes, my hand a needle better fits,
A Poets Pen, all scorne, I should thus
wrong;
For such despight they cast on female
wits:
If what I doe prove well, it wo'nt advance,
They'l say its stolne, or else, it was by
chance.
6. But sure the antick *Greeks* were far
more milde,

Else of our Sex, why feigned they those
nine,
And poesy made, *Calliope's* owne
childe,
So 'mongst the rest, they plac'd the Arts
divine:
But this weake knot they will full soone
untye,
The *Greeks* did nought, but play the
foole and lye.
7. Let *Greeks* be *Greeks,* and Women
what they are,
Men have precedency, and still excell,
It is but vaine, unjustly to wage war,
Men can doe best, and Women know it
well;
Preheminence in each, and all is yours,
Yet grant some small acknowledgement
of ours.
8. And oh, ye high flown quils, that
soare the skies,
And ever with your prey, still catch your
praise,
If e're you daigne these lowly lines, your
eyes
Give wholsome Parsley wreath, I ask no
Bayes:
This meane and unrefined stuffe of mine,
Will make your glistering gold but more
to shine.

Before the Birth of One of My Children

All things within this fading world hath
end,
Adversity doth still our joys attend;
No ties so strong, no friends so dear and
sweet,
But with death's parting blow is sure to
meet.
The sentence past is most irrevocable,
A common thing, yet oh inevitable;
How soon, my dear, death may my steps
attend,

How soon it may be thy lot to lose thy
friend,
We both are ignorant, yet love bids
me
These farewell lines to recommend to
thee,
That when the knot's untied that made
us one,
I may seem thine, who in effect am
none;
And if I see not half my days that's due,

What nature would, God grant to yours
  and you;
The many faults that well you know I
  have,
Let be interred in my oblivious grave;
If any worth or virtue were in me,
Let that live freshly in thy memory
And when thou feel'st no grief, as I no
  harms,
Yet love thy dead, who long lay in thine
  arms:
And when thy loss shall be repaid with
  gains,

Look to my little babes my dear
  remains;
And if thou love thy self, or loved'st me
These O protect from step dame's
  injury;
And if chance to thine eyes shall bring
  this verse,
With some sad sighs honour my absent
  hearse;
And kiss this paper for thy love's dear
  sake,
Who with salt tears this last farewell did
  take.

Sor Juana Inés De La Cruz (c. 1648–1695): The New World's First Major Writer

Sor Juana Inés de la Cruz was the first major literary figure in the New World, and one of Latin America's most important writers. She was a poet, playwright, composer, and intellectual who wrote works in nearly every major genre popular in Spain's Golden Age. Her works include 65 sonnets, 62 romances, 3 one-act plays, 2 comedies, and a 975-verse work, *First Dream,* that is regarded as the "most important philosophical poem in the Spanish language" (Arena and Powell 1994, 17). She also composed 32 preludes to plays that were sung and performed, a song/dance for play intermissions, and at least 15 sets of carols for religious services. Not surprisingly, she was called the "Mexican Phoenix" or, like other early women poets, the "tenth muse." Her most famous work, *La Respuesta,* brought her the title "First Feminist of America," bestowed by Mexico in 1974. (Arena and Powell 1994, 17)

She was born Juana Ramirez de Asbaje in 1648 or 1651, the illegitimate third child of Doña Isabel Ramirez. Her mother was a strong, independent woman. She had six illegitimate children by two men, but never married, and managed her father's hacienda for over 30 years after his death. Although Juana's mother was uneducated, her grandfather was a learned man with a large library in which she spent hours as a child. Unlike most learned women of her time who had tutors, she was largely self-taught. When she was around ten, she was sent to Mexico City and presented at court. She spent five years in the service of the Vicereine Doña Leonor Carreto, with whom she developed a deep friendship. De la Cruz wrote her first poem while at court and continued her studies. At age 13, she took a public oral examination with 40 leading professors and intellectuals, amazing everyone with her answers to questions on science, mathematics, music, literature, philosophy, and theology.

In 1668, she turned her back on court life and entered an aristocratic but strict convent. She left the convent when she became ill, but within the year entered Santa Paula, a wealthy and more lenient uncloistered convent where she lived until her death. Sor Juana enjoyed comfortable quarters, complete with several servants and a mulatto slave. She was allowed to acquire books, continue her studies, write, and compose. Her plays and music, which were performed by the sisters and used in services, enriched convent life, and commissions she received for her poetry helped finance the institution. She was the center of a *salon* where scholars, religious leaders, friends from court, and others she invited met to exchange ideas. She entertained visitors and corresponded with many people. Two women were particularly important to her intellectual and literary career. Vicereine Doña Leonor Carreto was a friend and patron until her death in 1674, and her successor, Vicereine Maria Luisa Manrique de Lara y Gonzaga, was also an important patron throughout the seven years she and her husband lived in Mexico. She arranged for the publication of Sor Juana's poems in Spain in 1689. The support of these two influential women also helped protect Sor Juana for many years from church officials who were opposed to her writing and interaction with the public.

In 1691, she wrote her famous *La Respuesta,* under the pseudonym Sor Philotea, in response to a letter from the Bishop of Puebla that attacked her for writing an "unchaste" poem. Her response was a classic defense of woman's right to learn, to think, and to speak out, and an important contribution to the "woman question" (*querelle des femmes*) debate. It was also the climax of her two-decades-long struggle with the church. Shortly thereafter, she stopped her studies and creative activities, sold her library which by then numbered several thousand volumes, and her scientific instruments. She devoted the rest of her life to serving the poor and using her knowledge of medicine and native herbal cures. In 1694 she signed a declaration of faith in blood, repenting the errors of her past life and formally renouncing her secular studies. She died in April 1695 while tending the sick during a plague.

La Respuesta is a revealing autobiographical as well as intellectual document, for it delineates her efforts to reconcile her personal aspirations with societal gender expectations. Compare her internal tensions, her struggles with her critics, and the arguments she uses to defend herself with those of the other women included in this chapter.

THE ANSWER/LA RESPUESTA (1691)*

[WHY SHE WRITES]

My writing has never proceeded from any dictate of my own, but a force beyond me—, I can in truth say, "You *have compelled me.*" One thing, however, is true, so that I shall not deny it. . . . For ever since the light of reason first dawned in me, my inclination to letters was marked by such passion and vehemence that neither the reprimands of others . . . nor reflections of my own . . . have sufficed to make me abandon my pursuit of this native impulse that God Himself bestowed on me. His Majesty knows why and to what end He did so, and He knows that I have prayed He snuff out the light of my intellect, leaving only enough to keep His Law. For more than that is too much, some would say, in a woman; and there are even those who say that it is harmful. His Majesty knows too that, not achieving this, I have attempted to entomb my intellect together with my name and to sacrifice it to the One who gave it to me; and that no other motive brought me to the life of Religion, despite the fact that the exercises and companionship of a community were quite opposed to the tranquility and freedom from disturbance required by my studious bent. And once in the community, the Lord knows . . . what I did to try to conceal my name and renown from the public; he did not, however, allow me to do this, telling me it was temptation, and so it would have been. . . .

[HER CHILDHOOD AND HER DECISION TO ENTER A CONVENT]

I remember that in those days, though I was as greedy for treats as children usually are at that age, I would abstain from eating cheese, because I heard tell that it made people stupid, and the desire to learn was stronger for me than the desire to eat—powerful as this is in children. Later, when I was six or seven years old and already knew how to read and write, along with all the other skills like embroidery and sewing that women learn, I heard that in Mexico City there were a University and Schools where they studied the sciences. As soon as I heard this I began to slay my poor mother with insistent and annoying pleas, begging her to dress me in men's clothes and send me to the capital, to the home of some relatives she had there, so that I could enter the University and study. She refused, and was right in doing so; but I quenched my desire by reading a great variety of books that belonged to my grandfather, and neither punishments nor scoldings could prevent me. And so when I did go to Mexico City, people marveled not so much at my intelligence as at my memory and the facts I knew at an age when it seemed I had scarcely had time to learn to speak.

I began to study Latin, in which I believe I took fewer than twenty lessons. And my interest was so intense, that although in women (and especially in the very bloom of youth) the natural adornment of the hair is so esteemed, I would cut off four to six fingerlengths of my hair, measuring how long it had been before. And I made myself a rule that if by the time it had grown back to the same length I did not know such and such a thing that I intended to study, then I would cut my hair off again to punish my dull-wittedness. And so my hair grew, but I did not yet know what I had resolved to learn, for it grew quickly and I learned slowly. Then I cut my hair right off to punish my dull-wittedness, for I did not think it reasonable that hair should cover a head that was so bare of facts—the more desirable adornment. I took the veil because, although I knew I would find in religious life many things that would be quite opposed to my character . . . , it would, given my absolute unwillingness to enter into marriage, be the least unfitting and most decent state I could choose, with regard to the assurance I desired of my salvation. For before this first concern . . . all the impertinent little follies of my character gave way and bowed to the yoke. These were wanting to live alone and not wanting to have either obligations that would disturb my freedom to study or the noise of a community that would interrupt the tranquil silence of my books. These things made me waver somewhat in my decision until, being enlightened by learned people as to my temptation, I vanquished it with divine favor and took the state I so unworthily hold. I thought I was fleeing myself, but—woe is me!—I brought myself with me, and brought my greatest enemy in my inclination to study, which I know not whether to take as a Heaven-sent favor or as a punishment. For when snuffed out or hindered with every [spiritual] exercise known to Religion, it exploded like gunpowder; and in my case the saying *"privation gives rise to appetite"* was proven true.

[HER THIRST FOR KNOWLEDGE CONTINUES]

I went back (no, I spoke incorrectly, for I never stopped)—I went on, I mean, with my studious task (which to me was peace and rest in every moment left over when my duties were done) of reading and still more reading, study and still more study, with no teacher besides my books themselves. What a hardship it is to learn from those lifeless letters, deprived of the sound of a teacher's voice and explanations; yet I suffered all these trials most gladly for the love of learning. . . . Nevertheless I did my best to elevate these studies and direct them to His service, for the goal to which I aspired was the study of Theology. Being a Catholic, I thought it an abject failing not to know everything that can in this life be achieved, through earthly methods, concerning the divine mysteries. And being a nun and not a laywoman, I thought I should, because I was in religious life, profess the study of letters—the more so as the daughter of such as St. Jerome and St. Paula; for it would be a degeneracy for an idiot daughter to proceed from such learned parents.* I argued in this way to myself, and I thought my own argument quite reasonable. However, the fact may have been (and this seems most likely) that I was merely flattering and encouraging my own inclination, by arguing that its own pleasure was an obligation.

I went on in this way, always directing each step of my studies, as I have said, toward the summit of Holy Theology; but it seemed to me necessary to ascend by the ladder of the humane arts and sciences in order to reach it; for who could fathom the style of the Queen of Sciences without knowing that of her handmaidens? . . .

[CHURCH CRITICISM SHE AND OTHER LEARNED WOMEN, SUCH AS
TERESA OF AVILA, EXPERIENCED]

Well, as for this aptitude at composing verses—which is doubly unfortunate, in my case, even should they be sacred verses—what unpleasantness have they not caused me, and indeed do they not still cause? Truly, my Lady, at times I ponder how it is that a person who achieves high significance—or rather, who is granted significance by God, for He alone can do this—is received as the common enemy. For that person seems to others to usurp the applause they deserve or to draw off and dam up the admiration to which they had aspired, and so they persecute that person.

. . . In all that I have said, my Lady, I do not wish (nor would I be capable of such foolishness) to claim that I have been persecuted because of my knowledge, but rather only because of my love for learning and letters, and not because I had attained either one or the other.

. . . I confess that I am far indeed from the terms of Knowledge and that I have wished to follow it, though *"afar off."* But all this has merely led me closer to the flames of persecution, the crucible of affliction; and to such extremes that some have even sought to prohibit me from study.

ENGLAND'S "FEMALE WITS"

Margaret Cavendish, Duchess of Newcastle (1623–1674)

Margaret Cavendish published 13 books including children's books, poetry, essays, fables (or fancies), social commentaries, two collections of plays, science fiction, an autobiographical essay, a biography of her husband, letters, and scientific and philosophical treatises published in *Philosophical and Physical Opinions* and *Observations Upon Experimental Philosophy* (1666). Her *Philosophical Letters* (1664) included letters she wrote in response to philosophers Thomas Hobbes, René Descartes, and Henry More. She was the first woman to submit a book of poems in English for publication.

*See Volume I, Chapter 13 for Jerome and Paula.

She lived in England during the tumultuous years of the first Stuart kings, the Puritan Revolution, and the Restoration of Charles II. Her father, Thomas Lucas, was a large landowner but had no aristocratic title. He died when she was an infant, and her mother raised their eight children, managed the estate alone, and hired tutors to educate the children. Margaret persuaded her mother to let her enter the queen's service as a maid-of-honor and accompanied the queen into exile in France during the civil wars. There she met William Cavendish whom she married in 1645. Cavendish, a widower 30 years older than she, had fled England in 1644 after the Puritans defeated the Royalist troops he commanded. They lived abroad, in Paris, then in Rotterdam and Antwerp for nearly 15 years.

They returned to England in 1660, and when William failed to obtain a position with Charles II, they moved to his country estates in the Midlands. Cavendish helped her husband restore and manage the estates that had fallen into disrepair during his exile. William, who was also a writer and patron of the arts, supported his wife's ambitions and interests. In 1667, she spent the spring in London, where she visited the royal family and attended plays. The highlight of her sojourn was an invitation to the Royal Society to see some scientific experiments. Although she longed to become a member of the society, she was thrilled to be the first woman even allowed entry into the all-male institution (Alic 1986, 82). The next year she published her second collection of plays. She died unexpectedly at age 50. In tribute to his wife, Cavendish published a collection of letters and poems in her honor written by famous people.

Cavendish was ridiculed for the strange dresses she wore and for her sometimes unconventional writings and eccentric ideas. Many thought she was weird simply because she wrote books, including some in verse, but she also earned praise from many of her contemporaries. Since the 1970s, she has won critical respect for her insightful critiques of seventeenth-century society, her analyses of the complex ways in which patriarchal structures affected women, and her sensitivity to women outside the aristocratic class. There has also been renewed interest in her utopian science fiction work *Blazing World* and in her plays, as demonstrated in the success of a 1995 London performance of *The Female Wits*.

Cavendish's play *Bell in Campo* is a witty portrayal of gender roles and a clever critique of the social order. The play begins with the town under siege from enemy troops and the defending army in disarray. The women of the town volunteer to help their men, but the general and his troops laugh at the suggestion that women might fight and reject their offer. Undeterred, Lady Victoria organizes the women, and when the men's army is routed, her army of "Amazons" comes to their defense. As in many of her other plays, the ending is happy, but utopian.

EXCERPTS FROM BELL IN CAMPO*

PART I, ACT 2, SCENE 9

[The women have agreed to follow Lady Victoria into battle against the enemy troops.]

Lady Victoria: Noble Heroickesses, I am glad to hear you speak all as with one voice and Tongue, which shows your minds are joyned together, as in one piece, without seam or rent; but let us not return unfit to do them service, so we may cause their

---

*From Margaret Cavendish, *Bell in Campo* in *Playes, Written by the Thrice Noble, Illustrious and Excellent Princess, the Lady Marchioness of Newcastle* (London: Printed by A. Warren, for John Martyn, James Allestry, and Tho. Dicas, 1662; Ann Arbor, MI: University Microfilms International, 1984), pp. 588–89, 609–10, 616–17, microfilm: Early English Books, 1641–1700; 1553:10. Reproduction of original in Huntington Library, San Marino, CA.

ruin by obstruction, which will wound us more than can their anger, wherefore let us strive by our industry to render our selves usefull to their service.

All the women: Propound the way, and set the Rules, and we will walk in the one, and keep strictly to the other.

Lady Victoria: Then thus, we have a Body of about five or six thousand women, which came along with some thirty thousand men, but since we came, we are not only thought unusefull but troublesome, which is the reason we were sent away, for the Masculine Sex is of an opinion we are only fit to breed and bring forth Children, but otherwise a trouble in a Commonwealth, for though we encrease the Commonwealth by our breed, we encomber it by our weakness, as they think, as by our incapacities, as having no ingenuity for Inventions, nor subtill wit for Politicians; nor prudence for direction, nor industry for execution; nor patience for opportunity, nor judgment for Counsellers, nor secrecy for trust; nor method to keep peace, nor courage to make War, nor strength to defend our selves or Country, or to assault an Enemy; also that we have not the wisdom to govern a Commonwealth, and that we are too partial to fit in the Seat of Justice, and too pittifull to execute rigorous Authority when it is needfull, and the reason of these erronious opinions of the Masculine Sex to the Effeminate, is, that our Bodyes seem weak, being delicate and beautifull, and our minds seem fearfull, being compassionate and gentle natured, but if we were both weak and fearfull, as they imagine us to be, yet custome which is a second Nature will encourage the one and strengthen the other, and had our educations been answerable to theirs, we might have proved as good Souldiers and Privy Counsellers, Rulers and Commanders, Navigators and Architectors, and as learned Sholars both in Arts and Sciences, as men are; for Time and Custome is the Father and Mother of Strength and Knowledge, they make all things easy and facil, wherefore if we would but accustome our selves we may do such actions, as may gain us such a reputation, as men might change their opinion, insomuch as to believe we are fit to be Copartners in their Governments, and to help to rule the World, where now we are kept as Slaves forced to obey; wherefore let us make our selves free, either by force, merit, or love, and in order, let us practise and endeavour, and take that which Fortune shall profer unto us, let us practice I say, and make these Fields as Schools of Martial Arts and Sciences, so shall we become learned in their disciplines of War, and if you please to make me your Tutoress, and so your Generalless, I shall take the power and command from your election and Authority, otherwise I shall most willingly, humbly, and obediently submit to those whom you shall choose.

All the women: You shall be our Generalless, our Instructeress, Ruler and Commanderess, and we will every one in particular, swear to obey all your Commands, to submit and yield to your punishments, to strive and endeavour to merit your rewards.

PART II, ACT 1, SCENE 3

Enter the Lady Victoria and her Heroickesses

Lady Victoria: Noble Heroickesses, I have intelligence that the Army of Reformations begins to flag, wherefore now or never is the time to prove the courage of our Sex, to get liberty and freedome from the Female Slavery, and to make our selves equal with men: for shall Men only sit in Honours chair, and Women stand as waiters by? shall only Men in Triumphant Chariots ride, and Women run as Captives by? shall only men be Conquerors, and women Slaves? shall only men live by Fame, and women dy in Oblivion? no, no, gallant Heroicks raise your Spirits to a noble pitch, to a deaticall height, to get an everlasting Renown, and infinite praises, by honourable, but unusual actions: for honourable Fame is got only by contemplating thoughts which lie lasily in the Womb of the Mind, and prove Abortive, if not brought forth in living deeds; but worthy Heroickesses, at this time Fortune disires to be the Midwife, and if the Gods and Goddesses did not intend to favour our proceedings with a safe deliverance, they would not have offered us so fair and fit an opportunity to be the Mothers of glorious Actions, and everlasting Fame, which if you be so unnatural to strangle in the Birth by fearfull Cowardize, may you be blasted with Infamy, which is worse than to dye and be forgotten; may you be whipt with the torturing tongues of our own Sex we left behind us, and may you be scorned and neglected by the Masculine Sex, whilst other women are preferr'd and beloved, and may you walk unregarded untill you become a Plague to your selves; but if you Arm with Courage and fight valiantly, may men bow down and worship you, birds taught to sing your praises, Kings offer up their Crowns unto you, and honour inthrone you in a mighty power.

May time and destiny attend your will,
Fame be your scribe to write your actions still;
And may the Gods each act with praises still.

All the women: Fear us not, fear us not, we dare and will follow you wheresoever and to what you dare or will lead us, be it through the jawes of Death. . . .

ACT 3, SCENE 8
Enter the Lady Victoria and many of her Amazons, then enters a Messenger from the Masculine Army
[He brings a letter from the Lord General and his commanders, in which they admit that the women are the victors. They then ask permission to] join our forces to yours, and to be your assistants, and as your Common Souldiers; but leaving all these affairs of War to your discretion, offering our selves to your service. . . .

All the women fall *into a great laughter, ha, ha, ha, ha.*

Lady Victoria: Noble Heroickesses, by your valours, and constant, and resolute proceedings, you have brought your Tyranes to be your Slaves; those that Commanded your absence, how humbly sue your presence, those that thought you a hindrance have felt your assistance, the time is well altered since we were sent to retreat back from the Masculine Army, and now nothing to be done in that Army without our advise, with an humble desire they may join their forces with ours: but gallant Heroickesses, by this you may perceive we were as ignorant of our selves as men were of us, thinking our selves shiftless, weak, and unprofitable Creatures, but by our actions of War we have proved our selves to be every way equal with men, for what we want of strength, we have supplied by industry, and had we not done what we have done, we should have lived in ignorance and slavery.

All the Female Commanders: All the knowledge of ourselves, the honour of renown, the freedome from slavery, and the submission of men, we acknowledge from you; for you advised us, counselled us, instructed us, and encouraged us to those actions of War: wherefore to you we owe our thanks, and to you we give our thanks.

Aphra Behn (1640–1689)

Aphra Behn is England's first professional woman writer, and the first professional female playwright. She also published poems, translations of French literary and philosophical works, and four works of prose fiction that were important in the development of the novel. We know little about her family or early life, but she was apparently born a gentlewoman and was related in some way to Lord Willoughby, the founder and governor of the colony of Surinam on the northern coast of South America. In 1663, she was in Surinam, perhaps with her foster family, but returned to England in 1664. She married a London merchant of Dutch background, who apparently died in the London plague of 1665. In 1666, she went to Antwerp to spy on Dutch naval activities for the government of Charles II during the Dutch wars. Unfortunately, she was never properly paid for her efforts and was either threatened with or actually sent to debtor prison upon her return to England, despite her petitions to the government for funds to repay a creditor. This experience prompted her decision to write for money. Her decision was particularly remarkable, because, although she was well read, she had not had the advantage of a classical education. She supported herself with her writing, though she ended her career in debt.

Between 1670 and 1682, Aphra Behn produced and published ten successful plays, beginning with *The Forc'd Marriage* (1670). The majority of her plays were farces, then in vogue in the Restoration theater, replete with complicated plots and subplots, amorous adventures, and intrigue. One comedy, *The Town Fop* (1676), shocked theatergoers with its brothel scenes. A staunch Tory and supporter of the Stuarts, she made the foibles of Whig politicians, knights, and merchants the targets of her political satires. Her plays of this period also included a tragedy, *Abdelazer.*

By the early 1680s, as theater audiences declined, she began to pursue additional literary avenues. Behn published a volume of her poems and began to supplement her income by doing French translations. Her most important such effort was her 1688 translation (and adaptation) of *La Pluralité des Deux Mondes* by Bernard de Fontenelle. She addressed this work specifically to women readers to make them acquainted with the rationalist philosophy and scientific ideas being discussed by leading intellectuals. She and other women who became known collectively as the "scientific ladies," were fascinated with the new ideas emerging from the Scientific Revolution. By publishing simplified versions of the latest scientific theories in new women's magazines, they helped popularize and spread scientific knowledge, thus contributing to the success of the Scientific Revolution. (Alic 1986, 77–88) Behn also published her prose narratives, most notably *Oroonoko: or, the Royal Slave,* the first fictional work to attack slavery, and, to many critics, the first English novel.

In nearly all of her work, beneath the humor and satire, Behn addressed serious societal issues, particularly gender inequities such as arranged marriages, the double standard, and women's powerlessness. She challenged traditional social mores and conventions by creating female characters who transgressed the boundaries of femininity in their dress and behavior. She wrote openly about sexuality and erotic desires, sometimes in reference to women's as well as male-female relationships. In many ways, she wrote in the same manner as men were writing for the stage, but because of her sex, she was attacked for being "loose." The selections that follow offer some examples of her forthright style, her societal concerns, and ways she transgressed gender boundaries.

"FRANCISCA'S SONG" FROM *THE DUTCH LOVER* (1673)*

[This song is sung by a maidservant, Francisca, to her mistress, Cleonte, in Act II, Scene 6. This comedy was Behn's third play.]

Amyntas led me to a Grove,	A many Kisses did he give,
Where all the Trees did shade us:	And I return'd the same;
The Sun it self, tho it had strove,	Which made me willing to receive,
Yet could not have betray'd us.	That which I dare not name.
The place secure from human eyes,	His charming eyes no aid requir'd,
No other fear allows;	To tell their amorous tale;
But when the Winds that gently rise	On her that was already fir'd,
Do kiss the yielding boughs.	'Twas easy to prevail.
Down there we sat upon the Moss,	He did but kiss, and clasp me round,
And did begin to play	Whilst they his thoughts exprest,
A thousand wanton tricks, to pass	And laid me gently on the Ground;
The heat of all the day.	Ah! who can guess the rest?

PREFACE TO *THE LUCKEY CHANCE, OR, AN ALDERMAN'S BARGAIN* (1686)**

The little Obligation I have to some of the witty Sparks and Poets of the Town, has put me on a Vindication of this Comedy from those Censures that Malice, and ill Nature have thrown upon it, tho in vain: The Poets I heartily excuse, since there is a sort of Self-Interest in their Malice, which I shou'd rather call a witty Way they have in this Age, of Railing at every thing they find with pain successful, and never to shew good Nature and speak well of any thing; but when they are sure 'tis damn'd, then they afford it that worse Scandal, their Pity. And nothing makes them so thorough-stitcht an Enemy as a full Third Day, that's Crime enough to load it with all manner of Infamy; and when they can no other way prevail it with the Town, they charge it with the old never failing Scandal—That 'tis not fit for the Ladys: . . . But I make a Challenge to any Person of common Sense and Reason . . . to read any of my Comedys and compare 'em with others of this Age, and if they find one Word that can offend the chastest Ear, I will submit to all their peevish Cavills; . . .

Ladies, for its further justification to you, be pleas'd to know, that the first Copy of this Play was read by several Ladys of very great Quality, and unquestioned Fame, and received their most favourable Opinion, not one charging it with the Crime, that some have been pleas'd to find in the Acting. Other Ladies who saw it more than once, whose Quality and Vertue can sufficiently justifie any thing they design to favour, were pleas'd

*From Aphra Behn, *The Dutch Lover: A comedy Acted at the Dukes Theatre, written by Mrs. A. Bhen (sic)* (London: Printed for Thomas Dring . . . , 1673; Ann Arbor, MI: University Microfilms, 1973), pp. 27–28, microfilm: Early English Books, 1641–1700; 445:32. Reproduction of original in Huntington Library, San Marino, CA.

**From Aphra Behn, *The Luckey Chance, or, An Alderman's Bargain: A Comedy as Is Acted by Their Majesty's Servants, by Mrs. A. Behn* (London: Printed by R.H. for W. Canning, 1687; Ann Arbor, MI: University Microfilms International, 1981), excerpts from the "Preface." Microfilm: Early English Books, 1641–1700; 1195:10. Reproduction of original in the Bodleian Library, Oxford University, UK.

to say, they found an Entertainment in it very far from scandalous; and for the Generality of the Town, I found by my Receipts it was not thought so Criminal. However, that shall not be an Incouragement to me to trouble the Criticks with new Occasion of affronting me, for endeavouring at least to divert; and at this rate, both the few Poets that are left, and the Players who toil in vain will be weary of their Trade.

. . . All I ask, is the Priviledge for my Masculine Part the Poet in me, (if any such you will allow me) to tread in those successful Paths my Predecessors have so long thriv'd in, to take those Measures that both the Ancient and Modern Writers have set me, and by which they have pleas'd the World so well: If I must not, because of my Sex, have this Freedom, but that you will usurp all to your selves; I lay down my Quill, and you shall hear no more of me, no not so much as to make Comparisons, because I will be kinder to my Brothers of the Pen, than they have been to a defenceless Woman; for I am not content to write for a Third day only. I value Fame as much as if I had been born a *Hero;* and if you rob me of that, I can retire from the ungrateful World, and scorn its fickle Favours.

Anne Kingsmill Finch, Countess of Winchilsea (1661–1720)

Anne Finch was born in Southampton, England, to parents from wealthy upper-class families. Tragedy struck repeatedly in her youth. Her father, Sir William Kingsmill, died when she was an infant, her mother when she was three, and her stepfather when she was ten. Nevertheless, she was raised in aristocratic circles and given an excellent education. In 1683, she became a lady-in-waiting to the duchess of York, whose husband became James II. She met her future husband, Heneage Finch, at court, where he was a gentleman of the bedchamber for King James. Finch pursued her relentlessly, and they wed in 1684. After their marriage they lived in London where Finch filled various government positions. Their ties with the crown ended, however, when James II was deposed, and Finch, out of loyalty to his former patron and king, refused to take an oath of allegiance to the new rulers, William and Mary. Exiled from court, they lived in semi-poverty, dependent upon various relatives, until 1690, when Finch's nephew, the earl of Winchilsea, invited them to his estate. In 1712, the earl died, leaving Finch his title and estate.

Anne and Heneage had an unusually happy marriage. He was able to pursue his scholarly interests at the country estate, and with no children or domestic responsibilities, she was free to write. They enjoyed rural life, and she extolled its beauty in her poetry. Yet, they were not culturally isolated. Through his nephew, they met numerous writers, and soon had their own circle of intellectuals. Henry Fielding, Jonathan Swift, and Alexander Pope were among their literary acquaintances.

Finch began writing poetry when she lived at court but fearing ridicule, she hid it from others. Once on their estate, with her husband's support and the interest of friends who read her poems, her output increased. Still she didn't publish any of her work until 1713, and then the collection was published anonymously. Some of her poetry was only published after her death, and that in which she expressed her most controversial opinions remained unpublished. Finch wrote passionate love poetry to her husband and satirized society and people she thought acted irrationally. She also wrote about her battle with depression. The first reading is the introduction to her first book. Note the concerns and themes that appear in this and the poem that follows and her use of women's history.*

*Poems from Anne Kingsmill Finch, *The Poems of Anne, Countess of Winchilsea, from the original edition of 1713 and from Unpublished Manuscripts,* ed. Myra Reynolds, vol. 5 of The Decennial Publications of the University of Chicago, Series 2 (Chicago: The University of Chicago Press, 1902), pp. 4–6, 150–51.

THE INTRODUCTION

Did I, my lines intend for publick view,
How many censures, wou'd their faults
persue,
Some wou'd, because such words they
do affect,
Cry they're insipid, empty, uncorrect.
And many, have attained, dull and
untaught
The name of Witt, only by finding fault.
True judges, might condemn their want
of witt,
And all might say, they're by a Woman
writt.
Alas! a woman that attempts the pen,
Such an intruder on the rights of men,
Such a presumptuous Creature, is
esteem'd,
The fault, can by no vertue be redeem'd.
They toll us, we mistake our sex and
way;
Good breeding, fashion, dancing, dress-
ing, play
Are the accomplishments we shou'd
desire;
To write, or read, or think, or to enquire
Wou'd cloud our beauty, and exaust our
time,
And interrupt the Conquests of our
prime;
Whilst the dull mannage, of a servile
house
Is held by some, our outmost art, and use.
    Sure 'twas not ever thus, nor are we
told
Fables, of Women that excell'd of old;
To whom, by the diffusive hand of
Heaven
Some share of witt, and poetry was
given.
On that glad day, on which the Ark
return'd,
The holy pledge, for which the Land had
mourn'd,
The joyfull Tribes, attend itt on the way,
The Levites do the sacred Charge convey,

Whilst various Instruments, before itt
play;
Here, holy Virgins in the Concert joyn,
The louder notes, to soften, and refine,
And with alternate verse, compleat the
Hymn Devine.
Loe! the yong Poet, after Gods own
heart,
By Him inspired, and taught the Muses
Art,
Return'd from Conquest, a bright
Chorus meets,
That sing his slayn ten thousand in the
streets
In such loud numbers they his acts
declare,
Proclaim the wonders, of his early war,
That Saul upon the vast applause does
frown,
And feels, itts mighty thunder shake the
Crown.
What, can the threat'n'd Judgment now
prolong?
Half of the Kingdom is already gone;
The fairest half, whose influence guides
the rest,
Have David's Empire, o're their hearts
confess't.
    A Woman here, leads fainting Israel
on,
She fights, she wins, she tryumphs with
a song,
Devout, Majestick, for the subject fitt,
And far above her arms, exalts her witt,
Then, to the peacefull, shady Palm with-
draws,
And rules the rescu'd Nation, with her
Laws.
How are we fal'n, fal'n by mistaken
rules?
And Education's, more then Nature's
fools,
Debarr'd from all improve-ments of the
mind,
And to be dull, expected and dessigned;

And if some one, wou'd Soar above the
rest,
With warmer fancy, and ambition
press't,
So strong, th' opposing faction still
appears,
The hopes to thrive, can ne're outweigh
the fears,
Be caution'd then my Muse, and still
retir'd;

Nor be dispis'd aiming to be admir'd;
Conscious of wants, still with contracted
wing,
To some few freinds, and to thy sorrows
sing;
For groves of Laurell, thou wert never
meant;
Be dark enough thy shades, and be thou
there content.

THE UNEQUAL FETTERS

Cou'd we stop the time that's flying
Or recall itt when 'tis past
Put far off the day of Dying
Or make Youth for ever last
To Love wou'd then be worth our cost.

Free as Nature's first intention
Was to make us, I'll be found
Nor by subtle Man's invention
Yeild to be in Fetters bound
By one that walks a freer round.

But since we must loose those Graces
Which at first your hearts have wonne
And you seek for in new Faces
When our Spring of Life is done
It wou'd but urge our ruine on

Marriage does but slightly tye Men
Whil'st close Pris'ners we remain
They the larger Slaves of Hymen
Still are begging Love again
At the full length of all their chain.

SUGGESTED READINGS

Altaba-Artal, Dolors. *Aphra Behn's English Feminism: Wit and Satire.* Selinsgrove, PA: Susquehanna University Press; London: Associated University Presses, 1999.

Merrim, Stephanie. *Early Modern Women's Writing and Sor Juana Inés de la Cruz.* Nashville, TN: Vanderbilt University Press, 1999.

Paz, Octavio. *Sor Juana or, The Traps of Faith.* Translated by Margaret Sayers Peden. Cambridge, MA: Harvard University Press, 1988.

Rosenmeier, Rosamund. *Anne Bradstreet Revisited.* Boston: Twayne, 1991.

Rosenthal, Laura. *Playwrights and Plagiarists in Early Modern England: Gender, Authorship, Literary Property.* Ithaca, NY: Cornell University Press, 1996.

Scheick, William J. *Authority and Female Authorship in Colonial America.* Lexington, University of Kentucky Press, 1998.

Wade, Elizabeth. *Anne Bradstreet, "The Tenth Muse."* New York: Oxford University Press, 1971.

Wilson, John H. *All the King's Ladies: Actresses of the Restoration.* Chicago: University of Chicago Press, 1958.

PART II

WOMEN AND CULTURE, 1750–1920

Part II investigates women's contributions to culture from the mid-eighteenth century to about 1920, with particular emphasis on the nineteenth century. The five chapters in this part are organized primarily along thematic lines and include documents by and about American as well as European women.

Chapter 6, "Age of the Enlightenment and Revolutions," begins by focusing on two artists whose careers spanned most of the second half of the eighteenth century. Their lives and work illustrate some of the momentous changes in political and artistic institutions, patronage, and popular tastes that occurred in the late eighteenth century. The second section examines women's involvement in the Enlightenment. It also shows how Enlightenment thinkers addressed the "woman question," and how American and French women addressed some of the political and gender issues raised during their respective revolutions.

Chapters 7 through 10 focus on women and culture in the nineteenth century, with particular attention to how the pervasive gender ideology popularly known as the Victorian ideal affected female creativity. Chapter 7, "The Victorian Ideal: Writers and Musicians," includes documents by a few of the many literary women who emerged in the nineteenth century and material by and about women musicians. It also introduces the new scientific theories that re-enforced traditional notions of gender differences. In Chapter 8, "The Victorian Ideal: The Performing and Visual Arts," we turn our attention to the visual and performing arts. Texts in this chapter treat us to glimpses of the lives, careers, and ideas of ballerinas, actresses, sculptors, and artists, many of whom pioneered new directions in their field. It also highlights the gains women had made in many professions by 1893. Chapter 9, "Challenging Orthodoxy: Women and Religion in America," is divided into three sections. The first section presents documents by and about women who were founders and leaders of religions in America. The second focuses on women's struggles to gain full participation in religious affairs. The final section consists of feminist critiques of the Bible and patriarchal features of established religions. Chapter 10, "The 'New Woman' and the Performing Arts," examines the "new woman" in the performing arts. It highlights the pioneers of modern dance and women involved in the development of new theater and the woman suffrage movement.

The documents in Part II illustrate the complex ways in which major developments in the eighteenth and nineteenth centuries affected women's lives and creative options. Those developments included an array of new ideas and expectations that emerged from the Enlightenment, the American and French Revolutions, the Scientific Revolution, and new social and economic ideologies such as Marxism and socialism. Women were also affected markedly by the Industrial Revolution and the new communications and transportation technology. Together these developments delayed marriage and child rearing; changed family roles; widened educational and employment opportunities; created new mass markets and audiences for writers, artists, and performers; and facilitated travel and the creation of international networks of people with similar interests.

While these developments brought greater opportunities for many women, particularly of the middle classes, barriers of gender, class, and race continued to inhibit the development and expression of female creativity. To some extent, these changes created a kind of backlash that re-enforced notions of essential gender differences and brought renewed pressure for women to remain in their traditional roles. Indeed, Enlightenment and revolutionary ideologies drew heavily from classical political and social theory, thus resulting in renewed emphases on separate spheres for men and women and the confinement of women to the private sphere.

As the documents reveal, however, there were other forces at work that countered the conservative trends. In particular, waves of evangelical revivals and the abolition movement in America, utopian and socialist movements in Europe and America, and the woman's rights movements of America and Western Europe helped foster female creativity. Men and women in the abolition, socialist, and utopian movements encouraged women to pursue new options and supported their creative and unconventional endeavors financially and emotionally. In particular, networks of woman's rights advocates provided significant moral, financial, and institutional support for their sisters in the arts. These social radicals enabled women of lower classes and minority groups (notably African-American women) to develop their talents as well. Finally, groups of creative women were able to pool their resources and create living arrangements and networks that enabled them to work and live independent lives.

For many reasons, then, Part II reveals a significant increase in women's public participation in creating culture and in the recognition creative women received.

Chapter 6

Age of the Enlightenment and Revolutions

ARTISTS IN THE EIGHTEENTH CENTURY

Women artists continued to face major gender barriers in the eighteenth century. They were still denied access to training in the art academies that nurtured male talent; forbidden to study and paint nude models, and hence unable to acquire the anatomical knowledge necessary for completing grand history paintings; and rarely achieved admission to the academies that opened doors to patronage. Nevertheless, a number of women artists emerged in France and elsewhere, generally by virtue of being born into artistic families and being trained by their fathers. These women specialized in flower painting or still life and portraiture, art genres that did not require knowledge of male anatomy. Several of these artists were admitted to the French Academy after Carriera: Anne Vallayer-Coster (still-life and flower painter, elected 1770) and portrait painters Adélaïde Labille-Guiard, and Elisabeth Vigée-Lebrun (1783). Unfortunately, most women left few documents other than their art. The two artists discussed in the following sections, however, are an exception, both by virtue of the letters and memoirs they left and also the recognition each earned. Note the factors that enabled each woman to build a successful career and how gender shaped the life, work, and public and critical reception of each artist.

Angelica Kauffmann (1741–1807): Swiss Neoclassical Artist

Angelica Kauffmann was an important Neoclassical painter, and one of the few women who produced history paintings. She was born in Switzerland but spent her childhood traveling in Switzerland, Italy, and Austria as her father filled art commissions. She received art training from her father, who also encouraged the development of her musical talent. For some time, Kauffmann was deeply torn between her twin passions for music and art but decided that to succeed professionally she would have to choose between painting and studying to be an opera singer. One of her most celebrated paintings, *The Artist Hesitating between the Arts of Music and Painting,* is a self-portrait that depicts her making the decision as the figure Painting points toward the temple of fame. In 1763, Kauffmann and her father moved to Rome where she met a group of painters who were in the vanguard of the Neoclassical movement. One of its leaders was the German classical scholar and art critic Abbé Winckelmann, whose description of her follows. She became one of the leading exponents of the new style.

Kauffmann moved to London in 1766, where she was an instant success, thanks in part to her friendship with Britain's leading artist Sir Joshua Reynolds. One London admirer noted: "She shared with hoops of extra magnitude, toupees of superabundant floweriness, shoe-heels of vividest scarlet and china monsters of superlative ugliness, the privilege of being the rage" (Manners 1924, 20). Initially she exhibited her paintings with the Free Society in the open art market and supported herself by painting portraits of Britain's aristocrats, intellectuals, and artists. After she was established however, she began to do history paintings based on classical and medieval subjects. She was the first female painter to challenge the male monopoly in history painting, the quintessential masculine genre that had been designated the highest art form by the royal academies. Kauffmann helped popularize Neoclassical art in England and was soon regarded as one of England's premier artists. In 1769, when the British Royal Academy was founded, she and Mary Moser, a flower painter, were the only women among the founding members. No other woman was admitted to the Academy until 1922. In 1767 she married a man who nearly squandered her earnings. His death freed her from financial ruin.

In 1781 Kauffmann married architect Antonio Zucchi, and they moved to Rome. Zucchi handled her business and was supportive of her career. She developed lasting friendships with many of her patrons and had a close relationship with the German writer Goethe. She completed some of her best history paintings in Rome. Several depicted famous women: *Sappho; Cleopatra Adorning the Tomb of Marc Antony;* and, perhaps her most famous work, *Cornelia Pointing to Her Children as Her Treasures.* When she died, artists from all over Europe and members of the Roman Academy of St. Luke, of which she was a member, marched in the funeral procession carrying some of her paintings aloft (Manners 1924, 111–13). The selections that follow reveal facets of her personality and her friendships and how she was regarded by contemporaries. Also note the light some shed on notions of gender.

Abbé Winckelmann to Mr. Franck, 16 July 1764*

> I have just been painted by a stranger, a young person of rare merit. She is very eminent in portraits in oil, mine is a half-length, and she has made an etching of it as a present to me. She speaks Italian as well as German, and expresses herself with the same facility in French and English, on which account she paints all the English who visit Rome. She sings with a taste which ranks her amongst our greatest *virtuosi.* Her name is Angelica Kauffmann.

A Critic's View of *Hector and Andromache,* the Painting That Ensured Kauffmann's Admission to the British Royal Academy**

> The defects in her method, (grave ones, I own), are in my opinion, counterbalanced by the many beauties of thought and feeling with which her work is permeated. . . .

*From Victoria A. E. Dorothy Manners, *Angelica Kauffmann, R.A., Her Life and Her Works,* by Lady Victoria Manners and Dr. G. C. Williamson* (London: John Lane, 1924), p. 14.

**Excerpt from letter of 15 September 1768 to unknown recipient written by Count Bernsdorff, art patron and Danish Prime Minister, quoted in Manners, *Angelica Kauffmann,* p. 37.

She shows great wisdom in her choice of a subject. . . . Her composition is full of grace, and the figures have the quiet dignity of the Greek models. Her women are most womanly, modest and loving, and she conveys with much art the proper relation between the sexes, the dependence of the weaker on the stronger, which appeals very much to her masculine critics.

GOETHE'S REFLECTIONS ON KAUFFMANN, 1788*

Considering her great talent and her fortune, she is not as happy as she deserved to be. She is tired of commissions, but her old husband thinks it is wonderful that so much money should roll in for what is often easy work. She would like to paint to please herself and have more leisure to study and take pains, and she could do exactly this. They have no children, and they cannot even spend the interest on her capital: indeed they could live on the money she earns every day by working moderately hard. But she does not do anything about it and she won't. She talks to me very frankly: I have told her my opinion, given her advice and I try to cheer her up whenever we meet. What's the use of talking about misery and misfortune when people who have enough of everything do not know how to use or enjoy it? For a woman she has extraordinary talent. One must look for what she does, not what she fails to do. How many artists would stand the test if they were judged only by their failings?

One of Kauffmann's closest friends after 1789 was a wealthy patron of the arts, Anna Amalia, duchess of Saxe-Weimar. During her residence in Italy from 1789 to 1791, the duchess was the center of a circle of prominent Romans and foreigners that included the pope, cardinals, government ministers, artists, musicians, and scholars. She and Kauffmann shared a love of art as well as affection and admiration for Goethe.

ANNA AMALIA TO ANGELICA: FROM NAPLES, 7TH OF SEPTEMBER, 1789**

The love and friendship which I feel for you, dear Angelica, makes me confident that you will forgive my disturbing your occupations with this letter, but it is *intolerable* to be so long without hearing from you. How is your health, my dear little woman, and are you always busy, always at your easel? Come to Naples, come to us! Tell dear old Zucchi to bring you, and put before him, in your own sweet way, what splendid designs and beautiful new ideas he will find here. Goethe is going to send you his Tasso, but perhaps you have it already. When you read it, think of the little room in the Villa d'Este; there one can enjoy it thoroughly. I will no longer take up your time, which is very much better employed at your delightful art, so farewell, dearest, best of little women; think of me often, as I do of you.—YOUR AMALIE.

---

*From Dorothy Moulton Mayer, *Angelica Kauffmann, R. A. 1741–1807* (Gerrards Cross, UK: Colin Smythe Ltd., 1972), p. 134. By permission of Colin Smythe, Ltd.

**From Victoria A. E. Dorothy Manners, *Angelica Kauffmann*, pp. 79–80.

Elisabeth Vigée-Lebrun on Kauffmann and Her Work*

ON SEEING A PORTRAIT BY KAUFFMANN IN THE UFFIZI GALLERY:

I noticed with a certain pride the portrait of Angelica Kauffmann, one of the glories of our sex.

VIGÉE-LEBRUN LETTER FROM ROME TO HUBERT ROBERT, 1 DECEMBER 1789

I found her very interesting, apart from her talents, on account of her intelligence and her knowledge. She is a woman of about fifty, very delicate, her health having suffered in consequence of her marriage in the first instance with an adventurer who had ruined her. She has since been married again, to an architect, who acts as her man of business. She has talked with me a great deal and very well, during the two evenings that I have spent with her. Her conversation is agreeable. . . . Angelica possesses some paintings by the great Masters. I saw several of her own works; her sketches pleased me more than her pictures, because their colouring is like that of Titian. . . .

Elisabeth Vigée-Lebrun (1755–1842): French Portrait Artist

Elisabeth Vigée-Lebrun was a prolific and popular portrait painter of the French aristocracy during the reign of Louis XVI and the European aristocracy and royalty into the early nineteenth century. She painted over 800 portraits and landscapes and was one of the highest paid artists of her time. In her early twenties, she became Marie Antoinette's official portrait painter and a close friend of the young queen. Despite opposition, she was one of four women elected to the French Royal Academy in the eighteenth century. After the election of both Vigée-Lebrun and Adélaïde Labille-Guïard in 1783, the Academy restored the prohibition on female members. Her most famous painting was a politically motivated work in a classical style, *Marie Antoinette and Her Children* (1787), in which she depicted the queen as a devoted mother. The portrait was intended to counter the slanderous depictions of the queen mounted by antiroyalists as a promiscuous, immoral, spendthrift.

Vigée-Lebrun got started in her career with the help of her father, a portrait painter who was influenced by Rosalba Carriera. He trained her and she took over his commissions when he died. When her mother remarried, her stepfather took control of her income. To escape him, she married Jean Lebrun. When the French Revolution broke out, she was forced to leave France because of her close connection with the royal family. She fled to Italy and then worked in courts all across Europe. She was elected to membership in the academies of Rome, Florence, Bologna, St. Petersburg (Russia), and Berlin. Thanks to a petition signed by over 200 French artists, Napoleon allowed her to return to France and even gave her some commissions. Her memoirs provide delightful glimpses of her life and the lifestyle of the European aristocracy and wonderful verbal sketches, drawn with a painter's eye, of her patrons and acquaintances. Some also illustrate the gender dynamics that nearly all women confronted.

---

*Excerpts from Vigée-Lebrun letter to unknown recipient in November, 1789, and letter to Hubert Robert, quoted in Manners, *Angelica Kauffmann*, p. 83.

Excerpts from Vigée-Lebrun's Memoirs, *Souvenirs**

[At boarding school, age 6–11]

. . . During that time, I scrawled on everything at all seasons; my copy-books, and even my schoolmates'. . . . on the walls of the dormitory I drew faces and landscapes with coloured chalks. So it may easily be imagined how often I was condemned to bread and water. . . . At seven or eight, I remember, I made a picture by lamplight of a man with a beard, which I have kept until this very day. When my father saw it he went into transports of joy, exclaiming, "You will be a painter, child, if ever there was one!"

[Her Marriage]

My stepfather having retired from business, we took up residence at the Lubert mansion. . . . M. Lebrun had just bought the house and lived there himself, and as soon as we were settled in it I began to examine the splendid masterpieces of all schools with which his lodgings were filled. . . . M. Lebrun was so obliging as to lend me, for purposes of copying, some of his handsomest and most valuable paintings. Thus I owed him the best lessons I could conceivably have obtained, when, after a lapse of six months, he asked my hand in marriage. I was far from wishing to become his wife, though he was very well built and had a pleasant face. I was then twenty years old, and was living without anxiety as to the future, since I was already earning a deal of money, so that I felt no manner of inclination for matrimony. But my mother, who believed M. Lebrun to be very rich, incessantly plied me with arguments in favour of accepting such an advantageous match. At last I decided in the affirmative, urged especially by the desire to escape from the torture of living with my stepfather, whose bad temper had increased day by day since he had relinquished active pursuits. So little, however, did I feel inclined to sacrifice my liberty that, even on my way to church, I kept saying to myself, "Shall I say yes, or shall I say no?" Alas! I said yes, and in so doing exchanged present troubles for others. Not that M. Lebrun was a cruel man: . . . he was . . . quite an agreeable person. But his furious passion for gambling was at the bottom of the ruin of his fortune and my own, of which he had the entire disposal, so that in 1789, when I quitted France, I had not an income of twenty francs, although I had earned more than a million. He had squandered it all.

[Marie Antoinette]

It was in the year 1779 that I painted the Queen for the first time; she was then in the heyday of her youth and beauty. Marie Antoinette was tall and admirably built, being somewhat stout, but not excessively so. Her arms were superb, her hands small and perfectly formed, and her feet charming. She had the best walk of any woman in France, carrying her head erect with a dignity that stamped her queen in the midst of her whole court, . . .

. . . I was so fortunate as to be on very pleasant terms with the Queen. When she heard that I had something of a voice we rarely had a sitting without singing some duets . . . , for she was exceedingly fond of music, although she did not sing very true. . . . the kindness she always bestowed upon me has ever been one of my sweetest memories.

*Excerpts from Elisabeth Vigée-Lebrun, *Memoirs of Madame Vigée Lebrun,* trans. Lionel Strachey (New York: Doubleday, Page & Company, 1903), pp. 3, 20–21, 25, 27, 34–35, 172, 188–89, 210.

[Election to Royal Academy, 1783]

[The picture**] delighted and inspired me to such a degree that I made a portrait of myself at Brussels, striving to obtain the same effects. I painted myself with a straw hat on my head, a feather, and a garland of wild flowers, holding my palette in my hand. And when the portrait was exhibited at the Salon I feel free to confess that it added considerably to my reputation. . . . Soon after my return from Flanders, the portrait I had mentioned, and several other works of mine, were the cause of Joseph Vernet's decision to propose me as a member of the Royal Academy of Painting. M. Pierre, then first Painter to the King, made strong opposition, not wishing, he said, that women should be admitted, although Mme. Vallayer-Coster, who painted flowers beautifully, had already been admitted, and I think Mme. Vien had been, too. M. Pierre, a very mediocre painter, was a clever man. Besides, he was rich, and this enabled him to entertain artists luxuriously. Artists were not so well off in those days as they are now. His opposition might have become fatal to me if all true picture-lovers had not been associated with the Academy, and if they had not formed a cabal, in my favour, against M. Pierre's. At last I was admitted, and presented my picture "Peace Bringing Back Plenty. . . ."

[Her Return to France]

I will not attempt to describe my feelings at setting foot on the soil of France, from which I had been absent twelve years. I was stirred by terror, grief and joy in turn. I mourned the friends who had died on the scaffold; but I was to see those again who still lived. This France, that I was entering once more, had been the scene of horrible crimes. But this France was my country.

[Her Response to an English Critic, 1802]

Sir: I understand that in your work on painting you speak of the French school. As, from what is reported to me concerning your remarks, I gather that you have not the least idea of that school, . . . I presume, in the first place, that you do not attack the great artists who lived in the reign of Louis XIV. . . . As for the artists of the day, you do the French school the greatest injustice in rating it by its achievements of thirty years ago. Since then it has made enormous strides in a branch totally different from that signalising its decline. . . . We have since produced David, . . . and a number of others I might cite.

It is not surprising that after criticising the works of David, which you evidently do not know at all, you do me the honour of criticising mine, which you know no better. . . .

[Rediscovering Her Portrait of Queen Marie Antoinette and Her Children]

Under Bonaparte, the large portrait I had made of the Queen and her children had been relegated to a corner of the palace of Versailles. I left Paris one morning to take a glance at it. Arrived at the royal gate, a guard escorted me to the room which contained the picture, and which was forbidden the public. The custodian who admitted us recognised me from having seen me in Rome, and exclaimed, "Oh, how glad I am to welcome Mme. Lebrun here!" He hastened to turn my picture round, which was facing the wall, since Bonaparte, after learning that many came to look at it, had ordered its removal. The order, as is plain, was very badly obeyed, since the exhibition of

___

**The picture referred to was Peter Paul Rubens's portrait of a woman, entitled *Straw Hat*.

the picture continued, and this to such a degree that the custodian, when I wanted to give him a trifle, persisted in declining it, saying that I had earned him enough money. When the Restoration came, this picture was reexhibited at the Salon. . . .

THE ENLIGHTENMENT, REVOLUTIONS, AND WOMEN

The intellectual ferment of the Enlightenment and the political upheavals wrought by the American and French Revolutions raised new possibilities for women. Critiques of European institutions and new theories of limited government and natural rights had the potential to profoundly change gender relations and women's legal, political, and economic status. Sensing this, women were eager participants in these intellectual and political movements. French women created salons that provided forums for the *philosophes* to present and argue their new theories of government and society, while some English women, known as the "bluestockings," debated the new ideas among themselves and with male intellectuals. Women in Europe and North America popularized and disseminated the new theories to others of their sex through women's magazines and discussed them in their informal societies. Women also participated in the American and French Revolutions as propagandists, combatants, spies, leaders of boycotts, and supporters of revolutionary leaders.

Inevitably, gender became part of the Enlightenment and revolutionary discourse. To some extent, woman served as an allegorical inspiration for revolutionaries. More importantly, discussions of natural rights and the right of the people to a voice in their government raised questions about women's rights. Were women included in the notion that "all men are equal" and entitled to "inalienable rights"? Did government by consent of the people include the fair sex? Did the demands of the Third Estate in France for participation in governance include the women of that class? Should the family be scrutinized and reshaped as well as political, religious, and economic institutions? Should property rights extend to women? These issues were discussed by both men and women, in philosophical as well as political terms. The promise of significant changes in gender relations, however, was circumscribed by the eighteenth-century reverence for classical models, notably, the Athenian and Roman Republics. Predictably, this resulted in a renewed emphasis on private virtue as a basis of political stability, on the division of society into distinct classes, and on separate spheres for men and women. For myriad reasons, the notion that women were equal to, but different from, men held sway.

The first reading, from a book by Jean Jacques Rousseau, is one of the more extreme examples of a *philosophe's* theories about women. The remaining documents show how women of diverse backgrounds and nationalities responded to the potential for change embodied in the ideas of the Enlightenment and the revolutions, participated in the debates, and struggled to reconcile conflicting notions of gender. They also illustrate the continuing clash between patriarchal definitions of woman and an emerging feminist vision. As you read the selections, look for the patriarchal or traditionalist definition of womanhood and its justifications as expressed implicitly and explicitly in Rousseau's work *and* in the women's writings. Note how women countered these views, how their visions of a new society compared with Rousseau's, and the extent to which they fundamentally challenged the social order.

Jean Jacques Rousseau (1712–1778): French Philosopher

Rousseau was a controversial figure even among the *philosophes,* or French philosophers. He offered a more radical critique of the social order as he championed the idea of the "natural man," unspoiled by civilization, and argued that individual freedom had been corrupted by the growth of society. Some of the *philosophes* did address the inequities of marriage and education and women's legal and economic status. None, however, proposed a radical restructuring of gender relations, or proposed that women be part of the body politic. Rousseau was one of the most misogynous of the *philosophes,* but his views of gender largely became the norm. His views are set forth in his novel *Émile,* which describes the education the "natural man" should receive. One chapter deals with the education Émile's mythical wife Sophie should receive and delineates the qualities and behavior appropriate to a woman. How should her education differ from his, and why?

THE EDUCATION OF WOMAN FROM *ÉMILE,* 1762*

In the union of the sexes each contributes equally toward the common end, but not in the same way. Hence arises the first assignable difference among their moral relations. One must be active and strong, the other passive and weak. One must needs have power and will, while it suffices that the other have little power of resistance.

The moment it is demonstrated that man and woman are not and ought not to be constituted in the same way, either in character or in constitution, it follows that they ought not to have the same education. In following the directions of Nature they ought to act in concert, but they ought not to do the same things; their duties have a common end, but the duties themselves are different. . . . After having tried to form the natural man, let us also see . . . how the woman is to be formed who is befitting to this man. . . .

. . . the whole education of women ought to be relative to men. To please them, to be useful to them, to make themselves loved and honored by them, to educate them when young, to care for them when grown, to counsel them, to console them, and to make life agreeable and sweet to them—these are the duties of women at all times, and what should be taught them from their infancy.

. . . Girls ought to be heedful and industrious, and this is not all; they ought early to be brought under restraint. . . . As long as they live they will be subject to the most continual and the most severe restraint—that which is imposed by the laws of decorum. They must early be trained to restraint, to the end that it may cost them nothing; and to conquer all their whims, in order to subject them to the wills of others . . . .

There results from this habitual restraint a docility which women need during their whole life, since they never cease to be subject either to a man or to the judgments of men, and they are never allowed to place themselves above these judgments. The first and most important quality of a woman is gentleness. Made to obey a being as imperfect as man, often so full of vices, and always so full of faults, she ought early to learn to suffer even injustice, and to endure the wrongs of a husband without complaint; . . .

For the reason that the conduct of woman is subject to public opinion, her belief is subject to authority. Every daughter should have the religion of her mother, and every wife that of her husband. Even were this religion false, the docility which makes the mother and the daughter submit to the order of nature expunges in the

*Excerpts from Jean Jacques Rousseau, *Émile: or, Treatise on Education,* trans. William H. Payne, vol. 20 International Education series, ed. William T. Harris (New York: D. Appleton, 1907), pp. 260–61, 263, 268, 270, 275–76, 281–82.

sight of God the sin of error. As they are not in a condition to judge for themselves, women should receive the decision of fathers and husbands as they would the decision of the Church. . . .

The search for abstract and speculative truths, principles, and scientific axioms, whatever tends to generalize ideas, does not fall within the compass of women; all their studies ought to have reference to the practical; . . . All the reflections of women which are not immediately connected with their duties ought to be directed to the study of men and to that pleasure-giving knowledge which has only taste for its object; for as to works of genius, they are out of their reach, nor have they sufficient accuracy and attention to succeed in the exact sciences; . . . Whatever her sex can not do for itself, and which is necessary or agreeable to her, she must have the art of making us desire. She must therefore make a profound study of the mind of man, not the mind of man in general, through abstraction, but the mind of men to whom she is subject, either by law or by opinion. She must learn to penetrate their feelings through their conversation, their actions, their looks, and their gestures. . . . Woman has more spirit and man more genius; woman observes and man reasons. . . .

Judith Sargent Murray (1751–1820): American Poet, Essayist, and Playwright

Judith Sargent Murray was the author of poetry, fiction, essays, and plays. She began to publish her essays and poetry in 1784 in various New England magazines under the pen name Constantia, and in 1798 she published a three-volume collection of her works as *The Gleaner*. Two of her comedies were produced and had a short run at Boston's Federal Street Theater. She was the first American-born woman whose work was performed in Boston. Her essays cover many subjects including politics, religion, morals, and money, but the majority of her works deal with gender relations. Hers was an important voice in America's post-revolutionary debate about women's place in the new republic.

Judith Sargent was a member of a prominent merchant family in Gloucester, Massachusetts. At an early age she became aware of her gender when she was given a limited education of some reading, writing, religion, and sewing instruction deemed appropriate for a girl. She resented the fact that her brother was able to study the classics under tutors and then attend the Boston Latin School and Harvard. Like many other girls in America and Europe, she was largely self-educated. She read widely in Enlightenment philosophy, Shakespeare, and European novels and also works by her countrymen and women. At age 25, she rejected the Puritan faith in which she was raised and converted to Universalism, a new, more egalitarian Protestant faith. Her conversion cost her dearly in terms of her social standing in the community, but it strengthened her intellectual independence and her determination to challenge all forms of tyranny. The Universalists' belief in individual interpretation of the Bible enabled her to develop biblical arguments for the equality of women. Through the Universalist Church, she also met her second husband, John Murray (her first had died early in their marriage). Pastor Murray was the leader of the church and became her mentor and loyal supporter throughout their marriage.

The readings are from some of her most famous works. She also wrote a four-part essay in which she used examples of many of the creative women from ancient history through the seventeenth century we have encountered in earlier chapters to make her case for the equality of the sexes. Compare her views with those of Rousseau and the women whose works follow.

DESULTORY THOUGHTS BY CONSTANTIA, 22 OCTOBER 1784*

... A young lady, growing up with the idea, that she possesses few, or no personal attractions, and that her mental abilities are of an inferior kind, imbibing at the same time, a most melancholy idea of a female, descending down the vale of life in an unprotected state; taught also to regard her character [as] ridiculously contemptible, will, too probably, throw herself away upon the first who approaches her with tenders of love, however indifferent may be her chance for happiness, [lest] ... she may never be so happy as to meet a second offer, and must then inevitably be stigmatised with that dreaded title, an Old Maid, must rank with a class whom she has been accustomed to regard as burthens upon society, and objects whom she might with impunity turn into ridicule! ... to prevent which great evil, I would early impress under proper regulations, a reverence of self; I would endeavour to rear to worth, and a consciousness thereof; I would be solicitous to inspire the glow of virtue, with that elevation of soul, that dignity, which is ever attendant upon self-approbation, arising from the genuine source of innate rectitude.

ON THE EQUALITY OF THE SEXES**

That minds are not alike, full well I
    know,
This truth each day's experience will show;
To heights surprising some great spirits
    soar,
With inborn strength mysterious depths
    explore;
Their eager gaze surveys the path of
    light,
Confest it stood to Newton's piercing
    sight. ....
Yet cannot I their sentiments imbibe,
Who this distinction to the sex
    ascribe,
As if a woman's form must needs
    enrol,
A weak, a servile an inferiour soul;
And that the guise of man must still
    proclaim,

Greatness of mind, and him, to be the
    same;
Yet as the hours revolve fair proofs arise,
Which the bright wreath of growing
    fame supplies;
And in past times some men have *sunk
    so low,*
That female records nothing less can
    show.
But imbecility is still confin'd,
And by the lordly sex to us consign'd;
They rob us of the power t' improve,
And then declare we only trifles
    love;
Yet haste the era, when the world shall
    know,
That such distinctions only dwell
    below;
The soul unfetter'd, to no sex confin'd,

*Excerpts from Constantia, "Desultory Thoughts, &c.," in *The Gentleman and Lady's Town and Country Magazine: or, Repository of Instruction and Entertainment* (Boston: Weeden and Barrett, 1784; Ann Arbor, MI: University Microfilms, 1942), I, no. 6 (October 1784), p. 253, microfilm: American Periodical Series, Eighteenth Century, 13.

**From Judith Sargent Murray, "On the Equality of the Sexes," *The Massachusetts Magazine, or Monthly Museum of Knowledge and Rational Entertainment* (Boston: Isaiah Thomas and Co.; Ann Arbor, MI: University Microfilms, 1942), II, no. 3 (March 1790), pp.132–35; II, no. 4 (April 1790), pp. 224–25, microfilm: American Periodical Series, Eighteenth Century, 15.

Was for the abodes of cloudless day
    designed
Mean time we emulate their manly fires,
Though erudition all their thoughts
    inspires,

Yet nature with *equality* imparts,
And *noble passions,* swell e'en *female
    hearts.*

Is it upon mature consideration we adopt the idea, that nature is thus partial in her distributions? Is it indeed a fact, that she hath yielded to one half of the human species so unquestionable a mental superiority? . . . Yet it may be questioned, from what doth this superiority, in this determining faculty of the soul, proceed. May we not trace its source in the difference of education, and continued advantages? Will it be said that the judgment of a male of two years old, is more sage than that of a female's of the same age? I believe the reverse is generally observed to be true. But from that period what partiality! how is the one exalted and the other depressed, by the contrary modes of education which are adopted! the one is taught to aspire, and the other is early confined and limited. As their years increase, the sister must be wholly domesticated, while the brother is led by the hand through all the flowery paths of science. . . .

Will it be urged that those acquirements would supersede our domestick duties. I answer that every requisite in female economy is easily attained; and, . . . that when once attained, they require no further *mental attention.* Nay, while we are pursuing the needle, or the superintendency of the family, I repeat, that our minds are at full liberty for reflection; that imagination may exert itself in full vigor; and that if a just foundation is early laid, our ideas will then be worthy of rational beings. . . . Should it still be vociferated, "Your domestick employments are sufficient"—I would calmly ask, is it reasonable, that a candidate for immortality, for the joys of heaven, an intelligent being, who is to spend an eternity in contemplating the works of Deity, should at present be so degraded, as to be allowed no other ideas, than those which are suggested by the mechanism of a pudding, or the sewing of the seams of a garment? Pity that all such censurers of female improvement do not go one step further, and deny their future existence; to be consistent they surely ought.

Yes, ye lordly, ye haughty sex, our souls are by nature *equal* to yours; the same breath of God animates, enlivens, and invigorates us; and that we are not fallen lower than yourselves, let those witness who have greatly towered above the various discouragements by which they have been so heavily oppressed; and though I am unacquainted with the list of celebrated characters on either side, yet from the observations I have made in the contracted circle in which I have moved, I dare confidently believe, that from the commencement of time to the present day, there, hath been as many females, as males, who, by *the mere force of natural powers,* have merited the crown of applause; who, *thus unassisted,* have seized the wreath of fame. I know there are those who assert, that as the animal powers of the one sex are superiour, of course their mental faculties also must be stronger; . . . But if this reasoning is just, man must be content to yield the palm to many of the brute creation, since by not a few of his brethren of the field, he is far surpassed in bodily strength. Moreover, was this argument admitted, it would prove too much, for occular demonstration evinceth, that there are many robust masculine ladies, and effeminate gentlemen. . . . Besides, were we to grant that animal strength proved anything, taking into consideration the accustomed impartiality of nature, we should be induced to imagine, that she had invested the female mind with superiour strength as an equivalent for the bodily powers of man. But waving this however palpable advantage, for *equality only,* we wish to contend.

[On Eve and Biblical Justifications for the Subordination of Women]

... woman was first in the transgression. Strange how blind *self love* renders you men; were you not wholly absorbed in a partial admiration of your own abilities, you would long since have acknowledged the force of what I am now going to urge. It is true some ignoramuses absurdly enough informed us, that the beauteous fair of paradise was seduced from her obedience, by a malignant demon, in the guise of *a baleful serpent*; but we, who are better informed, know that the fallen spirit presented himself to her view, *a shining angel still*; for thus, saith the criticks in the Hebrew tongue, ought the word to be rendered. Let us examine her motive— Hark! the seraph declares that she shall attain a perfection of knowledge; ... It doth not appear that she was governed by any one sensual appetite; but merely by a desire of adorning her mind; ... a thirst for knowledge impelled the predilection so fatal in its consequences. Adam could not plead the same deception; ... His gentle partner stood before him, a melancholy instance of the direful effects of disobedience; he saw her not possessed of that wisdom which she had fondly hoped to obtain, but he beheld the once blooming female, disrobed of that innocence, which had heretofore rendered her so lovely. To him then deception became impossible, as he had proof positive of the fallacy of the argument, which the deceiver had suggested. ... What mighty cause impelled him to sacrifice myriads of beings yet unborn, and by one impious act, which *he saw* would be productive of such fatal effect, entail undistinguished ruin upon a race of beings, which he was yet to produce. Blush, ... ye haughty lords of the creation; blush when ye remember, that he was influenced by no other motive than a bare pusillanimous attachment to a woman! by sentiments so exquisitely soft, that all his sons have, from that period, when they have designed to degrade them, described as highly feminine. Thus it should see, that all the arts of the grand deceiver ... were requisite to mislead our general mother, while the father of mankind forfeited his own, and relinquished the happiness of posterity, merely in compliance with the blandishments of a female.

Olympe de Gouges (1748–1793): French Writer and Royalist

Olympe de Gouges was a novelist, playwright, and political pamphleteer. Born Marie Gouze, she was the self-educated daughter of a French butcher. She assumed her pen name after moving to Paris. Despite the radical nature of some of her works, she was a royalist and addressed her political pamphlets to her royal patrons. Her *Les Droits de la femme* (*The Rights of Woman*) was addressed to Marie Antoinette, whom she urged to take up the cause of women and lead a revolution of morals. By defending the "unfortunate sex," she argued, the queen would win the support of half of the kingdom and many men as well (Bell and Offen 1983, 98–99). Her appeal is modeled after the *French Declaration of the Rights of Man* (1789). In similar fashion, American feminist Elizabeth Cady Stanton would model her 1848 feminist manifesto *The Declaration of Sentiments* after the American Declaration of Independence. De Gouges, however, went beyond the traditional rights of man and ended her appeal with a provocative proposal (not included in the following excerpt) for a new marriage contract that would protect women from exploitation by men and guarantee legitimacy and financial support to children born out of wedlock. In 1793, she was guillotined by the Jacobins for her royalist politics and for challenging the gender order. Note how she uses Enlightenment principles of natural rights in the declaration and consider why her work might be deemed radical.

THE RIGHTS OF WOMAN, PARIS, 1791*

Man, are you capable of being just? It is a woman who asks you this question; at least you will not deny her this right. Tell me! Who has given you the sovereign authority to oppress my sex? Your strength? Your talents? Observe the creator in his wisdom; regard nature in all her grandeur, with which you seem to want to compare yourself; and give me, if you dare, an example of this tyrannical empire. Go back to the animals, consult the elements, study the plants, then glance over all the modifications of organized matter, and cede to the evidence when I offer you the means. Seek, search, and distinguish, if you can, the sexes in the administration of nature. Everywhere you will find them mingled, everywhere they cooperate in harmony with this immortal masterpiece.

Only man has fashioned himself a principle out of this exception. Bizarre, blind, bloated by science and degenerate, in this century of enlightenment and wisdom, he, in grossest ignorance, wishes to exercise the command of a despot over a sex that has received every intellectual faculty; he claims to rejoice in the Revolution and claims his rights to equality, at the very least.

Declaration of the Rights of Woman and Citizen,

To be decreed by the National Assembly in its last meetings or in those of the next legislature.

PREAMBLE

The mothers, daughters, and sisters, representatives of the nation, demand to be constituted a national assembly. Considering that ignorance, disregard of or contempt for the rights of women are the only causes of public misfortune and of governmental corruption, they have resolved to set forth in a solemn declaration, the natural, inalienable and sacred rights of woman; to the end that this declaration, constantly held up to all members of society, may always remind them of their rights and duties; to the end that the acts based on women's power and those based on the power of men, being constantly measured against the goal of all political institutions, may be more respected; and so that the demands of female citizens, henceforth founded on simple and indisputable principles, may ever uphold the constitution and good morals, and may contribute to the happiness of all.

*Excerpts from Olympe de Gouges, *Les Droits de la femme* (Paris, 1791), trans. Nupur Chaudhuri with Susan Groag Bell and Karen M. Offen, from Bell, Susan Groag, and Karen M. Offen, eds., WOMEN, THE FAMILY, AND FREEDOM. THE DEBATE IN DOCUMENTS, Volume One, 1750–1880, pp.104–106. Copyright © 1983 by the Board of Trustees of the Leland Stanford Junior University. With the permission of Stanford University Press, *www.sup.org*.

Consequently, the sex that is superior in beauty as well as in courage of maternal suffering, recognizes and declares, in the presence and under the auspices of the Supreme Being, the following rights of woman and citizen.

Article One. Woman is born free and remains equal in rights to man. Social distinctions can be founded only on general utility.

II. The goal of every political association is the preservation of the natural and irrevocable rights of Woman and Man. These rights are liberty, property, security, and especially resistance to oppression.

III. The principle of all sovereignty resides essentially in the Nation, which is none other than the union of Woman and Man; no group, no individual can exercise any authority that is not derived expressly from it.

IV. Liberty and justice consist of rendering to persons those things that belong to them; thus, the exercise of woman's natural rights is limited only by the perpetual tyranny with which man opposes her; these limits must be changed according to the laws of nature and reason.

V. The laws of nature and of reason prohibit all acts harmful to society; whatever is not prohibited by these wise and divine laws cannot be prevented, and no one can be forced to do anything unspecified by the law.

VI. The law should be the expression of the general will: all female and male citizens must participate in its elaboration personally or through their representatives. It should be the same for all; all female and male citizens, being equal in the eyes of the law, should be equally admissible to all public offices, places, and employments, according to their capacities and with no distinctions other than those of their virtues and talents.

VII. No woman is immune; she can be accused, arrested, and detained in such cases as determined by law. Women, like men, must obey these rigorous laws.

VIII. Only punishments strictly and obviously necessary may be established by law. No one may be punished except under a law established and promulgated before the offense occurred, and which is legally applicable to women.

IX. If any woman is declared guilty, then the law must be enforced rigorously.

X. No one should be punished for their opinions. Woman has the right to mount the scaffold; she should likewise have the right to speak in public, provided that her demonstrations do not disrupt public order as established by law.

XI. Free communication of thoughts and opinions is one of the most precious rights of woman, since this liberty assures the legitimate paternity of fathers with regard to their children. Every female citizen can therefore freely say: "I am the mother of a child that belongs to you," without a barbaric prejudice forcing her to conceal the truth; she must also answer for the abuse of this liberty in cases determined by law.

XII. Guarantee of the rights of woman and female citizens requires the existence of public services. Such guarantee should be established for the advantage of everyone, not for the personal benefit of those to whom these services are entrusted.

XIII. For the maintenance of public forces and administrative expenses, the contributions of women and men shall be equal; the woman shares in all forced labor and all painful tasks, therefore she should have the same share in the distribution of positions, tasks, assignments, honors, and industry.

XIV. Female and male citizens have the right to determine the need for public taxes, either by themselves or through their representatives. Female citizens can agree to this only if they are admitted to an equal share not only in wealth but also in public administration, and by determining the proportion and extent of tax collection.

XV. The mass of women, allied for tax purposes to the mass of men, has the right to hold every public official accountable for his administration.

XVI. Any society in which the guarantee of rights is not assured, or the separation of powers determined, has no constitution. The constitution is invalid if the majority of individuals who compose the Nation have not cooperated in writing it.

XVII. The right of property is inviolable and sacred to both sexes, jointly or separately. No one can be deprived of it, since it is a true inheritance of nature except when public necessity, certified by law, clearly requires it, subject to just and prior compensation.

Mary Wollstonecraft (1759–1797): English Author and Feminist

Mary Wollstonecraft, who is often called the "grandmother of feminism," was born in London, the second child of Edward and Elizabeth Wollstonecraft. The family moved often, as her father repeatedly failed in his farming attempts. As his inheritance dwindled, he took his frustrations out on his often pregnant wife, who, in turn, made demands on Mary. As a child, Mary received little education, rarely enjoyed parental affection, and had few friends. A minister and his wife opened their hearts to the lonely girl, shared their books with her, and introduced her to Fanny Blood. Fanny, who was well educated, supported her family with her drawing and sewing, since her father was also an incompetent provider. With her guidance, Wollstonecraft educated herself and developed her writing skills.

In 1778, the 19-year-old struck out on her own. She took a position as companion to an elderly widow but in 1780 returned home to nurse her dying mother. After working as a governess in Ireland, she moved in with Fanny's family in 1782, and in late 1784, opened a boarding school for girls, with Fanny and her two sisters as teachers. In 1785, Fanny married and moved to Lisbon, Portugal. When Fanny became ill during pregnancy, Wollstonecraft nursed her until she and the baby died shortly after delivery. Forced financially to close her school in 1786, Wollstonecraft took a job as a governess and then moved to London in 1787 to begin a new life.

Mary's decision to pursue a writing career had its genesis in the publication of her book of essays *Thoughts on the Education of Daughters* in 1786. Her London publisher hired her as a translator and reviewer for a journal he edited. Between 1787 and 1790, she learned German and Italian (she knew French); published a novel, *Mary, a Fiction;* wrote articles and reviews; edited an anthology, *A Female Reader;* and translated important works by continental male authors. By 1790, Mary was an enthusiastic supporter of the ideas of the French Revolution, and, when Edmund Burke wrote his denunciation of the new French government, *Reflections on the Revolution in France,* she responded with a work that propelled her into the public arena. Her pamphlet, *A Vindication of the Rights of Man, in a Letter to the Right Honourable Edmund Burke,* was a forceful document that made her a central figure in the political debates of the time. Her next publication made her famous in feminist history.

She wrote *A Vindication of the Rights of Woman* in response to a *Report on Public Instruction* by Talleyrand that set forth a plan for national education. His plan proposed that girls be educated with their brothers to the age of eight, at which time they would remain at home and focus on domestic duties. She dedicated her response to Talleyrand, and, in the preface, urged him to revise his plan and to extend democratic rights to women. Many of her comments, however, were directed at Rousseau.

Wollstonecraft's life after publication of this important work took on tragic overtones. She suffered bouts of depression had a painful infatuation with a married man who rejected her, and then had a passionate affair with American Gilbert Imlay by whom she had a daughter Fanny. When Imlay left her, she tried to commit suicide. In 1796, she met William Godwin for a second time, and after she became pregnant they married. After their March 1797 marriage, however, they kept separate apartments but communicated constantly. Wollstonecraft gave birth to a daughter, Mary Wollstonecraft Godwin, August 30, but died of childbirth complications September 10, 1797. In 1798, Godwin published her four-volume *Posthumous Works* which included her incomplete novel *The Wrongs of Women: or, Maria.*

A VINDICATION OF THE RIGHTS OF WOMAN (1792)*

I have turned over various books written on the subject of education, and patiently observed the conduct of parents and the management of schools; but what has been the result?—a profound conviction that the neglected education of my fellow-creatures is the grand source of the misery I deplore; and that women, in particular, are rendered weak and wretched by a variety of concurring causes, originating from one hasty conclusion. The conduct and manners of women, in fact, evidently prove that their minds are not in a healthy state; for, like the flowers which are planted in too rich a soil, strength and usefulness are sacrificed to beauty; and the flaunting leaves, after having pleased a fastidious eye, fade, disregarded on the stalk, long before the season when they ought to have arrived at maturity. One cause of this barren blooming I attribute to a false system of education, gathered from the books written on this subject by men who considering females rather as women than human creatures, have been more anxious to make them alluring mistresses than rational wives; and the understanding of the sex has been so bubbled by this specious homage, that the civilized women of the present century, with a few exceptions, are only anxious to inspire love, when they ought to cherish a nobler ambition, and by their abilities and virtues exact respect. . . .

Let us examine this question. Rousseau declares that a woman should never, for a moment, feel herself independent, that she should be governed by fear to exercise her *natural* cunning, and made a coquettish slave in order to render her a more alluring object of desire, a *sweeter* companion to man, whenever he chooses to relax himself. . . .

What nonsense! When will a great man arise with sufficient strength of mind to puff away the fumes which pride and sensuality have thus spread over the subject! If women are by nature inferior to men, their virtues must be the same in quality, if not in degree, or virtue is a relative idea; consequently, their conduct should be founded on the same principles, and have the same aim. . . .

How women are to exist in that state where there is to be neither marrying or giving in marriage, we are not told. For though moralists have agreed that the tenor

*Excerpts from Mary Wollstonecraft, *A Vindication of the Rights of Woman: with Strictures on Political and Moral Subjects* (London: Printed for J. Johnson, 1792), pp. 1–2, 47–48, 65–66, 68–69, 82–85, 87–88, 92–93, 120–21, 331, 333, 342, 394–95.

of life seems to prove that *man* is prepared by various circumstances for a future state, they constantly concur in advising *woman* only to provide for the present. Gentleness, docility, and a spaniel-like affection are, on this ground, consistently recommended as the cardinal virtues of the sex; . . . She was created to be the toy of man, his rattle, and it must jingle in his ears whenever . . . he chooses to be amused. . . .

But . . . frankly acknowledging the inferiority of woman, according to the present appearance of things, I shall only insist that men have increased that inferiority till women are almost sunk below the standard of rational creatures. Let their faculties have room to unfold, and their virtues to gain strength, and then determine where the whole sex must stand in the intellectual scale. . . .

But should it be proved that woman is naturally weaker than man, from whence does it follow that it is natural for her to labour to become still weaker than nature intended her to be? Arguments of this cast are an insult to common sense. . . . The *divine right* of husbands, like the divine right of kings, may, it is to be hoped, in this enlightened age, be contested without danger, . . .

. . . To preserve personal beauty, woman's glory! the limbs and faculties are cramped with worse than Chinese bands, and the sedentary life which they are condemned to live, whilst boys frolic in the open air, weakens the muscles and relaxes the nerves.—As for Rousseau's remarks . . . that they have naturally, that is from their birth, . . . a fondness for dolls, dressing, and talking—they are so puerile as not to merit a serious refutation. That a girl, condemned to sit for hours together listening to the idle chat of weak nurses, or to attend at her mother's toilet, will endeavour to join the conversation, is, indeed, very natural; and that she will imitate her mother or aunts, and amuse herself by adorning her lifeless doll, as they do in dressing her, poor innocent babe! is undoubtedly a most natural consequence. . . .

I have, probably, had an opportunity of observing more girls in their infancy than J. J. Rousseau—I can recollect my own feelings, and I have looked steadily around me; yet, . . . I will venture to affirm, that a girl, whose spirits have not been damped by inactivity, or innocence tainted by false shame, will always be a romp, and the doll will never excite attention unless confinement allows her no alternative. Girls and boys, in short, would play harmlessly together, if the distinction of sex was not inculcated long before nature makes any difference. I will go further, and affirm, as an indisputable fact, that most of the women, in the circle of my observation, who have acted like rational creatures, or shown any vigour of intellect, have accidentally been allowed to run wild. . . .

Let not men then in the pride of power, use the same arguments that tyrannic kings and venal ministers have used, and fallaciously assert that woman ought to be subjected because she has always been so. But, when man, governed by reasonable laws, enjoys his natural freedom, let him despise woman, if she do not share it with him; and, till that glorious period arrives, in descanting on the folly of the sex, let him not overlook his own.

It is time to effect a revolution in female manners—time to restore to them their lost dignity—and make them, as a part of the human species, labour by reforming themselves to reform the world. . . .

I lament that women are systematically degraded by receiving the trivial attentions which men think it manly to pay to the sex, when, in fact, they are insultingly supporting their own superiority. . . . So ludicrous, in fact, do these ceremonies appear to me that I scarcely am able to govern my muscles, when I see a man start with eager and serious solicitude to lift a handkerchief, or shut a door, when the *lady* could have done it herself, had she only moved a pace or two. . . .

The being who discharges the duties of its station is independent; and, speaking of women at large, their first duty is to themselves as rational creatures, and the next, in point of importance, as citizens, is that which includes so many, of a mother. . . .

But, to render her really virtuous and useful, she must not, if she discharge her civil duties, want, individually, the protection of civil laws; she must not be dependent on her husband's bounty for her subsistence during his life, or support after his death—for how can a being be generous who has nothing of its own? or, virtuous, who is not free?. . .

Would men but generously snap our chains, and be content with rational fellowship instead of slavish obedience, they would find us more observant daughters, more affectionate sisters, more faithful wives, more reasonable mothers – in a word, better citizens. We should then love them with true affection, because we should learn to respect ourselves; and the peace of mind of a worthy man would not be interrupted by the idle vanity of his wife, nor his babes sent to nestle in a strange bosom, having never found a home in their mother's. . . .

I know that libertines will also exclaim, that woman would be unsexed by acquiring strength of body and mind, and that beauty, soft bewitching beauty! would no longer adorn the daughters of men! I am of a very different opinion, for I think that, on the contrary, we should then see dignified beauty, and true grace; . . . such as appears to make us respect the human body as a majestic pile fit to receive a noble inhabitant. . . .

Germaine de Staël (1766–1817): French Writer

Germaine de Staël, originally Anne-Louise-Germaine Necker, was born into a wealthy family in Geneva, Switzerland, but lived and worked in France until she was expelled by Napoleon. Through marriage she became Baronne de Staël-Holstein. She was a prolific writer of novels and essays and earned an international reputation. She became one of the most famous women in Europe when exiled for her anti-Napoleon political activities. The following excerpt from her 1807 novel *Corinna* compares the educational and intellectual opportunities of Continental and British women.

CORINNA; OR, ITALY (1807)*

Lord Edgermond was my father. I was born in Italy by his first wife, who was a Roman lady; and Lucilia, whom you were destined to espouse, is my sister by the father's side. She is the fruit of the second marriage of my father with an English lady.

Now listen to me. Educated in Italy, I lost my mother when I was only ten years old; but, as she had on her deathbed expressed a wish that my education might be finished before I should go to England, my father left me with an aunt of my mother at Florence, where I remained until I was fifteen. My talents, my taste, even my character were formed, when the death of my aunt made my father determine on bringing

*Excerpts from Germaine de Staël, *Corinna; or, Italy, by mad. De Stael Holstein* (Philadelphia: Printed for Hopkins and Earle; Fry and Kammerer, 1808), pp. 254–57.

me to his own country. He lived in a small town in Northumberland, which I am sensible could give me but a poor idea of England; but it was all that I had an opportunity of knowing of that country during the six years I lived in it. In my infancy my mother had frequently impressed upon my mind, that not to live in Italy was a misfortune; and my aunt often repeated that the fear of leaving her country had caused the death of my mother. My good aunt was also persuaded that a catholic must be damned who lived in a protestant country, and though I was far from participating in this opinion, the idea of going to England gave me much uneasiness.

... [My stepmother] received me very well, but I readily perceived that my manner greatly surprised her, and that she resolved to change it if she could. Not a word was spoken during dinner, notwithstanding some neighbors were invited. This silence was so oppressive to me, that in the midst of the dinner I attempted to say a few words to an elderly gentleman who sat next to me. I understood English very well, as my father had taught it me in my infancy, and, in the course of the conversation, I quoted some very elegant Italian verses, in which the subject of love was introduced. My mother-in-law [stepmother], who knew Italian, looked at me, blushed, and made a signal for the ladies to retire much sooner than usual to the tea-table, the gentlemen being left alone at the dessert. I did not understand this custom, which would appear very extraordinary in Italy, where men can find no pleasure in society without women; but I supposed for a moment that my mother-in-law was so displeased at my conduct, that she would not stop in the room with me. I was undeceived, however, when she made a sign to me to follow her, and when I found that she did not reproach me during the three hours which we remained in the drawing-room, until the gentlemen joined us.

My mother-in-law said to me, softly, at supper, that it was not the custom for young ladies to speak with so much freedom as I had shown in conversation, and in particular that it was very wrong to say a word about love. "Miss Edgermond," said she, "you must endeavor to forget everything connected with Italy; it would have been better for you had you never known that country." I passed the night in tears; my heart was oppressed with sorrow. In the morning I went out to walk, and found myself enveloped in a frightful fog: I could not see the sun, which at least would have reminded me of Italy. My father came to me and said: "My dear child, it is not here as in Italy: with us, women have no employ but their domestic duties: the talents which you possess will enable you to employ your time in solitude: perhaps you may meet with a husband to whom your accomplishments will afford pleasure; but in a small town like this, everything that attracts attention excites envy, and you will find few men disposed to marry you, if it be believed that you have tastes and pursuits inconsistent with our manners. Here the whole routine of existence must be subject to our ancient provincial customs . . . "

... About the end of autumn my father generally went on hunting parties, and sometimes did not return until midnight; during his absence I remained the greater part of the day in my room and endeavored to cultivate my talents, which displeased my stepmother. "What is all this good for?" she used to say, "will it render you more happy?" This question threw me into despair. What is happiness, said I to myself, if it consists not in the development of our faculties? Is not moral as bad as physical suicide? And if I must stifle my understanding and repress all the emotions of my heart, why preserve the wretched remains of an existence which agitates me to no useful purpose? I took care, however, not to repeat these thoughts to my mother-in-law. I did once or twice break silence on this subject, but she replied to me that the business of a woman was to manage the affairs of her family, and to take care of the health of her children; that all pretensions to superior accomplishments only led to evil and the best advice she could give me, if I possessed them, was to conceal them.

SUGGESTED READINGS:

Artists

Roworth, Wendy Wassyng, ed. *Angelica Kauffman: A Continental Artist in Georgian England.* Brighton, UK: The Royal Pavilion Art Gallery and Museums; London: Reaktion Books, 1992.
Sheriff, Mary D. *The Exceptional Woman: Elisabeth Vigée-LeBrun and the Cultural Politics of Art.* Chicago and London: University of Chicago Press, 1996.

Enlightenment and Revolutionary Europe

Flexner, Eleanor. *Mary Wollstonecraft: A Biography.* New York: Coward, McCann and Geoghegan, 1972.
Hufton, Olwen H. *Women and the Limits of Citizenship in the French Revolution.* Toronto: University of Toronto Press, 1992.
Myers, Sylvia Harcstark. *The Blue Stocking Circle: Women, Friendship and the Life of the Mind in Eighteenth-Century England.* Oxford: Oxford University Press, 1990.
Scott, Joan Wallach. *Only Paradoxes to Offer: French Feminists and the Rights of Man.* Cambridge, MA: Harvard University Press, 1996.

Enlightenment and Revolutionary America

Kerber, Linda. *Women of the Republic: Intellect and Ideology in Revolutionary America.* Chapel Hill: Published for the Institute of Early American History and Culture by the University of North Carolina Press, 1980.
Norton, Mary Beth. *Liberty's Daughters: The Revolutionary Experience of American Women, 1750–1800.* Boston and Toronto: Little, Brown and Co., 1980.

Chapter 7

The Victorian Ideal:
Writers and Musicians

Throughout the nineteenth century a gender ideology commonly referred to as the "Victorian ideal" prevailed, most notably in England, France, and the United States. The Victorian ideal evolved from the Enlightenment ideal of separate spheres and the belief that men and women were innately different and had distinct roles to fill. It was re-enforced by political instability, demographic shifts, and social-economic changes associated with the Commercial and Industrial Revolutions. This ideology was at its core a middle-class belief system, intended to elevate the status of the new bourgeoisie and set members of that class apart from the decadent elite, on the one hand, and the "depraved" masses on the other. The ideology meshed neatly with the post-revolutionary emphases on virtue, self-restraint, and civic order, particularly in America. It also provided a way to grant women special status in lieu of legal and political equality. In reality, the Victorian ideal or "cult of true womanhood" was hardly new; it echoed the gender ideology of classical Athens and the Roman Republic, the Renaissance lady ideal, and the arguments traditionalists such as Rousseau made in the long-running debate over the "woman question" or *querelle des femmes*. In essence, women were to find fulfillment and exert their influence through service to husbands and children in their domestic roles. They were to set an example of moral rectitude, quietly influence their husbands to be virtuous citizens, prepare their daughters to assume their domestic duties, and rear their sons to be future leaders. Any who departed from the norm were unfeminine or "hens that crow," and to enter the public arena was akin to losing one's virtue. Religious teachings underscored this ideal, as did popular ladies' magazines and fiction.

In the second half of the century, new scientific "evidence" re-enforced these views. Medical experts warned that education, clerical work, professional occupations, and physical exercise would irreparably damage the female reproductive organs, rendering women infertile or incapable of producing normal offspring. Evolutionary biologists and social scientists "proved" that male and female brains were significantly different. Males (and those of the Anglo-Saxon race) had far more rational capacity than females (and males of all other races). They "proved," moreover, that sex differences were greatest among the most "civilized" races and therefore argued that for women to abandon domesticity and seek equality with men in any field would destroy civilization. (Trecker 1974; Haller and Haller 1977, chs. 1, 2) Yet, the increasingly shrill and repetitive discussion of woman's true nature and place suggested that all was not well in Western culture. Indeed, the seeming preoccupation with the issue of gender roles paralleled significant changes in women's behavior, lifestyles, and opportunities. Likewise, the linking of gender with racial/ethnic ideologies reflected Western colonialism and reaction to new immigration patterns in America.

As you read the introductions and documents in this and the following chapters, be attentive to the underlying societal expectations and pressures women experienced and note how individually and sometimes collectively they responded. In what ways did women challenge the Victorian gender ideology—implicitly and openly? How did gender shape their cultural contributions?

LITERARY WOMEN

Mary Wollstonecraft Godwin Shelley (1797–1851): British Writer

Mary Shelley was the daughter of William Godwin and Mary Wollstonecraft. Her mother died ten days after her birth, and she was raised by her father, a novelist and philosopher. She was essentially self-educated. She was a curious child, and her father let her read whatever she wished. She read her parents' works, the new Romantic poetry and eighteenth-century Gothic novels. She also met the literary men who comprised her father's circle: Charles Lamb, Samuel Taylor Coleridge, and the Romantic poet Percy Bysshe Shelley. In 1814, she and Shelley "eloped," despite the fact he was married. They married two years later when his wife died. She bore four children, only one of whom survived to adulthood, and was widowed in 1822, when Percy died in a boating accident. *Frankenstein* was her first story, written in 1817 when she was only 19. It was published anonymously in 1818 with a preface by her husband that emphasized the story's moral value. Shelley subsequently wrote five more novels, numerous tales and essays, and prepared notes to Percy's works after his death. A journal entry reveals her mother's influence on her thought: "If I have never written to vindicate the Rights of women, I have ever befriended women when oppressed—at every risk I have defended and supported victims to the social system" (Shelley 1987, 557).

Frankenstein was written one weekend when she, Percy, and some friends were confined indoors during a storm. Someone suggested they have a competition to see who could write the best ghost story. Her story won. Although some reviewers described the story as revolting with no lessons for the reader, it was a bestseller and has continued to be. Indeed, it has had a powerful influence on modern culture. It was so influential that the term "Frankenstein" entered the Oxford English Dictionary and the Oxford American Dictionary, defined as a "thing which becomes formidable to the person who created it." As you read the following excerpt, consider the relevance of the dictionary definition and compare popular culture's portrayal of Frankenstein with Shelley's character. Also consider how her comment about her social conscience might relate to the novel. *Frankenstein*, however, is much more than a ghost story. It incorporates several strains of thought prevalent in the eighteenth and early-nineteenth centuries: Enlightenment ideas of the social contract and rationalism, themes common to romanticism (nature, individual genius, etc.), and her mother's concerns about societal treatment of women (reflected, in part, in the creature).Watch for some of these elements as you read.

FRANKENSTEIN; OR, THE MODERN PROMETHEUS (1818)*

> [Victor frankenstein creates life]
> It was on a dreary night of November, that I beheld the accomplishment of my toils.
> With an anxiety that almost amounted to agony, I collected the instruments of life

*Excerpts from Mary W. Shelley, *Frankenstein; Or, The Modern Prometheus* (New York: John W. Lovell Co., 1890), pp. 44–46, 77–79, 101–03, 115.

around me, that I might infuse a spark of being into the lifeless thing that lay at my feet. It was already one in the morning; the rain pattered dismally against the panes, and my candle was nearly burnt out, when, by the glimmer of the half-extinguished light, I saw the dull yellow eye of the creature open; it breathed hard, and a convulsive motion agitated its limbs.

How can I describe my emotions at this catastrophe, or how delineate the wretch whom with such infinite pains and care I had endeavoured to form? His limbs were in proportion, and I had selected his features as beautiful. Beautiful!— Great God! His yellow skin scarcely covered the work of muscles and arteries beneath; his hair was of a lustrous black, and flowing; his teeth of a pearly whiteness; but these luxuriances only formed a more horrid contrast with his watery eyes, that seemed almost of the same colour as the dun-white sockets in which they were set, his shrivelled complexion, and straight black lips.

The different accidents of life are not so changeable as the feelings of human nature. I had worked hard for nearly two years, for the sole purpose of infusing life into an inanimate body. For this I had deprived myself of rest and health. I had desired it with an ardour that far exceeded moderation; but now that I had finished, the beauty of the dream vanished, and breathless horror and disgust filled my heart. Unable to endure the aspect of the being I had created, I rushed out of the room, and continued a long time traversing my bed-chamber, unable to compose my mind to sleep. . . . I started from my sleep with horror; . . . when, by the dim and yellow light of the moon, as it forced its way through the window-shutters, I beheld the wretch— the miserable monster whom I had created. He held up the curtain of the bed; and his eyes, if eyes they may be called, were fixed on me. His jaws opened, and he muttered some inarticulate sounds, while a grin wrinkled his cheeks. He might have spoken, but I did not hear; one hand was stretched out, seemingly to detain me, but I escaped, and rushed down stairs. . . .

Oh! no mortal could support the horror of that countenance. A mummy again endued with animation could not be so hideous as that wretch. I had gazed on him while unfinished; he was ugly then; but when those muscles and joints were rendered capable of motion, it became a thing such as even Dante could not have conceived. I passed the night wretchedly. . . .

[Many months later the monster approaches Victor Frankenstein]
. . . his countenance bespoke bitter anguish, combined with disdain and malignity, while its unearthly ugliness rendered it almost too horrible for human eyes. . . .

"Devil!" I [Frankenstein] exclaimed, "do you dare approach me? and do not you fear the fierce vengeance of my arm wreaked on your miserable head? Begone, vile insect! or rather stay, that I may trample you to dust! and, oh, that I could, with the extinction of your miserable existence, restore those victims whom you have so diabolically murdered!"

"I expected this reception," said the daemon. "All men hate the wretched; how then must I be hated, who am miserable beyond all living things! Yet you, my creator, detest and spurn me, thy creature, to whom thou art bound by ties only dissoluble by the annihilation of one of us. . . . Do your duty towards me, and I will do mine towards you and the rest of mankind. If you will comply with my conditions, I will leave them and you at peace; but if you refuse, I will glut the maw of death, until it be satiated with the blood of your remaining friends."

"Abhorred monster! fiend that thou art! the tortures of hell are too mild a vengeance for thy crimes. Wretched devil! you reproach me with your creation; come on then, that I may extinguish the spark which I so negligently bestowed." . . .

[The Creature spoke]

"Be calm! I entreat you to hear me, before you give vent to your hatred on my devoted head. Have I not suffered enough, that you seek to increase my misery? . . . Oh, Frankenstein, be not equitable to every other, and trample upon me alone, to whom thy justice, and even thy clemency and affection, is most due. Remember, that I am thy creature: I ought to be thy Adam; but I am rather the fallen angel, whom thou drivest from joy for no misdeed. Every where I see bliss, from which I alone am irrevocably excluded. I was benevolent and good; misery made me a fiend. Make me happy, and I shall again be virtuous."

"Begone! I will not hear you. There can be no community between you and me; we are enemies. Begone, or let us try our strength in a fight, in which one must fall."

"How can I move thee? Will no entreaties cause thee to turn a favourable eye upon thy creature, who implores thy goodness and compassion. Believe me, Frankenstein: I was benevolent; my soul glowed with love and humanity: but am I not alone, miserably alone? You, my creator, abhor me; what hope can I gather from your fellow-creatures, who owe me nothing? they spurn and hate me. . . . Shall I not then hate them who abhor me? I will keep no terms with my enemies. I am miserable, and they shall share my wretchedness. Yet it is in your power to recompense me, and deliver them from an evil which it only remains for you to make so great, that not only you and your family, but thousands of others, shall be swallowed up in the whirlwinds of its rage. Let your compassion be moved, and do not disdain me. Listen to my tale: when you have heard that, abandon or commiserate me, as you shall judge that I deserve. But hear me. The guilty are allowed, by human laws, bloody as they may be, to speak in their own defence before they are condemned. Listen to me, Frankenstein. You accuse me of murder; and yet you would, with a satisfied conscience, destroy your own creature. Oh, praise the eternal justice of man! Yet I ask you not to spare me: listen to me; and then, if you can, and if you will, destroy the work of your hands." . . .

[His story]

. . . "Who was I? What was I? Whence did I come? What was my destination? These questions continually recurred, but I was unable to solve them. . . .

. . . Like Adam, I was created apparently united by no link to any other being in existence; but his state was far different from mine in every other respect. He had come forth from the hands of God a perfect creature, happy and prosperous, guarded by the especial care of his Creator; he was allowed to converse with, and acquire knowledge from beings of a superior nature: but I was wretched, helpless, and alone. Many times I considered Satan as the fitter emblem of my condition; for often, like him, when I viewed the bliss of my protectors, the bitter gall of envy rose within me.

Another circumstance strengthened and confirmed these feelings. . . . I discovered some papers in the pocket of the dress which I had taken from your laboratory. . . . Here they are. Everything is related in them which bears reference to my accursed origin; the whole detail of that series of disgusting circumstances which produced it is set in view; the minutest description of my odious and loathsome person is given, in language which painted your own horrors, and rendered mine ineffaceable. I sickened as I read. 'Hateful day when I received life!' I exclaimed in agony. 'Cursed creator! Why did you form a monster so hideous that even you turned from me in disgust? God in pity made man beautiful and alluring, after his own image; but my form is a filthy type of your's, more horrid from its very resemblance.' Satan had his companions, fellow-devils, to admire and encourage him; but I am solitary and detested. . . .

. . . I now indulge in dreams of bliss that cannot be realized. What I ask of you is reasonable and moderate; I demand a creature of another sex, but as hideous as myself—the gratification is small, but it is all that I can receive, and it shall content me. It is true, we shall be monsters, cut off from all the world; but on that account we shall be more attached to one another. Our lives will not be happy, but they will be harmless, and free from the misery I now feel, Oh! my creator, make me happy; let me feel gratitude towards you for one benefit! Let me see that I excite the sympathy of some existing thing; do not deny me my request!"

I was moved. I shuddered when I thought of the possible consequences of my consent; but I felt that there was some justice in his argument. His tale, and the feelings he now expressed, proved him to be a creature of fine sensations; and did I not, as his maker, owe him all the portion of happiness that it was in my power to bestow? . . .

Charlotte Brontë [Currer Bell] (1816–1855): British Novelist

Charlotte Brontë was one of England's pre-eminent women novelists. Her father was a Yorkshire parson of Irish descent who wrote poetry, a novel, and published a collection of sermons. Her mother managed to write essays despite bearing six children before she died. Her widowed father sent his four oldest girls to a school for daughters of impoverished clergy. It was a miserable place, and two of the sisters died of typhoid fever which struck the school, but Charlotte and Emily escaped the disease. Brontë taught briefly at the school and was then employed as a governess but hated the job, so in 1842 moved to Brussels where she and Emily studied French and German for two years in preparation for opening their own school. Unfortunately, Charlotte fell in love with her Belgian instructor, who was married and the father of numerous children. When she returned to England, the school never materialized, so she and her remaining two sisters began to write. Emily published the powerful novel *Wuthering Heights.* All used pen names; Charlotte published under the name Currer Bell. Her second and most famous novel, *Jane Eyre,* was quite controversial because it portrayed a heroine who was open about her passion for her employer, a married man, and openly expressed her desire for liberty. It also introduced a new form of novel that departed markedly from the sentimental fiction most women wrote and read. Her literary success was marred by the deaths of her brother and last two sisters shortly after its publication. She published *Shirley* in 1849 and *Villette* in 1853.

Through her novels, Brontë expressed her own views on marriage and passion. She married in 1854, became pregnant, and died in March 1855, probably of tuberculosis. *Shirley* was an even more daring novel than *Jane Eyre,* for through its dialogues, Brontë explored the position of middle-class women, their family relationships, and personal desires in a more direct manner than any other work of Victorian fiction. Based on this excerpt, why might Victorian readers be taken aback by the novel? How might women respond to it?

EXCERPTS FROM *SHIRLEY: A TALE**

[Shirley Keeldar and Caroline Helstone discuss life and women's options]

"I often wonder, Shirley, whether most men resemble my uncle in their domestic relations; whether it is necessary to be new and unfamiliar to them, in order to seem agreeable or estimable in their eyes, and whether it is impossible to their natures to retain a constant interest and affection for those they see every day."

"I don't know: I can't clear up your doubts. I ponder over similar ones myself sometimes. But, to tell you a secret, if I were convinced that they are necessarily and universally different from us—fickle, soon petrifying, unsympathizing—I would never marry. I should not like to find out that what I loved did not love me, that it was weary of me, and whatever I might make to please would hereafter be worse than useless, since it was inevitably in its nature to change and become indifferent. That discovery once made, what should I long for? To go away—to remove from a presence where my society gave no pleasure."

"But you could not if you were married."

"No, I could not—there it is. I could never be my own mistress more. A terrible thought! It suffocates me! Nothing irks me like the idea of being a burden and a bore—an inevitable burden—a ceaseless bore! Now, when I feel my company superfluous, I can comfortably fold my independence round me like a mantle, drop my pride like a veil, and withdraw to solitude. *If married, that could not be.*"

"I wonder we don't all make up our minds to remain single," said Caroline; "we should if we listened to the wisdom of experience. My uncle always speaks of marriage as a burden; and I believe whenever he hears of a man being married, he invariably regards him as a fool, or, at any rate, as doing a foolish thing."

"But, Caroline, men are not all like your uncle; surely not—I hope not."

She paused and mused.

"I suppose we each find an exception in the one we love, till we are married," suggested Caroline.

"I suppose so: and this exception we believe to be of sterling materials; we fancy it like ourselves; we imagine a sense of harmony. We think his voice gives the softest, truest promise of a heart that will never harden against us. We read in his eyes that faithful feeling—affection. I don't think we should trust to what they call passion at all, Caroline. I believe it is a mere fire of dry sticks, blazing up and vanishing. But we watch him, and see him kind to animals, to little children, to poor people. He is kind to us, likewise—good—considerate. He does not flatter women, but he is patient with them, and he seems to be easy in their presence, and to find their company genial. He likes them not only for vain and selfish reasons, but as *we* like him—because we like him. Then we observe that he is just—that he always speaks the truth—that he is conscientious. We feel joy and peace when he comes into a room—we feel sadness and trouble when he leaves it. We know that this man has been a kind son— that he is a kind brother. Will any one dare to tell me that he will not be a kind husband?"

"My uncle would affirm it unhesitatingly. 'He will be sick of you in a month,' he would say."

*Excerpts from Charlotte Brontë [Currer Bell, pseud.], *Shirley: A Tale* (New York: Derby & Jackson, 1857), pp. 190–92, 203, 491–92.

"Mrs. Pryor would seriously intimate the same."

"Mrs. Yorke and Miss Mann would darkly suggest ditto." . . .

[Later, the two women continue their conversation]

"Caroline," demanded Miss Keeldar, abruptly, "don't you wish you had a profession—a trade?"

"I wish it fifty times a day. As it is, I often wonder what I came into the world for. I long to have something absorbing and compulsory to fill my head and hands, and to occupy my thoughts."

"Can labor alone make a human being happy?"

"No, but it can give varieties of pain, and prevent us from breaking our hearts with a single tyrant master-torture. Besides, successful labor has its recompense; a vacant, weary, lonely, hopeless life has none."

"But hard labor and learned professions, they say, make women masculine, unwomanly."

"And what does it signify whether married and never-to-be-married are unattractive and inelegant or not? provided only they are decent, decorous and neat, it is enough. The utmost which ought to be required of old maids, in the way of appearance, is that they should not absolutely offend men's eyes as they pass them in the street; for the rest they should be allowed, without too much scorn, to be as absorbed, plain-looking, and plain-dressed as they please."

"You might be an old maid yourself, Caroline, you speak so earnestly."

"I shall be one; it is my destiny. I will never marry a Malone or a Sykes—and no one else will ever marry me."

[Shirley responds to her uncle and former guardian after an argument about marriage.]

"Mr. Sympson . . . I am sick at heart with all this weak trash; I will hear no more. Your thoughts are not my thoughts, your aims are not my aims, your gods are not my gods. We do not view things in the same light; we do not measure them by the same standard; we hardly speak in the same tongue. Let us part."

"It is not," she resumed, much excited—"It is not that I hate you; you are a good sort of man; perhaps you mean well in your way; but we cannot suit—, we are ever at variance. You annoy me with small meddling, with petty tyranny; you exasperate my temper, and make and keep me passionate. As to your small maxims, your narrow rules, your little prejudices, aversions, dogmas, bundle them off. Mr. Sympson, go; offer them a sacrifice to the deity you worship; I'll none of them. I wash my hands of the lot. I walk by another creed, light, faith, and hope than you."

"Another creed! I believe she is an infidel."

"An infidel to *your* religion; an atheist to *your* god."

"*An atheist!*"

"Your god, sir, is the world. In my eyes, you, too, if not an infidel, are an idolater. I conceive that you ignorantly worship. In all things you appear to me too superstitious. Sir, your god, your great Bel, your fish-tailed Dagon, rises before me as a demon. You, and such as you, have raised him to a throne, put on him a crown, given him a sceptre. Behold how hideously he governs! See him busied at the work he likes best—making marriages. He binds the young to the old, the strong to the imbecile. He stretches out the arm of Mezentius, and fetters the dead to the living. In his realm there is hatred—secret hatred; there is disgust—unspoken disgust; there is treachery—family treachery; there is vice—deep, deadly, domestic vice. In his dominions, children grow unloving between parents who have never loved: infants are nursed on deception from their very birth; they are reared in an atmosphere corrupt with lies. Your god rules at the bridal of kings—look at your royal dynasties! Your deity is the deity of foreign aristocracies—analyze the blue blood of Spain! Your god is the Hymen of France—what is French domestic life? All that surrounds him hastens to decay—all declines and degenerates under his sceptre. *Your* god is a masked Death."

"This language is terrible! My daughters and you must associate no longer, Miss Keeldar: there is danger in such companionship. Had I known you a little earlier— but, extraordinary as I thought you, I could not have believed–"

"Now, sir do you begin to be aware that it is useless to scheme for me?—that in doing so, you but sow the wind to reap the whirlwind? I sweep your cobweb-projects from my path, that I may pass on unsullied. I am anchored on a resolve you cannot shake. My heart, my conscience, shall dispose of my hand—*they only.* Know this at last."

George Sand (1804–1876): French Novelist

George Sand was born Amantine-Lucile-Aurore Dupin to a family of moderate means. In her twenties she married François Dudevant and tried to settle into life at his family's estate. Ultimately, she became depressed and bored, so she left her husband of nine years and her two children and settled in Paris, where she intended to support herself by writing. When her mother-in-law once visited her and learned she was writing, she was rather shocked but suggested that Amantine would never harm the Dudevant name by publishing under her real name. In truth, Amantine had already decided to publish under the pen name George Sand. Sand corresponded with numerous people, had a series of lovers, and frequently appeared in public dressed in male attire. Her flaunting of convention in her personal life and her success as a novelist made her something of an idol of other women who were trying to pursue professional aspirations and create new living arrangements outside of conventional marriage. Composer Frederik Chopin was one of her lovers and closest friends. Sand, like other literary men and women, was influenced by some of the utopian movements of the nineteenth century, particularly the Saint-Simonian and Fourierist communities that experimented with alternative family and work structures to ensure women's equality with men.

In her novels and life, Sand was among the vanguard of the new Romantics who challenged Victorian sensibilities and institutions. Note how she does so in the following excerpt from her autobiography and her first successful novel *Indiana* (1832). *Indiana* is the story of a woman trapped in a loveless marriage from which there is no escape. The selected scene follows her unsuccessful attempt to convince her lover to take her away with him and her own attempted suicide from which her cousin Ralph had rescued her the night before.

EXCERPT FROM *MY LIFE,* SAND'S AUTOBIOGRAPHY*

[On leaving her husband]
. . . My husband was not mean; he refused me nothing. I had no needs, I desired nothing outside the household budget he had drawn up, and content to forgo all responsibility, I left him unlimited authority. . . .

*Excerpts from George Sand, *My Life,* translation of *Histoire de ma vie,* trans. Dan Hofstadter (New York: Harper & Row, 1979), pp. 196–97. © 1979 by Dan Hofstadter. With permission of the Balkin Agency, Inc., Amherst, MA.

Amid the nunnish life that I led at Nohant . . . a need to live on my own grew at last within me. I suffered from being useless. . . .

. . . slavery is something antihuman which one accepts only on the condition that one may dream of freedom. I was not my husband's slave, he gladly left me to my readings and my juleps; but I was enslaved in a preordained social condition, and it was not he who could emancipate me. . . .

EXCERPT FROM *INDIANA**

Madame Delmare, when she heard her husband's imprecations, felt stronger than she expected. She preferred this fierce wrath, which reconciled her with herself, to a generous forbearance which would have aroused her remorse. She wiped away the last trace of her tears and summoned what remained of her strength, which she was well content to expend in a day, so heavy a burden had life become to her. Her husband accosted her in a harsh and imperious tone, but suddenly changed his expression and his manner and seemed sorely embarrassed, overmatched by the superiority of her character. He tried to be as cool and dignified as she was; but he could not succeed.

"Will you condescend to inform me, madame," he said, "where you passed the morning and perhaps the night?"

That perhaps indicated to Madame Delmare that her absence had not been discovered until late. Her courage increased with that knowledge.

"No, monsieur," she replied, "I do not propose to tell you."

Delmare turned green with anger and amazement.

"Do you really hope to conceal the truth from me?" he said, in a trembling voice.

"I care very little about it," she replied in an icy tone. "I refuse to tell you solely for form's sake. I propose to convince you that you have no right to ask me that question."

"I have no right, ten thousand devils. Who is master here, pray tell, you or I? Which of us wears a petticoat and ought to be running a distaff? Do you propose to take the beard off my chin? It would look well on you, hussy!"

"I know that I am the slave and you the master. The laws of this country make you my master. You can bind my body, tie my hands, govern my acts. You have the right of the stronger, and society confirms you in it; but you cannot command my will, monsieur; God alone can bend it and subdue it. Try to find a law, a dungeon, an instrument of torture that gives you any hold on it! you might as well try to handle the air and grasp space."

"Hold your tongue, you foolish, impertinent creature; your high-flown novelist's phrases weary me."

"You can impose silence on me, but not prevent me from thinking."

"Silly pride! pride of a poor worm! you abuse the compassion I have had for you! But you will soon see that this mighty will can be subdued without too much difficulty."

"I don't advise you to try it; your repose would suffer, and you would gain nothing in dignity."

---

*From George Sand [Amandine Lucille Aurore Dupin, Baroness Dudevant], *Indiana,* trans. George Burnham Ives (Philadelphia: G. Barrie, 1900), pp. 204–08.

"Do you think so?" he said, crushing her hand between his thumb and forefinger.

"I do think so," she said, without wincing.

Ralph stepped forward, grasped the colonel's arm in his iron hand and bent it like a reed, saying in a pacific tone:

"I beg that you will not touch a hair of that woman's head."

Delmare longed to fly at him; but he felt that he was in the wrong and he dreaded nothing in the world so much as having to blush for himself. So he simply pushed him away, saying: "Attend to your own business."

Then he returned to his wife.

"So, madame," he said, holding his arms tightly against his sides to resist the temptation to strike her, "you rebel against me, you refuse to go to Ile Bourbon with me, you desire a separation? Very well! *Mordieu!* I too—"

"I desire it no longer," she replied. "I did desire it yesterday, it was my will; it is not so this morning. You resorted to violence and locked me in my room; I went out through the window to show you that there is a difference between exerting an absurd control over a woman's actions and reigning over her will. I passed several hours away from your domination; I breathed the air of liberty in order to show you that you are not morally my master, and that I look to no one on earth but myself for orders. As I walked along I reflected that I owed it to my duty and my conscience to return and place myself under your control once more. I did it of my own free will. My cousin *accompanied* me here, he did not *bring me back.* If I had not chosen to come with him, he could not have forced me to do it, as you can imagine. So, monsieur, do not waste your time fighting against my determination; you will never control it, you lost all right to change it as soon as you undertook to assert your right by force. Make your preparations for departure; I am ready to assist you and to accompany you, not because it is your will, but because it is my pleasure. You may condemn me, but I will never obey anyone but myself."

"I am sorry for the derangement of your mind," said the colonel, shrugging his shoulders.

And he went to his room to put his papers in order, well satisfied in his heart with Madame Delmare's resolution and anticipating no further obstacles; for he respected her word as much as he despised her ideas.

Frances Ellen Watkins Harper (1825–1911): American Poet and Novelist

Frances Watkins Harper contributed to the abolition movement and the struggle for racial justice through her poems, prose, speeches, and articles. She was born in Baltimore, Maryland, to free Negro parents, orphaned at three, and raised by her uncle, a clergyman. She attended his school for free Negroes, which provided a broad education in the classics, rhetoric, and the Bible to prepare its students for teaching careers. At age 14 she became a live-in maid for a white family. The Armstrongs gave her free access to the books in their home library and in Mr. Armstrong's bookstore when she had finished her chores. Her first volume of poetry was published around 1846. After leaving the Armstrongs, she was hired as the first female instructor at Union Seminary. In the early 1850s, she moved to a town near Philadelphia where she became active in the antislavery movement as a propagandist and lecturer and in the Underground Railroad. She withdrew from activist causes after she married Fenton Harper in her mid-thirties and had one daughter. Four years later, after his death in 1864, she resumed lecturing and toured the South speaking to black and mixed-race audiences. Before she died at 85, Harper had published several volumes of poetry, written and delivered countless speeches, and completed a novel *Iola Leroy; or, Shadows Uplifted* (1892). The work was the first novel about Reconstruction by a black author and the first to challenge the racial stereotypes that pervaded the works of New South writers (Foster 1988, xxx). After the Civil War, she was active in the temperance movement and the American Woman Suffrage Association, director of the American Association of Education of Colored Youth, and vice-president of the National Association of Colored Women.

Her pre–Civil War poetry described the horrors and pathos of slavery and the ways slave women subverted the system to preserve black culture. Her poems of the postwar years dealt with race discrimination, global injustice, politics, and women's rights, as well as family relations, religion, and Southern black life. Hers was a powerful voice for justice and peace for all. The poems that follow are from a complete collection of her poetry.*

AUNT CHLOE'S POLITICS

Of course, I don't know very much
   About these politics,
But I think that some who run 'em,
   Do mighty ugly tricks.

I've seen 'em honey-fugle round,
   And talk so awful sweet,
That you'd think them full of kindness
   As an egg is full of meat.

Now I don't believe in looking
   Honest people in the face,

And saying when you're doing wrong,
   That 'I haven't sold my race.'

When we want to school our children,
   If the money isn't there,
Whether black or white have took it,
   The loss we all must share.

And this buying up each other
   Is something worse than mean,
Though I thinks a heap of voting,
   I go for voting clean.

AN APPEAL TO MY COUNTRY WOMEN

You can sigh o'er the sad-eyed Armenian
   Who weeps in her desolate home.
You can mourn o'er the exile of Russia
   From kindred and friends doomed to
      roam.

You can pity the men who have woven
   From passion and appetite chains
To coil with a terrible tension
   Around their heartstrings and brains.

You can sorrow o'er little children

Disinherited from their birth,
The wee waifs and toddlers neglected,
   Robbed of sunshine, music and mirth.

For beasts you have gentle compassion;
   Your mercy and pity they share.
For the wretched, outcast and fallen
   You have tenderness, love and care.

But hark! from our Southland are floating
   Sobs of anguish, murmurs of pain,
And women heart-stricken are weeping

*From Frances E. W. Harper. *Complete Poems of Frances E. W. Harper,* ed. Maryemma Graham, Schomburg Library of Nineteenth-Century Black Women Writers Series, Henry Louis Gates, Jr., gen. ed. (New York: Oxford University Press, 1988), pp. 127, 193–95.

Over their tortured and their slain.

On their brows the sun has left traces;
    Shrink not from their sorrow in scorn.
When they entered the threshold of being
    The children of a King were born.

Each comes as a guest to the table
    The hands of our God has outspread,
To fountains that ever leap upward,
    To share in the soil we all tread.

When we plead for the wrecked and
        fallen,
    The exile from far-distant shores,
Remember that men are still wasting
    Life's crimson around our own doors.

Have ye not, oh, my favored sisters,
    Just a plea, a prayer or a tear,
For mothers who dwell 'neath the
        shadows
    Of agony, hatred and fear?

Men may tread down the poor and lowly,
    May crush them in anger and hate,

But surely the mills of God's justice
    Will grind out the grist of their fate.

Oh, people sin-laden and guilty,
    So lusty and proud in your prime,
The sharp sickles of God's retribution
    Will gather your harvest of crime.

Weep not, oh my well-sheltered sisters,
    Weep not for the Negro alone,
But weep for your sons who must gather
    The crops which their fathers have
        sown.

Go read on the tombstones of nations
    Of chieftains who masterful trod,
The sentence which time has engraven,
    That they had forgotten their God.

'Tis the judgment of God that men reap
    The tares which in madness they sow,
Sorrow follows the footsteps of crime,
    And Sin is the consort of Woe.

WOMEN AND MUSIC

Many women musicians emerged in the nineteenth century, thanks in large part to the emphasis on musical training as part of every elite and middle-class girl's education. Many were singers, others pianists, and a surprisingly large number also composed. Few, however, became professional musicians and fewer still actually published their compositions. Yet, new works by women are still being discovered. The two women presented reflect many of the social dynamics that sometimes encouraged women to become accomplished musicians but then inhibited their full development as professionals.

Fanny Mendelssohn Hensel (1805–1847): German Musician

Fanny was the sister of the well-known composer Felix Mendelssohn. She was the eldest of four children born to banker Abraham Mendelssohn and his wife Lea Solomon, and the granddaughter of a famed philosopher and theologian, Moses Mendelssohn. Her family was part of the leading musical and intellectual circles in Berlin. Fanny received the same education and musical training as Felix (who was four years younger than she), and, like Felix, was a *wunderkind* or child prodigy. Their mother, who came from a musical family, gave the children their early piano lessons. When she was 12, Fanny could play 24 preludes of Bach's *Well-Tempered Clavier* by memory. She began to compose soon after she and Felix began to study composition and music theory at the elite Berlin Sing Academy. In 1821, however, the careers and lives of Fanny and her brother began to take different paths. Felix was prepared for a career in music, while Fanny was guided toward her destiny as wife and mother.

After her marriage in 1829 to court painter Wilhelm Hensel and the subsequent birth of their only child, she set aside her composing and assumed responsibility for organizing weekly Sunday musical gatherings at their home. She was the hostess and center of these large gatherings, and occasionally performed in this private and intimate setting. Others also performed her compositions. Fanny composed well over 400 pieces and sent many to Felix for his feedback. He published some of her works under his name and in letters reported positive audience response when he performed her works. (Criton 1984, 12–13) Nevertheless, although her husband and some musician friends continually encouraged her, anticipated family opposition, particularly from her beloved Felix, caused her to limit her composing, and she refused to publish her works until the end of her life. At one point, their mother wrote Felix begging him to give Fanny his blessing to publish, but he refused to do so. Ironically, though he was reluctant to endorse his sister's desire to publish, his encouragement led another woman, Josephine Lang, to publish her compositions. Near the end of her life, Fanny followed the advice of friends and her husband and published without having obtained his approval.

The excerpts that follow reveal the family pressures Fanny experienced as a composer, how the Victorian ideal shaped her life, and her dreams and love of music.

EXCERPTS FROM MENDELSSOHN FAMILY LETTERS AND JOURNALS*

ABRAHAM MENDELSSOHN TO HIS DAUGHTER, FANNY (AGE 14), 16 JULY 1820

. . . What you wrote to me about your musical occupations with reference to and in comparison with Felix was both rightly thought and expressed. Music will perhaps become his profession, whilst for you it can and must only be an ornament, never the root of your being and doing. We may therefore pardon him some ambition and desire to be acknowledged in a pursuit which appears very important to him, because he feels a vocation for it, whilst it does you credit that you have always shown yourself good and sensible in these matters; and your very joy at the praise he earns proves that you might, in his place, have merited equal approval. Remain true to these sentiments and to this line of conduct; they are feminine, and only what is truly feminine is an ornament to your sex. . . .

FANNY TO HER MUSICIAN FRIEND, KLINGEMANN, 15 JULY 1836

. . . I inclose two pianoforte-pieces which I have written since I came home from Dusseldorf. I leave it to you to say whether they are worth presenting to my unknown young friend, but I must add that it is a pleasure to me to find a public for my little pieces in London, for here I have none at all. Once a year, perhaps, some one will copy a piece of mine, or ask me to play something special . . . ; and now that

*From Sebastian Hensel. *The Mendelssohn Family (1729–1847) from Letters and Journals,* trans. Carl Klingemann and an American collaborator, 2d rev. ed., vols. I and II (New York: Harper & Brothers, 1881), vol. I, p. 82; vol. II, p. 31.

Rebecca [her sister] has left off singing, my songs lie unheeded and unknown. If no-body ever offers an opinion, or takes the slightest interest in one's productions, one loses in time not only all pleasure in them but all power of judging of their value. Felix, who is alone a sufficient public for me, is so seldom here that he cannot help me much, and thus I am thrown back entirely on myself. But my own delight in music and Hensel's sympathy keep me awake still, and I cannot help considering it a sign of talent that I do not give it up, though I can get nobody to take an interest in my efforts. But enough of this uninteresting topic.

LETTER FROM FANNY TO FELIX, BERLIN, 9 JULY 1846*

. . . Actually I wouldn't expect you to read this rubbish now, busy as you are, if I didn't have to tell you something. But since I know from the start that you won't like it, it's a bit awkward to get under way. So laugh at me or not, as you wish: I'm afraid of my brother at age 40, as I was of father at age 14—Or, more aptly expressed, desirous of pleasing you and everyone I've loved throughout my life. And when I now know in advance that it won't be the case, I thus feel rather uncomfortable. In a word, I'm be-ginning to publish. I have Herr Bock's sincere offer for my lieder and have finally turned a receptive ear to his favorable terms. And if I've done it of my own free will and cannot blame anyone in my family if aggravation results from it (friends and ac-quaintances have indeed been urging me for a long time), then I can console myself, on the other hand, with the knowledge that I in no way sought out or induced the type of musical reputation that might have elicited such offers. I hope I won't dis-grace all of you through my publishing, as I'm no *femme libre* and unfortunately not even an adherent of the Young Germany movement. I trust *you* will in no way be bothered by it, since, as you can see, I've proceeded completely on my own in order to spare you any possible unpleasant moment. I hope you won't think badly of me. If it succeeds—that is, if the pieces are well liked and I receive additional offers—I know it will be a great stimulus to me, something I've always needed in order to cre-ate. If not, I'll be as indifferent as I've always been and not be upset, and then if I work less or stop completely, nothing will have been lost by that either. . . .

A month after her confessional letter to Felix, Fanny received the response she had longed for years to hear and recorded her relief in her diary. Nine months later on May 14, 1847, she died of a sudden stroke.

FELIX GIVES HIS BLESSINGS TO FANNY**

FELIX TO FANNY, LEIPZIG, 12 AUGUST 1846

My dearest Fance,—Not till to-day, just as I am on the point of starting, do I, unnat-ural brother that I am, find time to thank you for your charming letter, and send you

*From Fanny Mendelssohn Hensel, *The Letters of Fanny Hensel to Felix Mendelssohn,* ed. and trans. Marcia J. Cit-ron, Musicological Series (New York: Pendragon Press, 1987), pp. 349, 351. Copyright © by Pendragon Press, 1987. With permission of Pendragon Press.

**From Hensel, *The Mendelssohn Family (1729–1847) from Letters and Journals,* vol. II, p. 326.

my professional blessing on becoming—a member of the craft. This I do now in full, Fance, and may you have much happiness in giving pleasure to others; may you taste only the sweets and none of the bitternesses of authorship; may the public pelt you with roses, and never with sand; and may the printer's ink never draw black lines upon your soul—all of which I devoutly believe will be the case, so what is the use of my wishing it! But it is the custom of the guild, so take my blessing under my hand and seal. . . .

FANNY'S DIARY ENTRY, 14 AUGUST 1846

At last Felix has written, and given me his professional blessing in the kindest manner. I know that he is not quite satisfied in his heart of hearts, but I am glad he has said a kind word to me about it.

Clara Schumann (1819–1896): German Composer and Concert Pianist

Clara Wieck Schumann was one of the great concert pianists of the nineteenth century. She began her concert career in 1838 at age 8. By the time she was 18, she had completed 10 years of successful concert tours in Paris, Vienna, and cities across Germany. She had also received Vienna's highest honor when the emperor named her "Royal and Imperial Chamber Virtuoso." This was an unprecedented honor for an 18-year-old woman, who was also a Protestant and a foreigner. Her final concert, celebrating the sixtieth anniversary of her first public performance in Leipzig, occurred in October 1878. No other pianist, male or female, had such a long career in the nineteenth century. Her career was particularly significant because of her sex. Few women continued to perform after marriage, let alone after having children. Moreover, as public concerts replaced private court performances, showmanship became an increasingly important aspect of success. Few could compare, for example, with Franz Liszt on the concert stage, yet Schumann was regarded as a peer of Liszt and other leading pianists such as Anton Rubinstein. Moreover, she was a success without developing a flamboyant style. She premiered the Beethoven sonatas and works of Chopin, Brahms, and her husband, Robert Schumann. Like other artists, she also arranged her concert tours. (Reich 1985, 262–63, 281–83) She also managed to compose a fairly large number of concertos and songs.

Clara Wieck was the daughter of Friedrich Wieck, a gifted piano teacher, and Marianne Tromlitz, a concert pianist and soprano. Her mother left her husband after the birth of her fifth child and returned to her family home. She was permitted to keep Clara only until her fifth birthday, at which time the child came under her father's legal control and was rarely permitted to see her mother. Clara received excellent training from her father, who recognized her unusual talent. She had little education other than music and languages, however, and her father discouraged her and his other female students from learning feminine arts such as sewing.

Clara met Robert Schumann when he began studying under her father. She was 9 and he was 18. Her father tried everything possible to break up their romance, partly, Robert suspected, to maintain control over her lucrative earning power. They finally married, despite his objections, in 1840, the day before her twenty-first birthday. Thus began a most interesting union of an early dual-career couple. Clara had eight children and one miscarriage during the 14 years she and Robert were together. They lived in three different cities in that period, and she assumed responsibility for setting up each new household, managing it and two or three servants, bearing and rearing the children, while fostering her husband's career as a composer, giving concerts herself, and composing as often as she could.

They always had two grand pianos, each in a different room, to enable both to compose and practice; however, "the evils of thin walls" made it impossible for both to play at the same time (Litzmann 1972, vol. I, p. 313).

The last two years of their marriage were very painful. Robert's long-standing mental problems became so severe that he was committed to a hospital. A few months after he was institutionalized she bore her eighth child. Too proud to seek financial help, she managed to pay their debts by embarking on another concert tour. In addition to Robert's death, she also lost four adult children. In each case, her method of coping was to turn to her work. She eased her pain at Robert's death by performing his music to ensure his recognition as a major composer. She also relied on the friendship and support of the young composer Johannes Brahms and violinist Joseph Joachim.

Clara and Robert kept a dual diary throughout their marriage, and the excerpts that follow shed light on many aspects of her personality, their marriage, and her creative work. The excerpts also illustrate the challenges they faced as a pioneering "dual-career couple." These challenges were particularly evident in the spring of 1842, when Clara went on an extended concert tour alone, after Robert decided his career required him to remain at home.

CLARA AND ROBERT SCHUMANN: DUAL-CAREER COUPLE*

CLARA TO HER FRIEND EMILIE LIST, MAY 30, 1842

. . . Yes, I really went to Copenhagen alone, . . . [she notes she had considered abandoning the trip] I thought the matter over, however. I am a woman, I shall not be neglecting anything, I earn nothing at home, why should I not by means of my talent, gain my mite for Robert? Could anyone think ill of me for so doing, or of my husband for going home to his child and his business? I laid my plan before Robert, and it is true that at first he shrank from it, but in the end he agreed, when I represented the matter to him as reasonably as possible. It was certainly a great step for a wife who loves her husband as I do, but I did it for love of him, and for that no sacrifice is too great or too hard for me. . . .

ROBERT'S DIARY ENTRY DURING CLARA'S TOUR, MARCH 14, 1842

The separation has once more made me very conscious of my peculiar and difficult position. Am I to neglect my own talent, in order to serve you as a companion on your journeys? Have you allowed your talent to lie useless, or ought you to do so, because I am chained to the paper and to the piano? Now, when you are young and in full possession of your powers? We found the solution. You took a companion with you, and I came back to the child and to my work. But what will the world say? Thus I torture myself with thinking. Yes, it is most necessary that we should find some means by which we can both utilise and develop our talents side by side.

*Excerpts from Berthold Litzmann, *Clara Schumann; An Artist's Life, Based on Material Found in Diaries and Letters,* trans. and abridged from the 4th ed. by Grace E. Hadow with preface by W. H. Hadow (Reprint of the 1913 ed., New York: Vienna House, 1972), vol. I, pp. 336–38.

CLARA'S THOUGHTS ABOUT MUSIC AND HER TALENT*

November, 1839: I once thought that I possessed creative talent, but I have given up this idea; a woman must not desire to compose—not one has been able to do it, and why should I expect to? It would be arrogance, though indeed, my Father led me into it in earlier days.

Oct. 2, 1846, after the First Rehearsal of Her Trio: There is nothing greater than the joy of composing something oneself, and then listening to it. There are some pretty passages in the trio, and I think it is fairly successful as far as form goes. . . . of course it is only a woman's work, which is always lacking in force, and here and there in invention.

COPING WITH ROBERT'S MENTAL ILLNESS**

March 1, 1854: . . . He, my glorious Robert, in an asylum!—How was it possible for me to bear it? And ah! I was forbidden even to clasp him once more to my heart. I had to make this greatest of all sacrifices for him, for my Robert.

May 16, 1854: Ah! how sad a morning dawned again to-day! The news from the doctor was painful in many respects. The delusions of hearing continue, and he speaks wildly. . . . But the most painful thing to me is that when he speaks of Dusseldorf he mentions the Hasenclevers, but does not say one syllable of me. . . . Ah! Robert, my love is so unending that you must feel it. . . . If only my child were born I could begin to set about some work—I cannot go on like this.—Besides I must see about earning something. Living is far too expensive, and Robert's money is gradually melting away. My chief endeavour now is to earn enough to pay for Robert's illness. If heaven sends him recovery, there must be nothing to remind him of this miserable time. . . . If only I could do something at once! . . .

CELEBRATING HER CAREER AS A CONCERT PIANIST, 1878***

Tuesday 21, October: To Leipsic . . . for the celebration of my jubilee . . . on the invitation of the *Gewandhaus* committee. It certainly was not my wish that this event which is so pleasant for me, should be celebrated in public, but . . . I could not refuse them. . . . It meant much to me to keep this festival in my native town and in the same room, in which I made my first public appearance 60 years ago. . . .

October 24th: A memorable day. In the morning I was overwhelmed with magnificent presents, addresses, flowers, wreathes, telegrams. . . . Concert in the evening. . . . only works by Robert were given. . . . The whole hall was decorated with wreathes and garlands of green and gold oak-leaves. As I stepped on to the platform the entire audience stood up and a rain of flowers began under which I was really buried. . . . It

*Excerpts from Berthold Litzmann, *Clara Schumann*, trans. and abridged from the 4th ed. by Grace E. Hadow with preface by W. H. Hadow, vols. I and II (Reprint of the 1913 ed., New York: Vienna House, 1972), vol. I, pp. 259, 410.

**Excerpts from Litzmann, *Clara Schumann*, vol. II, pp. 60, 72–73.

***Excerpts from Litzmann, *Clara Schumann*, vol. II, pp. 342–43.

was a long time before I could seat myself at the piano. Once or twice I felt as if I should be overcome, I trembled violently, but I controlled myself and played the concerto perfectly quietly, and it went splendidly . . . At the end when I was recalled, Reinecke handed me a magnificent gold laurel-wreath, a present from the orchestra. . . . It is exquisitely made, on every leaf is the name of one of the composers whose works I have played in the course of my career . . . After the concert . . . I went to the Freges, and was greeted on my entrance by some beautiful songs. . . . Besides this I found all my friends and acquaintances gathered together. . . . They were all so merry and friendly that I found the end of the day as stimulating as the rest of it had been. . . . And so I went to bed with a very grateful heart because God had allowed me to enjoy this day in the full possession of my artistic powers.

Women Musicians: Seizing Control of Their Artistic Lives

Many talented European and American women musicians dreamed of careers other than teaching music, but they were denied the opportunity even to try out for membership in orchestras. In response, they began to create all-female orchestras of their own. The following article suggests some of the public reaction to this strategy. It also reveals the music critic's own assumptions or gender biases.

THE VIENNA LADY ORCHESTRA, NEW YORK TIMES, 13 SEPTEMBER 1871*

The first performance of the Vienna Lady Orchestra was given at Steinway Hall on Monday evening, to the expressed pleasure of a very large and fashionable audience. The spectacle was certainly a novel one. The platform was changed into a bower, and under the roses were sheltered, instead of the familiar *profanuns vulgus* of music-makers, a score of blushing maidens attired in purest white, and armed, after the orthodox style, for their harmonious work. The sight of the instrumentalist of the gentler sex has little rarity about it, but the view of an organized force of female musicians was, until Monday, never offered in this country. On this fact was founded a very large share of the first success of the Vienna Lady Orchestra, and on it will rest their prospective triumphs. We would not, however, underrate the cleverness and culture the company displayed. Its members execute with precision and spirit the rather unpretentious selections whereof their programme is made up, and some of the solo talent is to be highly commended. The chief opportunity for fault-finding is suggested by the lack of heavy wood and string instruments, and by the absence of brass. . . .

A Late Nineteenth Century Debate: Can Women Become Composers?

In the late nineteenth and early twentieth centuries, increasing numbers of women emerged as performers, teachers, and patrons of music. More women also began to compose, particularly popular music and dance music, but more also emerged as composers of classical music in Europe and America.

*Excerpt from "The Vienna Lady Orchestra," *New York Times* (Rochester, NY: Eastman Kodak Co. for Recordac Corp.), September 1871, p. 5, col. 4, microfilm: NP1.

Alarmed by the growing number of women composers, some music critics feared that music would become "feminized" and that the quality of music would decline. They argued that women were innately incapable of composing great music, drawing, in part, on scientific "evidence" of female mental inferiority.

George Upton, a Chicago music critic, was among the first to set forth this theory in his influential book *Woman in Music,* published in 1880. Upton acknowledged that women could interpret music, notably as singers, but insisted that they could not write "great" music. Consider the arguments or evidence he uses to support his theory and whether he grants women any role in the creation of "great" music.

George Upton, Why Women Are Incapable of Being Composers*

> . . . even assuming that woman had the disposition and the leisure to devote to musical composition, would she *then* succeed? The bluntest answer to this is, that she has not succeeded when she has had the opportunity. . . . If music . . . simply addressed itself to the senses, if it were but an art composed of ravishing melody, of passionate outbursts, of the attributes of joy, grief, and exaltation, and vague, dreamy sensations without any determinate ideas, woman possibly would have grasped it long ago, and flooded the world with harmony . . . ; but music is all this and more. . . . It is not only an art, but an exact science, and, in its highest form, mercilessly logical and unrelentingly mathematical. . . . The mere possession of the poetical imagination and the capacity to receive music in its fullest emotional power will not lead one to the highest achievements in musical art. With these subjective qualities must be combined the mastery of the theoretical intricacies, the logical sequences, and the mathematical problems, which are the foundation principles of music. In this direction woman, except in very rare instances, has never achieved great results. . . .
>
> For these and many other reasons growing out of the peculiar organization of woman, the sphere in which she moves, the training which she receives, and the duties she has to fulfil, it does not seem that woman will ever originate music in its fullest and grandest harmonic forms. She will always be the recipient and interpreter, but there is little hope she will be the creator.
>
> However this may be, there is a field in which she has accomplished great results; namely, her influence upon the production of music. . . . it is not exaggeration to claim that . . . the great composers have written through her inspiration, and that she has, in numerous notable instances, been their impulse, support, and consolation.

In the next excerpt, Helen Clarke is responding to an article by Edith Brower, "Is the Musical Idea Masculine?" that appeared in the *Atlantic Monthly* in March 1894. Like Upton, Brower had argued that women were incapable of the abstract thought necessary to create music. Note the explanations Clarke gives for the lack of women composers in her rebuttal of Brower, Upton, and other such critics, and consider what these two excerpts suggest about the importance of women's history.

*Excerpts from George Upton, *Woman in Music,* 3rd ed. (Chicago: A. C. McClurg and Co., 1890), pp. 29–32.

HELEN J. CLARKE, *WHY HAS IT BEEN DIFFICULT FOR WOMEN TO COMPOSE?**

. . . All of the great composers . . . were thoroughly trained, either through their own efforts, or through the aid of teachers and experience, in all that pertains to the technic of composition and not a few were educated men in other respects. . . .

As for their musical education, there is not one from Bach down who did not have it. They were usually taught several instruments, were drilled in the laws of counterpoint and pored over the scores of the great composers who preceded them. In fact, no art can boast a more continuous record of special training than that of music, and no art requires special training more than music. And to man almost exclusively in the past has fallen the lot of special training. . . .

Another way in which conditions have been peculiarly favorable for the development of the composing faculty in men is that they have always breathed in the midst of musical environments. When a Bach or a Haydn is discovered to have a voice, he immediately becomes a choir boy, and being a boy he knows he may someday become choir master, so he observes the effects which may be produced from the organ, or the effects in chorus singing—all of which he lays up in his mind and digests as artistic food.

Likewise, when a Handel or a Beethoven plays an instrument ere long he plays in an orchestra, and so has constant opportunity of observing the qualities and capabilities of the instruments, the timbre, the intensity of sound and so on. Only by such means can he hope ever to use instruments effectively. And this artistic expression is no more than artistic diet without which the artistic faculty can no more grow and develop than could a human body develop physically without food. . . .

. . . I do not intend to argue from these facts that women are great composers. . . . I think, however, as I have tried to show, that the nature of music is such that certain conditions in the past have militated greatly against her highest development in the art, . . .

Until women have had the same sort of training, above all, the same musical environments, the same opportunity to devote themselves body and soul to the art of composition, it is manifestly unfair to declare them mentally and emotionally incapable of great work.

The difficulties that women must overcome are far greater than those which meet men at the dawn of their musical career. They must come into competition with all the great works which have preceded them, and they must struggle in the face of a prejudice against their possession of genius so deeprooted and widespread that even their faith in themselves wavers, and the desire to attain without which no goal can be made is thus shorn of the strong impulse that should "aim at the stars" and is content if it but "hits the moon."

*From Helen J. Clarke, "The Nature of Music and Its Relation to the Question of Women in Music," in *Music, a Monthly Magazine; Devoted to the Art, Science, Technic and Literature of Music* (Chicago: W. S. B. Mathews, 1895) 7 (March 1895), pp. 458–61.

SUGGESTED READINGS

Literature

Coultrap-McQuin, Susan Margaret. *Doing Literary Business: American Women Writers in the Nineteenth Century.* Chapel Hill: University of North Carolina Press, 1990.

Gorsky, Susan Rubinow. *Femininity to Feminism: Women and Literature in the Nineteenth Century.* New York: Twayne; Toronto: Maxwell Macmillan Canada; New York: Maxwell Macmillan International, 1992.

Prentis, Barbara. *The Brontë Sisters and George Eliot: A Unity of Difference.* Basingstoke, UK: Macmillan, 1988.

Seymour, Miranda. *Mary Shelley.* New York: Grove Press, 2000.

Music

Ammer, Christine. *Unsung: A History of Women in American Music.* Portland, OR: Amadeus, 2001.

Hyde, Derek. *New Found Voices: Women in Nineteenth Century English Music.* Cornwall, England: Belvedere Press Ltd., 1984.

Tillard, Françoise. *Fanny Mendelssohn.* Translated by Camille Naish. Portland, OR: Amadeus Press, 1987.

Audio Sources

Hensel, Fanny Mendelssohn. *Gartenlieder (Choral Music, Selections).* CPO, 1988. Compact disc 999 012–2.

Schumann, Clara. *Pieces pour Piano.* Calliope, 1987. Compact disc CAL 9211.

Chapter 8

The Victorian Ideal:
The Performing and Visual Arts

WOMEN ON STAGE

During the nineteenth century, women continued to make further inroads onto the stage in ballet and theater. In both art forms, female superstars emerged, and in dance, the *prima ballerina* even eclipsed the premier male dancers. Dance and theater also became important occupational fields for lower-class girls seeking jobs other than factory or servant positions. Because being on stage was tantamount to prostitution in the eyes of many in society, however, respectable middle-class families often opposed their daughters' desire to try for stardom. In fact, rank-and-file dancers and actresses could barely make a living on their meager incomes. The few superstars, however, commanded high salaries and the kind of public acclaim modern pop stars enjoy. (Kendall 1979, 4–7; Johnson 1987, 66–74) Women in both dance and theater introduced a number of innovations that added to the popularity of the performing arts, such as more revealing dance costumes and *breeches roles* in theater where actresses performed male roles in male attire. The titillating promise of more views of female legs on stage drew the curious to the theater or ballet but then won over more converts to each. Ballerinas were critical to the success of the new romantic ballets while actresses helped shift staple theater productions from melodrama to more realistic plays. The two women discussed in this section illustrate these and other patterns in the performing arts.

Marie Taglione (1804–1884): Italian Prima Ballerina

Marie Taglione was an awkward-looking child whose father molded her into the world's premier ballerina of the mid-nineteenth century. In the 1820s, female dancers were exploring *en pointe* (toe) dancing, a technique that gave the dancer a light and ethereal or floating appearance. Although it gave the impression of frailty, toe dancing required incredible strength and skill, particularly in the early years before block toe shoes were invented to support the foot. Taglione's father drilled her in *en pointe* dancing, added proper shoes with toe support, and choreographed movements specifically designed for her type of body and movement. He also wrote a new ballet, *La Sylphide,* to showcase her particular talents and unique style. *La Sylphide,* created in 1831, was the first fully developed Romantic ballet. It also introduced a new costume for the ballerinas, designed to enhance the dancer's beauty and the other-worldly character of the star. It featured a tight bodice, with an off-shoulder look, and full fluffy skirt. The white costume, together with clever point work, gave the dancer the appearance of floating above the stage. (Hill 1967, 13–14, 82–83) That image was further enhanced by the use of harnesses and wires that enabled the ballerina to fly across the stage. Gas lighting also contributed to the effect by creating a soft misty ambiance and focusing the light and hence audience attention on the stage.

The combination of new staging, new costumes, and point work made Taglione an instant celebrity and ensured the success of Romantic ballet. Although Marie was married for a short period of time and had some children, the public knew little of her private life. Her brother, who was also trained by her father, was her partner in many of her performances. Her father supervised most ballets in which she appeared in order to ensure that she was allowed to dance in ways that showcased her special style and talent. Other prima ballerinas emerged in her shadow, and, as had happened in the seventeenth century, great rivalries ensued among the dancers, particularly between Taglione and Fanny Elssler, and their fans. Taglione and Romantic ballet brought the ballerina to center stage. The story revolved around her and the choreography featured her skills. The male dancers receded into the background and assumed the role of assisting and lifting the prima ballerina. By the end of the century, some lamented that women had made the male dancer nearly invisible (Levinson 1977, 110–11). The newspaper accounts that follow suggest the excitement that Taglione generated, her particular talents, and the differing styles of her major rivals.

TIMES (LONDON), 3 JUNE 1840: REVIEW OF LA GITANA*

> Mademoiselle Taglioni made her first appearance last night in her favourite ballet of *La Gitana*. . . . The beauties of her dancing have been dwelt on again and again; but they are of that high order that they are always new, and the last appearance always seems to be attended with some fresh charm. . . . In the *pas de trois* last night Taglioni threw complete meaning into her slow movements; there was a gentle tenderness about them, a feeling for which her graceful motion seemed the natural expression. Then came the dart into the quick movement, as if some joyous fancy had suddenly entered the mind of the dancer, and sent her less bounding than flying along the stage with the wanton glee of a bacchante. Her mazurka was very fine: at times she seemed to sink into mere indolence, as if the dance had grown so habitual that she might listlessly leave her limbs to take their own course, her face expressing little more than a happy contentment; then would her countenance suddenly light up, a new animation possessed her frame, and she was wafted along by its influence. Every one of her *pas,* from the mazurka to the concluding *cachucha,* drew down thunders of applause.
>
> The Queen Dowager was at the theatre, which was exceedingly well attended.

*From "Her Majesty's Theatre," *Times* (London; New Haven, CT: Research Publications, 1977), 3 June 1840, p. 6, col. 2, microfilm: NP 12.

Times (London), 14 July 1845: Review of the *Pas de Quatre**

On Saturday night was the greatest Terpsichorean exhibition that ever was known in Europe—we repeat the phrase—that ever was known in Europe. Taglioni, [Fanny] Cerito [Cerrito], Carlotta Grisi, and Lucile Grahn were all combined in one *pas de quatre,* and such a combination was altogether unprecedented, nay, might have been declared impossible. For secret history will ooze its way even through the pores of curtain, and then do we learn that those ethereal looking creatures, whom mortals call *danseuses, . . .* are not remarkable for love towards each other, and that the task of getting four of them into one *pas,* supposes a power of persuasion and argumentation bordering on the preternatural. There is not the slightest doubt that even to half past 10 o'clock on Saturday night there were sundry sceptics who believed that the announced *pas* would never take place, . . . Certainly people had seen a *pas de deux* by Elssler and Cerito, danced amid an enthusiastic warfare that threatened to revive the blue and green factions of the Hippodrome, but then—how great the difference between two and four! For the difficulty in these cases does not merely progress in the geometrical ratio of the number of artists, but must be estimated by squares, like the velocity of falling bodies.

Therefore, we say, when the curtain rose for the impossible *pas de quatre,* and the marvellous four entered, all in a line, hand holding hand, as a testimony of amity, the house burst forth into a tumult, not only of admiration, but of amazement. . . . The slow movement of the *pas* began, and the four ladies formed a series of groups matchless for taste and elegance, Taglioni usually occupying the central position. Then came the quick movements with the variations . . . [the steps each dancer executes *sola* in a grand *pas* are called "variations"] and here was the period for the greatest excitement, now was the question to be decided how each would put forth her strength. Taglioni displayed all her common long manner, relying much on that advancing step, of which we believe, she was the inventress, and astonishing by some of her bounds. Lucile Grahn, a *disciple* of the same school, danced with a breadth and vigour which showed a determination not to be outdone by her elder competitors. Cerito entered into the contest with that revolving step which invariably delights; and Carlotta Grisi, forming a striking contrast, gave a *piquant,* coquettish sort of variation with her wonted fascination. . . . Never was such a *pas* before, and there is no reason to believe that after the present season there will ever be such a *pas* again. The excitement which a competition so extraordinary produced in the artists roused them to a pitch of energy which would have been impossible under other circumstances, and hence every one did her utmost, the whole performance being a complete inspiration. . . .

The manifestation of enthusiasm on the part of the audience was scarcely less remarkable than the manifestation of energy on the part of the artists. The whole long *pas* was danced to a running sound of applause, which, after each variation swelled to a perfect hurricane, the *furor* of partisanship being added to the weight of general admiration. Bouquets flew from every point, in immense profusion, as each *danseuse* came forward. . . .

*From "Her Majesty's Theatre," *Times* (London; New Haven, CT: Research Publications, 1977), 14 July 1845, p. 5, col. 3, microfilm: NP 12.

Charlotte Cushman (1816–1876): American Actress

Charlotte Cushman was one of America's first important actresses. Like other actresses and many other American artists of the nineteenth century, however, she spent a good part of her professional life abroad. Most of her professional career was spent in England, but she also spent time in Rome, where she was the center of a group of American artists and sculptors who moved there for the opportunities that city afforded aspiring artists. Like many other career women of the period, she adopted an alternative lifestyle, making her life with other women. When she returned to the United States, she continued to perform and was instrumental in building public interest in theater. She also established a second career doing public "readings" after she had left the stage and worked to interest young students in theater. During the Civil War she raised funds to help clothe and supply Union soldiers.

She was among a generation of actresses who assumed *breeches roles* in order to play more demanding roles. She and her sister Susan appeared together in a number of plays and enjoyed great success. In taking male roles and donning male attire, Cushman and others were reversing theatrical conventions of the Shakespearean theater in which men and boys played all the female roles. They attracted huge audiences initially because of the novelty of seeing women on stage with their legs on display. The notion of women playing male roles also was a box-office draw. Once in the theater, however, Cushman's acting talent overshadowed the novelty aspect of the performance. The following excerpts also reveal how ambitious women looked to successful women in other fields as well as their own for inspiration. You will meet some of these role models later in this chapter. All of the selections are from *Charlotte Cushman. Her Letters and Memories of Her Life.**

English Critic James Sheridan Knowles's Review of Cushman's Romeo

I witnessed with astonishment the Romeo of Miss Cushman. Unanimous and lavish as were the encomiums of the London press, I was not prepared for such a triumph of pure genius. You recollect, perhaps, Kean's third act of Othello. Did you ever expect to see anything like it again? I never did, and yet I saw as great a thing last Wednesday night in Romeo's scene with the Friar, after the sentence of banishment, quite as great! I am almost tempted to go further. It was a scene of topmost passion; not simulated passion,—no such thing; real, palpably real; the genuine heart-storm was on,—on in wildest fitfulness of fury; and I listened and gazed and held my breath, while my blood ran hot and cold. I am sure it must have been the case with every one in the house; but I was all absorbed in Romeo, till a thunder of applause recalled me to myself. I particularize this scene because it is the most powerful, but every scene exhibited the same truthfulness. The first scene with Juliet, for instance, admirably personated by her beautiful sister, was exquisitely faithful,—the eye, the tone, the general hearing,—everything attesting the lover smit to the core at first sight, and shrinkingly and falteringly endeavoring, with the aid of palm and eye and tongue, to break his passion to his idol.

My heart and mind are so full of this extraordinary, most extraordinary performance, that I know not where to stop or how to go on. Throughout it was a triumph equal to the proudest of those which I used to witness years ago, and for a repetition

*Excerpts from *Charlotte Cushman. Her Letters and Memories of Her Life,* Edited by Her Friend Emma Stebbins (Boston and NY: Houghton, Mifflin, 1899), pp. 63, 182, 186–87, 262–64.

of which I have looked in vain till now. There is no trick in Miss Cushman's performance; No thought, no interest, no feeling, seems to actuate her, except what might be looked for in Romeo himself were Romeo reality.

CUSHMAN ON GEORGE SAND

. . . My one sole reason for not knowing or seeking to know her has been my reverence. I cannot speak French; I cannot make myself sufficiently understood to intrude upon the life and time of a great woman like Madame Dudevant, . . . To George Sand I should bring nothing but my reverence and my admiration. She would produce in me the same feeling and the same silence she did in Mrs. Browning. Therefore I have hesitated to know her. But one of these days we will go together to see her and thank her for all that she has been to both of us; for to me she revealed my religion, and she has ever been able to produce nothing but good in me.

FUNDRAISING FOR THE U.S. SANITARY COMMISSION DURING THE CIVIL WAR

The President of the United States Sanitary Commission feels it to be a great pleasure to call universal attention to the patriotic munificence of our distinguished countrywoman, Miss Charlotte Cushman, who, from the vessel in which she leaves our shores, modestly sends him the full account of her splendid donations to the sick and wounded through the United States Sanitary Commission. They are as follows:

Benefit at Academy of Music, Philadelphia, September 12	$1,314.27
Benefit at Academy of Music, Boston, September 26	2,020.75
Benefit at Grover's Theatre, Washington, October 17	1,800.00
Benefit at Ford's Theatre, Baltimore, October 19 (this small receipt is attributable to the negligence and carelessness of the manager. C.C.)	360.00
Benefit at Academy of Music, New York, October 22	2,772.27
Total	$8,267.29

This magnificent product of the genius of Miss Cushman, devoted to the relief of our suffering soldiers, is only the most striking exemplification yet made of woman's power and will to do her full part in the national struggle. Inspired with love and pity, American women have been, by their labors and sympathies, a real part of the army, and their ranks, under leaders like Miss Cushman, will not break while their sons, brothers, and husbands are faithful in the field.

It is due to Miss Charlotte Cushman to say that this extraordinary gift of money, so magically evoked by her spell, is but the least part of the service which, ever since the war began, she has been rendering our cause in Europe. Her earnest faith in the darkest hours, her prophetic confidence in our success, her eloquent patriotism in all presences, have been potent influences abroad, and deserve and command the gratitude of the whole nation. . . .

Henry W Bellows, President United States Sanitary Commission. November 7, 1863

Cushman's Farewell New York Performance, *Macbeth*, 1874

[After the performance at 11:00 p.m., a group came on stage to salute her; first with an ode and flowers, then] Mr. William Cullen Bryant then delivered the following address:

MADAM: The members of the Arcadian Club have desired me to present you with a crown of laurel. . . . Be pleased to receive it as both a token of their proud admiration of your genius and their high esteem for your personal character. . . . The laurel is the proper ornament for the brow of one who has won so eminent and enviable a renown by successive conquests in the realm of histrionic art. You have taken a queenly rank in your profession; you have carried into one department of it after another the triumphs of your genius; you have interpreted through the eye and ear to the sympathies of vast assemblages of men and women the words of the greatest dramatic writers; what came to your hands in the skeleton form you have clothed with sinews and flesh, and given it warm blood and a beating heart. Receive, then, the laurel crown . . . as a symbol of the regal state in your profession to which you have risen. . . .

CUSHMAN'S REPLY:

. . . I thank you, gentlemen, for the great honor you have offered me. I thank you, not only for myself, but for my whole profession, to which, through and by me, you have paid this very graceful compliment. . . .

I say this to the beginners in my profession, and I am sure all the associates in my art, who have honored me with their presence on this occasion, will indorse what I say in this. Art is an absolute mistress; she will not be coquetted with or slighted; she requires the most entire self-devotion, and she repays with grand triumphs. . . .

To my public—what shall I say? From the depths of my heart I thank you, who have given me always consideration, encouragement, and patience; who have been ever my comfort, my support, my main help. I do not now say farewell to you in the usual sense of the word. In making my final representations upon the mimic scene in the various cities of the country, I have reserved to myself the right of meeting you again where you have made me believe that I give you the pleasure which I receive myself at the same time,—at the reading-desk [lecture series]. To you, then, I say, may you *fare* well and may I *fare* well, until at no distant day we meet again—*there*. . . .

SCULPTORS AND ARTISTS

Women had more access to artistic training in the nineteenth century than ever before. In England, France, and America, the need for teachers and governesses led to the creation of female schools of art and design. Expanding industries also needed artisans with training in engraving, illustrations, textile design, and furniture carving and were delighted to find cheaper female artists. Despite new training options, however, the academies remained resistant to women, particularly the most prestigious European institutions. American artists, like actresses, however, still felt the need to go to Europe for training or to get established. This was particularly true of a group of female sculptors who went to Rome where they had access to marble and skilled workmen, great sculptures to study, and an atmosphere congenial to artists. These women were referred to as the "white marmorean flock." (Rubinstein 1990, 32–80) The two women discussed next were part of that group of expatriates.

Harriet Hosmer (1830–1908): American Neoclassical Sculptor

Harriet Hosmer was the most famous woman sculptor of the century. Her father raised her as a tomboy, gave her a liberal education, and built her a studio so she could pursue her art. A friend of her father's who was a physician, arranged private anatomy lessons for her. After seeing Hosmer's first work, Charlotte Cushman persuaded Harriet's father to send her to Europe. She was ridiculed by her male colleagues, because she was the first woman to try to break into the all-male clique of neoclassical sculptors, however, she earned their respect in time. She was able to support herself after selling over 30 copies of a decorative statue, *Puck on a Toadstool*. Within ten years she was so successful that she opened a large studio in Rome and hired a staff of male stonecutters to work under her. She was a petite woman and made quite a picture when standing on scaffolding to sculpt her large figures. She had a zest for life and loved racing on horseback at night through the streets of Rome. *Zenobia in Chains* is one of her most famous works. Her other works include a large statue of Senator Thomas Hart Benton, as well as statues of Queen Isabella of Spain and Beatrice Cenci (Percy Shelley's tragic heroine). The following excerpts shed light on her personality, her relationships with patrons, and public response to her work. They also tell us something about her philosophy of art, life, and women's history. All the selections are from *Harriet Hosmer. Letters and Memories.**

HOSMER TO WAYMAN CROW, 12 OCTOBER 1854

Dear Mr. Crow:

On returning last night I found your letter waiting for me. Indeed, I frankly confess that I don't know what to say, except that it seems a God's providence that it has relieved my mind of a burden. The fact is that at the time of my "bankruptcy" I was in debt. I had two or three bills coming due for marble, and at the same time had to pay for work already going on. It is very true that when one has a name, sculpture is a mine of wealth, but it is equally true that name or no name, one must spend a good deal before one can hope to make one. Now, as I said in my last letter, I have spent money with too little thought, but no one has an idea of how expensive an affair it is, at first. You, dear Mr. Crow, know that one must have a good capital to begin business at all, much more to begin with advantage. It is exactly the same thing in sculpture. A painter has no expense of the kind; he buys his canvas, his paints, which cost little and he is made; but from the time a sculptor begins, he finds that without funds he is at a standstill. Some seem to think that statues can be made like rail-fences. I do not agree with them. It is work, work, work, and if they try their hands at it, they would become aware of the length of time one must study, before one can hope to do anything. Sometimes I cannot help thinking that too much is expected of me in so short a time as I have been here. Why, it is not three years yet, and

*From Cornelia Carr, ed., *Harriet Hosmer. Letters and Memories* (New York: Moffat, Yard and Company, 1912), pp. 37–39, 191–92, 331–33.

what is that for learning so difficult an art in, an art which requires years and years to master? And when we consider that the first year I was kept copying the antique, it leaves rather a short time for me to have made my fortune in, as I am afraid I was expected to do. My master [sculptor under whom she worked] is the one to know if I have made progress, and he is satisfied with me, and is not one easily satisfied either.

Now dear Mr. Crow, I dare say you will say "What is the girl driving at?" Why, simply that you have understood my case well enough to lay me under an obligation, so great that if I were to realize your fondest hopes of me, I could never repay you. One thing is past denial, that however successful I may become in my profession, it is to you that I owe all. . . . Every successful artist in Rome who is living, or who has ever lived, owes his success to *his* Mr. Crow. . . .

Lydia Maria Child, Letter to the *Boston Transcript* about Hosmer's *Zenobia**

This is the third week of the exhibition, and nearly fifteen thousand people have paid homage to the Queen, while the gallery continues to be crowded daily.

In the notices I have seen, it is assumed that the face is altogether ideal; but the fact is, the features were copied from an ancient coin of the Queen of Palmyra, to which the artist has imparted the mingled expression of her dignified character and her fallen fortunes. . . . Cleopatra and Zenobia were descended from the same line of Macedonian kings, and both received a wonderful inheritance of beauty; . . . It was [Zenobia's] womanly modesty, her manly courage, and her intellectual tastes, which first attracted Miss Hosmer toward her; and the result of her loving study of the character is this marble embodiment of the Queen of the East, by a Queen of the West. . . .

Hosmer's Philosophy of Art**

I did unreservedly criticise, as I shall ever criticise and deplore, the limited range of our art as displayed in our public parks and squares. . . .

We erect a portrait statue to one of our heroes, clad in the outrageous costume of our time, and then feel, in a general way, that we have done something for art. We have done something for history, if you will, but all we do for art by the erection of these bronze photographs is to banish true art farther and farther from its legitimate realm. For what is the meaning of art? Its true signification implies creation, and, may I ask, what opportunity has the most imaginative sculptor when executing a work of modern portraiture, fettered by the necessity of adhering to an uncouth costume, to display the creative faculty or his sense of beauty and grace? . . .

Another point. As a disciple of classic art I am supposed "to inveigh against the modern realistic school." Not in the least. Give us everything and the fittest will survive, but against the term "realistic" as opposed to the "classic school" I rebel. Never

---

*The statue depicts captive Zenobia, as she was marched in chains through Rome's streets, after the defeat of her army by Rome in 272 A.D.

**Hosmer shared her philosophy of art in her response to San Franciscans who objected to her criticisms of the city's statues.

was a grosser misapplication of terms. "Realistic" I take to mean "real," "true to nature," and therefore I claim that what is known as the classic school furnishes the most commanding examples of realistic art—who, save Nature herself, reality itself, could conceive of the form of The Fighting Gladiator . . . or of the Venus of Milo . . . ? These statues, one and all, are portrait statues—wrought by the ancient masters with a patience, a knowledge and a keenness of vision, of which few artists are now capable. But one and all reflect Nature in her noblest, happiest mood, which should be the end and aim of all art. . . .

Deprived of these magnificent monuments of human genius, we could form no conception of the beauty of which the human form is capable. Think what advantages the Greek sculptors enjoyed as compared with the status of art in our time. Their models were furnished by a race supreme in the world's history for physical perfection. Their climate, their games, all their modes of life, fostered and developed this perfection of form. The study of physical beauty was reduced to a science. . . .

Edmonia Lewis (1843?–ca. 1911): American Sculptor

Edmonia Lewis is known as America's first important black sculptor. She was the daughter of a Chippewa woman and a black man. She was raised by her mother's tribe who gave her the name Wildfire. Throughout her career she received support from abolitionists. They also financed her education at Oberlin College, the first coeducational college in America and the first to admit black students along with whites. The readings that follow reveal much about her life, the subjects she chose to sculpt, and the praise her work earned. While the documents tend to focus on her sculptures that relate to black history, she also did some exquisite small sculptures of Native Americans, notably her *Old Indian Arrow Maker and His Daughter.*

A NEGRO SCULPTRESS, ROME, FEBRUARY 1866*

An interesting novelty has sprung up amongst us in a city where all our surroundings are of the olden time. Miss Edmonia Lewis, a lady of colour, has taken a studio in Rome, and works as a sculptress in one of the rooms formerly occupied by the great master Canova. She is the only lady of her race in the United States who has thus applied herself to the study and practice of sculptural art, and the fact is so remarkable and unique that a brief sketch of her life, given almost in her own words, will I am sure, be acceptable to the wide circle of your readers. "My mother," she told me only last Monday, "was a wild Indian, and was born in Albany, of copper colour, and with straight, black hair. There she made and sold moccasins. My father, who was a negro, and a gentleman's servant, saw her and married her. I was born at Greenhigh, in Ohio. Mother often left her home, and wandered with her people, whose habits she could not forget, and thus we her children were brought up in the same wild manner. Until I was twelve years old I led this wandering life, fishing and swimming," she added with great glee, "and making moccasins. I was then sent to school for three years in M'Graw, but was declared to be wild—they could do nothing with me. Often they said to me, 'Here is your book, the book of Nature; come

*From H.W. [Henry Wreford], "A Negro Sculptress," *Athenaeum*, no. 2001 (London), 3 March 1866, p. 302.

and study it.' From this school I was sent to another, at Oberlin, in Ohio, where I remained four years, and then I thought of returning to wild life again; but my love of sculpture forbade it. Some friends recommended me to go to England, but I thought it better first to study in Rome." And here she is, the descendent and member of a much-injured race, struggling against ignorant prejudice, but with genius enough to prove that she bears the image of Him who made all nations under the sun. . . . Her first ideal group was to be executed under promise for some gentlemen in Boston, and, in the true spirit of a heroine, she has selected for her subject "The Freedwoman on first hearing of her Liberty." She has thrown herself on her knees, and, with clasped hands and uplifted eyes, she blesses God for her redemption. Her boy, ignorant of the cause of her agitation, hangs over her knees and clings to her waist. She wears the turban which was used when at work. Around her wrists are the half-broken manacles, and the chain lies on the ground still attached to a large ball. "Yes," she observed, "so was my race treated in the market and elsewhere." It tells, with much eloquence, a painful story.

THE REVOLUTION* ON EDMONIA LEWIS**

One of the first studios which we visited in Rome was that of Edmonia Lewis, the colored sculptor. We were interested in her even before we saw her, or any of her works; not only because of her sex, but of her race, and our acquaintance with her and her works has only heightened the interest which we felt in her. . . .

. . . On her first visit to Boston, she saw a statue of Benjamin Franklin. It filled her with amazement and delight. She did not know by what name to call "the stone image," but she felt within her the stir of new powers.

"I, too, can make a stone man," she said to herself; and at once she went to visit Lloyd Garrison and told him what she knew she could do, and asked him how she should set about doing it.

Struck by her enthusiasm, Garrison gave her a note of introduction to Brackett, the Boston sculptor, and after a little talk with her, Mr. Brackett gave her a piece of clay and a mould of a human foot, as a study. "Go home and make that," said he, "if there is anything in you, it will come out."

Alone, in her own room, the young girl toiled over her clay, and when she had done her best, carried the result to her master. He looked at her model, broke it up and said, "Try again."

She did try again, modelled feet and hands, and at last undertook a medallion of the head of John Brown, which was pronounced excellent.

The next essay was a bust of the voting hero Colonel Shaw, the first man who took the command of a colored regiment and whose untimely and glorious death, and the epitaph spoken by the South, "Bury him with his niggers," have made him an immortal name in the history of our civil war. . . .

*The Revolution was the newspaper of suffragists Elizabeth Cady Stanton and Susan B. Anthony.

**From "Edmonia Lewis," The Revolution (New York [S.B. Anthony, et. al.]; Westport, CT: Greenwood Publishing Co.), vol. 8 (20 April 1871), p. 1, microfilm: PR 1836.

Of this bust she sold one hundred copies and with that money she set out for Europe, full of hope and courage.

"I thought I knew everything when I came to Rome," she said naively, "but I soon found that I had everything to learn."

At once she devoted herself to hard study and hard work, and here she made her first statue: a figure of Hagar in her despair in the Wilderness. It is a work full of feeling, for as she says: "I have a strong sympathy for all women who have struggled and suffered. For this reason the Virgin Mary is very dear to me." . . .

A fine bust, also, of [Longfellow], is about to be put in marble, which has been ordered by Harvard College, and in this instance, at least, old Harvard has done itself honor. If it will not yet open its doors to women who ask education at its hands, it will admit the work of a woman who has educated herself in her chosen department. . . .

HER CLEOPATRA*

An even more remarkable sculpture from the hand of a female . . . which was in the [1876] Centennial Exhibition was the Cleopatra of Edmonia Lewis. This was not a beautiful work, but it was a very original and very striking one, and it deserves particular comment, as its ideal was so radically different from those adopted by Story and Gould in their statues of the Egyptian Queen. Story gave his Cleopatra Nubian features, and achieved an artistic if not a historical success by so doing. The Cleopatra of Gould suggests a Greek lineage. Miss Lewis, on the other hand, has followed the coins, medals, and other authentic records in giving her Cleopatra an aquiline nose and a prominent chin of the Roman type, . . . This Cleopatra, therefore, more nearly resembled the real heroine of history than either of the others, . . .

. . . Miss Lewis, up to the time of the opening of the Centennial Exhibition, did not keep herself very prominently before the public, and to many of the visitors to that Exhibition who only knew of her by vague report, the real power of her Cleopatra was a revelation.

Rosa Bonheur (1822–1899): French Animal Artist

Rosa Bonheur was the most famous animal artist of the nineteenth century and was the first woman artist to be honored with the Cross of the Legion of Honor, the highest award of the French government. She carefully studied animal anatomy and depicted both wild and domesticated animals in a realistic natural way. She loved animals and acquired a virtual zoo on her estate outside Paris. Once her reputation was established, she was able to sell her paintings and engravings of animals to private individuals and could avoid the large exhibitions. One interesting aspect of French society was the necessity for her to obtain a police permit to wear trousers when she was painting or working in the stockyards. The regulation of dress was a means of enforcing proper gender roles and behavior. Bonheur enjoyed smoking and hunting and maintained a wide correspondence with artists, intellectuals, students, and family over her lifetime. Her work was quite popular in England, and the French government selected one of her paintings to exhibit as representative of French culture at the Chicago World's Fair in 1893. Bonheur spent a good part of her life with Natalie Micas, and after her death, with Anna

*From William J. Clark, *Great American Sculptors,* (Philadelphia: Gebbie & Barrie, 1878; Ann Arbor, MI, Xerox University Microfilms, 1974), pp. 141–42, microfilm: American Culture Series, Reel 598, no. 5.

Klumpke. The following excerpts shed light on her philosophy of life and art, her relationships with friends, family, and patrons, and her personality. Note again the importance of role models.

HER EARLY YEARS AND DISCOVERY OF ART*

I was truly indomitable. I refused positively to learn to read, but I was not four years old when I had already the greatest passion for drawing, and used to smear the whitewashed walls as high up as I could reach with crude drawings. Another one of my delights was to cut figures out of paper.

By this time I had begun to work at the Louvre. . . . The drawings by old masters had a special fascination for me. How many happy hours of work have I passed in those endless rooms filled with *chef-d'oeuvres*. How many of them I have copied, and I cannot repeat sufficiently to young beginners who wish to adopt the hard life of the artist, to do as I have done: stock their brains with studies after the old masters. It is the real grammar of art, and time thus employed will be profitable to the end of their career.

EXCERPTS FROM BONHEUR'S (AUTO)BIOGRAPHY**

[Her Father's Dreams for Her Future]
"Seek your way, daughter," my father said again and again. "Seek your way, try to surpass Mme Vigée-Lebrun, whose name is on everyone's lips these days. She's a painter's daughter, too, and she did so well that by the age of twenty-eight she got into the Royal Academy, and now she's a member of the Academies of Rome, Saint Petersburg, and Berlin." . . .

Alas! I cannot help feeling a twinge of pain whenever I think of my *Ploughing in the Nivernais*. . . . A few days before my father died, he made another proud inspection of my work. He embraced me and said: "You're right on the heels of Vigée-Lebrun. So it's not in vain that I made her your role model." Poor Father, . . . he had no idea that the money I got for this painting was meant to pay for his funeral expenses.
*[Empress Eugenie and the "Cross of the Legion of Honor," 10 June 1865***]*
"Mademoiselle," she said, "I am bringing you a jewel from the Emperor. His Majesty has given me permission to inform you that you've been made a knight in the Imperial Order of the Legion of Honor."

As she spoke, she opened up a little jewel case and removed a gold cross. Deeply moved, I knelt at her feet, . . . and the Empress pinned the red ribbon with that glorious star over my heart. Then she raised me up and kissed me, saying: "You're finally a knight. I am so pleased to be the godmother of the first woman artist to receive this high honor. I wanted to devote my last act as regent to showing that, as far as I'm concerned, genius has no sex. Moreover, to underscore the importance

*From Rosa Bonheur, "The Story of My Life," *The Ladies Home Journal* 14 (December 1896), pp. 13–14.
**The Empress made a surprise visit to Bonheur's workshop on June 10th.
***Excerpts from Anna Klumpke, *Rosa Bonheur: The Artist's (Auto)biography,* trans. Gretchen van Slyke, (Ann Arbor: University of Michigan Press, 1997), pp. 112, 130, 172–73, 204, 206, 239–40, 232. Copyright © 1997 by The University of Michigan. With permission of The University of Michigan Press.

that I attach to this great act of justice, you won't be part of a "batch." Your nomination will be announced a day later than the others, but in a special decree headlined in the *Moniteur.*"

[On Her Dress]

. . . I strongly disapprove of women who refuse to wear normal clothes because they want to pass themselves off as men. . . .

If you see me dressed this way, it's not in the least to make myself stand out, as too many women have done, but only for my work. Don't forget I used to spend days and days in slaughterhouses. Oh! You've got to be devoted to art to live in pools of blood, surrounded by butchers. I was also passionate about horses; and what better place to study them than at horse fairs, mingling with all those traders? Women's clothes were quite simply always in the way. That's why I decided to ask the prefect of police for permission to wear men's clothing. . . .

[The St. Simonian View of Women She Inherited from Her Father]

Why shouldn't I be proud to be a woman? My father, that enthusiastic apostle of humanity, told me again and again that it was woman's mission to improve the human race, that she was the future Messiah. To his doctrines I owe my great and glorious ambition for the sex to which I proudly belong, whose independence I'll defend till my dying day. Besides, I'm convinced the future is ours. . . .

[On Women Artists]

. . . I think young artists bear me more of a grudge for being a woman than for being old. They can't forgive me for having proved that the sex of the artist doesn't matter. I'm afraid this tension will never be resolved. Yet today women can compete for the Rome prize. That's great, since I'm not afraid of a fight. Otherwise, we'd have to resign ourselves to women-only shows. I can't bring myself to that. I can't even see that kind of show without thinking about Muhammad's notion of paradise, where our Muslim sisters have to have their own Garden of Eden. . . .

My stand is altogether different. I think that as soon as women can aspire to the highest honors, there's no reason for them to form groups that shut out men. They'd do better to seize every opportunity to show that we women can be as good as men and sometimes even better. . . .

[Bonheur Speaks about Her Long-time Partner, Nathalie Micas]

. . . What would my life have been without her love and devotion! Yet people tried to give our love a bad name. They were flabbergasted that we pooled our money and left all our earthly goods to each other. Had I been a man, I would have married her, and nobody could have dreamed up all those silly stories. I would have had a family, with my children as heirs, and nobody would have had any right to complain.

Mary Cassatt (1844–1926): American Impressionist

Mary Cassatt was one of many American expatriates who went to Paris, the center of the art world, in the late 1860s to pursue her art. She is widely regarded as the best American artist of her generation. She was an active participant in the Impressionist movement, and up to date with all the latest art currents in Paris. For example, some of her works incorporated Japanese print and photography techniques. She chose to show her work in the Impressionists' free exhibitions and consistently fought against juried shows that she believed were biased in favor of academy members or the old guard. Although she was influenced by Degas and other Impressionists, she kept growing and developing her own style. In 1893, she completed a large mural for the Woman's Building at the Chicago World's Fair, and in 1904 was awarded the prestigious medal of the French Legion of Honor.

Cassatt was born in Pittsburgh, Pennsylvania, into an upper-middle-class family. Her family supported her initial training at the Pennsylvania Academy of Fine Arts, but her father was appalled when she said she wanted to be a professional artist. She finally went to Paris, allegedly as a tourist, but once there signaled her determination to stay. Her father, Robert, relented, and took great pride in her successes. Her parents and sister joined her in Paris in 1877. She remained single all her life. Although Cassatt lived most of her life in Paris, she worked to improve American art and opportunities for artists in America. She was a patron of the arts, and prodded museums and art dealers to search for American talent instead of filling the walls with European works. She also was a supporter of woman suffrage.

MARY CASSATT TO CLARENCE GIHON, 13 SEPTEMBER 1905*

Dear Mr. Gihon,

Your card has just reached me. I am sorry I cannot be of any use to you in this matter of the Exhibition—The truth is I have not served on the jury, never will serve on any jury, nor be the means of repressing the works of another painter. I think the whole system wrong & have written to Mr. Beatty requesting him to withdraw my name

You may be surprised after this statement that my name should have appeared as a member of the jury. Some years ago Mr. Beatty told me that Whistler had suggested my being asked, it was I think the first year of the exhibitions at the Carnegie Institute, I accepted on the condition I was never asked to serve, & in the hopes of being able to get the Trustees to invest some of the funds in the purchase of genuine Old Masters & thus form the beginning of a Museum, & thereby give to American artists some of the advantages of the artists on this side—My hopes have proved vain, no such pictures have been bought by the Institute they have gone to private collections.

As for this years exhibition, I saw from a letter in the Herald that only one American was on the jury & only five American pictures were accepted. The American artists have the remedy in their own hands, let them refuse to send until the conditions of admission are changed. Our group were the founders of the "Independents". After we gave up our exhibitions the name & principles were adopted by a younger set & have prospered—Our profession is enslaved, it is for us to set it free. The jury system has proved a failure since hardly a single painter of talent in the last fifty years in France has not been a victim to the system—Amongst those refused again & again, are Corot, Courbet, Millet & hosts of others, these men were kept back for years. We need a new system, the old one is used up—I hope you will help to inaugurate a new one; I do regret I cannot be of use to you in this case but if it helps to raise you against juries, I will regret it less. . . .

*Excerpt from letter, Mary Cassatt to Clarence Gihon, 13 September 1905, reprinted in Mathews, ed. *Cassatt and Her Circle,* 1984), p. 297. Original letter in the Carnegie Institute, Museum of Art Records, Archives of American Art, Smithsonian Institution.

MARY CASSATT TO COLONEL PAINE, 28 FEBRUARY 1915*

My dear Colonel Paine,

I come to appeal to you as a patriotic American to lend your Degas to the exhibition Mrs Havemeyer is arranging. The sight of that picture may be a turning point in the life of some young American painter. The first sight of Degas pictures was the turning point in my artistic life.

Never mind the object of the exhibition. Think only of the young painters. As to the suffrage for women it must come as a result of this awful war. With the slaughter of millions of men women will be forced, are now being forced to do their work, & we have only begun. Far worse is yet to come these next months. . . .

MARY CASSATT TO LOUISINE HAVEMEYER, 5 JULY 1915**

Dearest Louie,

I feel like a perfect brute having written you those letters, but indeed dear I was upset, you dont know all I do. Joseph [Durand-Ruell] was here, & as to the exhibition he said it was *the cause* [italics mine] which kept many people away, "society" it seems is so against suffrage. Many regretted to him that they missed seeing a fine exhibition but their principles forbade their going. Also he said that if women voted it would be for peace at any price. . . .

I am so glad you spoke to all those people, surely it will do good. Do you think if I have to stop work on account of my eyes I could use my last years as a propagandist? It wont be necessary if the war goes on, as it must. Women are now doing most of the work. I never felt so isolated in my life as I do now. . . .

MARY CASSATT TO BERTHA PALMER, 11 OCTOBER 1892***

My dear Mrs. Palmer

Your letter of Sept. 27th only arrived this morning, so unfortunately this will not reach you by the 18th as you desired. Notwithstanding that my letter will be too late for the ladies of the committee, I should like very much to give you some account of the manner I have tried to carry out my idea of the decoration [for the Woman's Building].

Mr. Avery sent me an article from one of the New York papers this summer, in which the writer, referring to the order given to me, said my subject was to be the "The Modern Woman as glorified by Worth"! That would hardly describe my idea,

---

*Excerpt from letter, Mary Cassatt to Colonel Paine, 28 February 1915, reprinted in Mathews, ed. *Cassatt and Her Circle*, p. 321. By permission of J. Robert Maguire, Executor/Trustee, Estate of Lois Cassatt Thayer.

**Excerpts from letter, Mary Cassatt to Louisine Havemeyer, 5 July 1915, reprinted in Mathews, ed. *Cassatt and Her Circle*, p. 324. By permission of J. Robert Maguire, Executor/Trustee, Estate of Lois Cassatt Thayer.

***Excerpts from letter, Mary Cassatt to Bertha Palmer, 11 October 1892. Bertha Palmer Collection, Ryerson and Burnham Archives, The Art Institute of Chicago. By permission of The Art Institute of Chicago.

of course I have tried to express the modern woman in the fashions of our day. . . . I took for the subject of the central & largest composition Young women plucking the fruits of knowledge or science &—that enabled me to place my figures out of doors & allowed of brilliancy of color—I have tried to make the general effect as bright as gay as amusing as possible. The occassion is one of rejoicing, a great national fete. I reserved all the seriousness for the execution, for the drawing & painting. My ideal would have been one of those admirable old tapestries brilliant yet soft. My figures are rather under life size although they seem as large as life. I could not imagine women in modern dress eight or nine feet high. An American friend asked me in rather a huffy tone the other day "Then this is woman apart from her relations to man?" I told him it was. Men I have no doubt, are painted in all their vigour on the walls of the other buildings; to us the sweetness of childhood, the charm of woman-hood, if I have not conveyed some sense of that charm, in one word if I have not been absolutely feminine, then I have failed— . . . I will still have place on the side panels for two compositions, one . . . is, young girls pursuing fame. This seems to me very modern & besides will give me an opportunity for some figures in clinging draperies. The other panel will represent the Arts Music . . . dancing & all treated in the most modern way. The whole is surrounded by a border, wide below, narrower above, bands of color, the lower cut with circles containing naked babies tossing fruit, &&c. I think, my dear Mrs. Palmer, that if you were here & I could take you out to my studio & show you what I have done that you would be pleased indeed with-out too much vanity—I may say I am almost sure you would.

When the work reaches Chicago, when it is dragged up 48 feet & you will have to stretch your neck to get sight of it all, whether you will like it then, is another question. Stillman, in a recent article, declares his belief that in the evolution of the race painting is no longer needed, the architects evidently are of that opinion. Paint-ing was never intended to be put out of sight. This idea however has not troubled me too much, for I have passed a most enjoyable summer of hard work. If painting is no longer needed, it seems a pity that some of us are born into the world with such a passion for line and color. After this grumbling I must get back to my work knowing that the sooner we get to Chicago the better.

You will be pleased, believe me, my dear Mrs. Palmer

WOMEN AT THE CHICAGO WORLD'S FAIR, 1893

Mary Cassatt was not the only woman whose work was celebrated at the Chicago World's Fair (also called the World Columbian Exhibition) in 1893. The Woman's Building was designed by architect So-phie Hayden, a graduate of the Massachusetts Institute of Technology. Inside it featured, in addition to Cassatt's mural, women's art, literature, sculpture, and music, offering marvelous examples of women's past and present achievements in all aspects of culture. It also provided evidence of the changing roles of contemporary women. In addition to the international displays, the building featured a child-care facility and lounge where visitors to the exhibits could meet other women from around the globe.

Women's presence at the fair was also evident in the general mixed assemblies and sessions held throughout the fair's existence to bring together people of different nationalities, interests, and profes-sions. The selections that follow provide a glimpse of how some of the women celebrated the achieve-ments of their sex and sought to build a world-wide network to ensure that progress would continue in the next century. Other examples are included in Chapter 9, "Challenging Orthodoxy: Women in Religion in America."

WOMEN'S CONGRESSES AT CHICAGO WORLD'S FAIR, 1893*

Mrs. May Wright Sewall, President of the National Woman's Council and Chairman of the International Woman's Congress, which is to be held at the Columbian Exposition from May 15 to May 23, told about 150 ladies many interesting things regarding the congress at the Fifth Avenue Hotel yesterday afternoon. . . .

Mrs. Sewall characterized the proposed congress as "the spiritual and intellectual exhibit" of the World's Fair, and as to the success which now seems promised for it, she said much was due to the efforts of Mrs. Potter Palmer and Mrs. Charles Henrotin of Chicago.

"The congress in which women were to be the leading spirits," she said, "was under the management of women, and in all the congresses which are to be held during the fair women would participate to an extent which she regarded as significant. More than 100 congresses had been arranged, and in all but two women are to take part in the discussions. . . .

"In this international congress we hope to represent all the activities in which women have distinguished themselves, whether by organized or by individual effort, and first we want it distinctly understood that this is not for the promotion of any one branch of woman's sphere. It is not a temperance movement. It is not a movement for the higher education of women. It is not for the propagation of any religious sect. It is not for the spread of the doctrines of the Presbyterians, or the Methodists, or even of the Catholics . . .

"Nor is the congress organized for the political equality of women. It is for the broadest possible discussion of the great question of advancing the interests, the work, and the condition of women all over the world. Forty-five woman's organizations in the United States, 12 in England, 2 in Finland, 2 in Sweden, 2 in Norway, 3 in Germany, and 2 in France—each a national organization—have agreed to send delegates. Individual representation will come from Spain, Italy, Austria, Russia, and Turkey." . . .

Considerable time was devoted to a description of the resources for managing the congress. An art palace is the new building in which it will be held. There will be two auditoriums, each with a capacity of from 2,500 to 3,000 and smaller rooms adjoining, in which the branch congresses will be held at the same time. The general division of topics for discussion will be education, philanthropic and charitable works, literature and art, social reforms, civil law, and government and religion. The particular topics will be many, among them civil and social evolution of woman, woman's administrative ability, and the political future of women. . . . Woman on the stage, woman in the pulpit, the ethics of dress, and women as patriots will be other prominent topics.

*From "Women at the Big Fair," *New York Times* (Rochester, NY: Eastman Kodak Co. for Recordak Corp.), 17 March 1893, p. 3, col. 3, microfilm: NP1.

Woman's contribution to the musical world will be given especial attention at the closing exercise of the congress, which will be a grand sacred concert, in which the compositions of women alone will be presented. . . .

SUGGESTED READINGS

Weimann, Jeanne Madeline. *The Fair Women: The Story of the Women's Building, World's Columbian Exposition.* Chicago: Academy Chicago, 1981.

Art

Ashton, Dore, and Denise Brown Hare. *Rosa Bonheur: A Life and a Legend.* New York, Viking Press 1981.

Garb, Tamar. *Sisters of the Brush: Women's Artistic Culture in Late Nineteenth-Century Paris.* New Haven, CT: Yale University Press, 1994.

Hartigan, Lynda Roscoe. "Edmonia Lewis." In *Sharing Traditions: Five Black Artists in Nineteenth-Century America: From the Collections of the National Museum of American Art.* Washington, DC: Published for the Museum by the Smithsonian Institution Press, 1985.

Hook, Bailey Van. *Angels of Art: Women and Art in American Society, 1876–1914.* University Park: Pennsylvania State University Press, 1996.

Mathews, Nancy Mowll. *Mary Cassatt: A Life.* New Haven, CT: Yale University Press, 1998.

Sherwood, Dolly. *Harriet Hosmer, American Sculptor, 1830–1908.* Columbia: University of Missouri Press, 1991.

Yeldham, Charlotte Elizabeth. *Women Artists in Nineteenth-Century England and France.* New York and London: 1984.

Dance and Theater

Merrill, Lisa. *When Romeo Was a Woman: Charlotte Cushman and Her Circle of Female Spectators.* Ann Arbor: University of Michigan Press, 1999.

Migel, Parmenia. *The Ballerinas, from the Court of Louis XIV to Pavlova.* New York: Macmillan, 1972.

Powell, Kerry. *Women and Victorian Theatre.* Cambridge, UK: Cambridge University Press, 1997.

Audiovisual Sources

Hearts and Hands: Influence of Women and Quilts on American Society. 1988. Produced and Directed by Pat Ferrero. 63 min. San Francisco, CA: Hearts and Hands Media Arts, 1988. Videocassette.

Picturing the Genders: Male and Female Views of Women in Art. 1998. Produced and Directed by Tony Coe. 30 min. Princeton, NJ: Films for the Humanities and Sciences, 2002. Videocassette; DVD BVL29902.

Chapter 9

Challenging Orthodoxy:
Women and Religion in America

This chapter focuses on women and religion in nineteenth-century America, a period in which successive waves of immigration, America's tradition of religious freedom, and the religious ferment unleashed by the Protestant Reformation transformed the United States into a truly pluralistic society. In virtually all faiths, denominations, and interdenominational crusades or revival meetings, women comprised the majority of worshipers. Their participation led to what came to be seen as the feminization of religion. Male clergy responded to women's preponderance among the faithful by exhorting them to help spread the faith through charitable works, fundraising, model behavior, and their roles as mothers and wives. Clergy preached to this audience by praising the so-called feminine virtues of humility and acceptance of divine will. Protestants stressed Jesus' love more than God's wrath and explored alternative concepts of the divine. In the early days of the many new religious sects and experimental Christian communities that emerged in the first half of the century, men also welcomed women as missionaries and even preachers. (Cott 1977, ch. 4; Welter 1976, ch. 6) Patriarchal values and institutional structures, however, held firm.

In this context, women of all classes, races, and religious traditions struggled to carve out appropriate roles for themselves and to express or live out their personal faith. Many accepted traditional mores but enlarged their roles within traditional boundaries as Sunday school teachers, charitable workers, and moral reformers. Others, however, challenged religious orthodoxy and insisted upon their right to follow the dictates of their faith. The readings in this chapter provide a small sample of the diverse ways women sought to live their faith in meaningful ways. Despite the different paths they took, there are some fascinating recurring patterns. Women sought to have a greater voice in governance of their religious institutions and to reshape these according to their beliefs. Their faith also impelled many to engage in social reform causes throughout the century. Even more interesting is the revival of mysticism or what the nineteenth century referred to as spiritualism or religious excitement. Visions and powerful experiences of the Divine impelled many to action that they might ordinarily not have taken. In this, they were like the great medieval women mystics, women of the Catholic Reformation, and Reformation pietists. Some created and led entirely new religions; others fought to preach; all sought some degree of independence or autonomy from male authorities. All, to some degree, critiqued religion and the male interpretations of religious doctrine. Watch for these themes and ask how each experienced the Divine, how their views related to the "woman question," and how their ideas and actions compared with religious women we've seen in earlier chapters in Volumes I and II.

WOMEN FOUNDERS AND LEADERS

Mother Ann Lee (1736–1784): Founder of the Shakers

The United Society of Believers in Christ's Second Appearing (commonly known as the Shakers) was the first religion in the North American colonies founded by a woman and led by a woman. It was also one of the most successful religious utopian societies in nineteenth-century America. Its founder, Ann Lee, was born in Manchester, England, one of eight children of a blacksmith. She had no formal schooling. In 1758 she joined a separatist group of Quakers who became known as Shakers because of their worship style which included shaking, dancing, shouting, and singing. In 1762, she married a blacksmith and had four children in rapid succession; all of them died soon after birth. After nearly dying after the last birth, she suffered an emotional breakdown, during which she had a religious experience of being born into God's kingdom. Soon she emerged as leader of the group and was arrested for breaking the Sabbath when preaching in the street in 1772 and 1773. While in prison, she had a vision and received her divine call to begin living a celibate life and complete Christ's work.

Another revelation after her release from prison foretold that the true faith would be established in New England, so she and a few followers (including her husband) sailed to New York in 1774. In 1776, they settled in the town of Watervliet near Albany. The New Light Baptist revival (new evangelical, millennial sects were called "New Light") helped the Shaker faith get established, for those disappointed that the millennium did not come as predicted flocked to hear the new prophetess and many converted. Between 1781 and 1783, she completed missionary missions in eastern New York and New England.

Mother Ann (Mother of the Last Creation), as she was called by the faithful, was regarded variously as a religious fanatic, a heretic, or by her followers as the manifestation of the Second Coming of the Lord. Her teachings, based upon her life experiences and her visions, became Shaker theology. She revived the ancient concept of an androgynous God whose feminine element was Sophia, Holy Wisdom. Thus, Jesus, the masculine manifestation of the Divine, had been sent to redeem humankind, and she, Ann Lee, the feminine manifestation, had been sent as the "second coming" to prepare believers for ultimate salvation. For Lee, carnal knowledge was the root of all sin, hence the core of her faith was celibacy. Seeking to re-create the early Christian church, she established a communal society, in which everything was held in common and all members were equal. Lee died from severe beatings she received from New York patriot authorities when imprisoned for heresy and for allegedly being a British spy.

Her theology guided the organization and the daily patterns of Shaker communities. Under her successors, Shaker communities were divided into "forms," or groups: men, women, and children. Upon entry into the community, married couples dissolved their unions, women resumed their maiden names, and children were placed under the guidance of selected adults. Members lived in large communal houses divided into separate dormitory-like quarters for women, men, and children. All shared common living and worship areas. To simplify their lives and focus more on worship, Shakers developed a simple style of furniture and architecture for which they are still famous. Shakers allowed converts who wished to maintain their family structure to be members of an "outer order." The "inner order" consisted of those who adopted the entire Shaker regimen.

In the readings that follow, note how Ann Lee and her followers envisioned the Deity and the nature of Ann's authority and influence.

SHAKER EUNICE GOODRICH SHARES A RECOLLECTION OF MOTHER ANN LEE, 1816*

. . . In the former part of the year 1781, a large assembly of the Believers were gathered at Watervliet. . . . Mother was at that time under great sufferings of soul. She came forth with a very powerful gift of God and reproved the people for their hardness of heart and unbelief in the second appearance of Christ. "Especially," said she, "ye men and brethren! I upbraid you of your unbelief and hardness of heart."

She spoke of the unbelieving Jews in his first appearance. "Even his own disciples," added she, "after he arose from the dead, though he had often told them that he should rise the third day, believed it not. They would not believe that he had risen, because he appeared first to a woman! So great was their unbelief that the words of Mary seemed to them like idle tales! His appearing first to a woman showed that his second appearing would be in a woman!" . . .

Anna White (1831–1910): Shaker Eldress and Reformer

Anna White was born in Brooklyn, New York. Her Quaker parents sent her to a Friends' boarding school in New York for her early education, and she became acquainted with the Shakers when her father took her to visit a Shaker community in Massachusetts. Her father joined the Shaker community at New Lebanon, New York, and she entered the community in September 1849. She spent the rest of her life as a member of the North "family," one of the units into which community was divided. In 1865, she was appointed associate eldress and she succeeded as eldress of the North family in 1887, a position she held until her death.

White was involved in reforms in the "outside" world, which was unusual for Shakers, but typical of one wing. She was active in international disarmament, served as vice-president of the Alliance of Women for Peace, and spoke widely on peace and arbitration. She was a member of the National American Woman Suffrage Association and vice-president of the National Council of Women of the United States. She was also interested in vegetarianism, in spiritualism (Shakers believed they could communicate with departed spirits), and in Christian Science.

White pursued her early interest in Shaker songs and history, compiling two books of Shaker music that included some of her own "gifts of song" (Andrews 1971, 584). In 1904, she published *Shakerism: Its Meaning and Message* in collaboration with Eldress Leila S. Taylor. This is the only published history of the movement by a member of the society. Her other books included *Woman's Mission, Voices from Mount Lebanon* (1899) and *The Motherhood of God* (1903).

SHAKERISM: ITS MEANING AND MESSAGE (1904)**

Among the revelations to Ann Lee and imparted through her life and teachings, were ideas new to the Christian world. . . . Among these great truths are:

*Excerpts from "Testimony of Eunice Goodrich" from [Rufus Bishop], *Testimonies of the Life, Character, Revelations and Doctrines of Our Ever Blessed Mother Ann Lee . . .* (1816), ch. xxiii, reprinted in *Mother's First-Born Daughters. Early Shaker Writings on Women and Religion,* ed. Jean M. Humez. Religion in North America Series, Catherine L. Albanese and Stephen J. Stein, eds. (Bloomington: Indiana University Press, 1993), p. 18. By permission of Indiana University Press.

**From Anna White and Leila S. Taylor. *Shakerism. Its Meaning and Message Embracing an Historical Account, Statement of Belief and Spiritual Experience of the Church from Its Rise to the Present Day* (Columbus, OH: Press of Fred. J. Heer, 1904; Glen Rock, NJ: Microfilming Corporation of America, 1976), pp. 255–58, microfiche, Western Reserve Historical Society Shaker Collection, mif 431; no. 289.

God is Dual

Shakers believe in One God—not three male beings in one, but Father and Mother. . . .

The ancient language of Scripture distinguishes God when power or truth are emphasized as masculine; when love or wisdom is the important attribute, the masculine name has the feminine complement. *O Theos agapa estin,* God is Love (feminine). The term Adam is well known to mean humanity, male and female. How can it "image" a Being utterly unlike itself? Simple and beautiful becomes the relation between God and the man when the true meaning is accepted. Hence comes

Equality of Sex

Woman appears in her rightful place, at once the equal of man in creation and office at the hand of God. Ann Lee's followers, 1900 years after Jesus uttered the words, "Neither do I condemn thee, go and sin no more," and sent Mary to tell the Good News of a risen Lord and living Savior, alone of all humanity, have taught the doctrines that have placed woman side by side with man, his equal in power, in office, in influence and in judgment. To Ann Lee may woman look for the first touch that struck off her chains and gave her absolute right to her own person. To Ann Lee may all reformers among women look as the one who taught and through her followers teaches still perfect freedom, equality and opportunity to woman. The daughters of Ann Lee, alone among women, rejoice in true freedom not alone from the bondage of man's domination, but freedom also from the curse of that desire "to her husband" by which, through the ages, he has ruled over her.

God the Father-Mother

Fatherhood-and-motherhood exist in the complete human being. One is correlative of the other. . . . And as all life in the "things that He has made" originates, as scientists tell us after most careful experiments, not from spontaneous generation, but always from seed or germinal principle, from a father and mother, so in the highest form of earth life, humanity, in the spiritual realm are souls born of God, the Absolute, Self-existent, infinite Perfection of Being, Father and Mother. The very name God, Almighty, in its original Hebrew form, El Shaddai, reveals the infinite quality. El, God, its first meaning, Strength; Shaddi, the plural whose singular, Shad, signifies a Breast and is feminine.

In the beautiful and lofty strains of that magnificent psalm found in the eighth chapter of Proverbs, "Doth not Wisdom Cry," etc., Wisdom [Sophia] is feminine, and all through the wondrous passage the Mother in Deity utters her voice. In the forty-fifth Psalm, the Queen is pictured standing at the right hand of the King. . . . We may look up through Nature to God. Our natural father and mother, with their united strength and wisdom, truth and love are types of that Perfect Parentage our Father and Mother which are in Heaven. . . .

Phoebe Worrall Palmer (1807–1874): Holiness Leader

Phoebe Worrall Palmer was the most famous female leader and lay evangelist of the mid-nineteenth century "Holiness revival." She was the fourth of ten children born to a New York City Methodist couple. At 19, she married a homeopathic physician, Walter Clark Palmer. Both had experienced powerful conversions to Methodism as teenagers, and when their two sons died shortly after birth, they interpreted the deaths as signs they should focus on religious activities. In 1832, during a revival in New York's Allen Street Methodist Episcopal Church, they dedicated themselves to "spiritual holiness." Phoebe began to lead a weekly afternoon prayer meeting for women. This became the Tuesday Meeting for the Promotion of Holiness, dedicated to seeking complete sanctification according to the doctrine of Christian perfection first preached by Methodist founder, Englishman John Wesley, and, in the 1830s, by American evangelists, such as Charles Grandison Finney. By 1839, these evangelical meetings included men and many Methodists, and by 1858, they attracted ministers and lay people from many denominations. The perfectionist movement thus evolved out of her women's prayer meeting.

Palmer's writings and her work as a traveling evangelist were important to the development of the movement. She first wrote for the *Guide to Holiness,* the movement's journal, and then published *The Way of Holiness* (1845) about her own religious experience. Seven other volumes followed, including a volume of personal testimonies, *Pioneer Experiences* (1868). In 1862, Phoebe's husband bought the monthly *Guide to Holiness* and Phoebe served as editor-in-chief until her death. In 1850, the Palmers began spending half of each year going to camp meetings and leading holiness revivals in the United States and Canada. They went to England in 1859 and led revivals for four years.

For Palmer, as for other religious women, sanctification led to service to others. In the 1840s, she distributed religious tracts in slums, visited prisons, and served as secretary of the New York Female Assistance Society for the Relief and Religious Instruction of the Sick Poor. Her most famous achievement was the 1850 founding of the Five Points Mission in New York City's worst slum. The mission was a precursor of the late nineteenth-century settlement houses, replete with 20 free apartments for indigents, a chapel, schoolroom, baths, and a House of Industry that employed 500 workers (White 1986, 63–64, 217–27; Raser 1987, 213–15).

Although Palmer avoided the women's rights movement, she was an articulate advocate for religious or "sanctified" feminism. She devoted over 400 pages of her major work, *Promise of the Father,* to analyses of biblical passages that showed the roles women had played in Christianity and to critiques of negative passages about women that she attributed to particular historical conditions. In essence, she argued that the "promise of the Father" could be fulfilled only when women achieved equality in the church and were able to carry out God's work. (Raser 1987, 204–10) Note Palmer's use of women's history and the strategies she employs to counter religious conservatives in this next selection.

PROMISE OF THE FATHER (1859)*

CHAPTER II: WOMAN

A QUESTION of grave interest is now demanding the attention of all Christians, irrespective of name or sect. Especially does it demand the attention of the Christian ministry. . . .

The question is this: Has not a gift of power, delegated to the church on the day of Pentecost, been neglected? . . .

. . . From whence has the doctrine obtained, that women may not open their mouth in supplication and prayer in the presence of their brethren? . . .

*Excerpts from Phoebe Palmer, *Promise of the Father.* ed. Donald W. Dayton, "The Higher Christian Life" Sources for the Study of the Holiness, Pentecostal, and Keswick Movements, a Garland Series, (Boston: H.V. Degen, 1859; reprint, New York: Garland Publishing, 1985), pp. 14–15, 143–44, 151–52.

CHAPTER X: REJECTED MESSAGE

Imagine, after our Lord had commissioned Mary to proclaim the gospel of a risen Christ to her brethren, that these brethren had turned away contemptuously, refusing to accept the message, because it fell from the lips of a woman.

We know of a church with whom the signs of spiritual life were well nigh extinct. . . .

About the time that this church was thus rapidly approximating towards spiritual death, God raised up an instrumentality by which he would have saved it. A female member of that church, the wife of one of the leading members, a lady of excellent reputation and intelligent piety, had fallen in with a book in which she saw the Bible view of Christian holiness illustrated with simplicity and force. She saw that this was the gift of power which that church must have in order to make it efficient in the evangelization of the world. . . .

Not more truly did the Saviour deliver a message, through the lips of a devoted female, to those erring disciples who forsook the Saviour, in the hour of his greatest extremity, and fled, than he would now have delivered a message to the brethren of this church community, through the lips of this devoted, intelligent female disciple. Such had been her evident manifestations of devotedness and supreme love of Christ, that we presume no one doubted she was a beloved disciple, as was the devoted Mary of Magdalene. . . .

But now that this beloved, newly-baptized disciple spake as the Spirit gave utterance, did her brethren receive this testimony for Jesus as it fell from her lips? No! not because the message did not come clothed with heart-thrilling pathos and divine power. No! many felt this. . . . And why did they reject this message, if coming thus from a known disciple of Christ, who had the confidence of the religious public, and whose wondrous message came clothed with divine authority, and the reception of which might, doubtless, have been the salvation of that church community? They rejected it because the church had imposed the cruel seal of silence on the lips of woman. . . . All knew that the fires of the Spirit were fast dying out in that church. . . .

And now one of their own number had, in obedience to the command of the Saviour, tarried at Jerusalem until, endued with power and filled with the Holy Ghost, she would fain have all seek the same needful grace, and, with the same power impelling her that impelled those women on the day of Pentecost to speak as the Spirit gave utterance, she utters before the multitude the great things God has done for her, and her testimony is contemptuously rejected because it falls from the lips of a woman. . . .

Ellen Gould Harmon White (1827–1915): Seventh-Day Adventist Founder and Prophetess

Ellen G. White was the founder and prophetess of the Seventh-Day Adventist Church which by the time of her death in 1915 was "one of America's largest indigenous denominations" (Numbers 1992, xiii). Her influence sprang from visions that occurred during trances and continued throughout her life. Her visions guided those Millerites who reorganized as Seventh-Day Adventists and stimulated the growth of the sect. Despite her importance to the religion, however, men always filled the formal leadership positions of the church.

Ellen was born in Portland, Maine, and experienced her first religious "awakening" at a Methodist camp meeting in the summer of 1840. She was baptized in 1842, when Millerite or Adventist excitement was sweeping Portland. William Miller preached that Christ's return was to occur around 1843, and the Harmons were among many who converted after hearing him. When Christ failed to return as predicted, many abandoned the new faith and returned to their old churches. In December 1844, Ellen went into a trance at a female prayer group meeting and reported her vision of Advent people in the sky on pilgrimage to the City of God. This was the first of over 2,000 visions she claimed to have had during her life. Although in poor health, she began to share her visions with audiences and, in 1845, at age 18, she embarked on an itinerant ministry. She re-interpreted Miller's message, claiming first that Christ's return was still imminent, but that no firm date was set. She then called for observance of the seventh-day Sabbath in accordance with a vision she had on April 7, 1847.

In August 1846, she married James Springer White, another young Adventist preacher. Of their four children, two survived childhood and became workers in the church. In 1849, at her urging, her husband inaugurated the *Advent Review and Sabbath Herald,* the movement's official newspaper. She published her autobiography and account of her early visions in 1851, and by the time she died, had some 50 books, many pamphlets, and over 4,000 articles in print (Goen 1974, 586).

In 1855, the Whites moved to Battle Creek, Michigan which became the base for Adventist operations for a half century. In 1860, the Battle Creek group chose the name Seventh-Day Adventists, and, in 1863, formally created the new denomination. During this formative period, White shaped critical decisions by the authority of her visions. She never claimed to be a prophetess, but her interpretations established Seventh-Day Adventist beliefs, and acceptance of her visions and their divine origin became a basic principle of the church. In 1855, she published a pamphlet of instructions for Adventists, *Testimonies for the Church,* which ultimately grew to nine volumes.

White was also involved in many reforms, and her ideas about health, education, and temperance became part of her religious instruction. She was instrumental in establishing the Battle Creek sanitarium, which, under Dr. John Harvey Kellogg, became a model for similar institutions Adventists established around the world. She advocated child-centered education, insisted that education be practical and available to all, and founded Battle Creek College in 1874. Her 1903 book *Education* became the basis of education in Adventist schools from elementary level through professional. She supported the antislavery cause, and made Battle Creek a stop on the Underground Railroad. In the late nineteenth century, she attracted thousands to her temperance lectures and spent the 1890s as a missionary to Australia. She was a powerful role model for many Adventist women. Compare her visions with those of other women in this chapter.

White's Vision of the Sabbath*

. . . [In 1847, she had the following vision during a Sabbath service.]

We felt an unusual spirit of prayer. And as we prayed the Holy Ghost fell upon us. We were very happy. Soon I was lost to earthly things and was wrapped in a vision of God's glory. I saw an angel flying swiftly to me. He quickly carried me from the earth to the holy city. In the city I saw a temple, which I entered. I passed through a door before I came to the first veil. This veil was raised, and I passed into

*From Ellen Gould Harmon White, *Early Writings of Mrs. White* (11th ed., 1907; Woodbridge, CT: Research Publications, 1977), pp. 32–33, microfilm, History of Women, Reel 780, no. 6234.

the holy place. Here I saw the altar of incense, the candlestick with seven lamps, and the table on which was the showbread. After viewing the glory of the holy, Jesus raised the second veil and I passed into the holy of holies.

In the holiest I saw an ark; on the top and sides of it was purest gold. On each end of the ark was a lovely cherub, with its wings spread out over it. Their faces were turned toward each other, and they looked downward. Between the angels was a golden censer. Above the ark, where the angels stood, was an exceeding bright glory that appeared like a throne where God dwelt. Jesus stood by the ark, and as the saints' prayers came up to Him, the incense in the censer would smoke, and He would offer up their prayers with the smoke of the incense to His Father. In the ark was the golden pot of manna, Aaron's rod that budded, and the tables of stone which folded together like a book. Jesus opened them, and I saw the Ten Commandments written on them with the finger of God. On one table were four, and on the other six. But the fourth, the Sabbath commandment, shone above them all; for the Sabbath was set apart to be kept in honor of God's holy name. . . .

Mary Baker Eddy (1821–1910): Founder, Church of Christ, Scientist

Mary Baker Eddy, the founder of Christian Science, was born in New Hampshire, the youngest of six children. From early childhood, she suffered chronic spinal problems and fevers, and, as a result, attended school irregularly. She married in December 1843, but six months later she was a widow and pregnant. Her health declined further after the birth of her son, so she gave him up to a foster family. In 1853, she remarried. During the 20 years of her second marriage, she was rarely healthy and sought cure after cure. She led a semi-nomadic existence, estranged from her husband, living in boarding houses or with acquaintances, teaching, healing, and gradually developing her ideas on religion and health. She had stormy relationships with followers, friends, and partners. In 1875, she settled in Lynn, Massachusetts, in what became the Christian Scientists' Home. She held classes and meetings, making a living from her students' tuition, and published the first edition of *Science and Health.* In 1877 she married one of her students and assistants, Asa Gilbert Eddy, who was her business consultant and supporter until his death in 1882.

In 1879, the Church of Christ (Scientist) was formally chartered, and in 1881, Eddy obtained a charter for the Massachusetts Metaphysical College as a degree-granting institution. She moved the church and college to Boston in 1882. The next year she founded the monthly *Christian Science Journal* as the official church organ and added a weekly journal, *Christian Science Sentinel,* in 1898. In the meantime, she published *Key to the Scriptures* that linked her theories to specific biblical passages. By 1910, this book had sold nearly half a million copies. Her church grew rapidly in the 1880s, but the following decade brought a series of divisions, reorganizations, and renewed power struggles between Eddy and various followers. Indeed, her church was constantly beset with conflicts between disaffected former students and its founder. She continually sought to centralize control over the church and its college and excommunicated followers who became too popular and independent. She replaced preachers with readers, insisting that they only read (with no interpretation) from texts prescribed for a particular day.

Mary Baker Eddy's legacy is a lasting church structure and a body of doctrine spelled out in her numerous writings and in official church journals. In 1908, she founded a daily newspaper, the *Christian Science Monitor.* The doctrines of Christian Science gained appeal as more people became interested in the relationship of the body and mind and in psychic well-being as a basis of health, peace, and prosperity. Its adherents had confidence in the power of positive thinking to bring about change. Its doctrine that worldly affluence proved its "truth" also appealed to successful, prosperous individuals. As you read this selection consider why urban women tended to comprise the bulk of her followers and adherents.

SCIENCE AND HEALTH, WITH KEY TO THE SCRIPTURES*

Revelation 12:1. And there appeared a great wonder in Heaven, a woman clothed with the sun, and the moon under her feet, and upon her head a crown of twelve stars.

Heaven represents harmony, and Divine Science interprets the Principle of heavenly harmony. The great miracle, to human sense, is divine love. . . .

. . . The Revelator beheld the spiritual idea from the mount of vision. Purity was the symbol of Life and Love. He saw also the spiritual ideal, as a woman clothed in light, a bride coming down from Heaven, wedded to the Lamb of Love. To him, the Bride and the Lamb represented the correlation of divine Principle and spiritual idea, bringing harmony to earth. . . .

John the Baptist prophesied the coming of the immaculate Jesus, and he saw in those days the spiritual idea as the Messiah, who would baptize with the Holy Ghost,— Divine Science. As Elias represents the Fatherhood of God, through Jesus, so the Revelator completes this figure with woman, as the spiritual idea or type of God's Motherhood. The moon is under her feet. This idea reveals the universe as secondary and tributary to Spirit, from which it borrows its reflected Substance, Life, and Intelligence.

The spiritual idea is crowned with twelve stars. The twelve tribes of Israel, with all mortals,—separated, by belief, from man's divine origin and the true idea,—shall through much tribulation yield to the activities of the divine Principle of man, in the harmony of Science. These are the stars in the crown of rejoicing. They are the lamps in the spiritual heavens of this age, which show the workings of the spiritual idea by healing the sick and the sinful, and by manifesting the light which shines "unto the perfect day," as the night of materialism wanes.

THE STRUGGLE FOR AUTONOMY, AUTHORITY, AND INCLUSION

Jarena Lee (1783–18?): African Methodist Episcopal Visionary and Preacher

Jarena Lee was the first female preacher in the African Methodist Episcopal Church (AME). She traveled extensively and published the record she kept of her ministry. She was the first black woman to write and publish an autobiography in America, 25 years before Harriet Jacobs's *Incidents in the Life of a Slave Girl* (1861), the first female slave narrative. Spiritual autobiographies, in fact, were the first forms of autobiography in African-American literature. Lee's autobiography was the first to describe the roles assigned women in black religion in America and to show women's resistance to gender restrictions. Women's spiritual autobiographies in general reveal a belief that they had been chosen by

*From Mary Baker Eddy, *Science and Health, with Key to the Scriptures,* 79th edition (Boston: E. J. Foster Eddy, 1893; Ann Arbor, MI: Xerox University Microfilms, 1974), pp. 540–42, microfilm, American Culture Series, reel 580:15.

God to speak to the unsaved, and that faith enabled them to live independent lives in a racist and sexist society.

Lee's parents were free, but not well off, so they hired her out at age 7 as a servant girl. In 1804, at 21, she converted to Christianity and joined Philadelphia's Bethel AME Church. Three weeks later, during the sermon, she rose up as she experienced salvation. For four years she doubted the legitimacy of the visions and was tempted to commit suicide. Then she met William Scott who told her of the doctrine of sanctification as preached by John Wesley. This convinced her she wasn't yet sanctified, but within months, she received sanctification from God. Around 1811, she felt a call to preach and she told her minister, Reverend Richard Allen. Thus began her struggle with the church.

In 1811, she married Joseph Lee, pastor of a black church near Philadelphia, but by 1817 her husband and four other family members were dead, and she was left with two young children. She returned to Philadelphia in 1818, and asked Allen (now an AME bishop) to let her have prayer meetings in her home, which he did. A year later, she interrupted the sermon in Bethel Church and began preaching on the text the preacher was using. Allen then endorsed the validity of her calling and she began her career as an itinerant preacher. She traveled to Philadelphia and all over the Mid-Atlantic and Northeastern states, preaching to black and white audiences. In 1835, she traveled over 700 miles and preached hundreds of sermons. She was accepted by AME preachers and leaders as a "traveling exhorter," but not as a licensed preacher. (Andrews 1986, 6) In 1840 she joined the American Antislavery Society to spread the gospel through abolitionism.

She wrote her autobiography to draw others to Christ and paid to have the book printed in 1836. She distributed it at camp meetings, on streets, and at Methodist churches. In 1839 she had more copies printed, and in 1849 she underwrote the printing of her *Religious Experience and Journal* updated to her fiftieth birthday. This is the last information we have about her, but she apparently inspired other women. At the 1850 annual meeting of the Philadelphia Conference of the AME church, a group of women, claiming a divine calling to preach, formed an informal organization to appoint members from their group to preaching roles in Philadelphia. The group disintegrated, however, and in 1852 the AME conference rejected a resolution calling for licensing women to preach.

Note the forms Lee's experiences of the divine calling took and how they enabled her to challenge church authority.

RELIGIOUS EXPERIENCES OF JARENA LEE*

Between four and five years after my sanctification, on a certain time, an impressive silence fell upon me, and I stood as if some one was about to speak to me, yet I had no such thought in my heart. But to my utter surprise there seemed to sound a voice which I thought I distinctly heard, and most certainly understood, which said to me, "Go preach the Gospel!" I immediately replied aloud, "No one will believe me." Again I listened, and again the same voice seemed to say, "Preach the Gospel; I will put words in your mouth, and will turn your enemies to become your friends."

At first I supposed that Satan had spoken to me, for I had read that he could transform himself into an angel of light, for the purpose of deception. Immediately I went into a secret place, and called upon the Lord to know if he had called me to

*Excerpts from Jarena Lee, *Religious Experience and Journal of Mrs. Jarena Lee, being an Account of Her Call to Preach the Gospel,* (Philadelphia: Printed and Published for the Author, 1849), pp. 10–11, 14, reprinted in *Spiritual Narratives,* Schomburg Library of Nineteenth-Century Black Women Writers, Henry Louis Gates, Jr., ed. (New York; Oxford: Oxford University Press, 1988 [1991 printing]).

preach, and whether I was deceived or not; when there appeared to my view the form and figure of a pulpit, with a Bible lying thereon, the back of which was presented to me as plainly as if it had been a literal fact.

In consequence of this, my mind became so exercised that during the night following, I took a text, and preached in my sleep. I thought there stood before me a great multitude, while I expounded to them the things of religion. So violent were my exertions, and so loud were my exclamations, that I awoke from the sound of my own voice, which also awoke the family of the house where I resided. Two days after, I went to see the preacher in charge of the African Society, . . . the Rev. Richard Allen, . . . to tell him that I felt it my duty to preach the gospel. . . .

I now told him, that the Lord had revealed it to me, that I must preach the gospel. He replied by asking, in what sphere I wished to move in? I said, among the Methodists. He then replied, that a Mrs. Cook, a Methodist lady, had also some time before requested the same privilege; who it was believed, had done much good in the way of exhortation, and holding prayer meetings; and who had been permitted to do so by the verbal license of the preacher in charge at the time. But as to women preaching, he said that our Discipline knew nothing at all about it—that it did not call for women preachers. . . . O how careful ought we to be, lest through our by-laws of church government and discipline, we bring into disrepute even the word of life. For as unseemly as it may appear now-a-days for a woman to preach, it should be remembered that nothing is impossible with God. And why should it be thought impossible, heterodox, or improper, for a woman to preach? seeing the Saviour died for the woman as well as for the man. . . .

Women in the Black Baptist Church

By the end of the nineteenth century, the Black Baptist church was the largest black religious group in America. In the antebellum decades, gender restrictions prevented women from preaching or attending business meetings in many of the free Black Baptist churches in the Northeast. Some congregations segregated church seating by sex, and even prohibited women from praying publicly. Yet women occasionally appeared as deaconesses, delegates to official meetings, and members of women's committees. After the Civil War and the abolition of slavery, the Black Baptist church grew rapidly in the South. Soon its ministers began to organize the independent Black Baptist churches into local and then state conventions in order to more effectively implement programs to sustain black communities and combat racism. In 1895, their efforts resulted in the formation of the National Baptist Convention (NBC). At all levels, however, women were excluded from participation in the conventions.

As a result, in the 1880s, women began to organize their own groups to spread the gospel and give women a voice in church affairs. Women's conventions aroused the bitter opposition of the clergy and male lay leaders who feared loss of control over the funds raised by women and over their female members in general. Nevertheless, determined leaders such as Virginia W. Broughton of Tennessee, Mary V. Cook of Kentucky, Nannie Helen Burroughs of Washington, D.C., and others forged ahead. By 1900, they had organized state conventions in 23 states and in the Indian Territory, Oklahoma Territory, and Washington, D.C. That same year, the male-led NBC finally voted to establish the Women's Convention (WC) Auxiliary to the NBC. Lewis Jordan and Charles Parrish, whose support led to the victory, were married to convention leaders.

Despite the poverty and pitiful wages of most black women, local and state women's unofficial conventions had a remarkable record of achievements. They organized low-income women and raised substantial sums of money. They created and financed orphanages, elder-care homes, day nurseries and kindergartens, vocational training programs, community health facilities, and settlement houses. At the height of Jim Crow (rigid racial segregation), leaders of the women's conventions broke with Booker T. Washington's policy of accommodation and spoke out against black disfranchisement, lynching, and segregation. They always championed black women's rights to education, jobs, and suffrage. Within the church, they attacked sexism, demanding a voice in church affairs, control over the funds they raised, and women's right to be missionaries and preachers.

Virginia Broughton (185?–19??): Black Baptist Leader

Virginia Broughton's father had purchased his and his wife's freedom from his Virginia master and raised their children as free blacks. Broughton was among the few freed children to be educated in a private school, and after the Civil War she was among the first class of students enrolled in Fisk University. She graduated from the college department in 1875, and, according to her autobiography, was the first female college graduate south of the Mason-Dixon Line. For over 12 years she was a teacher and school administrator in Memphis, Tennessee. In 1887 she was invited to a women's missionary meeting that subsequently decided to organize Bible Bands. Thus began her long involvement in the crusade for women's full participation in the Baptist church. She led the effort in Tennessee for women to form Bible Bands for the study and interpretation of the scriptures and published *Women's Work, as Gleaned from the Women of the Bible* (1904) to demonstrate biblical precedents for gender equality in the church. This book brought together the themes she addressed as a teacher, lecturer, grass-roots organizer, and in her correspondence. It also exemplified the feminist theology that guided her work and that of Cook, Burroughs, and other Baptist activists (Higginbotham 1993, 121–49).

The excerpts from her autobiography reveal some of the struggles and achievements of this determined woman. They also suggest why some opposed her work. The selection begins with Broughton's account of women's pioneering work shortly after the Board of Directors of the Bible and Normal Institute decided to begin missionary work among the black women of Tennessee in 1888.

TWENTY YEARS' EXPERIENCE OF A MISSIONARY (1907)*

> . . . Miss E. B. King and Virginia [Broughton] were the two women appointed. These two consecrated women with Bibles in hand went forth, . . . Everywhere these women went the people were aroused, some for them and many against them. Bible Bands were organized throughout the district. Exciting days were those! Bibles were being searched as never before by that people to find out if there was any divine authority for such work; women were rising up and striving to get to the meetings to hear what new doctrine those women missionaries were teaching, and men were discussing and opposing. . . .
>
> The Lord permitted a few of our Bible women to grow strong under this special ministry of grace known as the Bible Band work. This strength led the women to contend for the Bible plan of church government in the discipline of members, in supporting churches, and in preaching and teaching the gospel. The common evil

*Excerpts from V. W. Broughton, *Twenty Year's Experience of a Missionary* (Chicago: Pony Press, Publishers, 1907), pp. 20–21, 34–35, 38–39, reprinted in *Spiritual Narratives*, Schomburg Library of Nineteenth-Century Black Women Writers, Henry Louis Gates, Jr., ed. (New York: Oxford; Oxford University Press, '88 [1991 printing]).

practices of intemperance in beer drinking, tobaco using, excessive eating and dressing, and the desecrating custom of using church houses for fairs, festivals and other worldly amusements were all strongly condemned by our Bible women, while righteousness, holiness, purity and all the kindred graces of Christianity were upheld and emphasized. Ministers and laymen, who looked with disdain upon a criticism that came from a woman, and all those who were jealous of the growing popularity of the woman's work, as if there was some cause of alarm for the safety of their own positions of power and honor, all rose up in their churches, with all the influence and power of speech they could summon to oppose the woman's work and break it up if possible. The work had taken root too deeply in the hearts of our women ever to be uprooted, but we were given a good shaking and thrashing, and for a season the work seemed to stand still. The separate associational meeting was broken up, many local Bible Bands disbanded, . . . Virginia continued to hold meetings where she could find an opportunity. As God has always provided some way of escape for his servants, He provided for Virginia, for there were some preachers who never closed their churches against our work, and hence an opportunity was given for self defense in the thickest of the fight. Brethren would come to our meetings to catch every word spoken, if thereby they might have some just cause to condemn our teaching, as being false doctrine. . . .

When the opposition raged fiercely, a certain minister, Bob T. by name, came to one of our churches with the expressed intention to throw Virginia out of the window. . . .

In some places church houses were locked against our Bible women, and violent hands even laid upon some. Dear Sister Nancy C. said had not Sister Susan S. come to her rescue she would have been badly beaten for attempting to hold a woman's meeting in her own church.

In another vicinity Brother F. P. became so enraged he drew a gun on his wife after she had gotten in a wagon to go to one of our Bible Band meetings, and threatened to take her life if she went a step farther. Of course she was obliged to stop that time and stay home, but that man soon died; he was not permitted to live long enough to prohibit that good woman a second time from going when her missionary sisters called a meeting. This incident did much to allay the persecution throughout that section. While men opposed and Satan strove our progress to retard, God was with us. . . .

Hannah Greenebaum Solomon (1858–1942): Jewish Leader

Hannah Greenebaum Solomon was the founder of the National Council of Jewish Women (NCJW) and an important philanthropic leader and social reformer in Chicago. She was the fourth of ten children born to Michael and Sarah Greenbaum, émigrés from the German Palatinate. Her father became a prosperous hardware merchant and leader in the Jewish community. He and his wife were members of the first Reform congregation of Judaism in Chicago. Hannah received her early education in a temple school, attended public high school for two years, and then chose to study piano with a private instructor. In 1879, she married a merchant, Henry Solomon. They had three children, one of whom died in 1899. Hannah and her husband shared interests in music and art, and he was one of her staunchest supporters as she became involved in women's club activities and community affairs. She was active in numerous Jewish social and cultural clubs, and she and her sister were the first Jewish members of the influential Chicago Woman's Club. After the Chicago World's Fair (Columbian Exhibition) in 1893, Solomon continued her reform efforts, working through the Chicago section of the NCJW. She also worked with Chicago's famous social reformer Jane Addams and other Hull House women to improve the plight of immigrants and slum dwellers. She helped establish the Cook County juvenile court and served on the board of the Illinois Industrial School for Girls. Her reform work, like her efforts to establish the NCJW, resulted from, and was shaped by, her religious values and faith.

The reading focuses on her role organizing the Jewish Women's Congress as part of the world's fair and her vision of the roles Jewish women should assume in America.

EXCERPTS FROM SOLOMON'S AUTOBIOGRAPHY*

Preparations for the World's Columbian Exposition entailed many exciting obligations on the part of the Chicago Woman's Club. Two of its members, Mrs. Potter Palmer and Mrs. Charles Henrotin, were made chairman and vice-chairman of the Board of Lady Managers. . . . Club members served on committees of all congresses. . . .

I was honored, by those who were planning the women's congresses by being made representative of the Jewish women, and was further authorized to call Jewish women together under whatever division or divisions I thought best. Since I believed then, as I do now, that when we use the word "Jewish" it must have a purely religious connotation, I felt that our place should be with the Parliament of Religions which was to be one of the great features of World's Fair year. A women's board was organized to aid in furthering the Parliament, and I was made chairman for Jewish women's participation. . . .

How gratifying the day when I could report definite progress and request two places for Jewish women on the general Parliament program. We had selected two remarkable speakers: Henrietta Szold, then secretary of the Jewish Publication Society, who chose as her topic, "What Judaism Has Done for Women", and Josephine Lazarus, a brilliant thinker who wielded a powerful pen, and who elected to discuss "The Outlook for Judaism." Both papers . . . paved the way for Jewish women, magnificently opening up for them many opportunities to speak on Judaism before women of other faiths.

When the Jewish men of Chicago gathered to make plans for their congress, I was invited to attend the meeting. After some preliminary business, the chairman turned to me, asking, "Mrs. Solomon, will you Jewish women cooperate with us in our sessions?"

"Well," I replied, "our plans are already far advanced, and assignments have been given our representatives in the general Parliament. We will, however, be very glad to join with you if you will accord us active participation in your program."

The program committee then retired to deliberate, and when they returned, lo and behold! not a single woman's name appeared in their recommendations!

*Excerpts from Hannah G. Solomon, *Fabric of My Life. The Autobiography of Hannah G. Solomon* (New York: Bloch Publishing Company, 1946), pp. 80, 82–83, 90. By permission of Bloch Publishing Company.

"Mr. Chairman," I inquired, "just where on your program are the women to be placed?"

"Well," hemmed and hawed the chairman, "the program seems complete just as it stands."

"Very well," I replied, "under these circumstances we do not care to cooperate with you, and I request that the fact of our presence at this meeting be expunged from the records."

The Jewish Women's Congress at the Chicago World's Fair

[At the final session, delegates created a permanent organization of Jewish women, and adopted the following resolutions defining its purpose.]

. . . "Resolved, that the National Council of Jewish Women shall (1) seek to unite in closer relation women interested in the work of Religion, Philanthropy and Education and shall consider practical means of solving problems in these fields; shall (2) organize and encourage the study of the underlying principles of Judaism; the history, literature and customs of the Jews, and their bearing on their own and the world's history; shall (3) apply knowledge gained in this study to the improvement of the Sabbath Schools, and in the work of social reform; shall (4) secure the interest and aid of influential persons, wherever and whenever and against whomever shown, and in finding means to prevent such persecutions." . . .

And so was born the National Council of Jewish Women . . . living symbol of world progress as demonstrated by the World Columbian Exposition. . . .

WOMEN MINISTERS IN SESSION, CHICAGO WORLD'S FAIR, 21 MAY 1893*

Eighteen ordained women ministers of the Gospel, representing thirteen different denominations, sat on the speaker's platform at the religious services held this morning in Washington Hall of the Memorial Art Palace by the World's Congress of Representative Women. . . .

Miss Anna H. Shaw delivered the sermon. She took the Sixty-eighth Psalm, verse 11, of the Revised Scriptures for her text and said in part: "All women who have spoken at these meetings have voiced the one cry—to be free; they have been expressing the one aspiration that truth shall be our guide, and not tradition. All the work has been imbued with the one great spirit which takes truth for authority, not authority for truth. We have learned that we have had enough of creed. The limited vision of those women who think that their truth must be the truth for all and will recognize no other creed than their own is disappearing through such work as has been done.

To teach toleration has been the mission of the congress, and those who have taken part shall go forth as women in whose souls have been planted the germs, not of one exclusive truth, but of many truths."

*From "Women Ministers in Session," *New York Times* (Rochester, NY: Eastman Kodak Co. for Recordak Corp.), 22 May 1893, p. 8, microfilm: NP1.

FEMINIST CRITIQUES OF RELIGION

Lucretia Coffin Mott (1793–1880): Quaker Minister, Abolitionist, and Feminist

Lucretia Coffin Mott was a Quaker minister who dedicated her life to the abolition of slavery, social justice, and the emancipation of women. She was born in Nantucket, Massachusetts, a seafaring Quaker community with a long tradition of strong women. Her father was a sea captain involved in the new China trade, and her mother was a shopkeeper. Since the men of Nantucket were often at sea for months at a time, women ran businesses and households. Daily life thus re-enforced the Quaker belief in equality. In 1804, the family moved to Boston, where Lucretia attended public and private Quaker schools and then spent two years teaching at a Friends' boarding school in New York. On April 10, 1811, Lucretia married a colleague, James Mott, and settled in Philadelphia. She bore six children between 1812 and 1828. For 57 years, they enjoyed a partnership marriage.

Mott was officially recognized as a minister by the Quakers in 1821. In 1827, when the Quakers broke into rival factions, she and James followed the liberal wing led by Elias Hicks. The Hicksite Friends, as they were called, rejected the increasing orthodoxy and control by the elders of the orthodox wing and, instead, emphasized the principles of equality and justice. With the Hicksites, she and James joined the antislavery cause and sided with the radical Garrisonian abolitionists. She was an organizer of the first Female Antislavery Society in Philadelphia and the first Antislavery Conventions of American Women in 1837 and 1838, and was one of the American women delegates denied seating and the right to speak at the World Antislavery Convention in London. In 1848, she joined with Elizabeth Cady Stanton and others to launch the woman's rights movement. In the post–Civil War years she worked for Negro suffrage and education and held leadership positions in the American and international peace movements and the woman's suffrage movement. She also raised funds for the coeducational Quaker college, Swarthmore (1864). Guided by her faith and interpretation of the Divine will, she was critical of religious orthodoxy, opposing Sabbath laws and all other measures that violated individual free conscience. She was an inspiration and role model for generations of young women who learned from her example that women could travel, speak in public, preach, and demand justice and equality.

In the reading that follows, note how Quaker beliefs in the equality of souls and direct access of all to God without intermediaries shaped her arguments and politics. Also note which aspects of nineteenth-century religion angered or disturbed her, and why.

SERMON DELIVERED AT CHERRY STREET MEETING, PHILADELPHIA, 4 NOVEMBER 1849*

> . . . The great error in Christendom is that the Bible is called the word, that it is taken as a whole, as a volume of plenary inspiration and in this way it has proved one of the strongest pillars to uphold ecclesiastical power and hireling priesthood. What has been the power of this book? Is it not uniformly taken among all the professors to establish their peculiar creeds, their dogmas of faith and their forms of worship, be they ever so superstitious? Is not the Bible sought from beginning to end for its

*Excerpts from Lucretia Mott, *Lucretia Mott: Her Complete Speeches and Sermons,* ed. Dana Greene, vol. 4 of Studies in Women and Religion Series (New York and Toronto: Edwin Mellen Press, 1980), pp. 124–25, 132–33. By permission of Edwin Mellen Press.

isolated passages wherewith to prove the most absurd dogmas that ever were palmed off upon a credulous people; dogmas doing violence to the divine gift of reason with which man is so beautifully endowed; doing violence to all his feelings, his sense of justice and mercy with which the Most High has seen fit to clothe him? The Bible has been taken to make man from his very birth a poor corrupt sinful creature, . . . We find the religionist, especially those whose greater interest it is to build up sect than to establish truth and righteousness in the earth, . . . ready to flee to the Bible for authority for all their mysteries, their nonsensical dogmas, that have been imposed as articles of belief, as essential doctrines of Christianity. But also my friends has there not been an unworthy resort to this volume to prove the rightfulness of war and slavery, and of crushing woman's powers, the assumption of authority over her, and indeed of all the evils under which the earth, humanity has groaned from age to age? . . .

. . . He that upholdeth truth designs that there should be no inspiration, no power delegated upon one portion of the people over another. Until we come to this, until there is an intelligent testimony born against ecclesiastical usurpations, against hierarchical institutions, against the favored few in the congregation, there must be divisions and subdivision among us. . . .

. . . The usurpations of the church and clergy, by which woman has been so debased, so crushed, her powers of mind, her very being brought low, and a low estimate set upon these, are coming to be seen in their true light. But woman must avail herself of the increasing means of intelligence, education and knowledge. She must rise also in a higher sphere of spiritual existence and suffer her moral nature to be developed, her mind to be made right in the sight of God. Then will the time speedily come when the influence of the clergy shall be taken off of woman, when the monopoly of the pulpit shall no more oppress her, when marriage shall not be a means of rendering her noble nature subsidiary to man, when there shall be no assumed authority on the one part nor admitted inferiority or subjection on the other. One of the abuses of the Bible . . . has been to bind silence upon woman in the churches, fasten upon her that kind of degrading obedience in the marriage relation which has led to countless evils in society and indeed has enervated, and produced for us a feeble race. Oh my friends, these subjects are subjects of religious interest and of vast importance. . . .

Elizabeth Cady Stanton (1815–1902): Feminist

Elizabeth Cady Stanton was a founder and leader of the American woman's rights movement and author of its "manifesto," *The Seneca Falls Declaration of Sentiments*. Stanton, the daughter of a prominent lawyer and a New York Supreme Court judge, first awakened to women's subordinate status upon hearing some of the tales of her father's female clients. She married abolitionist Henry B. Stanton over her father's objections. In 1848, bored and isolated in western New York, she and a few others placed an ad in the local newspaper, inviting people to attend the first woman's rights convention. Over three hundred people showed up in Seneca Falls and, by a majority, adopted her *Declaration*. With that act, the American woman's rights movement was born. From then on, while rearing seven children, Stanton devoted her life, her pen, her voice, and her energies to the movement to emancipate women. She was a popular speaker because of her sense of humor, and she never failed to arouse controversy by advocating dress reform (bloomers); divorce; an end to the double standard;

economic, legal, and educational equality for women; and, of course, suffrage. She also supported temperance and the antislavery cause.

After the Civil War, Stanton refused to subordinate women's rights to Negro rights, noting that half of the freed people were women. In 1869, she began a 12-year lecture career on the grueling Lyceum circuit. She was co-author of the multivolume *History of Woman Suffrage* and author of an autobiography and hundreds of articles and speeches. In the 1880s, frustrated by the depth of opposition to woman suffrage, she began to publicly attack organized religion for its role in oppressing women. In 1895, at a gathering in the New York Metropolitan Opera House honoring her eightieth birthday, she shocked many by insisting that women demand an equal place in the church. That same year she published *The Woman's Bible. The Woman's Bible* was a collaborative effort, but she was its guiding force and author of many sections. The work challenged and reinterpreted the Bible's derogatory references to women in light of other biblical passages and common sense. While popular, the book aroused a storm of protest and resulted in the National American Woman Suffrage Association adopting a resolution that, in essence, censured the mother of the movement. Her uncompromising decision to criticize religion and its role in women's oppression resulted in her near erasure from the history of the movement for many years. Younger suffragists looked to her friend and partner of half a lifetime, Susan B. Anthony, as the movement's leader and forgot Stanton's critical role and lifetime commitment. Were the ideas in the reading new? Why, do you think, her *Woman's Bible* was so controversial?

THE WOMAN'S BIBLE (1895–98)*

Chapter I.

Genesis i; 26, 27, 28.

26. And God said, let us make man in our image, after our likeness; and let them have dominion over the fish of the sea, . . . and over every creeping thing that creepeth upon the earth.

27. So God created man in his own image, in the image of God created he him; male and female created he them.

28. And God blessed them, and God said unto them Be fruitful, and multiply, and replenish the earth, and subdue it; and have dominion . . . over every living thing. . . .

Here is the sacred historian's first account of the advent of woman; a simultaneous creation of both sexes, in the image of God. It is evident from the language that there was consultation in the Godhead, and that the masculine and feminine elements were equally represented. Scott in his commentaries says, "this consultation of the Gods is the origin of the doctrine of the trinity." But instead of three male personages, as generally represented, a Heavenly Father, Mother, and Son would seem more rational.

The first step in the elevation of woman to her true position, as an equal factor in human progress, is the cultivation of the religious sentiment in regard to her dignity and equality, the recognition by the rising generation of an ideal Heavenly Mother, to whom their prayers should be addressed, as well as to a Father.

If language has any meaning, we have in these texts a plain declaration of the existence of the feminine element in the Godhead, equal in power and glory with the

*From Elizabeth Cady Stanton. *The (Original) Feminist Attack on the Bible (The Woman's Bible)* (reprint of 1895–98 edition. New York: Arno Press, 1974), pp. 14–19.

masculine. The Heavenly Mother and Father! "God created man in his *own image, male and female.*" Thus Scripture, as well as science and philosophy, declares the eternity and equality of sex—the philosophical fact, without which there could have been no perpetuation of creation, no growth or development in the animal, vegetable, or mineral kingdoms, no awakening nor progressing in the world of thought. The masculine and feminine elements, exactly equal and balancing each other, are as essential to the maintenance of the equilibrium of the universe as positive and negative electricity, the centripetal and centrifugal forces, the laws of attraction which bind together all we know of this planet whereon we dwell and of the system in which we revolve.

In the great work of creation the crowning glory was realized, when man and woman were evolved on the sixth day, the masculine and feminine forces in the image of God, that must have existed eternally, in all forms of matter and mind. All the persons in the Godhead are represented in the Elohim the divine plurality taking counsel in regard to this last and highest form of life. Who were the members of this high council, and whether a duality or a trinity? Verse 27 declares the image of God male and female. How then is it possible to make woman an afterthought? We find in verses 5–16 the pronoun "he" used. Should it not in harmony with verse 26 be "they," a dual pronoun? We may attribute this to the same cause as the use of "his" in verse II instead of "it." The fruit tree yielding fruit after "his" kind instead of after "its" kind. The paucity of a language may give rise to many misunderstandings.

The above texts plainly show the simultaneous creation of man and woman, and their equal importance in the development of the race. All those theories based on the assumption that man was prior in the creation, have no foundation in Scripture.

As to woman's subjection, on which both the canon and the civil law delight to dwell, it is important to note that equal dominion is given to woman over every living thing, but not one word is said giving man dominion over woman.

Here is the first title deed to this green earth given alike to the sons and daughters of God. No lesson of woman's subjection can be fairly drawn from the first chapter of the Old Testament. E. C. S.

Charlotte Perkins Gilman (1860–1935): Author, Feminist, and Social Critic

Charlotte Perkins Stetson Gilman was a noted feminist, author, and lecturer. She is probably best known for her short story "The Yellow Wallpaper." She had a miserable, lonely childhood and limited education but supported herself in her teens as a commercial artist and governess. In 1884, she married artist Charles W. Stetson. Their only child, Katharine Beecher, was born within a year. Charlotte suffered a nervous breakdown but discovered her depression ended when she was away from home, so she divorced her husband, let him and his new wife keep their daughter, and embarked on an independent course. Moving to California, she supported herself by writing, and, in 1898, published her most important work, *Women and Economics,* a feminist manifesto that called for women's economic independence as the basis of social progress. She also wrote *The Home Concerning Children,* an indictment of how woman's traditional roles stifled her growth and, by extension, her children's development. In addition to her social critiques, she wrote some utopian fiction, including *Herland,* which addressed gender roles with humor and insight. Her works reflected nineteenth-century socialist, feminist, and sociological theories, including the new concept of evolution.

Like many social critics, Gilman saw religion (along with other manmade institutions) as a prime source of women's inequality. In addressing the topic, however, she drew on another popular strain of thought: the notion of fundamental gender differences. As you read the excerpt from *His Religion and Hers,* ask why she thinks men and women would create different kinds of religions and how effectively she makes her case.

HIS RELIGION AND HERS (1923)*

What would have been the effect upon religion if it had come to us through the minds of women? . . .

Had the religions of the world developed through her mind, they would have shown one deep, essential difference, the difference between birth and death. The man was interested in one end of life, she in the other. He was moved to faith, fear, and hope for the future; she to love and labor in the present.

To the death-based religion the main question is, "What is going to happen to me after I am dead?"—a posthumous egotism.

To the birth-based religion the main question is, "What must be done for the child who is born?"—an immediate altruism. . . .

The death-based religions have led to a limitless individualism, a demand for the eternal extension of personality. Such good conduct as they required was to placate the deity or to benefit one's self—to "acquire merit," as the Buddhist frankly puts it. The birth-based religion is necessarily and essentially altruistic, a forgetting of oneself for the good of the child, and tends to develop naturally into love and labor for the widening range of family, state, and world. . . .

As the thought of God slowly unfolded in the mind of woman, that great Power would have been apprehended as the Life-giver, the Teacher, the Provider, the Protector—not the proud, angry, jealous, vengeful deity men have imagined. She would have seen a God of Service, not a God of Battles. It is no wonder that Christianity was so eagerly adopted by woman. Here was a religion which made no degrading discrimination against her, and the fulfillment of which called for the essentially motherly attributes of love and service.

Women have adhered to all previous religions, of course, having no others; but the new teachings of Jesus were widely accepted by them and widely spread through their efforts. They were not, however, the interpreters, the disputers, the establishers of creeds. They did not gather together to decide whether or not men had souls. They did not devise the hideous idea of hell, the worst thought ever produced by the mind of man. It cannot be attributed to women any more than to Jesus that his wise, tender, practical teaching of right living was twisted and tortured into a theory of right dying. . . .

*Excerpts from Charlotte Perkins Gilman, *His Religion and Hers: A Study of the Faith of Our Fathers and the Work of Our Mothers* (New York and London: Century Co., 1923), pp. 50–52.

SUGGESTED READINGS

Andrews, Edward Deming. *The People Called Shakers; A Search for the Perfect Society.* New York: Oxford University Press, 1953.

Braude, Ann. *Radical Spirits: Spiritualism and Women's Rights in Nineteenth-Century America.* Boston: Beacon Press, 1989.

Chmielewski, Wendy E., Louis J. Kern, and Marlyn Klee-Hartzell, eds. *Women in Spiritual and Communitarian Societies in the United States.* Syracuse, NY: Syracuse University Press, 1992.

Coburn, Carol, and Martha Smith, eds. *Spirited Lives: How Nuns Shaped Catholic Culture and American Life, 1836–1920.* Chapel Hill: University of North Carolina Press, 1999.

Hardesty, Nancy A. *Women Called to Witness: Evangelical Feminism in the 19th Century.* Knoxville: University of Tennessee Press, 1999.

Thomas, Robert David. *"With Bleeding Footsteps": Mary Baker Eddy's Path to Religious Leadership.* New York: Knopf, 1994.

Chapter 10

The *New Woman*
and the Performing Arts

The end of the nineteenth century brought exciting new developments in the performing arts. Women in dance and theater began to seize control of their personal and professional lives and pursue new avenues of artistic expression. In the process, they often created new institutions and support networks of like-minded women and men. Both dance and theater performers broke with traditional art forms as they searched for ways to express their artistic impulses and perspectives on life and art. Unable to change existing male-dominated institutions of ballet and theater, women began to manage their own careers, produce their own dances and plays, and create their own dance schools and theater companies. They also became the artistic creators, writing plays and choreographing their own dances. Many of these independent artists also lived unconventional lives that defied the societal norm of a monogamous marriage and family. Some had several marriages, some numerous affairs and children out of wedlock, and others established lasting relationships with other women. Finally, these women supported the movement for women's suffrage and espoused broader feminist principles. American women's quest for artistic freedom took them to Europe where theater and dance were more established institutions and where audiences tended to be more receptive to new ideas. In their quest for personal independence and freedom of artistic expression, they introduced exciting new art forms that had a lasting impact on Western culture.

They also played significant roles in the emergence of the "new woman" of the early twentieth century: a self-confident, assertive, and independent woman ready to participate in full partnership with men in every aspect of society. The "new woman" was epitomized by the "flapper" of the twenties, who bobbed her hair, abandoned her corset, donned short skirts, smoked cigarettes, played sports, and drank with the men. More seriously, she was often a college graduate who delayed marriage to earn her living or to pursue a profession.

PIONEERS OF MODERN DANCE

The three American women featured in this section were the creators of modern dance, an entirely new art form. This new art form emerged from a number of developments in the late nineteenth century: the dress reform movement that sought to free women from restrictive Victorian clothing and improve their health; a physical fitness movement that encouraged female exercise; and women's quest for free intellectual and artistic expression. It also grew out of ballet's belated acceptance by the American public and the availability of ballet training for American girls. Women's health and fashions were especially important to these pioneers and to their reform-minded mothers.

One important precursor of modern dance was a new craze among elite women: Delsarte parties. François Delsarte, an actor who lost his voice, created a nonverbal form of dance training that used movements to evoke emotions. He popularized his system through recitals and classes in which his students performed in bare feet and light tunics. (Kendall 1979, 24–25) His system became a popular form of exercise for women, particularly because it did not take them into the public arena. More importantly, it created opportunities for the modern dance pioneers to begin their careers by teaching dance as a form of exercise. They also benefited from, and contributed to, the fashion revolution that allowed them to lift their arms and move naturally.

As the readings that follow reveal, the originators of modern dance rebelled against ballet as a dance form but did not seek to replace it with a single new system. Each sought to elevate dance in American eyes to a serious art form, equal in value to great music and painting. All three performed to classical music and linked their expression to other art forms.

Loie Fuller (1862–1928)

Loie Fuller was the first of the modern dance pioneers. She grew up in Chicago, where she made her debut as a child actress. After a reported stint as a temperance lecturer in her mid-teens, she appeared in plays with a touring company, wrote and produced a play herself, and, in the 1880s, had roles in several plays in New York City. She made her debut as a dancer in 1891, in *Quack, M.D.*, a play about a doctor who hypnotized and then seduced his patients. Although the play was a failure, the experience inspired her to embark on a dance career. With no formal training in dance, she developed a unique style that was based primarily on her novel use of costumes that she designed and made herself and innovative lighting. In 1892, she performed the first of her creations, *The Serpentine Dance*, in a New York extravaganza. Her success resulted in her own shows and engagements in several theaters. But Fuller yearned to be accepted as an artist, not simply as a novelty, so she set sail for Germany where she had a contract to perform, and then went to Paris, the cultural center of Europe.

In October 1892, Fuller made her debut at the Folies Bergere, a theater renowned for its spectacular stage extravaganzas and scantily clad female performers. She was an instant success and became the rage of the city's artists, writers, intellectuals, art critics, students, and society women. She quickly attracted a group of young students with whom she toured and performed across Europe.

Costumes and lighting were key features of her dances, leading some critics to say she was not really a dancer. Ignoring critics, Fuller pursued her own individual style and continued to experiment with the effects of fabrics and lighting on her movements. She gained fame as an inventor, acquired patents for a number of her innovations, and became a respected member of the French scientific community. Her costumes were made of the finest, lightest silk available. To manipulate the fabrics, she patented special wands that allowed her to create a variety of shapes and re-form these in ever-changing patterns. She also patented secret dyes for her silks, at one time employing over a dozen scientists in her basement laboratory. She once asked her friend Marie Curie for some of her newly discovered radium to add to her dye so her costumes would glow in the dark. Madame Curie refused, saying radium was far too dangerous to use, so Fuller used sulphur (sea) salts to achieve her "glow" effect (Current and Current 1997, 153). Her most important staging inventions were her designs for gels and her lighting techniques. Gels were colored sheets of gelatin she placed in front of lights to throw colors onto the stage. She created a round gel, divided into pielike sections, each with a different color.

She spun this in front of a light, thus throwing changing colors onto the stage. Her experiments benefited from the advent of electric lights which opened an array of new staging possibilities.

One of her famous dances and innovations involved underlighting. She placed her multicolored gel against a square plate of glass in the floor, with lights placed underneath. She appeared on stage in *Dance of Flame* wearing one of her trademark costumes made of dozens of yards of fabric that she lifted with long wands in waves high above her head as she moved on the glass plate. From a semidarkened stage, as the underlight came up, her costume turned red and orange, the silk fabric glowing as if she had burst into flames. It was an awesome visual experience for audiences. Her dancing required continual and rapid movement in order to manipulate the fabric and get the costumes in the air; once up, the light silk floated as if alone. During her career, her costumes grew larger and larger, and her lighting ever more complex.

Though she toured the United States in the 1920s, Fuller spent most of her life in Europe. She had a huge impact on art nouveau, a new European art trend. To many her dances, lighting, and costumes epitomized this new style, and images or variations of her dances appeared on art nouveau posters, and in shapes and colors of art nouveau lamps, vases, and works of glass art. Her impact on dance was even more important. Fuller helped Isadora Duncan begin her European career and was an inspiration to the groups of young dancers who performed until the late 1930s as the Loie Fuller Dancers. Ruth St. Denis acknowledged the debt that she, Isadora Duncan, and all modern dancers owed Fuller for her "magnificent contributions" in theater lighting with a spectacular show, *The Ballet of Light,* at the Hollywood Bowl on August 3, 1954, in which she performed dances billed as "Reminiscences of Loie Fuller" (Current and Current 1997, 337). Finally, Fuller introduced audiences to new types of dancing, proved that women could survive independently of male impresarios, and helped make women dancers respectable.

The excerpts that follow illustrate many of these aspects of her career and the impact her art had on audiences. They also reveal the importance of role models in the lives of pioneering women in all fields.

EXCERPTS FROM FULLER'S AUTOBIOGRAPHY*

[On Actress Sarah Bernhardt]
. . . *She* appeared, and there was an almost painful silence in the great overcrowded hall.

. . . Suddenly pandemonium was let loose. . . . Finally silence was restored. Sarah Bernhardt came forward and began to read her lines. I believe I understood her soul, her life, her greatness. She shared her personality with me! The stage settings were lost on me. I saw and heard only her. . . .

I was dancing at the Folies-Bergere. At a matinee some one came to say that Sarah Bernhardt was in a box with her little daughter. Did I dream? My idol was there. And to see me! Could this be possible? . . . I danced and, although she could not know it, I danced for her. I forgot everything else. I lived again through the famous day in New York, and I seemed to see her once more, marvellous as she was at the matinee. And now here was a matinee to which she had come for the purpose of seeing me—my idol, to see me. . . .

[French Sculptor Auguste Rodin's Tribute to Fuller, 19 January 1908]
Mme. Loie Fuller, whom I have admired for a number of years, is, to my mind, a woman of genius, with all the resources of talent. All the cities in which she has appeared, including Paris, are under obligations to her for the purest emotions. She has

*Excerpts from Loie Fuller, *Fifteen Years of a Dancer's Life: with Some Account of Her Distinguished Friends,* with intro. by Anatole France (Boston: Small, Maynard, 1913; New Haven, CT: Research Publications, 1977), pp. 91–92, 127, 227–28, 282, microfilm, History of Women Collection, reel 814, no. 6538.

reawakened the spirit of antiquity. . . . Her talent will always be imitated, from now on, and her creation will be reattempted over and over again, for she has re-created effects and light and background, all things which will be studied continually, and whose initial value I have understood. She has even been able, by her brilliant reproduction, to make us understand the Far East. I fall far below what I ought to say about this great personality; my language is inept for that, but my artistic heart is grateful to her.

[Fuller on Seeing Isadora Duncan Dance]

All at once she made her entrance, calm and indifferent, looking as if she did not care in the least what our guests thought of her. But it was not her air of indifference that surprised me most. I could hardly refrain from rubbing my eyes. She appeared to me nude, or nearly so, to so slight an extent did the gauze which she wore cover her form. She came to the front and, while the orchestra played a prelude from Chopin she stood motionless, her eyes lowered, her arms hanging by her side. Then she began to dance.

Oh, that dance, how I loved it! To me it was the most beautiful thing in the world. I forgot the woman and all her faults, her absurd affectations, her costume, and even her bare legs. I saw only the dancer, and the artistic pleasure she was giving me. . . .

[A Male Dance Critic's Reflections after Seeing Fuller Rehearse Salome*]*

The other evening, I had, as it were, a vision of a theatre of the future, something of the nature of a feministic theatre. Women are more and more taking men's places. They are steadily supplanting the so-called stronger sex. The court-house swarms with women lawyers. The literature of imagination and observation will soon belong to women of letters. In spite of man's declaration that there shall be no woman doctor for him the female physician continues to pass her examinations and brilliantly. Just watch and you will see woman growing in influence and power; and if, as in Gladstone's phrase, the nineteenth century was the working-man's century, the twentieth will be the women's century. . . .

FULLER TALKS ABOUT HER ART IN AN INTERVIEW, MARCH 1896*

. . . To be an artist at your business calls for a life's experience. Your profession is so full of subtleties that you have never done learning.

I leave nothing to chance. I drill my light men; drill them into doing just what I want. I tell them to throw the light so, or so, and they have to do their business with the exactitude of clockwork. This one has to throw a yellow light up to here—that man a blue one no further than there—the man with the red lamp has to follow suit and to keep within his circuit also. If you watch the ins and outs of the dance you will see that the colors fall as they do through a prism. How this is done by limelights is my secret. I arrange the light colors pretty much as an artist arranges his colors on his palette. You must know about colors, the effect of one color on another, and of

*From "Why She Does Not Think Much of [?] Twirling and Toe-Kicking Imitators," *New York Times*, 1 March 1896, p.10, col. 5.

their combinations also, just as the painter does, and be able to tell how they will appear at such and such an angle.

Theme, style, time, all differ in one dance from another. A dance is not built up in a day. The "Fleur-de-lys" . . . I had in hand three years before I produced it. . . .

My gowns, or skirts, are made after my own models, and generally of fine gossamer silk. No, they don't come all right at once. A good deal of tinkering is necessary to get quite the right thing. Why, for the lily dance I had 500 yards of dress stuff. In the making up it all disappeared somehow. The dress is twenty feet high, and I fancy something like 100 yards around the skirt. It is made loose from the neck. . . .

FULLER'S ACTIVITIES AFTER HER DANCE CAREER ENDS*

. . . for a decade or so she has not appeared at all, but has contented herself with arranging and staging ballets for the Opéra Comique and with preparing her dancers for engagements all over Europe. Her time is concerned chiefly with experiments in lighting and the blending of colors and lights, and at her home, . . . she maintains research laboratories where she works out lighting problems along the Einstein theories. She is said to know more about scientific light problems than any other woman in the world. . . .

Isadora Duncan (1878–1927)

Isadora Duncan was born and raised in San Francisco. Her parents were divorced shortly after her birth, and she and her three siblings were left to fend for themselves during the day while their mother worked to support them. Not surprisingly, Duncan became an independent, free-spirited girl. She also acquired some of her mother's unconventional attitudes, including a dislike of religion and disdain for material possessions. Duncan attended public school for five years but left at age ten to concentrate on the dance classes she had begun to teach when she was six. By the time she was eleven, she and her sister had also begun attracting adult students from the city's best families. In her late teens, she and her mother moved to Chicago and then to New York where, in 1896, she joined a theatrical company as an actress and dancer. In a short time, Duncan left the theater and began dancing solo performances at the homes of prominent citizens. In 1900, she moved to London and then to the Continent, developing her own unique style of dance and building a following in numerous cities. Like Loïe Fuller and artist Mary Cassatt, she was drawn to Paris where audiences were known to be open to new art forms. Fuller encouraged and aided her upon her arrival.

Her unconventional personal life hurt her with potential American audiences but made her more fascinating to Europeans. She had a series of lovers and two illegitimate children who died in a tragic automobile accident. A third baby (son of a third lover) died shortly after birth. After these personal tragedies, she returned to dancing and was planning to open a new school when World War I broke out. She and her students returned to the United States, where she tried to establish a dance school in New York City. After touring South America, highly successful performances in New York and San Francisco, and unsuccessful attempts to gain financial support for opening a school in Greece or France, she went to Moscow in 1921. She danced there, but the Soviet government reneged on its

*From *New York Times*, 1 November 1925, pt. 8, p. 2, col. 6.

promise of support for her school. During the last year of her life, Duncan gave a powerful performance in Paris, and wrote her autobiography, *My Life*. She died in 1927 when her shawl got caught in the spokes of a wheel and broke her neck as she started to drive away in her convertible.

As the following excerpts reveal, Isadora Duncan's concept of dance and her style differed markedly from Loie Fuller's, yet they shared some commonalities. Both sought to elevate modern dance to a high art form, and both broke away from nineteenth-century ballet. They also linked their dance to other art forms.

DANCE OF THE FUTURE*

I am asked to speak upon the "dance of the Future,"—yet how is it possible? In fifty years I may have something to say. . . .

If we seek the real source of the dance, if we go to nature, we find that the dance of the future is the dance of the past, the dance of eternity, and has been and will always be the same. . . .

The school of the ballet of to-day vainly striving against the natural laws of gravitation or the natural will of the individual, and working in discord in its form and movement with the form and movement of nature, produces a sterile movement which gives no birth to future movements, but dies as it is made.

. . . All the movements of our modern ballet school are sterile movements because they are unnatural; their purpose is to create the delusion that the law of gravitation does not exist for them. . . .

To those who nevertheless still enjoy the movements from historical or choreographic or whatever other reasons, to those I answer: They see no farther than the skirts and tights. But look—under the skirts, under the tights are dancing deformed muscles.—Look still farther—underneath the muscles are deformed bones: a deformed skeleton is dancing before you. This deformation through incorrect dress and incorrect movement is the result of the training necessary to the ballet.

The ballet condemns itself by enforcing the deformation of the beautiful woman's body. . . .

. . . the dance was once the most noble of all arts—and it shall be again. . . . The dancer of the future shall attain so great a height that all other arts shall be helped thereby.

To express what is the most moral, healthful and beautiful in art—this is the mission of the dancer, and to this I dedicate my life. . . .

To find those primary movements for the human body from which shall evolve the movements of the future dance in every varying natural, unending sequences, that is the duty of the new dancer of to-day. . . .

The Greeks in all their painting, sculpture, architecture, literature, dance and tragedy evolved their movements from the movement of nature . . . This is why the art of the Greeks is not a national or characteristic art, but has been and will be the art of all humanity for all time.

*Excerpts from Isadora Duncan, *The Dance* (New York: Forest Press, 1909), pp.11–14, 20–21.

Therefore, dancing naked upon the earth, I naturally fall into Greek positions, for Greek positions are only earth positions.

The noblest in art is the nude. This truth is recognized by all, and followed by painters, sculptors and poets; only the dancer has forgotten it, who should most remember it, as the instrument of her art is the human body itself. . . .

This may seem a question of little importance, a question of differing opinions on the ballet and the new dance. But it is a great question. It is not only a question of true art, it is a question of race, of the development of the female sex to beauty and health, of the return to the original strength and to natural movements of woman's body. It is a question of the development of perfect mothers and the birth of healthy and beautiful children. The dancing school of the future is to develop and to show the ideal form of woman. It will be, as it were, a museum of the living beauty of the period. . . .

. . . From what I have said you might conclude that my intention is to return to the dances of the old Greeks or that I think that the dance of the future will be a revival of the antique dances or even of those of the primitive tribes. No, the dance of the future will be a new movement, a consequence of the entire evolution which mankind has passed through. But the dance of the future will have to become again a high religious art, as it was with the Greeks. For art which is not religious is not art; it is mere merchandise.

The dancer of the future . . . will dance not in the form of nymph, nor fairy, nor coquette, but in the form of woman in its greatest and purest expression. She will realize the mission of woman's body and the holiness of all its parts. She will dance the changing life of nature, showing how each part is transformed into the other. From all parts of her body shall shine radiant intelligence, bringing to the world the message of the thoughts and aspirations of thousands of women. She shall dance the freedom of woman. Oh, what a field is here awaiting her! Do you not feel that she is near, that she is coming, this dancer of the future? She will help womankind to a new knowledge of the possible strength and beauty of their bodies and the relation of their bodies to the earth nature and to the children of the future. She will dance the body emerging again from centuries of civilized forgetfulness, emerging not in the nudity of primitive man, but in a new nakedness, no longer at war with spirituality and intelligence, but joining itself forever with this intelligence in a glorious harmony. . . .

Oh, she is coming, the dancer of the future: the free spirit, who will inhabit the body of new women; more glorious than any woman that has yet been; more beautiful than the Egyptian, than the Greek, the early Italian, than all women of past centuries—the highest intelligence in the freest body!

Ruth St. Denis (1879–1968)

Ruth St. Denis became famous for her extravagant dance spectacles. Her liberated mother, who was one of the first woman M.D.s in the United States, added St. to her daughter's name for respectability. St. Denis is the only modern dance pioneer who performed primarily in the United States and thus helped to popularize dance as an art form in America. More importantly, she and her husband Ted Shawn established the Denishawn Dance School (1915) in Los Angeles, California. Their school was referred to as the "cradle of modern dance" because it trained a generation of dancers, including Martha Graham, who passed the new dance form with their own interpretations and variations on to subsequent generations.

Ted Shawn was studying to become a minister when he saw St. Denis perform. Instantly, he resolved to become a dancer and her partner. They were one of the first "celebrity couples" when both silent film and Hollywood were emerging. Many of their students were silent film stars who were studying movement. While Ruth devised her new spectacles, Ted was striving to make dance acceptable for men. To do so, he built an all-male company. The novelty helped build audiences, for many had never seen large groups of men on stage. The couple also published a short-lived journal, *The Denishawn Magazine: A Quarterly Review Devoted to the Art of the Dance*, to spread their philosophy of dance.

St. Denis's dances had simple choreography but utilized elaborate costumes and stage sets to suggest visions of ancient and foreign cultures. They played to the popular fascination with foreign themes and exotic places but made no pretense of historical accuracy. Her portrayals of real and imagined goddesses such as Ishtar, Isis, Egypta, and Radha, however, were also genuine expressions of her deep spirituality.

From Her Autobiography*

[Origins of Her Spiritual Dances]

[One day, St. Denis saw a poster advertising cigarettes that featured a modernized image of the Egyptian goddess Isis seated on a throne.]

. . . I identified myself in a flash with the figure of Isis. She became the expression of all the somber mystery and beauty of Egypt, and I knew that my destiny as a dancer had sprung alive in that moment. I would become a rhythmic and impersonal instrument of spiritual revelation rather than a personal actress of comedy or tragedy. . . .

[Dance and Spirituality]

The whole Christian world has been greatly concerned, in seventy years, with physical healing by spiritual means. Mary Baker Eddy sounded the first great popular call to arms, and the influence of her message and the success of the Christian Science Church confirms the need for this development in our spiritual life. This is as it should be. Health of mind and body precedes, in the line of complete realization, every other development. But I have maintained for many years that the next plane of demonstration should be in the arts, and to this neither the traditional church in any of its sects, nor the modern metaphysical church has applied itself. The discipline of spiritual consciousness is the only force that can enlarge the artist's capacities and free him from his own temperamental limitations. I have tried to dance my spiritual awareness, but alas, the human too often thwarted my ideals.

[Her Advice to Young Dancers]

. . . Dare to dance your own dance. Do not be bound by the techniques that you have learned, or the criticisms you fear to endure. I call to you not to be mere followers, . . . but to speak your own voice. . .

*From Ruth St. Denis. *Ruth St. Denis. An Unfinished Life. An Autobiography* (London: George G. Harrap & Co., 1939), pp. 52, 72–73, 330.

THE DANCE AS LIFE EXPERIENCE*

I see men and women dancing rhythmically and in joy, on a hilltop bathed in the saffron rays of a setting sun.

I see them moving slowly, with flowing, serene gestures in the glow of the risen moon.

I see them giving praise; praise for the earth and the sky and the sea and the hills, in free, happy movements that are projections of their moods of peace and adoration.

I see the Dance being used as a means of communication between soul and soul—to express what is too deep, too fine for words.

I see children growing straight and proportioned, swift and sure of movement, having dignity and grace and wearing their bodies lightly and with power.

I see our race made finer and quicker to correct itself—because the Dance reveals the soul.

The Dance is motion, which is life, beauty, which is love, proportion, which is power. To dance is to live life in its finer and higher vibrations, to live life harmonized, purified, controlled. To dance is to feel one's self actually a part of the cosmic world, rooted in the inner reality of spiritual being. . . .

Artificial and limited ideas of the dance have done cruel and grotesque things to its servants, indeed, they have to most artists of the stage. The spectacle of a singer or dancer or actor continuing on the stage in parts too young for him is tragic enough—but still more tragic is the situation of the artist who, in his maturity, having grown to the most interesting and beautiful stage of his consciousness, is forced to withdraw from his active career, because of the childish demand of the public for mere youth. . . . Some day our conceptions will expand to take in, with the loveliness and freshness of childhood, the gracious dignity of age in art as well as in life.

Dancing is the natural rhythmic movements of the body that have long been suppressed or distorted, and the desire to dance would be as natural as to eat, or to run, or swim, if our civilization had not in countless ways and for divers reasons put its ban upon this instinctive and joyous action of the harmonious being. Our formal religions, our crowded cities, our clothes, and our transportation, are largely responsible for the inert mass of humanity that until very lately was encased in collars and corsets. But we are beginning to emerge, to throw off, to demand space to think in and to dance in. . . .

THE *NEW WOMAN* IN THEATER

Women's theater activities at the turn of the century are closely intertwined with the British and American suffrage movements. Actresses' search for more challenging roles led them to embrace the new realistic drama and to write plays themselves that addressed issues central to women's lives. In order to produce such plays, however, they discovered they had to go outside the theatrical establishment with its male managers and producers and assume those managerial roles as well. The process helped

*From Ruth St. Denis, "The Dance as Life Experience," *The Denishawn Magazine: A Quarterly Review Devoted to the Art of the Dance* (New York, Ruth St. Denis and Ted Shawn School of Dancing) 1, no. 1 (1924), pp. 1, 3.

crystallize their feminism. From their experiences of sex discrimination in theater, they saw the need for the vote. Equally important, the suffrage movement in both countries needed them. Few women were prepared to take to the streets and halls to deliver suffrage speeches; actresses, however, had already broken the public speaking barrier by appearing on stage. Their roles as movement orators, propagandists, and leaders of organizations such as the British Actresses Franchise League were indispensable to the success of the movement. Concurrently, their participation garnered more support for their efforts to reform theater and helped them develop support networks of other women. Finally, these actresses/playwrights/suffragists contributed immensely to the vitality of British theater through their own works and by introducing new types of drama from other countries to British audiences.

Elizabeth Robins (1862–1952): American Actress, Playwright, Novelist

Elizabeth Robins was an American expatriate who spent most of her adult life in England. She is best known as an actress who helped introduce Henrik Ibsen's plays and thus realistic theater to England and as a supporter of the British women's suffrage movement. She also had a distinguished career as a novelist and playwright. Her work includes more than 20 published books, including novels, memoirs, collections of essays, and speeches on theater, politics, and feminism.

Robins was born in Louisville, Kentucky, during the Civil War. From an early age, she dreamed of becoming an actress, despite her family's negative response to the idea. In the fall of 1881, she moved to New York, and landed a job with a touring company. To keep her acting secret from her relatives, she adopted the stage name Claire Raimond. In 1883 she signed a contract with the Boston Museum Theater and began to send money home to help support her family. After a year's courtship, she married another company actor, in January 1885. He committed suicide 18 months later. In 1888, Robins moved to England to seek better stage opportunities.

In London, Robins quickly discovered it was difficult for a new actress to break into the actor-manager system without influential connections, money, or a willingness to "compromise" oneself. As a result, she turned to writing to support herself. For a decade she chose to remain anonymous, submitting much of her fiction under the pen name C. E. Raimond. She also did interviews with prominent theatrical figures, including Ellen Terry, for journals. Between 1890 and 1892, her acting opportunities improved, she made a number of friends and literary contacts, and she began to focus on her dream of elevating the standards of theater through an association of people devoted to art for art's sake.

A turning point in her life came in 1891 when she and Marion Lea (another American expatriate) produced and performed in Henrik Ibsen's *Hedda Gabler*. This was the first English production of the controversial play, and it won wide acclaim for the two actresses and their initiative. Lea's return to America ended their dreams of further joint ventures, but Robins was a hit in Henry James's *The American* and was soon discussing her dreams about a new independent theater with James, Oscar Wilde, and other actresses. Concurrently, she completed a novel about the theater, *The Coming Woman* (1892). In the next decade and a half, she gained acclaim as a novelist.

In 1906, Robins was drawn into the English suffrage campaign. Her first contribution, a play, *Votes for Women!*, established her reputation as a playwright as well as an actress and novelist. Through this play she expressed the feminist convictions that she had also expressed in her novels. She began to attend the mass outdoor suffrage meetings organized by the Women's Social and Political Union (WSPU), and she interviewed the WSPU leaders Emmeline and Christabel Pankhurst, whose flamboyant tactics she found appealing. They urged her to speak at suffrage rallies, as other actresses were doing, but Robins refused, choosing instead to lend her "voice" to the cause through her plays and novels. Her novel *The Convert* (1907) was a major contribution to the cause. By 1908, Robins was writing essays on suffrage, the oppression of women, and prostitution or "white slavery." Her essay "Woman's Secret" was a penetrating critique of how patriarchal society's insistence on the male norm in literature affected women writers (Gates 1994, 166–67). She also began giving public lectures. During and after World War I she engaged in relief and home mobilization efforts in England and organized groups on behalf of peace, women's health initiatives, and women's full equality.

The excerpt from *The Convert* is based upon Pankhurst's powerful street corner suffrage speeches. The novel, like her play *Votes for Women!* on which it was based, shows women who are reluctant to embrace suffrage gradually being won over. It also skillfully delineates the working-class roots of the British suffrage movement that are often overlooked. As the excerpt suggests, both the novel and play went beyond suffrage and addressed women's economic and sexual liberty as well. Consider what audiences or readers might have learned about sex discrimination and suffragists' goals from this speech.

THE CONVERT (1907)*

[The speaker] stemmed another torrent. "Be quiet, while I tell you something. You men have taught us that women can get a great deal by coaxing, often far more than we deserve! But justice isn't one of the things that's ever got that way. Justice has to be fought for. Justice has to be won."

Howls and uproar.

"You men—" (it began to be apparent that whenever the roaring got so loud that it threatened to drown her, she said, "You men—" very loud, and then gave her voice a rest while the din died down that they might hear what else the irrepressible Ernestine had to say upon that absorbing topic). "You men discovered years ago that you weren't going to get justice just by deserving it, or even by being men, so when you got tired of asking politely for the franchise, you took to smashing windows and burning down Custom Houses, and overturning Bishops' carriages; while we, why, we haven't so much as upset a curate off a bicycle!"

Others might laugh, not Ernestine.

"You men," she went on, "got up riots in the streets—real riots where people lost their lives. It may have to come to that with us. But the Government may as well know that if women's political freedom has to be bought with blood, we can pay that price, too."

Above a volley of boos and groans she went on, "But we are opposed to violence, and it will be our last resort. We are leaving none of the more civilized ways untried. We publish a great amount of literature—I hope you are all buying some of it—you can't understand our movement unless you do! We organize branch unions and we hire halls—we've got the Somerset Hall to-night, and we hope you'll all come and bring your friends. We have very interesting debates, and we answer questions, politely!" she made her point to laughter. "We don't leave any stone unturned. Because there are people who don't buy our literature, and who don't realize how interesting the Somerset Hall debates are, we go into the public places where the idle and the foolish, like that man just over there!—where they may point and laugh and make their poor little jokes. But let me tell you we never hold a

*Excerpt from Elizabeth Robins, *The Convert* (London: Methuen & Co.,1907), pp. 137–41.

meeting where we don't win friends to our cause. A lot of you who are jeering and interrupting now are going to be among our best friends. All the intelligent ones are going to be on our side."

Above the laughter, a rich groggy voice was heard, "Them that's against yer are all drunk, miss" (hiccough). "D-don't mind 'em!"

Ernestine just gave them time to appreciate that, and then went on—

"Men and women were never meant to fight except side by side. You've been told by one of the other speakers how the men suffer by the women more and more underselling them in the Labour market—"

"Don't need no tellin'."

"Bloody black-legs!"

"Do you know how that has come about? I'll tell you. It's come about through your keeping the women out of your Unions. You never would have done that if they'd had votes. You saw the important people ignored them. You thought it was safe for you to do the same. But I tell you it isn't ever safe to ignore the women!"

High over the groans and laughter the voice went on, "you men have got to realize that if our battle against the common enemy is to be won, you've got to bring the women into line."

"What's to become of chivalry?"

"What has become of chivalry?" she retorted; and no one seemed to have an answer ready, but the crowd fell silent, like people determined to puzzle out a conundrum.

"Don't you know that there are girls and women in this very city who are working early and late for rich men, and who are expected by those same employers to live on six shillings a week? Perhaps I'm wrong in saying the men expect the women to live on that. It may be they *know* that no girl can—it may be the men know how that struggle ends. But do they care? Do *they* bother about chivalry? Yet they and all of you are dreadfully exercised for fear having a vote would unsex women. We are too delicate—women are such fragile flowers." The little face was ablaze with scorn. "I saw some of those fragile flowers last week—and I'll tell you where. Not a very good place for gardening. It was a back street in Liverpool. The 'flowers'" (oh the contempt with which she loaded the innocent word!)—"the flowers looked pretty dusty—but they weren't quite dead. I stood and looked at them! hundreds of worn women coming down steep stairs and pouring out into the street. What had they all been doing there in that garden, I was going to say!—that big grimy building? They had been making cigars!—spending the best years of their lives, spending all their youth in that grim dirty street making cigars for men. Whose chivalry prevents that? Why were they coming out at that hour of the day? Because their poor little wages were going to be lowered, and with the courage of despair they were going on strike. No chivalry prevents men from getting women at the very lowest possible wage—(I want you to notice the low wage is the main consideration in all this)—men get these women, that they say are so tender and delicate, to undertake the almost intolerable toil of the rope-walk. They get women to make bricks. Girls are driven—when they are not driven to worse—they are driven to being lodging-house slaveys or overworked scullions. *That's* all right! Women are graciously permitted to sweat over other people's washing, when they should be caring for their own babies. In Birmingham"—she raised the clear voice and bent her flushed face over the crowd—"in

Birmingham those same 'fragile flowers' make bicycles to keep alive! At Cradley Heath we make chains. At the pit brows we sort coal. But a vote would soil our hands! You may wear out women's lives in factories, you may sweat them in the slums, you may drive them to the streets. You do. But a vote would unsex them."

Her full throat choked. She pressed her clenched fist against her chest and seemed to admonish herself that emotion wasn't her line.

"If you are intelligent, you know as well as I do that women are exploited the length and the breadth of the land. And yet you come talking about chivalry! Now, I'll just tell you men something for your future guidance." She leaned far out over the crowd and won a watchful silence. "*That talk about chivalry makes women sick.*" In the midst of the roar, she cried, "Yes, they mayn't always show it, for women have had to learn to conceal their deepest feelings, but depend on it that's how they feel."

Then, apparently thinking she'd been serious enough,

"There might be some sense in talking to us about chivalry if you paid our taxes for us," she said; while the people recovered their spirits in roaring with delight at the coolness of that suggestion.

"If you forgave us our crimes because we are women! If you gave annuities to the eighty-two women out of every hundred in this country who are slaving to earn their bread, many of them having to provide for their children; some of them having to feed sick husbands or old parents. But chivalry doesn't carry you men as far as that! No! No further than the door! You'll hold that open for a lady and then expect her to grovel before such an exhibition of chivalry! We don't need it, thank you! We can open doors for ourselves."

She had quite recovered her self-possession, and it looked, as she faced the wind and the raindrops, as if she were going to wind up in first-class fighting form. The umbrellas went down before a gleam of returning sun. An aged woman in rusty black, who late in the proceedings had timidly adventured a little way into the crowd, stood there lost and wondering. She had peered about during the last part of Miss Blunt's speech with faded incredulous eyes, listened to a sentence or two, and then, turning with a pathetic little nervous laugh of apology, consulted the faces of the Lords of Creation. When the speaker was warned that a policeman had his eye on her, the little old woman's instant solicitude showed that the dauntless Suffragist had both touched and frightened her. She craned forward with a fluttering anxiety till she could see for herself. Yes! A stern-looking policeman coming slow and majestic through the crowd. Was he going to hale the girl off to Holloway? No; he came to a standstill near some rowdy boys, and he stared straight before him—herculean, impassive, the very image of conscious authority. Whenever Ernestine said anything particularly dreadful, the old lady craned her neck to see how the policeman was taking it. When Ernestine fell to drubbing the Government, the old lady, in her agitation greatly daring, squeezed up a little nearer as if half of a mind to try to placate that august image of the Power that was being flouted. But it ended only in trembling and furtive watching, till Ernestine's reckless scorn at the idea of chivalry moved the ancient dame faintly to admonish the girl, as a nurse might speak to a wilful child. "Dear! Dear!" and then furtively trying to soothe the great policeman she twittered at his elbow, "No! No! she don't mean it!"

When Ernestine declared that women could open doors for themselves, some one called out—"When do you expect to be a K.C.?"

"Oh, quite soon," she answered cheerfully, with her wind-blown hat rakishly over one ear, while the boys jeered.

"Well," said the policeman, "she's pawsed 'er law examination!" As some of the rowdiest boys, naturally surprised at this interjection, looked round, he rubbed it in. "Did better than the men," he assured them. . . .

Edith Craig (1869–1947): British Suffragist and Theater Pioneer

No theatrical woman had a greater impact on the British suffrage movement and the development of "new theater" than Edy Craig. Craig was the daughter of Ellen Terry, the greatest star of the English stage in the late nineteenth century and the first actress to be knighted (1925). Her father, Edwin Godwin, was an architect. She grew up in a liberated household and was raised to believe girls could do anything. She began her theater career as an actress and toured in America and with Ibsen's supporters in Britain. She also worked as a costumier and served as stage manager and producer for her mother during her American tour and in Britain. She was most important as the manager and producer of suffrage plays, the founder and director of Pioneer Players, and a leader in the new theater movement. Her work in the suffrage movement also included public speaking and selling suffrage pamphlets on street corners. She was an important role model for women and a demanding task mistress. The following selections illustrate the knowledge and skills she brought to her craft, and how she was regarded by her friends and colleagues.

Edy Craig, *Producing a Play**

When it was first announced that I was to be the stage-director for my mother, Miss Ellen Terry, during her American tour, there was quite a flutter in the . . . London newspapers.

I was the first woman stage-manager on record; I had started a new profession for women; I was the pioneer of a new departure in theatrical enterprise! No one could have been more surprised than I when reporters came and asked me how I felt under the grave responsibilities of a revolutionary! . . .

[Advice for Stage Managers]

. . . Lighting, like every other branch of stage decoration, should be considered as a means of helping the acting. There are some situations which demand light; others which do not suffer from shadow—and the wise stage-manager will remember this before arranging his lights.

The bad old way of helping the actors is by following them all over the stage with the lime-light. It is hardly necessarily to say how completely this plan destroys the sincerity of a situation, or how pictorially ugly it is. It is quite possible to have the actors in the light when they need it and at the same time to preserve an atmosphere of beauty and an illusion of nature. . . .

The importance of an intelligent staff, of individuals as opposed to machines, and the vital question of lighting ought to occupy the attention of every stage-manager; but only as a *means to an end*, as servants of the acting. . . .

The next thing in the stage-manager's jurisdiction is the music. Let us once for all abolish the stupidity of having music which is supposed to be on the stage played

*From Edith Craig, "Producing a Play," *Munsey's Magazine*, 37, no.3 (June 1907), pp. 311–14.

from the orchestra. . . . It is not always possible to have the instrumentalists on the stage, but we can always have them at the side with supers doing the accompaniment in pantomime on the stage. . . .

It is often argued that in the performance of a play only the acting matters, and that elaborate stage effects are distracting and unnecessary; but from the very first I was trained to see that the actor is the better, not the worse, for being surrounded by the right atmosphere. . . .

So far, my experience as stage-manager in America has been confined to New York, and there "please" has acted like magic.

I shall continue to try it in other cities. It has the objective recommendation of destroying the last obstacle to a woman occupying the position of stage-manager—anyway, in America. In England men create another objection by resenting a woman "bossing" them in a professional capacity. I have found the Americans startlingly and charmingly free from this prejudice.

In this review in *Time and Tide*, Craig's partner and colleague, Christopher St. John, deplored sex discrimination, linking Craig's position with that of Margaret Bondfield, a Labour Party member of Parliament. Bondfield, however, ultimately became England's first female cabinet minister.

CHRISTOPHER ST. JOHN LAMENTS CRAIG'S LACK OF RECOGNITION*

> While I was delighted at the impetuosity with which these writers let themselves go over the talents of my friend Edith Craig, I was sorry none of them commented on the irony of her not being in control of a single one of London's many stages. Does Lady Astor's theory of 'sub-conscious jealousy' explain this as well as Miss Margaret Bondfield's not being in the Cabinet? If it does, the more reason for the women of England who are in the majority among playgoers to bestir themselves and give Edith Craig an opportunity before it is too late, of showing how many plays can reach and delight audiences, when handled by a genuine artist of the theatre. . . . It is conceivable that the whole history of the English stage might be changed if Edith Craig could hand on to some young people working under her in a theatre the secret of her power to make a play alive as well as the less mysterious one of her technical efficiency.

A Pageant of Great Women

A Pageant of Great Women, a dramatic production written by Cicely Hamilton, is an excellent example of the contributions Edy Craig and her circle of theatrical friends made to the British suffrage movement. The *Pageant* "introduced" audiences to eleven learned women, seven artists (poets and painters), four saintly women, four heroic women, eight rulers, and ten warriors from ancient times to the twentieth century. It was a huge success all over England. The selections that follow describe the genesis of the project, the planning involved in producing it in towns across England, and some of the strategies Craig and her colleagues utilized to win converts to women's suffrage. How might the *Pageant* have affected the women who appeared in it and its audiences?

*From Christopher St. John, "Well Done Leeds!" *Time and Tide*, 1 February 1924, pp. 106–07, quoted in Katherine Cockin, *Edith Craig (1869–1947): Dramatic Lives* (London and Washington: Cassell, 1998), p. 13.

Cicely Hamilton on Edy Craig and the *Pageant of Great Women**

Edy came to me one day full of the idea of a pageant of great women which she would stage and which, she suggested, I should write for her. "Suggested" perhaps is the wrong word to use; if I remember aright her suggestion was more like an order. . . . though the actual writing of the pageant was mine, its subject matter was largely a joint affair, with Edy planning its details. Suggesting what characters were to be included in the groups of famous women—rulers, artists, saints—and arranging their appropriate music. She gave the pageant its first production . . . to an audience of enthusiastic suffragists. The cast she had got together consisted largely of well-known names, headed by that of her mother . . . Edy had cast herself as Rosa Bonheur and no one who heard the applause that greeted her entrance—palette in hand clad in painter's smock—could have had any doubt of her popularity among the adherents of "the movement." . . .

Although the cast was a large one, . . . there were only three speaking parts . . . and players for these parts Edy brought with her from London. The rest of . . . the thirty or forty actresses from whom no speech was required, she would rehearse and dress on her arrival—for she always provided the whole wardrobe. The secretary of the local suffrage movement was furnished beforehand with a list of the types required for the various parts; this list . . . was marked "strictly confidential" as well it might be, since it contained such items as "Need not be good looking" and, in the case of one character whose face was all but concealed beneath her head-dress, "Any old thing will do." . . .

Advertisement for *Pageant of Great Women***

You believe that women have been great, that they are great. Come to the Public Hall, Beckenham, on Saturday, September 24th and realise your beliefs! As learned women and saintly women, artists, heroines, rulers, and warriors pass before you, as you hear of the work they have accomplished, give rein to your enthusiasm, let your hands proclaim your pride in Womanhood; as these illustrious ones of all nations appear, let every woman present thank god that she belongs to the sex that, in spite of fearful odds, has left such splendid record upon the annals of history.

---

*Excerpts from Cicely Hamilton, "Triumphant Women by Cicely Hamilton" in *Edy. Recollections of Edith Craig*, Eleanor Adlard, ed. (London: Frederick Muller Ltd., 1949), pp. 41, 42.

**Advertisement for performance of the *Pageant of Great Women* in Kent in *Vote*, 10 September 1910, p. 231, quoted in Katherine Cockin, *Edith Craig (1869–1947): Dramatic Lives* (London and Washington: Cassell, 1998), p. 83.

A PAGEANT OF GREAT WOMEN*

Justice: (enthroned)

(To her enters Woman, pursued by Prejudice. Woman kneels at the feet of Justice)

Justice: Why dost thou cling to me? What dost thou ask?

Woman: I cling to Justice and I cry for freedom! . . .

Prejudice: She weeps for that she is not fit to have; She is a very child in the ways of the world, a thing protected, covered from its roughness

Woman: Have I not felt its roughness, suffered and wept?

Justice: Let him speak on—let him accuse—, then answer.

Prejudice: Freedom is born of wisdom—springs from wisdom—

And when was woman wise? Has she not ever looked childlike up to man?

Has she not ever put the outward show before the inward grace?

Scorned learning, lest it dim the light of her eye?

Shunned knowledge, lest long study pale her cheek?

Is not her day a day of petty cares, of petty hates and likings?

When has she stood godlike in her wisdom, great of soul?

What is her prize in life—a kiss, a smile, The right to claim caresses!

Yet she cries for freedom!

An she had it, she would sell it for a man's arm round her waist!

Woman: Oh, well, indeed, well does this come from you,

Who held the body as all, the spirit as naught—

From you who saw us only as a sex!

Who did your worst and best to quench in us

The very spark and glow of the intellect:

Who blew a jeer at the leap and glimmer of it

And smothered it with laughter! . . .

So were we trained to simper, not to think:

So were we bred for dimples, not for brains!

Not souls, but foolish flesh—so, you desired us

And, God have pity, made us! . . .

Oh, think you well what you have done to make it hard for her

To dream, to write, to paint, to build, to learn—

Oh, think you well! And wonder at the line

Of those who knew that life was more than love

And fought their way to achievement and to fame!

(The Learned Women enter.) [Each figure steps forward as Woman "introduces" her.]

Hypatia, she whose wisdom brought her death,

Heads the brave line; and see, the saintly nun,

Teresa, guide and leader unto God,

Writer of living words! . . .

*Excerpts from Cicely Hamilton, *A Pageant of Great Women*, arranged by Edith Craig, 1910, (New Haven, CT: Research Publications, 1976), pp. 21, 23, 25, 27, 29, 31, 45, 47, 49. microfilm History of Women, Reel 733, no. 5864.

What of the keen De Staël, quick of tongue,

Polished of pen? . . .

'twas a woman's hand

That penned a novel first—de Scudery's!

And on her follow her disciples twain,

English Jane Austen and George Sand of France.

. . . And where is the man

Stands higher in the rank of science today

Than Madame Curie? Last of all the train

Comes the girl graduate of a modern day,

Working with man as eagerly and hard—

And oft enough denied a man's reward.

And though you barred from us the realms of art—

Decreeing Love should be our all in all—

Denying us free thought, free act, free word—

Yet some there have been burst the silken bonds

(Harder to burst than steel) and lived and wrought.

(The Artists enter.)

Thy voice, oh Sappho, down the ages rings!

Woven of passion and power, thy mighty verse

Streams o'er the years, a flaming banner of song!

Inspiring others and herself inspired,

Vittoria Colonna sweeps us by—

Poet and noble dame . . . Ah, Madame Kauffmann,

In your day were our painters more gallant,

Admitting women to due share of honour!

Vigee le Brun, your sitters live for us

From far-off years . . . A man? No—Rosa Bonheur!

Back from the horse-fair, virile in her garb

As virile in her work! Who follows? . . .

Lo, Camargo comes

A dancer, a dancer, a poem—song herself!

Lyric of movement, ballad of gliding grace;

Rhythm of lifted hand and poised foot—

Music made manifest! . . . Come we last of all

To the living art of the actor

Nance Oldfield: By your leave,

Nance Oldfield does her talking for herself!

If you, Sir Prejudice, had had your way,

There would be never an actress on the boards.

Some lanky, squeaky boy would play my parts:

And, though I say it, there'd have been a loss!

The stage would be as dull as now 'tis merry—

No Oldfield, Woffington, or—Ellen Terry! . . .

Justice: I give thee judgment—and I judge thee worthy to attain thy freedom:

but 'tis thou alone canst show that thou art worthy to retain it.

O Woman with thy feet on an untried path,

O Woman with thine eyes on the dawn of the world,

Thou hast very much to learn.

Woman: But I shall learn it!

Justice: Yea, truly; but with suffering.

(The Woman kneels before her silent.)

Go forth: the world is thine . . . Oh, use it well!

Thou hast an equal, not a master, now.

(rising) I have an equal, not a master, now.

I will go speak with him as peer with peer, free woman with free man.

Justice: Then let thy words be just and wise.

Woman: They shall be wise and just;

Free words, and therefore honest . . . Thus I'll speak him!

I have no quarrel with you; but I stand

For the clear right to hold my life my own:

The clear, clean right! To mould it as I will,

Not as you will, with or apart from you.

To make of it a thing of brain and blood,

Of tangible substance and of turbulent thought—

No thin, grey shadow of the life of man!

Your love, perchance, may set a crown on it;

But I may crown myself in other ways—

(As you have done who are one flesh with me)

. . . henceforth, This you must know:

The world is mine, as yours,

The pulsing strength and passion and heart of it:

The work I set my hand to, woman's work, Because I set my hand to it.

Henceforth for my own deeds myself am answerable, to my own soul.

For this in days to come You, too, shall thank me.

Now you laugh, but I Laugh too, a laughter without bitterness;

Feeling the riot and rush of crowding hopes, dreams, longings and vehement powers; and knowing this

'Tis good to be alive when morning dawns!

The Pioneer Players

Edy Craig created the Pioneer Players Society in 1911 to introduce new drama to British audiences. It was organized as a subscription society. Membership fees helped underwrite the production of plays that were unlikely to get support from patrons or to be produced at major London theaters. Members included middle- and upper-class women and men. Pioneer Players also provided jobs for women in all areas of theater, from actresses to technicians. Equally important, women involved in its productions were able to work without the discrimination they often faced in theater.

Craig produced and directed its plays on a shoestring by using innovative lighting and few props or scenery. She also arranged productions in public halls instead of commercial theaters. Her staging innovations were widely praised and adopted by other producers. Craig, her friend Christopher St. John, and the Pioneer Players also contributed to women's history in 1914 by producing the first play in English translation by the tenth-century convent dramatist Hrotswitha of Gandersheim. (See Vol. I, Chapter 14, "Medieval Culture: The Religious Context.") After World War I, students at several American women's colleges used St. John's translations to mount productions.

The Pioneer Players played a significant role in the development of new drama. The group rarely produced a play more than twice; instead they solicited new plays. This practice was an important catalyst for those who sought out plays that had been ignored in England. It also stimulated English translations of Continental drama. The society helped keep theater alive during World War I, even producing controversial war dramas and foreign plays including Russian, French, and Japanese works.

Higher costs of production and more competition led to the demise of the society in the twenties. Its last production was Susan Glaspell's challenging work *The Verge* in 1925. Rediscovery of the work of the Pioneer Players in the 1980s was one stimulus to the rise of new feminist theater in England. The excerpt reveals more about the goals and the controversies surrounding the society.

PURPOSE OF THE PIONEER PLAYERS*

> It has more than once been suggested in the Press that we are a Society formed for the purpose of suffragist propaganda only; but this suggestion is a misleading one. It is obviously quite impossible nowadays to produce thoughtful plays written by thoughtful people which do not bear some traces of the influence of the feminist movement—an influence which no modern writer, however much he may wish it, can entirely escape. But those responsible for the selection of the plays that we have performed have never had either the wish or the intention of narrowing their choice to works dealing with one phase only of modern thought. All we ask of a play is that it shall be interesting; and if many of those who have sent us plays have found inspiration in various aspects of the feminist movement, we must conclude that it is because the feminist movement is, in itself, not without dramatic interest. This is confirmed by the fact that the leading provincial Repertory Companies have recently produced several new plays with a strong "feminist" element.

SUGGESTED READINGS

Dance

Duncan, Doree, Carol Pratl, and Cynthia Splatt, eds. *Life into Art: Isadora Duncan and Her World*. New York: W. W. Norton, 1993.

Harris, Margaret Haile. *Loie Fuller, Magician of Light: A Loan Exhibition at the Virginia Museum, March 12–April 22, 1979*. Richmond: The Virginia Museum, 1979.

Kurth, Peter. *Isadora: A Sensational Life*. Boston, New York and London: Little Brown, 2001.

Shelton, Suzanne. *Ruth St. Denis: A Biography of the Divine Dancer*. Austin: University of Texas, 1990.

Theater

Auster, Albert. *Actresses and Suffragists: Women in the American Theater, 1890–1920*. New York: Praeger, 1984.

Friedl, Bettina, ed. *On to Victory: Propaganda Plays of the Woman Suffrage Movement*. Boston: Northeastern University Press, 1987.

John, Angela. *Elizabeth Robins: Staging a Life, 1862–1952*. London and New York: Routledge, 1995.

Newlin, Keith, ed. *American Plays of the New Woman*. Chicago: Ivan R. Dee, 2000.

Whitelaw, Lis. *The Life and Rebellious Times of Cicely Hamilton: Actress, Writer, Suffragette*. London: Women's Press, 1990.

Audiovisual Sources

Ruth St. Denis, the Dancing Prophet. 1999. Dance Series. Produced by Edmund Penny and Gertrude Marks. Directed by Edmund Penney. 30 min. Derry, NH: Chip Taylor Communications, Videocassette.

---

*From *Pioneer Players Annual Report* (1911–12), pp. 7–8, quoted in Katherine Cockin, *Women and Theatre in the Age of Suffrage: The Pioneer Players, 1911-1925* (Hampshire, UK and New York: Palgrave Publishers, 2001), p. 42.

PART III

WOMEN AND CULTURE
IN THE TWENTIETH CENTURY

The final part of Volume II focuses on the cultural contributions of women in the twentieth century. The readings in these five chapters attest to the richness and diversity of women's creative work. As we have already seen with the pioneers of modern dance and "new" theater, twentieth-century women did not merely reflect cultural trends in their fields, they also shaped them. Women were often innovators. They developed new art forms, pioneered new styles of expression, experimented with new mediums, addressed themes rarely explored, and devised new ways of producing art. Many also reclaimed women's traditional forms of creative expression in art and language and demanded that they be recognized as "true art" and valued as highly as masculine forms.

The issue of selection looms particularly large in Part III. We take comfort in the fact that today there are myriad books and anthologies by and about women who are creating culture. Some are country specific; others focus on women of particular ethnic, racial, or religious groups; and many cover a particular discipline or time period. Here we have tried to provide an eclectic balance of varied voices from different fields, countries, and backgrounds, and a balance between familiar and hopefully new voices. We have also supplemented traditional written documents with a number of interviews.

Chapter 11, "New Directions in Literature and the Arts," focuses on women involved in culture between ca. 1900 and World War II. It continues the theme of women "breaking away" from the restrictive Victorian ideal and finding their own creative voices. Texts in Chapter 12, "Mid-Century Cultural Ferment," provide an eclectic sampling of female creativity around mid-century. The featured women reflect the challenges posed by the Depression and World War II and the cultural ferment that characterized the postwar, postcolonial, cold war era.

The last three chapters focus on women's diverse contributions to culture since the mid-sixties, with particular attention to the relationship between the feminist movement and women's creative endeavors. In Chapter 13, "Reclaiming Their Heritage: Women and Religion," we explore women's efforts to reclaim their religious heritage and eliminate patriarchal features that marginalize and exclude women from their respective religious traditions. Texts also show women again creating new religions and new forms of worship that reflect their experiences and fulfill their spiritual needs. Chapter 14, "Feminism, Social Change, and Female Creativity," examines the impact of feminism and broader forces of social change on women in several cultural fields. It also addresses some of the issues contemporary women confront in their professional lives, as well as themes they explore and approaches they utilize in their works.

We end Volume II with a sampling of the diverse voices of creative women in contemporary society. The selections in Chapter 15, "Contemporary Voices," provide insights into the ways women of different racial, ethnic, and cultural backgrounds have sought to express their own traditions and their multiple identities within the framework of a dominant Eurocentric culture. They also show women's continuing efforts to express their perspectives and experiences as females through their work within a culture that is still largely androcentric.

A number of themes and patterns are evident in Part III, many of which were identified in earlier parts of Volume II and even in Volume I. One is the persistent strength of a gender construct that relegates women to the private sphere and reserves the public sphere for men, and in so doing denies women opportunities for personal growth and creative expression. A related theme is the continuing struggle of women to combine their private roles as family members with their professional creative lives. The documents in Part III and indeed throughout the two volumes of this anthology clearly show that women have made many significant contributions to Western culture, despite the barriers they faced.

Evidence presented in these last chapters demonstrates that women have been able to contribute most fully when they have had the support of an organized women's movement that effectively challenged the legal and institutional barriers that for generations restricted women's access to education, money, jobs, and professional recognition in cultural fields. We again see women utilizing a strategy of separatism to overcome exclusionary and discriminatory practices and creating their own networks, professional associations, and women-directed institutions from orchestras to museums. The biographies and many of the documents also attest to the emergence of new "patrons" or sources of support for artists, in particular, grants from private, nonprofit foundations and, more importantly, university positions, fellowships, and research grants. Despite persistent discrimination, more women (and non-majority males) now have greater access to financial support and recognition while pursuing their creative endeavors than ever before.

Chapter 11

New Directions
in Literature and the Arts

The first decades of the twentieth century, as we have seen in the previous chapter, were marked by tremendous cultural ferment and social change. New forms of art, literature, music, and theater emerged, only to be challenged by still other examples of avant-garde expression. Nationalism and competing ideologies including communism, socialism, democracy, and fascism fostered political instability. World War I, the postwar years of reconstruction and retrenchment, the Depression, and the outbreak of World War II disrupted lives in Europe and America and generated swings of political and social liberalism and conservatism. New occupational, educational, and professional opportunities opened for women between 1880 and 1920, though at varying times and rates, in Europe and the Western Hemisphere. Numerous women's civic and labor organizations, plus the temperance, suffrage, and the international women's peace movements, created influential networks that helped bring changes in women's political, legal, and economic status. Change, particularly when it involved changes in gender relationships, also produced backlash, such as occurred in the 1920s when women were encouraged to return to traditional domestic roles and assume new gender-related roles as consumers.

The lives and works of women included in this chapter reflect these competing and changing trends. They illustrate the cross-pressures nontraditional women felt, the new opportunities they enjoyed, and the persistent barriers they faced. The examples in this chapter illustrate some of the strategies women used to enhance their own professional opportunities and to ensure that women after them would enjoy the same or additional options. Some also reveal women's recognition of the importance of foremothers and women's history. Again, we find in this and subsequent chapters the significance of partnerships between men and women and support networks among women. And we see that women are leaders in cultural change and pioneers in new art forms.

MUSIC

Ethel Smyth (1858–1944): British Composer, Author, and Suffragist

Ethel Smyth (pronounced like "scythe") was an outspoken advocate for woman's suffrage and equal rights for women musicians, a pioneer who succeeded in the male genre of opera, and a writer of note. One of eight children born to a British army officer and his Paris-educated wife, she grew up in the English countryside and received a typical middle-class Victorian "female" education. She was tutored at home and then sent to a boarding school that offered music, art, French, German, and literature and a smattering of science and math. At 17 she had her first lessons with a local composer, and in 1877, she went to Germany to study at Europe's finest music school, the Leipzig Conservatory.

The decade Smyth spent in Leipzig was an important period in her life. The city offered rich musical fare and her fellow students included such talented composers as Grieg, Dvořák, and Tchaikovsky. After a year at the conservatory, she began private lessons with Austrian composer Heinrich von Herzogenberg. Through Herzogenberg and his wife Elizabeth (Lisl), she met Brahms, Clara Schumann, and other musical luminaries. Meanwhile, she composed a string quartet, sonatas for violin and piano and cello and piano, and two sets of German *lieder* (songs). She also convinced a publisher to publish her songs despite his belief that few women could compose and that a woman's compositions would not sell (Smyth 1923, 236–37). Around 1885, she began an affair with Lisl's married brother-in-law, Henry Brewster (H. B.). By 1889, Smyth had composed an orchestral overture and a four-movement serenade. Her serenade was performed in London in 1890, marking her debut as a composer in her native land. In 1891, she composed her most important work to date, a Mass in D. It was performed at London's Royal Albert Hall in 1893 by the Royal Choral Society.

Between 1894 and 1904, Smyth composed three operas in collaboration with Brewster, who wrote the libretti. Her first opera debuted in Weimar, Germany, in 1898, and her second, *Der Wald,* was performed in Berlin in 1902 and subsequently at Covent Garden, London. In 1903, it had a historic premiere as the first opera by a woman performed at New York's Metropolitan Opera House. She completed her best-known opera, *The Wreckers,* in 1904. This phase of her life ended with Brewster's death in 1908. Their relationship was a mainstay of Smyth's life for over 40 years.

Between 1910 and 1913, Smyth devoted her energies to the British suffragist movement. She enlisted as the cause entered its most violent stage of imprisonments and hunger strikes and spent two months in prison for smashing a window of a cabinet minister's home. Her most famous contribution was her "March of the Women" that she dedicated to the Women's Social and Political Union, founded by her friend Emmeline Pankhurst. Cicely Hamilton wrote the stirring words. Smyth conducted the "March" from her prison window as WSPU activists sang outside and protested the imprisonment and forced feedings of their sisters. In 1913, a rejuvenated Smyth completed her most popular work, *The Boatswain's Mate,* a two-act comedy with feminist overtones that included "March of the Women" and "1910," another suffragist choral piece (Bernstein 1987, 316). She completed two more operas between 1922 and 1925, a Concerto for Horn, Violin, and Orchestra (1927), and, in 1930, a symphonic work for chorus and orchestra based on a text by Brewster.

During World War I she began a new career as a writer and published ten books and numerous articles before her death. Her descriptions of famous people, her comments about musicians and their works, and her witty, provocative insights about society make her books quite entertaining. Smyth often championed the cause of women musicians in her books and articles.

SMYTH'S REFLECTIONS ON MEN, WOMEN, AND MUSIC*

> By and by, students at our musical colleges began clamouring to learn stringed instruments, and presently half the string band consisted of girls. Later on the mouthpiece of certain wind instruments was permitted to insert itself between feminine

*Excerpts from Ethel Smyth, *Female Pipings in Eden,* (2d ed. [London] Peter Davies Ltd., 1934; Printed by T. and A. Constable Ltd. at the University Press, Edinburgh), pp. 8, 11–12, 25, 31, 48–49. By permission of David Higham Associates Limited, London.

lips, and, to cut a long story short, to-day there is not an instrument in the orchestra that is not taught to female musical students. . . .

As regards the B.B.C. band, perhaps the *attitude* of the cello player is considered an unseemly one for women? The B.B.C. is nothing if not proper, and once men's vicarious sense of modesty gets to work you never know where it will break out next. In my youth they strained at that harmless gnat, a girl on a bicycle; since then they have had to swallow something far worse than camels—horses with girls riding them cross-legged! To-day, engulfed by the rising flood of woman's independence, perhaps they are clinging to the violoncello as the drowning cling to a spar, . . . If not propriety, the idea can only be to keep women in their place. . . .

In the other London orchestras . . . not a woman is to be seen, unless occasionally plucking the strings of the 2nd Harp. The harp being a cumbrous and rather unlucrative instrument, woman has been permitted by ancient tradition to play it. Indeed I think her colleagues rather cherish this solitary white-armed presence in their midst, much as the men in the Welch regiment cherish the regimental goat.

In the meantime, our sex being admitted only on sufferance as it were to the outskirts of the musical scene, all the really interesting and educative jobs in our institutions, such as the training of choruses, stage management, conducting, the manipulation of the electric light, etc., etc.—exercising which people learn the meaning of the word authority and how best to use it—all these jobs, I say, fall automatically into the hands of youthful males. Now and then, favoured by the god of chance, some woman of quite exceptional gifts, an Ellen Terry, or a Lilian Baylis, achieves a commanding position; but Edith Craig, perhaps our greatest producer, has still to explain to casual stage hands who work under her that she really *does* know something about electricity! . . .

When it comes to the Lords of Creation considering the creative work of women on a field that has not yet become, willy-nilly, one of their recognised provinces, many other factors besides clannishness come into play; for instance prejudice, . . . and, more subtle still, . . . an honest incapacity to understand what women are driving at. . . .

My point is this. The hatred and enmity excited by every great innovating genius is one thing; this damping down *on principle* of feminine efforts is another. Great innovating geniuses are few and far between, but there are plenty of composers who earn a nice little income and give a good deal of pleasure. It is this possibility that is denied to women; for among the consequences of exclusion from the ranks of the performed are: no royalties, no performing fees; unwillingness of publishers to act for you (which means you pay for your own MS. if you can afford it, and forgo all chance of getting known even at home, let alone abroad); resultant unwillingness of gramophone companies to make records of works that are never performed, and so on and so on.

And there is a worse consequence than all this. . . . you cannot get giants like Mt. Blanc and Mt. Everest without the mass of moderate sized mountains on whose shoulders they stand. It is the upbuilding of this platform that is impossible so long as full music life is denied to women. . . .

Another thing that rather depresses those who take interest in the future of women musicians is, that nearly every woman possessed of power is busy running some man, or underpinning some male show. They cannot but be aware that their sex has a hard fight to keep its head above the water. . . .

Take the case of the British Women's Symphony Orchestra, one of the finest instances you can find of persistence, from sheer idealism and at immense personal sacrifice, in a noble enterprise—that of creating a First-Class Women's Orchestra. They believe in rehearsing, play magnificently, and have at last found a woman worthy to conduct them. It is common knowledge that no first-class orchestra, in London or elsewhere, makes both ends meet; one hears of one of the best of them being subsidised to the extent of £1000 per annum by a wealthy music lover, and all get help of some kind. But no woman can be found to endow this women's orchestra! . . .

American Musicians Organize

The document that follows is an example of strategies women used to create new opportunities in music. Compare their efforts with those of women in dance, theater, and other occupations.

WOMEN MUSICIANS URGE EQUAL RIGHTS, 1938*

FULL OPPORTUNITY FOR JOBS IS ASKED AT RALLY
OF NEW ORGANIZATION HERE

Full opportunity of employment for professional women musicians was proclaimed as a right yesterday morning at Steinway Hall at the first mass meeting of the six-weeks-old committee for the recognition of women in the musical profession. Nearly 125 women musicians heard invited speakers and officers of the group discuss organizational plans and programs to combat "an unjust discrimination" for which, according to one speaker, "there was absolutely no reason except habit."

The first speaker, Antonia Brico, conductor of the New York Women's Symphony Orchestra, protested against the existing "prejudice" as regards engaging women in leading musical organizations.

"The law, medicine, economics, politics, and many other professions are open to women," she said, "why then should not music be equally open to them? There is no lack of opportunity to study, what with the tuitionless schools, music colleges, private teachers. And the union admits us to its ranks. But what after that? Where shall we work, when so many organizations will not only not accept us but not even give us auditions?"

Jean Schneider, the committee's director of organization, stressed that the group's two main present considerations were the recognition of women's rights within the Musician's Union and the bringing of the problem to the attention of the public.

As to the first, she proposed the resolution, which was unanimously passed, that women take a greater active part in the union.

*"Women Musicians Urge Equal Rights," *New York Times* (Rochester, NY: Eastman Kodak Co. For Recordak Corp.), 19 May 1938, p. 24, microfilm: NP1. By permission of *The New York Times.*

As to the second consideration, Ruth Wilson, director of public relations, reported that various clubs and societies that have been informed of the committee's grievances have offered support.

Mary Dreier, vice president of the Women's Trade Union League, congratulated the new group on their determination to take active part in union affairs. She urged the body to organize and insist on their rights.

Felice Lauria, secretary of the Consumer's League, suggested that the committee "get a good rousing song" to dramatize their problem. Other speakers were Catherine Newton, financial secretary of the committee, and Isobel Soule of the League of Women Shoppers.

LITERATURE

Virginia Woolf (1882–1941): English Writer and Feminist

Virginia Woolf wrote nearly a dozen novels as well as short stories, essays, and reviews. Her works include *Jacob's Room* (1922); *To the Lighthouse* (1927); *Orlando* (1928); *Three Guineas* (1938); and a revealing diary. For years she was best known for her fiction which was widely praised for its aesthetic quality. She also earned respect as an avant-garde writer for her experimentation with new modes of expression, and as a literary critic. Ironically, her contemporaries and literary critics generally ignored her essays, although Woolf herself believed that essays were perhaps the most important literary genre. In the 1970s, however, her essays were "rediscovered" by a new generation of women scholars. Today, her *Room of One's Own* is recognized as a classic of feminist literature, and new readings have uncovered feminist elements in most of her fiction and essays. In effect, by ignoring the ideas in her work, Woolf's early critics silenced her and stifled feminist discourse.

Woolf was the third of four children born to Leslie Stephen and Julia Duckworth. It was the second marriage for both parents, and the household in which Woolf grew up included her mother's other three children. Her father was editor of a magazine as well as the *Dictionary of National Biography* and a prominent literary figure; her mother wrote occasionally. Their circle of friends included Americans James Russell Lowell and Henry James, British novelist George Meredith, actress Ellen Terry, and poet Alfred Lord Tennyson, among others. In addition to these contacts, Woolf enjoyed unlimited access to her father's extensive library and her mother's support of her desire to write. Unfortunately, she also experienced a series of painful events that probably contributed to the periodic bouts of mental instability she suffered throughout her life. These included sexual advances she and her sister suffered at the hands of their stepbrother, and the deaths of her mother when Woolf was 13 and two years later her oldest stepsister who had become "surrogate" mother to the clan.

Other experiences served as a catalyst for her feminism. When her brother Thoby went to Cambridge University, she and her sisters stayed home where they were tutored and given training in feminine skills. She was subjected to the increasingly arbitrary demands of her lonely father and the rigid Victorian mores of her half brother. After her father's death in 1904, she and her three siblings moved to the Bloomsbury district of London, where for the first time she experienced a life free of the expectations of a patriarchal household. Their Bloomsbury home became a center for Thoby's Cambridge friends, including economist John Maynard Keynes and Leonard Woolf, who gathered for freewheeling debates. Both Virginia and her sister Vanessa married men from this circle. Meanwhile, Woolf learned Greek on her own, taught at a college for working women in South London, worked in a suffrage office, wrote reviews for a literary magazine, and began writing fiction.

In 1912, Virginia married Leonard Woolf. Her husband was always supportive of her writing and cared for her during her periodic illnesses. He also founded the Hogarth Press in part to engage her interest and ward off a mental breakdown. In the early 1920s, Virginia Woolf fell passionately in love with Victoria (Vita) Sackville-West, a lesbian poet/novelist. She committed suicide by drowning on March 28, 1941.

Her essay *A Room of One's Own* addresses many of the feminist concerns that appear in her other works as well. Its conversational, meandering style is also illustrative of her avant-garde writing. The essay grew out of talks she had given at Newnham and Girton, Cambridge University's only colleges for women. The title relates to her somewhat controversial thesis about what a woman must have in order to write. What exactly does she think is necessary, and why? How convincing is she? What is the significance of the library incident? Her research at the British museum? Shakespeare's sister? How do you think students in her audience responded to her talk?

EXCERPTS FROM *A ROOM OF ONE'S OWN*, 1929*

[Denied Entry to the University Library]

What idea it had been that had sent me so audaciously trespassing I could not now remember. . . . but here I was actually at the door which leads into the library itself. I must have opened it, for instantly there issued, like a guardian angel barring the way with a flutter of black gown instead of white wings, a deprecating, silvery, kindly gentleman, who regretted in a low voice as he waved me back that ladies are only admitted to the library if accompanied by a Fellow of the College or furnished with a letter of introduction.

That a famous library has been cursed by a woman is a matter of complete indifference to a famous library. . . . [N]ever will I ask for that hospitality again, I vowed as I descended the steps in anger. . . .

So I went back to my inn, and as I walked through the dark streets I pondered this and that, as one does at the end of the day's work. . . . and I thought of the queer old gentlemen I had seen that morning . . . and of the shut doors of the library; and I thought how unpleasant it is to be locked out; and I thought how it is worse perhaps to be locked in; and, thinking of the safety and prosperity of the one sex and of the poverty and insecurity of the other and of the effect of tradition and of the lack of tradition upon the mind of a writer, [she decided to call it a day.]

[Observations While Doing Research at the British Museum]

. . . Have you any notion how many books are written about women in the course of one year? Have you any notion how many are written by men? Are you aware that you are, perhaps, the most discussed animal in the universe? . . . It was a most strange phenomenon; and apparently . . . one confined to the male sex. Women do not write books about men. . . . What could be the reason, then, of this curious disparity, I wondered . . . [Surveying many books, she reacted to one:] . . . it was the professor's statement about the mental, moral and physical inferiority of women. My heart had leapt. . . . I had flushed with anger. . . . One does not like to be told that one is naturally the inferior of a little man. . . . Soon my own anger was explained and done with; but . . . how explain the anger of the professors?

. . . Possibly when the professor insisted a little too emphatically upon the inferiority of women, he was concerned not with their inferiority, but with his own superiority. That was what he was protecting rather hot-headedly . . . , because it was a jewel to him of the rarest price. . . . Without self-confidence we are as babes in the cradle. And how can we generate this imponderable quality . . . most quickly? By thinking that other people are inferior to oneself. By feeling that one has some innate superiority—it may be wealth, or rank, [or] a straight nose, . . . Hence the enormous importance to a patriarch who has to conquer, who has to rule, of feeling that great numbers of people, half the human race indeed, are by nature inferior to himself. It must indeed be one of the chief sources of his power. . . . Women have served all these centuries as looking-glasses possessing the magic and delicious power of reflecting the figure of man at twice its natural size. Without that power probably the earth would still be swamp and jungle. The glories of all our wars would be unknown. . . . Whatever may be their use in civilised societies, mirrors are essential to all violent and heroic action. That is why Napoleon and Mussolini both insist so emphatically upon the inferiority of women, for if they were not inferior, they would cease to enlarge. That serves to explain in part the necessity that women so often are to men. And it serves to explain how restless they are under her criticism; . . . For if she begins to tell the truth, the figure in the looking-glass shrinks; his fitness for life is diminished. How is he to go on giving judgement, civilising natives, making laws, writing books . . . unless he can see himself at breakfast and at dinner at least twice the size he really is? So I reflected, crumbling my bread and stirring my coffee. . . .

[What Happened to Shakespeare's "Sister"?]

. . . it is unthinkable that any woman in Shakespeare's day should have had Shakespeare's genius. For genius like Shakespeare's is not born among labouring, uneducated, servile people. . . . How, then, could it have been born among women whose work began . . . almost before they were out of the nursery, who were forced to it by their parents and held to it by all the power of law and custom? . . . When, however, one reads of a witch being ducked, of a woman possessed by devils, of a wise woman selling herbs, . . . then I think we are on the track of a lost novelist, a suppressed poet . . . who dashed her brains out on the moor or mopped and mowed about the highways crazed with the torture that her gift had put her to. Indeed, I would venture to guess that Anon, who wrote so many poems without signing them, was often a woman. . . .

. . . any woman born with a great gift in the sixteenth century would certainly have gone crazed, shot herself, or ended her days in some lonely cottage outside the village, half witch, half wizard, feared and mocked at. . . . No girl could have walked to London and stood at a stage door and forced her way into the presence of actor managers without doing herself a violence and suffering an anguish which may have been irrational . . . but were none the less inevitable. . . . Chastity had then, it has even now, a religious importance in a woman's life, and has so wrapped itself round with nerves and instincts that to cut it free and bring it to the light of day demands courage of the rarest. To have lived a free life in London in the sixteenth century would have meant for a woman who was poet and playwright a nervous stress and dilemma which might well have killed her. Had she survived, whatever she had written would have been twisted and deformed. . . . And undoubtedly . . . her work would have gone unsigned. That refuge she would have sought certainly. It was the relic of the sense of chastity that dictated anonymity to women even so late as the nineteenth century. Currer Bell, George Eliot, George Sand . . . sought ineffectively to veil themselves by using the name of a man. Thus they did homage to the convention, which if not implanted by the other sex was liberally encouraged by them . . . , that publicity in women is detestable. Anonymity runs in their blood. The desire to be veiled still possesses them. . . .

[What Do Women Need in Order to Write?]

. . . The extreme activity of mind which showed itself in the later eighteenth century among women . . . was founded on the solid fact that women could make money by writing. . . . Thus, towards the end of the eighteenth century a change came about which, if I were re-writing history, I should describe more fully and think of greater importance than the Crusades or the Wars of the Roses. The middle-class woman began to write. . . . Without those forerunners, Jane Austen and the Brontës and George Eliot could no more have written than Shakespeare could have written without Marlow. . . . Jane Austen should have laid a wreath upon the grave of Fanny Burney. . . . All women together ought to let flowers fall upon the tomb of Aphra Behn . . . , for it was she who earned them the right to speak their minds. . . .

. . . Intellectual freedom depends upon material things. Poetry depends upon intellectual freedom. And women have always been poor, not for two hundred years merely, but from the beginning of time. Women have had less intellectual freedom than the sons of Athenian slaves. Women, then, have not had a dog's chance of writing poetry. That is why I have laid so much stress on money and a room of one's own. However, thanks to the toils of those obscure women in the past, . . . years later, these evils are in the way to be bettered. . . .

. . . For my belief is that if we live another century or so . . . and have five hundred a year each of us and rooms of our own; if we have the habit of freedom and the courage to write exactly what we think; . . . if we face the fact . . . that there is no arm to cling to, but that we go alone, . . . then the opportunity will come and the dead poet who was Shakespeare's sister will put on the body which she has so often laid down. Drawing her life from the lives of the unknown who were her forerunners, as her brother did before her, she will be born. . . . I maintain that she would come if we worked for her, and that so to work, even in poverty and obscurity, is worth while.

Zora Neale Hurston (1891–1960): American Author and Folklorist

Zora Neale Hurston is widely regarded as one of the most important African-American writers of the twentieth century. She was a folklorist, novelist, playwright, and anthropologist whose works provide a view of Southern black culture that differs in significant ways from that of her male contemporaries. Hurston's work was shaped by her family and community. Her mother encouraged her daughter to set her sights high and try anything. Her father was a Baptist minister and three-term mayor of her hometown, Eatonville, Florida. Eatonville was the first incorporated, self-governing all-black town in the United States, hence its citizens enjoyed a degree of autonomy few African Americans experienced.

Hurston early exhibited the independent spirit and initiative instilled by her mother. Her mother died when she was 9, and at age 14, after her father's remarriage, she left Eatonville to make her own way. She supported herself working as a wardrobe girl for a touring theater group and then settled in the Washington, D.C., area, where she took odd jobs while attending Morgan Academy in Baltimore and Howard University. In 1925, she moved to New York City and enrolled in Barnard College, Columbia University's sister college for women, where she was the only black student. There she studied with Franz Boas, a leading anthropologist, and completed her degree in 1928. While working her way through Barnard, Hurston became involved with artists and intellectuals of the Harlem Renaissance and their prominent white supporters and began to gain recognition as a writer. One of her stories appeared in an anthology, *The New Negro* (1925), and she helped edit a quarterly journal, *Fire!,* founded in1926 by Langston Hughes and Wallace Thurman. She also won literary awards for some stories and plays.

The 1930s was the most prolific period of Hurston's life. She continued folklore research in Eatonville that she had begun in1927. In 1934, she taught at Bethune-Cookman College, founded by Mary McLeod Bethune. In the second half of the decade, Hurston enjoyed support from prestigious fellowships and New Deal programs to combat unemployment among America's artists and intellectuals. She enrolled at Columbia University in 1935 to study anthropology, did dramatic coaching for the Federal Theater Project in New York in 1935–36, conducted anthropological research in the Caribbean on Guggenheim Fellowships in 1936 and 1937, and was an editor for the Federal Writers' Project in Florida in 1938.

She also had two brief marriages during the decade and published two of her most successful works, *Mules and Men* (1935) and *Their Eyes Were Watching God* (1937). *Mules and Men* was based on her anthropological studies in Florida and Louisiana in which she participated in Hoodoo initiation rites to learn more about that African-based faith. Her work helped define Hoodoo as a "suppressed religion," not mere superstition. These and other works were instrumental in rescuing and preserving black language and folklore. Her work also celebrated black cultural traditions, and showed how Southern blacks were able to break free of white control and live their lives with a measure of autonomy.

Hurston's works were quite popular in the late 1920s and 1930s. In the 1940s and 1950s, however, she was the target of sharp criticism from leading black male authors such as Richard Wright, who contended that her works, particularly *Their Eyes Were Watching God,* perpetuated white stereotypes of blacks as happy and carefree. Wright and others thought black writers should portray the racism and oppression blacks experienced. They also attacked her for publishing anticommunist essays, and, in particular, for her stance on the 1954 Supreme Court school desegregation decision, *Brown* v. *Board of Education.* While welcoming the Court's attack on segregation in principle, Hurston criticized it because it denied the value of existing black institutions. In the increasingly angry climate of the civil rights movement, Hurston's emphasis on the positive aspects of the black experience and the communities she studied seemed out of step. She published her last novel in 1948 but was unable to get anything published thereafter. She died penniless and was buried in an unmarked grave.

Hurston's work was rediscovered in black bookstores in the late 1960s, often by women in the new black studies programs. These women, newly admitted to the traditionally white and male professorial ranks in American colleges and universities, repeatedly petitioned Modern Language Association conventions to get Hurston's novels back in print. By the late 1970s, thanks to their efforts and to Robert Hemenway's *Zora Neale Hurston: A Literary Biography,* a Hurston "Renaissance" was under way. Many black women, including Alice Walker, declared Hurston's *Their Eyes* the most important book they had read. They responded to her positive and realistic image of black cultural traditions and particularly to her portrayal of Janie (Washington 1990, viii–xi).

As you read the following selections, consider the debate that raged at mid-century over her portrayal of Southern black communities, as well as the positive response the book has elicited in recent decades. How do you read her portrayal of Janie?

THEIR EYES WERE WATCHING GOD, 1937*

Janie found out very soon that her widowhood and property was a great challenge in South Florida. Before Jody had been dead a month, she noticed how often men who had never been intimates of Joe, drove considerable distances to ask after her welfare and offer their services as advisor.

"Uh woman by herself is uh pitiful thing," she was told over and again. "Dey needs aid and assistance. God never meant 'em tuh try tuh stand by theirselves. You ain't been used tuh knockin' round and doin' fuh yo'self, Mis' Starks. You been well taken keer of, you needs uh man."

Janie laughed at all these well-wishers because she knew that they knew plenty of women alone; that she was not the first one they had ever seen. But most of the others were poor. Besides she liked being lonesome for a change. This freedom feeling was fine. These men didn't represent a thing she wanted to know about. She had already experienced them through Logan and Joe. . . .

[Losing Tea Cake]

[Janie shocked the community by running off with Tea Cake, a much younger man with no steady job or visible financial resources. We pick up the story as he is dying from injuries suffered when he saved Janie during a hurricane that swept the Everglades.]

Tea Cake began to cry and Janie hovered him in her arms like a child. She sat on the side of the bed and sort of rocked him back to peace.

"Tea Cake, 'tain't no use in you bein' jealous uh me. In de first place Ah couldn't love nobody but yuh. And in de second place, Ah jus' uh ole woman dat nobody don't want but you."

"Naw, you ain't neither. You only sound ole when you tell folks when you wuz born, but wid de eye you'se young enough tuh suit most any man. Dat ain't no lie. Ah knows plenty mo' men would take yuh and work hard fuh de privilege. Ah done heard 'em talk."

"Maybe so, Tea Cake, Ah ain't never tried tuh find out. Ah jus' know dat God snatched me out de fire through you. And Ah loves yuh and feel glad."

"Thank yuh, ma'am, but don't say you'se ole. You'se uh lil girl baby all de time. God made it so you spent yo' ole age first wid somebody else, and saved up yo' young girl days to spend wid me."

"Ah feel dat uh way too, Tea Cake, and Ah thank yuh fuh sayin' it."

"Tain't no trouble tuh say whut's already so. You'se uh pretty woman outside uh bein' nice."

"Aw, Tea Cake."

"Yeah you is too. Everytime Ah see uh patch uh roses uh somethin' over sportin' they selves makin' out they pretty, Ah tell 'em 'Ah want yuh tuh see mah Janie sometime.' You must let de flowers see yuh sometimes, heah, Janie?"

"You keep dat up, Tea Cake, Ah'll believe yuh after while," Janie said archly and fixed him back in bed. . . .

*Excerpts from pp. 86, 171–72, 180, 182–84, from THEIR EYES WERE WATCHING GOD by ZORA NEALE HURSTON. Perennial Library (New York: Harper & Row, 1990). Copyright 1937 by Harper and Row, Publishers, Inc. Renewed 1965 by John C. Hurston and Joel Hurston. Reprinted by permission of HarperCollins Publishers Inc.

Janie buried Tea Cake in Palm Beach. She knew he loved the 'Glades but it was too low for him to lie with water maybe washing over him with every heavy rain. Anyway, the 'Glades and its waters had killed him. She wanted him out of the way of storms, so she had a strong vault built in the cemetery at West Palm Beach. Janie had wired to Orlando for money to put him away. Tea Cake was the son of Evening Sun, and nothing was too good. The Undertaker did a handsome job and Tea Cake slept royally on his white silken couch among the roses she had bought. He looked almost ready to grin. Janie bought him a brand new guitar and put it in his hands. He would be thinking up new songs to play to her when she got there.

Sop and his friends had tried to hurt her but she knew it was because they loved Tea Cake and didn't understand. So she sent Sop word and to all the others through him. So the day of the funeral they came with shame and apology in their faces. They wanted her quick forgetfulness. So they filled up and overflowed the ten sedans that Janie had hired and added others to the line. Then the band played, and Tea Cake rode like a Pharaoh to his tomb. No expensive veils and robes for Janie this time. She went on in her overalls. She was too busy feeling grief to dress like grief. . . .

[Janie Returns to Her Home Town]

. . . She had given away everything in their little house except a package of garden seed that Tea Cake had bought to plant. The planting never got done because he had been waiting for the right time of the moon when his sickness overtook him. The seeds reminded Janie of Tea Cake more than anything else because he was always planting things. She had noticed them on the kitchen shelf when she came home from the funeral and had put them in her breast pocket. Now that she was home, she meant to plant them for remembrance.

Janie stirred her strong feet in the pan of water. The tiredness was gone so she dried them off on the towel.

"Now, dat's how everything wuz, Pheoby, jus' lak Ah told yuh. So Ah'm back home agin and Ah'm satisfied tuh be heah. Ah done been tuh de horizon and back and now Ah kin set heah in mah house and live by comparisons. Dis house ain't so absent of things lak it used tuh be befo' Tea Cake come along. It's full uh thoughts, 'specially dat bedroom.

"Ah know all dem sitters-and-talkers gointuh worry they guts into fiddle strings till dey find out whut we been talkin' 'bout. Dat's all right, Pheoby, tell 'em. Dey gointuh make 'miration 'cause mah love didn't work lak they love, if dey ever had any. Then you must tell 'em dat love ain't somethin' lak uh grindstone dat's de same thing everywhere and do de same thing tuh everything it touch. Love is lak de sea. It's uh movin' thing, but still and all, it takes its shape from de shore it meets, and it's different with every shore."

"Lawd!" Pheoby breathed out heavily, "Ah done growed ten feet higher from jus' listenin' tuh you, Janie. Ah ain't satisfied wid mahself no mo'. Ah means tuh make Sam take me fishin' wid him after this. Nobody better not criticize yuh in mah hearin.'"

"Now, Pheoby, don't feel too mean wid de rest of 'em 'cause dey's parched up from not knowin' things. Dem meatskins is *got* tuh rattle tuh make out they's alive. Let 'em consolate theyselves wid talk. 'Course, talkin' don't amount tuh uh hill uh beans when yuh can't do nothin' else. And listenin' tuh dat kind uh talk is jus' lak openin' yo' mouth and lettin' de moon shine down yo' throat. It's uh known fact, Pheoby, you got tuh *go* there tuh *know* there. Yo' papa and yo' mama and nobody else can't tell yuh and show yuh. Two things everybody's got tuh do fuh theyselves. They got tuh go tuh God, and they got tuh find out about livin' fuh theyselves."

There was a finished silence after that so that for the first time they could hear the wind picking at the pine trees. It made Pheoby think of Sam waiting for her and getting fretful. It made Janie think about that room upstairs—her bedroom. Pheoby hugged Janie real hard and cut the darkness in flight.

Soon everything around downstairs was shut and fastened. Janie mounted the stairs with her lamp. The light in her hand was like a spark of sun-stuff washing her face in fire. Her shadow behind fell black and headlong down the stairs. Now, in her room, the place tasted fresh again. The wind through the open windows had broomed out all the fetid feeling of absence and nothingness. She closed in and sat down. Combing road-dust out of her hair. Thinking.

The day of the gun, and the bloody body, and the courthouse came and commenced to sing a sobbing sigh out of every corner in the room; out of each and every chair and thing. Commenced to sing, commenced to sob and sigh, singing and sobbing. Then Tea Cake came prancing around her where she was and the song of the sigh flew out of the window and lit in the top of the pine trees. Tea Cake, with the sun for a shawl. Of course he wasn't dead. He could never be dead until she herself had finished feeling and thinking. The kiss of his memory made pictures of love and light against the wall. Here was peace. She pulled in her horizon like a great fishnet. Pulled it from around the waist of the world and draped it over her shoulder. So much of life in its meshes! She called in her soul to come and see.

VISUAL ART

Käthe Kollwitz (1867–1945): German Graphic Artist

Käthe (Kaethe) Kollwitz was a leading graphic artist of the first half of the twentieth century whose work is commonly associated with German Expressionism. She worked in several art forms, including drawings, prints, woodcuts, lithographs, and sculpture, and experimented with various combinations of techniques and media. Her works are highly personal and convey in powerful, images the horrors of war, poverty, and oppression and the heroism of oppressed people fighting for their rights. She worked only in black and white, in part to make her work affordable for lower-middle-class buyers.

Her life spans a volatile period in German and Western European history, from the unification of Germany through World War I, the upheavals of the interwar years, the rise of the Nazis, and World War II. She was born in the East Prussian seaport town of Königsberg, the daughter of Karl and Katharina Rupp Schmidt. Both parents encouraged their children's talents, encouraging them to read and arranging art lessons for the girls.

In 1885, 17-year-old Käthe went to Berlin to study at the art school for girls. Her brother Konrad enrolled at the university in Berlin, which, like all German universities and government-sponsored schools of fine arts, was closed to women. Her school was one of three independent art schools established and run by a German women's professional art association, the Verein der Künstlerinnen. Its tuition was six times that charged male students at the Prussian Royal Academy and its course of study was shorter and less demanding, but at least it and its sister schools in Munich and Karlsruhe trained aspiring women artists (Radycki 1982, 11–13). During her year in Berlin, Käthe became engaged to Karl Kollwitz, a medical student. Her father, who thought that his plain-looking daughter would never attract a husband, had decided she should become a professional artist, and when he saw his plans for her were endangered, he sent her to study at the female Munich art school in 1888–89.

Her professional career began soon after she and Karl married in 1891 and settled in a working-class district in Berlin. When Käthe married, her father urged her to abandon thoughts of a career and devote herself to marriage. She again ignored his advice and pursued her work, despite bearing two sons, Hans in 1892 and Peter in 1896. In the 1890s, she completed *The Revolt of the Weavers*, a six-part print series that brought her recognition as a leading graphic artist. The inspiration for her prints was a play she attended by Gerhart Hauptmann about an 1844 revolt of desperate Silesian weavers. Her series was recommended for a gold medal; however, Kaiser Wilhelm refused to give her the medal because of the work's alleged socialist content. She also taught at the women's art school in Berlin for several years. During the first decade of the twentieth century she completed a second print series, *The Peasant War*, based on a sixteenth-century uprising led by a woman known as "Black Anna."

World War I and its aftermath had a profound impact on her art. Her son Peter was killed in the war, and she turned to sculpture to express her grief and that of so many other mothers. She also depicted the agony mothers felt at their children's suffering in the immediate postwar years. Although her work was strongly political in its critique of exploitation, political oppression, and war, she was never active in a particular political party. She was, however, active in feminist causes. She was a founder in 1913 of the German Women's Art Union (*Frauenkunstverband*) that fought to open public art schools to female students and teachers and was elected its president in 1914 (Radycki 1982, 11). In 1926 she helped found another feminist group GEDOK (Society for Women Artists and Friends of Art) whose purpose was to show, sponsor, and facilitate the work of women artists (Kearns 1976, 192). Germany's defeat in World War I also brought her the official recognition she deserved. Under the government of Kaiser Wilhelm, the Prussian Royal Academy did not admit women as members. That policy changed with the collapse of the government, and in 1919, Kollwitz became the first woman to be admitted to the renamed Prussian Academy of Fine Arts. From 1928 until 1933, she served as director of the academy's graphic arts department. She was forced to resign from that position when the Nazis came to power and condemned the work of Expressionists as "degenerate" art. World War II brought more sorrow into her life. Her husband died in 1940, and her grandson, named after her son Peter, was a war casualty in 1942. Nevertheless, she continued to work into her seventies and derived much pleasure from her son Hans and his family. The selections that follow provide glimpses of her work, relationships, and beliefs.

EXCERPTS FROM KOLLWITZ'S *DIARY AND LETTERS**

HER EARLY LIFE, WRITTEN 1941

A great event took place during this time [1892]: the . . . premiere of [Gerhart] Hauptmann's *The Weavers*. . . .

That performance was a milestone in my work. I . . . set to work on *The Weavers*. At the time I had so little technique that my first attempts were failures. For this reason the first three plates of the series were lithographed, and only the last three successfully etched: the *March of the Weavers, Storming the Owner's House,* and

*Excerpts from Hans Kollwitz, ed., *The Diary and Letters of Kaethe Kollwitz,* trans. Richard Winston and Clara Winston (Evanston, IL: Northwestern University Press, 1988), pp. 42, 43, 72, 96, 111. By permission of Krishna Winston.

The End. My work on this series was slow and painful. But it gradually came, and I wanted to dedicate the series to my father. . . . But meanwhile my father fell critically ill, and he did not live to see the success I had when this work was exhibited. On the other hand, I had the pleasure of laying before him the complete *Weavers* cycle on his seventieth birthday. . . . He was overjoyed. I can still remember how he ran through the house calling again and again to Mother to come and see what little Kaethe had done. . . .

I should like to say something about my reputation for being a "socialist" artist, which clung to me from then on. Unquestionably my work at this time, as a result of the attitudes of my father and brother and of the whole literature of the period, was in the direction of socialism. But my real motive for choosing my subjects almost exclusively from the life of the workers was that only such subjects gave me in a simple and unqualified way what I felt to be beautiful. For me the Koenigsberg longshoremen had beauty; the Polish *jimkes* on their grain ships had beauty; the broad freedom of movement in the gestures of the common people had beauty. Middle-class people held no appeal for me at all. . . . The proletariat, on the other hand, had a grandness of manner, a breadth to their lives. . . .

FROM HER DIARY: AUGUST 22, 1916

Stagnation in my work. When I feel so parched, I almost long for the sorrow again. And then when it comes back I feel it stripping me physically of all the strength I need for work.

Made a drawing: the mother letting her dead son slide into her arms. I might make a hundred such drawings and yet I do not get any closer to him. I am seeking him. As if I had to find him in the work. And yet everything I can do is so childishly feeble and inadequate. I feel obscurely that I could throw off this inadequacy, that Peter is somewhere in the work and I might find him. And at the same time I have the feeling that I can no longer do it. I am too shattered, weakened, drained by tears. I am like the writer in Thomas Mann: he can only write, but he has not sufficient strength to live what is written. It is the other way round with me. I no longer have the strength to form what has been lived. A genius and a Mann could do it. I probably cannot.

For work, one must be hard and thrust outside oneself what one has lived through. As soon as I begin to do that, I again feel myself a mother who will not give up her sorrow. Sometimes it all becomes so terribly difficult. . . .

FROM HER DIARY: JANUARY 4, 1920

I have again agreed to make a poster for a large-scale aid program for Vienna. I hope I can make it, but I do not know whether I can carry it out because it has to be done quickly and I feel an attack of grippe coming on.

I want to show Death. Death swings the lash of famine—people, men, women and children, bowed low, screaming and groaning, file past him.

While I drew, and wept along with the terrified children I was drawing, I really felt the burden I am bearing. I felt that I have no right to withdraw from the responsibility of being an advocate. It is my duty to voice the sufferings of men, the never-ending sufferings heaped mountain-high. This is my task, but it is not an easy one to fulfill. Work is supposed to relieve you. But is it any relief when in spite of my poster people in Vienna die of hunger every day? And when I know that? Did I feel relieved when I made the prints on war and knew that the war would go on raging? Certainly not. Tranquillity and relief have come to me only when I was engaged on one thing: the big memorial for Peter. Then I had peace and was with him.

FROM HER DIARY: NEW YEAR'S EVE, 1925

Recently I began reading my old diaries. Back to before the war. Gradually I became very depressed. The reason for that is probably that I wrote only when there were obstacles and halts to the flow of life, seldom when everything was smooth and even. So there were at most brief notes when things went well with Hans, but long pages when he lost his balance. And I wrote nothing when Karl and I felt that we belonged intimately to one another and made each other happy; but long pages when we did not harmonize. As I read I distinctly felt what a half-truth a diary presents. Certainly there was truth behind what I wrote; but I set down only one side of life, its hitches and harassments. I put the diaries away with a feeling of relief that I am safely out of those times. Yet they were times which I always think of as the best in my life. . . . Then came the war and turned everything topsy-turvy. . . .

Frida Kahlo (1907–1954): Mexican Artist

Frida Kahlo's semitragic life, her tumultuous relationship with Diego Rivera, her unique autobiographical art, and her zest for life have captured the attention of art lovers and lay people alike. Her efforts to convey Mexican culture and its indigenous roots and to reconcile her own mixed European and Mexican ancestry in her art have made her a powerful role model for American Chicanos, and particularly for Chicanas. Kahlo's personal life shaped, and was reflected in, her art to an unusual extent. She was the daughter of a European immigrant of Hungarian and German background and a Mexican woman. Her father, who was a photographer and artist, encouraged her to paint. The bond between father and daughter grew even closer after she contracted polio at age 14 because he too suffered physically from epilepsy. In 1922 she entered the National Preparatory School in Mexico City, the best school in the country. She was one of only 35 girls among the 2,000 students. The school had begun to admit girls as part of its post-revolutionary shift from a European to a Mexican institution.

In September 1925, her life changed drastically when she was impaled on a metal bar in a bus accident. She recovered after a two-year convalescence but experienced a life of pain. She had over 30 operations on her spine and right foot before she died 29 years later. Painting became a means of expressing her suffering, as well as a profession in lieu of medicine which she had intended to study. Much of her art is related to her body and things that happened to it over her short life. Her early work, particularly in the thirties, also employed religious artifacts and symbols.

In 1929, Kahlo met the famous Diego Rivera and, with her father's blessing, became the third wife of the 41-year-old painter. Theirs was a stormy, relationship (with a divorce and remarriage), but also a rewarding artistic partnership. When she was well, she nurtured him and his ego, and he continually encouraged her to paint and to show her work. When she was ill, he often cared for her. Each had various lovers (in her case, men and women). One of her most famous paintings, *Las Dos Fridas,* portrays her as twins, one symbolizing her European side, the other her Mexican/indigenous side that she believed Rivera preferred. It also depicts her heartbreak over their recent divorce. At the time of their marriage, her paintings began to reflect her *Mexicanidad* (a romantic form of nationalism), especially her self-portraits in traditional native costumes. Kahlo and Diego also shared a commitment to the Communist Party's efforts to continue the Mexican Revolution on behalf of the poor and the forgotten Indians and sought through their art to further the socialist cause.

Kahlo's career soared in the late 1930s and early 1940s, when her works were shown in major exhibitions of surrealist art and in shows in Europe, the United States, and Mexico. Although she said she detested surrealism, she benefited from being linked with the movement. Kahlo also taught art. In her teaching, as in her painting, her pride in all things Mexican was evident. In the late forties and early fifties, her health declined markedly, aided in part by drugs and alcohol taken to alleviate pain. Still, between bouts of depression and attempted suicides, she retained her zest for life and her work. This was evident in what to some was surrealist theater in April 1953 at the opening of her first one-person exhibition in Mexico City. She was too ill to attend, but suddenly an ambulance appeared at the gallery, and she was carried in and put on her canopy bed in the center of the hall. There she sat, greeting everyone who came to pay their respects. When she died a year later, she left behind a revealing illustrated diary and a legacy of fascinating art. The selections that follow illustrate her life and work, and give glimpses of the personality of this complex woman. The selections are from Hayden Herrera's biography of Kahlo.*

To Art Historian, Antonio Rodríguez

My father had had for many years a box of oil colors and some paintbrushes in an old vase and a palette in a corner of his little photography workshop. Purely for pleasure he would go to paint at the river in Coyoacán, . . . Ever since I was a little girl, . . . I had been casting an eye in the direction of the box of colors. I could not explain why. Being so long in bed, I took advantage of the occasion and I asked my father for it. Like a little boy whose toy is taken away from him and given to a sick brother, he "lent" it to me. My mother asked a carpenter to make an easel, if that's what you would call a special apparatus that could be attached to my bed where I lay, because the plaster cast did not allow me to sit up. In this way I began to paint.

Letter to Lucienne Bloch, 14 February 1938

Since I came back from New York [in 1935] I have painted about twelve paintings, all small and unimportant, with the same personal subjects that only appeal to myself and nobody else. I send four of them to a gallery, which is a small and rotten place, but the only one which admits any kind of stuff, so I send them there without any enthusiasm, four or five people told me they were swell, the rest think they are

*EXCERPTS TOTALING 1059 WORDS from FRIDA: A BIOGRAPHY OF FRIDA KAHLO by Hayden Herrera. Copyright © 1983 by Hayden Herrera. Reprinted by permission of HarperCollins Publishers Inc. Selections from pp. 64, 225, 254–55, 317, 330–31, 397, 402, 420.

too crazy. . . . To my surprise, Julian [sic] Levy wrote me a letter, saying that somebody talked to him about my paintings, and that he was very much interested in
having an exhibition in his gallery, I answered sending few photographs of my last
things, and he send another letter very enthusiastic about the photos, and asking me
for an exhibition of thirty things on October of this year. I don't know what they see
in my work Why do they want me to have a show? [She agreed, and the show in
Levy's Manhattan gallery was a success.]

FRIDA SPEAKING ABOUT HER ART

I never knew I was a Surrealist till Andre Breton came to Mexico and told me I was.
The only thing I know is that I paint because I need to, and I paint always whatever
passes through my head, without any other consideration.
[To Antonio Rodríguez]
I adore surprise and the unexpected. I like to go beyond realism. For this reason, I
would like to see lions come out of that bookshelf and not books. My painting naturally reflects these predilections and also my state of mind. And it is doubtless true
that in many ways my painting is related to that of the Surrealists. But I never had
the intention of creating a work that could be considered to fit in that classification.

. . . my paintings are . . . the most frank expression of myself, . . . I have painted
little, and without the least desire for glory or ambition, but with the conviction
that, before anything else, I want to give myself pleasure and then, that I want to be
able to earn my living with my craft. . . . many lives would not be enough to paint
the way I would wish and all that I would like.

FRIDA AS REMEMBERED BY HER STUDENTS

I remember her entering the school of Painting and Sculpture. . . . She appeared
there all of a sudden like a stupendous flowering branch because of her joyfulness,
kindness, and enchantment. This was owed, surely, to the Tehuana dress that she
wore, and that she always wore with such grace. . . . She chatted with us briefly after
greeting us very affectionately, and then immediately told us in a very animated way:
"Well, kids, let's go to work; I will be your so-called teacher, I am not any such thing,
I only want to be your friend, I never have been a painting teacher, nor do I think I
ever will be, since I am always learning. It is certain that to paint is the most terrific
thing that there is, but to do it well is very difficult, it is necessary to do it, to learn
the skill very well, to have very strict self-discipline and above all to have love, to feel
a great love for painting. . . . I want you to know, dear children, that there does not
exist in the whole world a single teacher who is capable of teaching art. To do that is
truly impossible." . . .

Frida's great teaching was to see through artist's eyes, to open our eyes to see the
world, to see Mexico. She did not influence us through her way of painting, but
through her way of living, of looking at the world and at people and at art. She made
us feel and understand a certain kind of beauty in Mexico that we would not have
realized by ourselves.

EXCERPTS FROM HER DIARY

[On Communism and Her Art, 1951]

I am very worried about my painting. Above all to transform it, so it will be something useful, since until now I have not painted anything but the honest expression of my own self, but absolutely distant from what my painting could do to serve the Party. I should struggle with all my strength for the little that is positive that my health allows me to do in the direction of helping the Revolution. The only real reason to live.

[Invalid Frida Writes about Diego]

If only I had his caress near me the way the air caresses the earth. The reality of his person would make me happier. It would distance me from the feeling that fills me full of gray. Nothing would then be so deep in me, so final. But how do I explain to him my enormous need for tenderness! My loneliness of many years. My structure ill adapted because it is inharmonious. I think it is better to go, to go, to *escape*. Let everything pass in a second, *Ojalá* [God grant].

[Shortly before Her Death, February 11, 1954]

They amputated my leg six months ago, they have given me centuries of torture and at moments I almost lost my "reason." I keep on wanting to kill myself. Diego is the one who holds me back because of my vanity in thinking he would miss me. He has told me so and I believe him. But never in my life have I suffered more. I will wait a little while.

I have achieved a lot.
I will be able to walk
I will be able to paint
I love Diego more
than I love myself.
My will is great

My will remains
Thanks to the magnif-
icent love of Diego. . . .
[and the expertise of
her doctors]

Georgia O'Keeffe (1887–1986): American Painter

Georgia O'Keeffe is best known for her bold flower paintings and abstract landscapes of the Southwest. Her work cannot be pigeonholed into any school of modern art; her style was highly individual. None of the European abstract movements influenced her. Instead, she wanted to create a uniquely American art. Toward the end of her career, she was honored with a major retrospective exhibition of her work in 1943 at the Art Institute of Chicago and again in 1946 at the Museum of Modern Art in New York City. She was "rediscovered" in 1970 when a retrospective exhibition of her works at the Whitney Museum in New York brought her to the attention of a new generation of art lovers and artists.

O'Keeffe was born in rural Wisconsin. Her introduction to art came at age 13 at a convent boarding school near Madison. She enjoyed her first attempts to draw a picture in the art class but recalled feeling terrible when the sister critiqued her work. Although her mother framed her pictures, O'Keeffe never liked them because the teacher made her feel she had not drawn them correctly. Still, by the end of eighth grade, she had decided that she was going to be an artist. In 1905, O'Keeffe studied anatomical drawing at the Art Institute of Chicago, and in 1907, she studied painting at the Art Students League (ASL) in New York City. Again, she felt at odds with her instructors and other students, for she disliked the ASL's emphasis on European art and its academic approach. She was thrilled when she discovered the theories of Arthur Wesley Dow who encouraged students to invent their own forms and express their own feelings, drawing on Oriental principles of harmony, patterning, and simplification. She used his principles when she taught art in Virginia, South Carolina, and Texas.

O'Keeffe's professional breakthrough came in 1916, when her art school friend Anita Politzer showed photographer Alfred Stieglitz some abstract charcoal drawings of Texas landscapes O'Keeffe had sent her. In 1918, he convinced her to return to New York, with a promise to support her for a year so she could paint full time. Not long after she accepted, Stieglitz left his family and moved in with O'Keeffe who was 25 years younger than he. They married in 1924. For over 20 years they supported each other's work and, with various side liaisons, were devoted to each other. She was the only woman who ever broke into his avant-garde artistic circle, and his display of her work in the 291 Gallery brought her to public attention. Until Stieglitz's death in 1946, she spent most of her time in New York City, with summers at Stieglitz's family home on Lake George. She felt stifled in the Northeast, however, and missed the stark, open landscape of the West. Thus in 1929, she began to spend most of each summer in New Mexico. She moved to Abiquiu, New Mexico, in 1949, where she spent the remaining years of her life.

O'Keeffe's work includes paintings of the New York skyline, large flowers, the Texas landscape, and numerous paintings of New Mexico's landscape, some buildings, and bones. Her flower paintings engendered some controversy as male critics, in particular, gave them a Freudian interpretation, suggesting they were abstract depictions of the female body. Male critics also spoke of her in gendered terms, in essence calling her the leading *female* artist. They praised her and other women artists for their "feminine perceptions," "feminine powers of expression," or "feminine intensity." (Chadwick 1990, 284–86) O'Keeffe resented this; she wanted recognition as a leading *artist*.

The following excerpts provide glimpses of her independent spirit, her creative processes, and her reaction to critics. They also shed light on some of her thoughts about gender, art, and society.

AUTOBIOGRAPHICAL EXCERPTS ABOUT HER WORK FROM EXHIBITION CATALOGS*

[Her Training and First Exhibition from "Anderson Galleries" 1923]

I grew up pretty much as everybody else grows up and one day seven years ago found myself saying to myself—I can't live where I want to—I can't go where I want to—I can't do what I want to—I can't even say what I want to. School and things that painters have taught me even keep me from painting as I want to. I decided I was a very stupid fool not to at least paint as I wanted to and say what I wanted to when I painted as that seemed to be the only thing I could do that didn't concern anybody but myself . . . I found that I could say things with color and shapes that I couldn't say in any other way—things that I had no words for. Some of the wise men say it is not painting, some of them say it is. Art or not Art—they disagree. Some of them do not care. Some of the first drawings done to please myself I sent to a girl friend [Politzer] requesting her not to show them to anyone. She took them to '29' and showed them to Alfred Stieglitz and he insisted on showing them to others. He is responsible for the present exhibition.

I say that I do not want to have this exhibition because, among other reasons there are so many exhibitions that it seems ridiculous for me to add to the mess— but I guess I'm lying. I probably want to see my things hang on a wall as other things hang so as to be able to place them in my mind in relation to other things I have seen done. And I presume, if I must be honest, that I am also interested in what anybody else has to say about them and also in what they don't say because that means something to me, too.

As a matter of fact, because of what I had seen in his gallery, I was more interested in what Stieglitz thought about my work than in what anyone else would think.

[Her Flower Paintings from "An American Place" 1939]

A flower is relatively small. Everyone has many associations with a flower—the idea of flowers. You put out your hand to touch the flower—lean forward to smell it—maybe touch it with your lips almost without thinking—or give it to someone to please them. Still—in a way—nobody sees a flower—really—it is so small—we haven't time—and to see takes time, like to have a friend takes time. If I could paint the flower exactly as I see it no one would see what I see because I would paint it small like the flower is small.

So I said to myself—I'll paint what I see—what the flower is to me but I'll paint it big and they will be surprised into taking time to look at it—I will make even busy New Yorkers take time to see what I see of flowers.

Well—I made you take time to look at what I saw and when you took time to really notice my flower you hung all your own associations with flowers on my flower and you write about my flower as if I think and see what you think and see of the flower—and I don't.

[An American Painting, Red, White, and Blue, from "An American Place" 1944]

That first summer I spent in New Mexico I was a little surprised that there were so few flowers. There was no rain so the flowers didn't come. Bones were easy to find so I began collecting bones. When I was returning East I was bothered about my work—the country had been so wonderful that by comparison what I had done with it looked very poor to me—although I knew it had been one of my best painting years. I had to go home—what could I take with me of the country to keep me working on it? I had collected many bones and finally decided that the best thing I could do was to take with me a barrel of bones—so I took a barrel of bones.

When I arrived at Lake George I painted a horse's skull—then another horse's skull and then another horse's skull. After that came a cow's skull on blue. In my Amarillo days cows had been so much a part of the country I couldn't think of it without them. As I was working I thought of the city men I had been seeing in the East. They talked so often of writing the Great American Novel—the Great American Play—the Great American Poetry. I am not sure that they aspired to the Great American Painting. Cézanne was so much in the air that I think the Great American Painting didn't even seem a possible dream. I knew the middle of the country—knew quite a bit of the South—I knew the cattle country—and I knew that our country was lush and rich. I had driven across the country many times. I was quite excited over our country and I knew that at that time almost any one of those great minds would have been living in Europe if it had been possible for them. They didn't even want to live in New York—how was the Great American Thing going to happen? So as I painted along on my cow's skull on blue I thought to myself, "I'll make it an American painting. They will not think it great with the red stripes down the sides—Red, White and Blue—but they will notice it."

After the Ninteenth Amendment was ratified in 1920, some suffragists insisted that their work was not over. In 1923, Alice Paul proposed an Equal Rights Amendment to the Constitution and initiated the National Woman's Party's campaign for its enactment. Challenging the conservatism and anti-feminism of the 1920s, 1930s, and 1940s, O'Keeffe and Politzer joined Paul's campaign. Note the case O'Keeffe makes as she tries to enlist the First Lady's support.

LETTER TO ELEANOR ROOSEVELT, 10 FEBRUARY 1944*

Having noticed in the N.Y. Times of Feb.1st that you are against the Equal Rights Amendment may I say to you that it is the women who have studied the idea of Equal Rights and worked for Equal Rights that make it possible for you, today, to be the power that you are in our country, to work as you work and to have the kind of public life that you have.

The Equal Rights Amendment would write into the highest law of our country, legal equality for all. At present women do not have it and I believe we are considered half the people.

Equal Rights and Responsibilities is a basic idea that would have very important psychological effects on women and men from the time they are born. It could very much change the girl child's idea of her place in the world. I would like each child to feel responsible for the country and that no door for any activity they may choose is closed on account of sex.

It seems to me very important to the idea of true democracy—to my country and to the world eventually—that all men and women stand equal under the sky.

I wish that you could be with us in this fight—You could be a real help to this change that must come.

Sincerely

Georgia O'Keeffe

SUGGESTED READINGS

Music

Neuls-Bates, Carol. "Women's Orchestras in the United States, 1925–45." In *Women Making Music.* Bowers and Tick, 1987.

St. John, Christopher. *Ethel Smyth: A Biography.* London: Longmans Green, 1959.

Walker-Hill, Helen, ed. *Black Women Composers: A Century of Piano Music (1893–1990).* Bryn Mawr, PA: Hildegard Publishing, 1992.

*Letter as it appears in Jack Cowart and Juan Hamilton, *Georgia O'Keeffe: Art and Letters* (National Gallery of Art, Washington, DC, in association with New York Graphic Society Books, Little, Brown and Company, Boston, MA, 1987), p. 235. Copyright © 1987 Estate of Georgia O'Keeffe. Reprinted by permission of The Georgia O'Keeffe Foundation. Original letter is in the Yale Collection of American Literature, Beinecke Rare Book and Manuscript Library.

Literature

Boyd, Valerie. *Wrapped in Rainbows: The Life of Zora Neale Hurston.* New York: Scribner, 2002.

Art

Behr, Shulamith. *Women Expressionists.* New York: Rizzoli, 1988.
Kahlo, Frida. *The Diary of Frida Kahlo: An Intimate Self-Portrait.* New York: Harry N. Abrams, 1995.
Lisle, Laurie. *Portrait of an Artist: A Biography of Georgia O'Keeffe.* Albuquerque: University of New Mexico Press, 1986; New York: Pocketbooks, 1987.
Prelinger, Elizabeth, et al. *Käthe Kollwitz.* Washington, DC: National Gallery of Art, 1992.
Udall, Sharyn Rohlfsen. *Carr, O'Keeffe, Kahlo: Places of Their Own.* New Haven, CT, and London: Yale University Press, 2000.

Audiovisual Sources

Smyth, Ethel. *Mass in D; Mrs. Waters Aria from The Botwswain's Mate; The March of the Women.* London, UK: Virgin Classics, 1991. Compact disc VC 7 91188–2.
Virginia Woolf. 1997. Produced by Bob Portway. 50 min. Princeton, NJ: Films for the Humanities and Sciences, 1997. Videocassette.
The Wreckers: Suffragettes Ethel Smyth and Sarah Bennett. 1997. Produced by Sam Organ. Directed by Kate Broome. 30 min. Princeton, NJ: Films for the Humanities and Sciences, 1997. Videocassette.

Chapter 12

Mid-Century Cultural Ferment

The professional careers of the women covered in this chapter spanned the tumultuous middle third of the twentieth century, roughly the early 1930s to the mid-1970s, although some worked for almost the entire century. They experienced the Great Depression, the rise of fascism, World War II, the horrors of the Holocaust, and the disintegration of colonial empires. They lived under the cloud of the atomic and hydrogen bombs and constant tension as the new superpowers, the Soviet Union and United States, faced off in the Cold War, and witnessed the reality of constant global conflicts in Korea, Vietnam, and the Middle East. American women experienced the social and political upheavals of the black civil rights movement and its rippling effect among Native Americans, Hispanics, and other ethnic groups. Finally, women on both sides of the Atlantic shaped, and were affected by, the new feminist movement that emerged as an organized force in the mid-1960s and early 1970s.

Women's creative endeavors in many respects reflected the shifting intellectual currents and cultural trends throughout this period. More importantly, however, women were often in the vanguard of intellectual, artistic, and social movements. Their ideas and artistic innovations shaped Western culture in profound ways. In their personal lives as well, they reflect the variety of lifestyles that existed in Western society, despite the pressures for a return to traditional family life and sex roles that pervaded Europe and America after World War II. Although most of these individuals benefited from the wider educational and professional opportunities that became available to women at the turn of the century, their options were still limited, particularly during the Depression and early postwar years. In pursuing their professional aspirations, however, these pioneers paved the way for the next generation of women, those born in the late 1930s. Most of them also opened new doors for the next generation by their conscious advocacy of feminism and/or equal opportunity for all.

LITERATURE

Simone de Beauvoir (1908–1986): French Philosopher, Writer, and Feminist

Simone de Beauvoir was an important literary figure, a journalist, and one of few renowned women philosophers of modern times. Her book *The Second Sex* (*Le deuxième sexe,* 1949) is regarded as a twentieth-century feminist classic. She grew up in Paris, the older of two daughters in a traditional bourgeois family. While still in her teens, she decided to become a writer, rejected her mother's Catholicism for atheism, and rebelled against the values that underlay her strict upbringing. She graduated from the Sorbonne with a degree in philosophy, taught philosophy in several schools between 1931 and 1941, and for the next two years, was a professor at the Sorbonne. She met Jean-Paul Sartre at the Sorbonne in 1929 and became part of his existentialist circle. They were companions until his death in 1980. Her relationship with Sartre linked her in most people's minds with existentialism, but she is not easily typed. In essays and some fiction, she called for intellectuals to take an active role in postwar political struggles, attacked France's colonial policies in Algeria, and professed socialist and sometimes Marxist views. Her works include a four-volume autobiography; a prize-winning novel, *The Mandarins;* and a novel *The Coming of Age,* that criticized society for its ill treatment of the elderly.

The Second Sex established her reputation as a feminist, even though when it was published, she proclaimed that the feminist movement was over and that she was not a feminist. It is a remarkable book, that generated tremendous hostility when published. The Catholic Church banned the work (and also *The Mandarins*), and some called her a lesbian on the grounds that no "real" woman would ever say the things she said in the book. Many intellectuals dismissed or attacked it because it covered so many areas of knowledge in an age when specialization in narrow topics was the norm. Instead of delineating and countering misogynist views of women, as many other works that contributed to the debate over the "woman question" did, she examined the historical, biological, and social factors that defined and perpetuated woman's status as "other." She also drew significant parallels between women and other oppressed groups. In sum, the book is a classic analysis of oppression and how it is perpetuated across all classes and through time, and a strong plea for women's independence.

In the 1970s, in contrast to her disavowals of feminism two decades earlier, de Beauvoir became a role model for a new generation of feminists and a leader in the radical French feminist movement that emerged in the spring of 1970. In the spring of 1971, the diverse radical women's groups the French press dubbed the Women's Libération Movement or MLF (Mouvement de la Libération des Femmes), began a campaign against the French ban on abortions. De Beauvoir was among around 300 women who publicly announced they had had an abortion (Rossi 1973, 672). In November 1971, she marched for abortion rights, and in February 1972, she helped organize a public tribunal, "Days of Denunciation of Crimes Against Women." The young feminists who organized the MLF were amazed at her ability to mobilize other women who shared her belief that women were not "by nature" fundamentally different from men (Schwarzer 1984, 13–15). Her activities expanded as the feminist agenda broadened. In 1974, she became president of the League of Women's Rights (modeled after the League for Human Rights), a position she still held in 1984, and in 1977, she assumed editorial responsibilities of a new journal, *Questions féministes* (Marks and Courtivron 1981, 35). She was a leader in the movement against domestic violence and helped establish shelters for battered women and their children. She also wrote a regular page with other women entitled "Everyday Sexism" for *Les Temps Modernes,* the journal she and Sartre published.

In the early 1970s, de Beauvoir acknowledged that she had previously opposed the idea of a separate feminist movement, and, like many other leftists, had believed that a socialist revolution would bring an end to the oppression of women. She stated, however, that she had come to the conclusion that an autonomous feminist movement was essential. (Schwarzer 1984, 32–33, 37–42) She and her work were an important bridge between the early twentieth-century feminist movement and the "new feminism." Compare her arguments in this reading with those of earlier participants in the *querelle des femmes*. In particular, consider the validity of her point that women participate in their own oppression and the persuasiveness of her analysis of woman as "other."

THE SECOND SEX (1949)*

For a long time I have hesitated to write a book on woman. The subject is irritating, especially to women; and it is not new. Enough ink has been spilled in the quarreling over feminism, now practically over, and perhaps we should say no more about it. It is still talked about, however, for the voluminous nonsense uttered during the last century seems to have done little to illuminate the problem. After all, is there a problem? And if so, what is it? . . .

But first we must ask: what is a woman? . . .

To state the question is, to me, to suggest, at once, a preliminary answer. The fact that I ask it is in itself significant. A man would never get the notion of writing a book on the peculiar situation of the human male. But if I wish to define myself, I must first of all say: "I am a woman"; on this truth must be based all further discussion. A man never begins by presenting himself as an individual of a certain sex; it goes without saying that he is a man. . . .

Thus humanity is male and man defines woman not in herself but as relative to him; she is not regarded as an autonomous being. . . . she is simply what man decrees; thus she is called, "the sex," by which is meant that she appears essentially to the male as a sexual being. . . . She is defined and differentiated with reference to man and not he with reference to her; she is the incidental, the inessential as opposed to the essential. He is the Subject, he is the Absolute—she is the Other.

The category of the *Other* is as primordial as consciousness itself. In the most primitive societies, in the most ancient mythologies, one finds the expression of a duality—that of the Self and the Other. This duality was not originally attached to the division of the sexes. . . .

Now, woman has always been man's dependent, if not his slave; the two sexes have never shared the world in equality. And even today woman is heavily handicapped, though her situation is beginning to change. Almost nowhere is her legal status the same as man's, and frequently it is much to her disadvantage. Even when her rights are legally recognized in the abstract, long-standing custom prevents their full expression in the mores. In the economic sphere men and women can almost be said to make up two castes; other things being equal, the former hold the better jobs, get higher wages, and have more opportunity for success than their new competitors. In industry and politics men have a great many more positions and they monopolize the most important posts. In addition to all this, they enjoy a traditional prestige that the education of children tends in every way to support, for the present enshrines the past—and in the past all history has been made by men. At the present time, when women are beginning to take part in the affairs of the world, it is still a world that belongs to men . . . To decline to be the Other, to refuse to be a Party to the deal—this would be for women to renounce all the advantages conferred upon them by their alliance with the superior caste. Man-the-sovereign will provide woman-the-liege with material protection and will undertake the moral justification of her existence; thus she can evade at once both economic risk and the metaphysical risk of a liberty in which ends and aims must be contrived without assistance. . . . When man makes of woman the *Other,* he may, then, expect her to manifest deep-seated tendencies toward complicity. Thus, woman may fail to lay claim to the status of subject because she lacks definite resources, because she feels the necessary bond that ties her to man regardless of reciprocity, and because she is often very well pleased with her role as the *Other.* . . .

. . . But the very fact that woman *is the Other* tends to cast suspicion upon all the justifications that men have ever been able to provide for it. These have all too evidently been dictated by men's interest. A little-known feminist of the seventeenth century . . . put it this way: "All that has been written about women by men should be suspect, for the men are at once judge and party to the lawsuit." Everywhere, at all times, the males have displayed their satisfaction in feeling that they are the lords of creation. "Blessed be God . . . that He did not make me a woman," say the Jews in their morning prayers, while their wives pray on a note of resignation: "Blessed be the Lord, who created me according to His will." The first among the blessings for which Plato thanked the gods was that he had been created free, not enslaved; the second, a man, not a woman. But the males could not enjoy this privilege fully unless they believed it to be founded on the absolute and the eternal; they sought to make the fact of their supremacy into a right. . . .

Legislators, priests, philosophers, writers, and scientists have striven to show that the subordinate position of woman is willed in heaven and advantageous on earth. The religions invented by men reflect this wish for domination. . . .

In proving woman's inferiority, the antifeminists then began to draw not only upon religion, philosophy, and theology, as before, but also upon science—biology, experimental psychology, etc. At most they were willing to grant "equality in difference" to the *other* sex. That profitable formula is most significant; it is precisely like the "equal but separate" formula of the Jim Crow laws aimed at the North American Negroes. As is well known, this so-called equalitarian segregation has resulted only in the most extreme discrimination. The similarity just noted is in no way due to chance, for whether it is a race, a caste, a class, or a sex that is reduced to a position of inferiority, the methods of justification are the same. "The eternal feminine" corresponds to "the black soul" and to "the Jewish character." True, the Jewish problem is on the whole very different from the other two—to the anti-Semite the Jew is not so much an inferior as he is an enemy for whom there is to be granted no place on earth, for whom annihilation is the fate desired. But there are deep similarities between the situation of woman and that of the Negro. Both are being emancipated today from a like paternalism, and the former master class wishes to "keep them in their place"—that is, the place chosen for them. In both cases the former masters lavish more or less sincere eulogies, either on the virtues of "the good Negro" with his dormant, childish, merry soul—the submissive Negro—or on the merits of the woman who is "truly feminine"—that is, frivolous, infantile, irresponsible—the submissive woman. In both cases the dominant class bases its argument on a state of affairs that it has itself created. . . .

I shall be told that [the idea of women's equality] is utopian fancy, because woman cannot be "made over" unless society has first made her really the equal of man. Conservatives have never failed in such circumstances to refer to that vicious circle; history, however, does not revolve. If a caste is kept in a state of inferiority, no doubt it remains inferior; but liberty can break the circle. Let the Negroes vote and they become worthy of having the vote: let woman be given responsibilities and she is able to assume them. . . . men have been led, in their own interest, to give partial emancipation to woman: it remains only for women to continue their ascent, and the successes they are obtaining are an encouragement for them to do so. It seems almost certain that sooner or later they will arrive at complete economic and social equality, which will bring about an inner metamorphosis.

. . . when we abolish the slavery of half of humanity, together with the whole system of hypocrisy that it implies, then the "division" of humanity will reveal its genuine significance and the human couple will find its true form. . . .

. . . It is for man to establish the reign of liberty . . . To gain the supreme victory, it is necessary . . . that by and through their natural differentiation men and women unequivocally affirm their brotherhood.

VISUAL ART

Margaret Bourke-White (1904–1971): Photojournalist and Author

Margaret Bourke-White was a pioneering photojournalist who helped stretch the boundaries of both journalism and art by forcing each field to expand to encompass photography. She had a remarkable career, working in some of the most male-dominated areas of photojournalism and became an important role model for many aspiring women photographers. She was born in the Bronx (New York), where her father worked in the printing industry as an engineer-designer. Between 1921 and 1927 she attended five universities and began to pursue photography. After graduation from Cornell University she began her career in Cleveland, Ohio, as a specialist in architectural and industrial photography. Like many Americans in the 1920s, she was enthralled with the beauty of the machine age and believed that industry, its machinery, and its products would provide the subjects for the art of the modern era.

In 1929, New York publisher Henry Luce, impressed by her photos of steel mill interiors, hired her as one of the first photographers for *Fortune,* his new industry-oriented magazine. In 1930, she made a photographic trip through the Soviet Union, which resulted in her first publication, *Eyes on Russia* (1931). In the mid-1930s, *Fortune* sent her to the Midwest to report on the dust bowl. Her article "The Drought" (October 1934) was the first of her powerful social documentaries.

In 1935, Bourke-White and other prominent photographers joined Luce in his experiment in photojournalism, *Life* magazine. Because of her industrial expertise, she was sent to Montana to report on a dam under construction, but she supplemented her photographs of construction forms with a human interest story of local frontier towns. Her material became the lead article and the cover of the inaugural edition of *Life;* it also marked the birth of a new journalistic form, the photo esssay. The next year, she toured the South for several months with writer Erskine Caldwell, documenting the appalling conditions of southern sharecroppers. Their book, *You Have Seen Their Faces* (1937), vividly illustrated the environmental, social, and personal disintegration of the region. It remains her most important historical documentary. She and Caldwell also covered the German attack on Moscow in 1941, at which time she was the only foreign photographer in the Soviet Union. *Shooting the Russian War* (1942) recounts that period.

Bourke-White was an official U.S. Army Air Force photographer during World War II. She followed the bomb squadrons to England and then to North Africa. She subsequently photographed action near Tunis and in Italy, recorded the final days of Hitler's regime as she accompanied General Patton and the Third Army in the Rhineland, and captured on film the horrors of Hitler's death camps. "The Living Dead of Buchenwald" (1945) is one of her most powerful photographs.

After World War II, *Life* sent her to cover the independence and partition of India, life in apartheid South Africa, and the Korean War. Her photo essays and book *Halfway to Freedom: A Study of the New India* (1949) captured the human drama and tragedy that unfolded as hatred between Muslims and Hindus erupted after the partition of India and Pakistan. Her final assignment was a study of the Jesuits, described in *A Report on the American Jesuits* (1956).

The excerpt below from her autobiography is from a meeting she had with Mahatma Gandhi, who was then 77, at the end of her trip to document the partition of India. She entered the meeting skeptical of Gandhi's idealistic approach to ending social conflict but quickly realized he was an extraordinary man. The interview on January 30, 1948, occurred at the time he had begun his sixteenth fast, this time, hoping his nonviolent principles would bring an end to Hindu-Muslim violence. The interview reflects one of her deep concerns, the nuclear threat.

GANDHI AND NONVIOLENCE IN A NUCLEAR WORLD, 1948*

I turned to the topic which I had most wanted to discuss with Gandhiji. . . .

I asked Gandhiji how he would meet the atom bomb. . . . "Ah," he said. "How shall I answer that? I would meet it by prayerful action. . . .

"I will go out and face the pilot so he will see I have not the face of evil against him. . . .

"I know the pilot will not see our faces from his great height, but that longing in our hearts that he should not come to harm would reach up to him, and his eyes would be opened. Of those thousands who were done to death in Hiroshima, if they had died with that prayerful action . . . then the war would not have ended as disgracefully as it has. It is a question now whether the victors are really victors or victims . . . of our own lust . . . and omission." . . . his words had become toneless and low. "The world is not at peace. . . . It is still more dreadful than before."

. . . a few hours later, on his way to evening prayers, this man who believed that even the atom bomb should be met with nonviolence was struck down by revolver bullets. . . . [She recounts the sea of mourners who gathered as his funeral pyre was lit.]

*Excerpts from Margaret Bourke-White, *Portrait of Myself* (New York: Simon & Schuster, 1963), pp. 296–97, 299.

. . . Nothing in all my life has affected me more deeply, and the memory will never leave me. I had seen men die on the battlefield for what they believed in, but I had never seen anything like this: one Christlike man giving his life to bring unity to his people.

Barbara Hepworth (1903–1975): British Sculptor

Barbara Hepworth is one of the major avant-garde sculptors of the twentieth century. She was born in Yorkshire, England, the first of three daughters and one son. Both parents encouraged her interest in art. She attended a girls' high school in Wakefield, whose headmistress, who also taught art, let her skip physical education to work in the art room and encouraged her to apply for a scholarship to Leeds School of Art. She entered Leeds with a scholarship in 1920. The next year, the 16-year-old entered the Sculpture School of the Royal College of Art in London. After graduating in 1924, she went to Paris and then Italy on a scholarship to study painting and sculpture. While in Florence she met and married another artist. They spent two years in Rome sculpting marble, while she developed techniques for carving her works directly in the stone. She had her first one-person exhibition in 1928, and the next year gave birth to a son, Paul. The marriage dissolved soon afterwards.

The 1930s was an important decade in her life and career. She married artist Ben Nicholson and spent 1932 and 1933 in Paris where they met numerous artists, including Pablo Picasso, Georges Braque, Jean Arp, and Piet Mondrian, whose work meshed with her growing interest in abstract organic geometric shapes. She also continued to collaborate with a college friend, Henry Moore, and began to explore sculpting shapes with open spaces or voids. In 1934, she gave birth again, but unexpectedly produced triplets. The Depression and World War II made it difficult for artists to sell works, so she maintained a garden, ran a school, pooled resources with friends, and engaged in war work.

In the 1950s Hepworth entered a new phase of life. Her marriage with Nicholson ended, and, in 1953, her son Paul, a pilot, was killed in Thailand. Grandchildren, however, entered her life, and her work took on new dimensions. She created abstract sets for theater and musical dramas and also designed costumes for a production at the Royal Opera House, Covent Garden. She continued to sculpt and traveled to Greece, New York, and Brazil, filling public and private commissions and participating in exhibitions. In 1959, she received the *Grand Prix* at the International Biennial Exhibition of Modern Art in São Paulo, Brazil. She was the first British artist to win that top prize. She had submitted examples of her work of the previous two decades, including over 20 sculptures, ranging from wood and marble carvings to works in bronze and stone, plus 17 drawings of her sculptures, to the competition.

Hepworth's work of the last decade of her life reflected her continuing fascination with the inside and outside of forms, but on a larger scale. Her abstract shapes and squares contained openings or piercings in which one could climb through, or look through for perspectives on nature—the sea, sun, moon, clouds. She also became fascinated with flight and space and created a 19-foot winged figure that graces an outside wall of the John Lewis Building on Oxford Street in London. She continued to do some smaller works in the pierced-form mode, including her 1962 alabaster sculpture *Merryn*, which is part of the permanent collection of the National Museum of Women in the Arts, Washington, D.C. Perhaps her most famous work is the 21-foot-high bronze sculpture *Single Form* that memorializes Dag Hammarskjöld, which stands in front of the United Nations building in New York. In 1965, Queen Elizabeth II honored this remarkable artist by making her a Dame of the British Empire. Her life's work was also featured in a retrospective exhibition at London's Tate Gallery.

In the excerpts that follow from her fascinating pictorial autobiography, Dame Hepworth shares her personal reflections about family and work and her philosophy of art and life.

EXCERPTS FROM HEPWORTH'S *PICTORIAL AUTOBIOGRAPHY*, 1970*

All my early memories are of forms and shapes and textures. Moving through and over the West Riding landscape with my father in his car, the hills were sculptures; the roads defined the form. Above all, there was the sensation of moving physically over the contours of fulnesses and concavities, through hollows and over peaks— feeling, touching, seeing, through mind and hand and eye. This sensation has never left me. I, the sculptor, *am* the landscape. I am the form and I am the hollow, the thrust and the contour. . . .

[On Combining Family and Work]

This was a wonderfully happy time. My son Paul was born, and, with him in his cot, or on a rug at my feet, my carving developed and strengthened. . . .

Friends and relations always said to me that it was impossible to be dedicated to any art and enjoy marriage and children. This is untrue, as I had nearly thirty years of wonderful family life; but I will confess that the dictates of work are as compelling for a woman as for a man. Not competitively, but as complementary, and this is only just being realised. . . .

These "working holidays" at Happisburgh were wonderful. We talked and walked, we bathed and played cricket, then we worked and danced. I think this idea of a working holiday was established in my mind very early indeed. My father took us each year to . . . stay in a house on the lovely beach. . . . My room was the right hand attic . . . and here I laid out my paints and general paraphernalia and crept at dawn to collect stones, seaweeds and paint, and draw by myself before somebody organised me! . . .

It made a firm foundation for my working life—and it formed my idea that a woman artist is not deprived by cooking and having children, nor nursing children with measles (even in triplicate)—one is in fact nourished by this rich life, provided one always does some work each day; even a single half hour, so that the images grow in one's mind.

I detest a day of no work, no music, no poetry.

[Triplets!] . . . Three pairs of eyes would watch every movement, and three pairs of ears listen to every word.

. . . my studio was a jumble of children, rocks, sculptures, trees, importunate flowers and washing.

[Art and the Artist]

I think the very nature of art is affirmative, and in being so it reflects the laws and the evolution of the universe—both in the power and rhythm of growth and structure as well as the infinitude of ideas which reveal themselves when one is in accord with the cosmos and the personality is then free to develop.

The artist works because he must! But he learns by the disciplines of his imagination. Through moments of ecstasy or great despair, when all thoughts of self are lost, a work seems to evolve which has not only the vivid uniqueness of a new creation, but also the seeming effortlessness and unalterable simplicity of a true idea

*Excerpts from Barbara Hepworth. *Barbara Hepworth: A Pictorial Autobiography* (New York: Praeger Publishers, Inc. and London: Tate Gallery Publications, 1970), pp. 9, 17, 20, 39, 24, 53, 96. © *Alan Bowness, Hepworth Estate.* Reprinted by permission of Alan Bowness.

relating to the universe. In our present time, so governed by fear of destruction, the artist senses more and more the energies and impulses which give life and are the affirmation of life. Perhaps by learning more and letting the microcosm reflect the macrocosm, a new way of life can be found which will allow the human spirit to develop and surmount fear.

[On Sculpture and the Meaning of Forms]

In sculpture there must be a complete realisation of the structure and quality of the stone or wood which is being carved. But I do not think that this alone supplies the life and vitality of sculpture. I believe that the understanding of the material and the meaning of the form being carved must be in perfect equilibrium. There are fundamental shapes which speak at all times and periods in the language of sculpture.

It is difficult to describe in words the meaning of forms because it is precisely this emotion which is conveyed by sculpture alone. Our sense of touch is a fundamental sensibility which comes into action at birth . . . the ability to feel weight and form and assess its significance. The forms which have had special meaning for me since childhood have been the standing form (which is the translation of my feeling towards the human being standing in landscape); the two forms (which is the tender relationship of one living thing beside another); and the closed form, such as the oval, spherical or pierced form. . . which translates for me the association and meaning of gesture in landscape; in the repose of say a mother and child, or the feeling of the embrace of living things, either in nature or in the human spirit. In all these shapes the translation of what one feels about man and nature must be conveyed by the sculptor in terms of mass, inner tension and rhythm, scale in relation to our human size and the quality of surface which speaks through our hands and eyes.

Address at the Unveiling of "Single Form" at the U.N., New York, 11 June 1964

It is very difficult for me to speak, because I can only communicate through my sculpture but I would like to offer these few words.

Dag Hammarskjöld spoke to me often about the evolution of the 'Single Form' in relation to compassion, and to courage and to our creativity. When I heard of his death, and was sharing my grief with countless thousands of people, my only thought was to carry out his wishes.

Dag Hammarskjöld had a pure and exact perception of aesthetic principles, as exact as it was over ethical and moral principles. I believe they were, to him, one and the same thing, and he asked of each of us the best we could give.

The United Nations is our conscience. If it succeeds it is our success. If it fails it is our failure. Throughout my work on the 'Single Form' I have kept in mind Dag Hammarskjöld's ideas of human and aesthetic ideology and I have tried to perfect a symbol that would reflect the nobility of his life, and at the same time give us a motive and symbol of both continuity and solidarity for the future.

DANCE

Martha Graham (1894–1991): Dancer, Choreographer, Teacher

Martha Graham probably had a greater impact on dance than any other person in the twentieth century. Her career spanned 70 years and affected every aspect of dance. She created a new dance language; introduced innovations in choreography, lighting, costumes, and stage design; trained several generations of dancers and choreographers; and influenced artists in numerous fields including film, theater, and music. She was also the first to employ African-American and Asian-American dancers. She performed at the White House for eight different presidents. In addition to the most prestigious dance awards, she received the Aspen Award in 1965, an international prize comparable to the Nobel Prize; was a 1979 Kennedy Center honoree; was a recipient of the Presidential Medal of Freedom, America's highest honor; and was awarded the Légion d'Honneur by the French government in 1984.

Graham was born in 1894 near Pittsburgh, Pennsylvania, but at age 14 moved to Santa Barbara, California, where her father practiced medicine. In 1911, Graham saw Ruth St. Denis perform at Mason Opera House in Los Angeles and was so inspired she decided to become a dancer. She studied theater and dance at an arts college and in 1916 enrolled in the new Denishawn School in Los Angeles. For eight years, she studied danced, and taught at Denishawn, working mainly with Ted Shawn. She won critical acclaim for her role as an Aztec maiden in *Xochitl,* a dance he created for her.

She left Denishawn in 1923 for New York City. She first performed with the Greenwich Village Follies where she was able to create her own dances. In 1926, she joined the faculty at the Eastman School of Music, where she began to develop her unique sudden movements to convey passionate, even violent, emotions. In 1927, she formed the Martha Graham School for Contemporary Dance and the Martha Graham Dance Company, one of the oldest dance troupes in the United States. In the late 1920s and 1930s, she choreographed a series of dances, many of which dealt with social problems. Her first group of works included *Immigrant, Lamentation, Vision of Apocalypse, Revolt,* and *Heretic.* All but *Heretic* were solo pieces. After 1935, she created *Chronicle,* an anti-imperialism piece; *Deep Song,* about the Spanish Civil War; and two works about Indian and Mexican culture, *Primitive Mysteries* and *Frenetic Rhythms.* She refused an invitation to dance at the 1936 Olympic Games in Berlin, in protest against Hitler's persecution of artists and Jews. When her company made its first postwar appearance in Berlin, she purposely chose to perform *Judith,* her powerful portrait of the biblical Jewish heroine, with a Jewish conductor in the orchestra pit. She made her first White House appearance in 1938, at the invitation of Eleanor Roosevelt.

Graham created some of her most famous and innovative works in the 1940s, including *El Penitente* and *Letter to the World* based on Emily Dickinson's poetry. She also created *Appalachian Spring* set to Aaron Copland's score. A number of her pieces involved her re-interpretation of mythology and often focused on the psychology of female characters. *Cave of the Heart* told Medea's story, *Night Journey* re-interpreted the Oedipus story, and *Clytemnestra* examined a key figure in Aeschylus' Greek trilogy *Orestia. Death and Entrances,* about the Brontë sisters, was another powerful psychological study. She also extended her collaboration with other artists, such as Copland, George Balanchine (with whom she created *Episodes*), her long-time friend Louis Horst, and the Japanese-American sculptor Isamu Noguchi. She had first collaborated with Horst and Noguchi in the mid-thirties when she created *Frontier,* a solo performance depicting the experiences of a pioneer woman. Horst had created an innovative sound design for the piece, while Noguchi had revolutionized stage sets by replacing the typical flat backdrops with sparse three-dimensional sculptures. Noguchi's sets and Horst's music meshed perfectly with the psychological dramas she depicted in her choreography.

In 1955, Graham introduced one of her finest works, *Seraphic Dialogue,* which depicted the inner struggles of Joan of Arc. She continued to dance until 1969 and to train new dancers and choreographers, including Alvin Ailey and Twyla Tharp, until her death. In 1990, she choreographed her one hundred ninety-first new work, *Maple Leaf Rag,* and finished her autobiography *Blood Memory.* When she died in 1991, she was choreographing *The Eye of the Goddess,* a ballet for the Barcelona Olympics.

GRAHAM'S THOUGHTS ABOUT THE NEW MODERN DANCE, 1941*

I am a dancer. My experience has been with dance as an art.

Each art has an instrument and a medium. The instrument of the dance is the human body; the medium is movement. The body has always been to me a thrilling wonder, a dynamo of energy, exciting, courageous, powerful; a delicately balanced logic and proportion. It has not been my aim to evolve or discover a new method of dance training, but rather to dance significantly. To dance significantly means "through the medium of discipline and by means of a sensitive, strong instrument, to bring into focus unhackneyed movement: a human being."

I did not want to be a tree, a flower, or a wave. In a dancer's body, we as audience must see *ourselves,* not the imitated behavior of everyday actions, not the phenomena of nature, not exotic creatures from another planet, but something of the miracle that is a human being, motivated, disciplined, concentrated.

The part a modern art plays in the world, each time such a movement manifests itself, is to make apparent once again the inner hidden realities behind the accepted symbols. Out of this need a new plasticity, emotional and physical, was demanded of the dance. This meant experiment in movement. The body must not only be strong, be facile, be brilliant, but must also be significant and simple. To be simple takes the greatest measure of experience and discipline known to the artist. . . .

Dance had its origin in ritual, the eternal urge toward immortality. Basically, ritual was the formalized desire to achieve union with those beings who could bestow immortality upon man. Today we practice a different ritual, and this despite the shadow over the world, for we seek immortality of another order—the potential greatness of man . . .

Although its concept was the product of Isadora Duncan and Ruth St. Denis, modern dance in its present manifestation has evolved since the World War. At that time a different attitude towards life emerged.

As a result of twentieth-century thinking, a new or more related movement language was inevitable. If that made necessary a complete departure from the dance form known as ballet, the classical dance, it did not mean that ballet training itself was wrong. It was simply found not to be complete enough, not adequate to the time, with its change of thinking and physical attitude.

A break from a certain rigidity, a certain glibness . . . was needed. There was need of an intensification, a simplification. For a time, this need manifested itself in an extreme of movement asceticism; there has now come a swing back from that extreme. All facilities of body are again being used fearlessly, . . .

No art ignores human values, for therein lie its roots. Directed by the authentic or perverted magnificence, which is man's spirit, movement is the most powerful and dangerous art medium known. This is because it is the speech of the basic instrument, the body, which is an instinctive, intuitive, inevitable mirror revealing man as he is.

Art does not create change; it registers change. The change takes place in the man himself. The change from nineteenth- to twentieth-century thinking and

---

*Excerpts from Martha Graham, "A Modern Dancer's Primer for Action," in *Dance: A Basic Educational Technique,* ed. Frederick Rand Rogers, (New York: Macmillan, 1941), pp. 178, 180–81. © 1980 by Dance Horizons, Brooklyn, New York. Reprinted by Permission of Dance Horizons.

attitude toward life has produced a difference in inspiration for action. As a result, there is a difference in form and technical expression in the arts.

In these excerpts from her autobiography Graham reflects on life, her art, and her career. In the first selection she responds to critics and politicians who attacked her dances as erotic and sought to censor her work. She contended the body and sex were beautiful expressions of life.

EXCERPTS FROM GRAHAM'S AUTOBIOGRAPHY, 1991*

I know my dances and technique are considered deeply sexual, but I pride myself in placing on stage what most people hide in their deepest thoughts. . . .

[Her Last Dance Appearance]

The last time I danced was in *Cortege of Eagles.* I was seventy-six years old. I had long been haunted by the image of Hecuba, the old and helpless Queen of Troy who watched as one by one, her loved ones died before her. I did not plan to stop dancing that night. It was a painful decision I knew I had to make.

[Final Reflections]

I'm asked so often at ninety-six whether I believe in life after death. I do believe in the sanctity of life, the continuity of life and of energy. I know the anonymity of death has no appeal for me. It is the now that I must face and want to face.

I have a new ballet to do for the Spanish government, and I have been brooding about pointing it toward the transmigration of the goddess figure, from India to Babylon, Sumer, Egypt, Greece, Rome, Spain . . . , and the American Southwest. And I am sure it will be a terror and a joy, and I will regret starting it a thousand times, and think it will be my swan song, and my career will end like this, and I will feel that I have failed a hundred times, and try to dodge those inevitable footsteps behind me. But what is there for me but to go on? That is life for me. . . .

Katherine Dunham (1909–): American Dance Pioneer and Anthropologist

Katherine Dunham is the most important pioneer in the development of black dance in America. This "Renaissance" woman has been a community activist, professor of dance and anthropology, and a priestess of the voodoo cult. She has choreographed over 100 original works; danced and sung to rave reviews in nightclubs, theatrical productions, and motion pictures; directed nearly a dozen theatrical works; and written six books primarily about dance. She is the recipient of numerous awards, including the 1979 Albert Schweitzer Music Award for her life's work devoted to music and to humanity; a Kennedy Center Honors Award (1983); the Samuel H. Scripps American Dance Festival Award (1987); the Southern Cross of Brazil; and the Grand Cross of Haiti. She was inducted into the Hall of Fame of the National Museum of Dance in Saratoga Springs, New York, in 1987 and has received Lifetime Achievement Awards from both the National Association for the Advancement of Colored People and the Urban League.

Dunham was born in Chicago and raised in the predominantly white community of Joliet, Illinois. Her mother was French Canadian and her father was African American. After high school, she followed her brother to the University of Chicago on a scholarship and received a degree in social anthropology in 1936. She began dance lessons in Chicago and danced her first leading role in 1933. Dunham taught dance to children and created a student dance company called Ballet Negre that performed with the Chicago Opera Company. After graduation, she toured the Caribbean on a fellowship,

*Excerpts from Martha Graham, *Blood Memory* (New York: Doubleday, 1991), pp. 211, 238, 276.

doing research in anthropology and dance. This began her lifelong study of how African religions, rituals, and dance evolved in the New World. She completed an M.A. degree in anthropology and pursued a Ph.D. at the University of Chicago where again she was the only black student in her classes.

In the late 1930s she decided to concentrate on dance instead of pursuing an academic career. She founded the Negro Dance Group in 1937, the first all-black modern dance company, and began to choreograph dances that blended African-American and the African-Caribbean dances she had studied. She premiered her work in New York City. Like Zora Neale Hurston, she was employed by the Federal Theater Project in Chicago, a New Deal program to combat unemployment. As dance director of the project's Negro Unit in 1937–1938, she choreographed dances for *Emperor Jones* and *Run Lil' Chillun* and presented her own work, *L'Ag'Ya,* a dance-drama based on a Martinique folktale and fighting dance. In 1939, she moved her company to New York City and began to create spectacular revues. Her revues, based on Caribbean folk material and music, Afro-Brazilian dance and rituals, and black American dances, showed the rich cultural links of the African diaspora. Her husband, artist and theatrical designer John Pratt, whom she married in the late 1930s, created the sets for her revues.

In the 1940s, the Katherine Dunham Dance Company toured Latin America, Europe, and the United States. The company also appeared with Dunham in the lead role in the Broadway show *Cabin in the Sky,* staged by George Balanchine. To raise money, the company performed in elite nightclubs. Dunham appeared in nine Hollywood productions and in foreign films. Her film credits include *Carnival of Rhythm* (1939), *Star-Spangled Rhythm* (1942), *Stormy Weather* (1943), and *Green Mansions* (1958). In 1945, she opened the Dunham School of Dance and Theater in New York. She continued to dance and direct Broadway productions until the mid-1960s.

In the 1960s, Dunham's career took new turns. In 1963, she choreographed the Metropolitan Opera production of *Aïda,* making history as the Met's first black choreographer. She also choreographed and staged dance sequences in Dino De Laurentiis's film *The Bible* and, in 1972, choreographed and directed Scott Joplin's opera *Treemonisha.* She served as an advisor to the cultural ministry in Senegal from 1965 to 1967, where she helped found the Ballet National de Senegal. In 1967, she moved to East Saint Louis, Illinois, where she began working with inner-city youth groups through the University of Southern Illinois. She also founded the Katherine Dunham Museum and the Katherine Dunham Center, which includes an Institute for Intercultural Communication and sponsors an annual international "Dunham Technique Seminar" for students of dance, music, theater, anthropology, and film.

Throughout her career, Dunham has protested race discrimination and fought for civil rights. She refused to perform until theaters made all seats available to blacks and hotels opened their doors to her troupe. She spent her first night in East Saint Louis in jail, after protesting police harassment of a young black gang. In 1993, the 84-year-old Dunham went on a 47-day hunger strike protesting America's policy toward Haitian refugees and its response to the overthrow of President Aristide.

The selections that follow shed light on some of the cultural and racial issues she has grappled with and her philosophy of dance. Compare her concepts of dance as an art form with Graham's and the pioneers of modern dance we met in Chapter 10 "The *New Woman* and the Performing Arts."

DUNHAM ON ETHNOLOGY AND DANCE*

[Her Studies of Dance and Ethnology in the Caribbean]
My desire was to see first-hand the primitive dance in its every-day relationship to
the people; and my anthropological studies which lead one to origins and the simple

*Quotations from Dorathi Bock Pierre, "Katherine Dunham. Cool Scientist or Sultry Performer," *Dance,* May 1947, pp. 12–13. By permission of *Dance Magazine.*

basic fundamentals of art which is made complex and esoteric by civilization, was the answer, I was sure. And I was in the Islands to find out for myself.

I spent six weeks in a tiny village waiting to get just one dance; and I spent much time on many small islands as well as Jamaica, Martinique, Haiti and Trinidad. I made innumerable records of the songs and music of the people. I took photographs and motion pictures, and became over-burdened with notebooks in which I carefully wrote down every movement and combination of movements I saw, as well as bits of life I saw about me—incidents I recognized immediately as having dramatic possibilities for the theater. I seemed always to live this sort of dual existence of having my intellect absorbed in searching out and annotating the real and authentic steps and movements, and an eye trained to see all of this color and movement and drama translated into theater idiom; and my notebooks, too, abound in marginal notes for use of the "real" material in the theater when I returned home, for I was more than ever determined to have a group of dancers who would be able to show the people of the United States what others have contributed to our culture. . . .

An Interview with Dunham, 1938*

[On the Unexpected Challenges She Faced When Starting Her School]
I carried on alone, . . . once again hoping for the best. I had been studying with Ludmilla Speranzeva, (of the Wigman School . . .) and she had agreed to help me with the training of the group. I brought together girls who were older and more interested, and we composed several numbers and gave two recitals. These were admittedly modern, but far from successful—the time was not ripe.

Can you believe it, . . . the Negro mothers immediately disapproved! They refused to send their children to me, for fear they *might* be taught Negro dancing! . . .

This aroused a small amount of interest and I was able to put my school on an almost paying basis. But the group itself improved slowly. Girls were constantly dropping out, and in each succeeding class there were new faces. It was disturbing, to say the least, for I had to re-teach them a dozen times a year! And the reason for it was simply that the Negro believes in a certain fallacy the white person has bequeathed him—namely, that the Negro is a *natural born* performer and needs no training. I am sure that any Negro will agree with me, if of course, he has reached any status in the artistic field, *that the one thing we face most often is a double standard of judgment, and the result is an appraisal of good for the Negro that is far below the expected good, of any other artist.* We are too quickly complimented and unless we are exceedingly strong and discerning our work is apt to be aborted in its very beginning. This ready acclamation retarded our progress.

. . . because our struggle for a permanent and dignified recognition must come through an outstanding contribution. We must always do *twice* as well and be *twice* as original to be accepted as genuine artists—and not on any basis of condescension, ever!

---

*From Frederick L. Orme, "The Negro in the Dance As Katherine Dunham Sees Him," *The American Dancer,* March, 1938, pp. 10, 46. By permission of *Dance Magazine.*

[Her Philosophy of Dance and Her Goals]

[Frederick Orme:] . . . will you state more simply just what you mean by your *anthropological* approach to dance?

[Dunham:] Certainly. It is to view it *functionally*—its meaning and significance in the personal and social lives of the people who participate in it; to grasp its ritual, its ceremonial, and its recreational values. Also, in a comparative analysis, a careful study of the dance form itself is necessary. Necessary for purposes of weighing its contact with other peoples and the results of such contact—best illustrated in Haiti, where West Africa meets eighteenth-century France, and does it so often in so many dances. . . .

[Orme:] And your plans?

[Dunham:] To establish a well-trained ballet group. To develop a technique that will be as important to the white man as to the Negro. To attain a status in the dance world that will give to the Negro dance-student the courage really to study, and a reason to do so. And to take *our* dance out of the burlesque—to make of it a more dignified art. We lack a tradition in the dance as we present it now, and the young Negro has no esthetically creative background.

A Conversation with Katherine Dunham, 1956*

> . . . I don't see any color in what we do. I see human emotions. It's only a fortunate accident that I've hit upon and used material chiefly of people with Negro background. But I would feel I'd failed miserably if I were doing dance confined in technique or audience-satisfaction to race, color or creed. I don't think that it would be art, which is something that has to do with universal truths and a set of fundamental ideas, evaluations and appreciations. . . .
>
> [Dunham defended her performances of dances from minstrel shows, arguing they are] an important part of American background, . . .
>
> And I only hope I've captured their spirit. For people to see the meaning of the Cuban or so-called 'exotic' material and not to see the meaning of the American Negro folk material—well that's precious. Besides, I'm not thinking of Negro history when presenting these dances but of American history, of which Negroes form an important part.

Maria Tallchief (1925–): American Prima Ballerina

Maria Tallchief was America's first *prima ballerina* and for two decades was one of the Western world's greatest female dancers and a guest star of the world's leading dance companies. She has received many awards and performed numerous times at the White House. In 1953, President Eisenhower honored her with the "Woman of the Year" Award. In 1967, she was the first Osage and the eighth woman to receive an Indian Achievement Award, sponsored annually by Indian Council Fire, a national organization. In 1996, she was a recipient of the John F. Kennedy Center for the Performing Arts Honors for lifetime achievement and was inducted into the National Women's Hall of Fame in Seneca Falls, New

---

*From Albert J. Elias, "Conversation with Katherine Dunham," *Dance Magazine*, February 1956, pp. 17, 18. By permission of *Dance Magazine*.

York. In 1997, the year she published her autobiography *America's Prima Ballerina,* she was honored with membership in the International Women's Forum Hall of Fame.

She was born Betty Marie Tall Chief in Fairfax, Oklahoma, the daughter of an Osage father and Scotch-Irish mother. She spent her childhood on the reservation of her father's people. In 1933 her family moved to Los Angeles, California, as many Oklahomans did during the Depression. She had music and dance lessons, but at 15, she chose to focus on dance. She was a student of Bronislava Nijinska, a former dancer and choreographer with the famed Russian Diaghilev Ballet Company and sister of the legendary Russian male dancer Nijinski. After studying with Nijinska for five years, she joined the Ballet Russe de Monte Carlo and emerged as a soloist in a variety of ballets. One of these was American choreographer George Balanchine's *Serenade.*

In 1946, she married Balanchine and was the inspiration for a number of his famed ballets. Most famous of all was *Firebird,* set to Igor Stravinsky's music, which he created specifically to showcase her technical abilities and unique artistry. She acquired an international reputation when they collaborated in performances at the Paris Opera on their working honeymoon. After their return to the United States, she danced many lead roles with his company, the famed New York City Ballet. She was a dedicated student of ballet and mastered all the demanding roles Balanchine created for her. She also showed amazing endurance, sometimes dancing eight exhausting performances in a week. She was not just a technician; she was also brilliant and captivating on stage.

After their marriage ended, Tallchief continued to dance with the New York City Ballet and then joined the Ballet Russe de Monte Carlo as a guest artist in 1955 and 1956. There she received the highest salary ever paid a dancer. She married a Chicago businessman, Henry (Buzz) Paschen, in 1956, but continued her career, taking her only leave of absence when she gave birth to a daughter, Elise, in 1958. She joined the American Ballet Theatre in 1960 and toured Russia and Eastern and Western Europe under the auspices of the U.S. State Department. She also performed in Asia. She was partnered by the premier male dancers of her time, including André Eglevsky and Denmark's Erik Bruhn. After his defection from Russia, Rudolf Nureyev chose to dance with her in his American debut on television in 1962. They were close friends until his untimely death.

Tallchief retired from the stage at the peak of her career in 1965 to spend more time with her family. She continued to teach ballet and has done educational outreach programs in public schools, particularly in inner-city neighborhoods. Her aim has been to introduce new audiences to the beauty of dance to inspire young people of different racial and ethnic backgrounds to consider dance as a career. In addition, she has devoted more time to Native American affairs, including serving on the board of Americans for Indian Opportunity, an organization founded by La Donna Harris. Despite her own career in a Western art form, she has always been committed to the preservation of Native American culture. In 1975, Tallchief became artistic director and teacher of the Chicago Lyric Opera Ballet. In 1981, she founded the Chicago City Ballet in collaboration with her sister Marjorie (who had a European career in ballet). She served as artistic director of the Chicago Ballet until 1987.

Excerpts from Tallchief's Autobiography, 1997*

> *[Her First Real Teacher: Madame Bronislava Nijinska]*
> The force of Madame Nijinska's personality, and her unwavering devotion to her art, helped me to understand that ballet was what I wanted to do with my life. . . .

*Excerpts from MARIA TALLCHIEF: AMERICA'S PRIMA BALLERINA by Maria Tallchief with Larry Kaplan, © 1997 by Maria Tallchief. Reprinted by permission of Henry Holt and Company, LLC. Excerpts from pp. 17, 58, 123, 130–31, 182–83, 302–303, 324.

. . . Before Nijinska, I liked ballet but believed that I was destined to become a concert pianist; . . . Now my goal was different. Two strong women, my mother and my teacher, were directing my destiny, and I loved them both. . . .

[Her Career and Partnership with Balanchine]

George's statement "Ballet is woman" has been so widely quoted that it's lost some of its meaning, but he believed it and lived it. Women fueled his creativity, fed his inspiration. All his previous wives had been dancers because his life was his work. It was simple, for him and for me.

. . . I understood that our marriage was a working arrangement, and that, although our public and private lives were bound together, the public life would dominate. George never said this in so many words, but he didn't have to. I was his wife, but I was also his ballerina. He was my husband, but he was also my choreographer. He was a poet and I was his muse. . . .

For five years, George and I spent fourteen hours of every day rehearsing and performing; all I had was practice and dance. . . . [O]n the road with Ballet Theatre, I was working so hard that one night my muscles staged a rebellion. In my hotel room after a performance of *Swan Lake,* . . . I lay out on the floor on my back and put my legs up against the wall opposite me, trying to soothe my spasmed muscles and inflamed tendons. Suddenly my feet started twitching and jerking. . . . I tried to get them to stop, but couldn't. I panicked. . . .

Perpetual exhaustion had become a way of life, and I often felt too tired to participate in the simplest activities. The evenings that George and I went out to museums or for dinner . . . I was too drained to enjoy myself. My legs ached when I stood for any length of time, and walking was just as uncomfortable. . . . I wasn't feeling sorry for myself, I loved everything I was doing. But I used to wonder if anyone on earth worked as hard as George and I. I didn't let up, though. I couldn't. . . .

[The Premier of Her Signature Ballet: "Firebird"]

Once the ballet began, I stopped thinking about . . . success or failure. . . . But when we started the pas de deux, I felt secure. Standing upstage, I took an extra breath and then made the flying leap into Frank's arms. Suddenly there I was being held by him upside down, my head practically touching the floor. An audible sigh rose in the audience. . . . It was as if they could barely believe what they had seen. One second before I had been at one end of the stage standing upright, yet now here I was at the other side, suspended in Frank's arms. No one could see how it had been done. I must have flown.

. . . I'd become this magical creature, the Firebird, yet I knew I had become the Firebird because George had made me the Firebird. His genius had never been as clear to me as it was in that instant. When we finished the pas de deux the audience applauded so loudly that Frank and I were stunned. . . .

Then the curtain rose again, and as long as I live I'll never forget the roar. A firestorm of applause erupted in the City Center, and the audience was on its feet clapping, stomping, and shouting. We just stood there, dumbfounded. People were screaming, "Bravo!" shouting themselves hoarse. It was pandemonium. The theater had turned itself into a football stadium, and the audience was in a frenzy . . . every time the curtain came down they started calling out my name until it went up again. . . .

[Women and Ballet in the 1990s]
The irony of George's remark that "ballet is woman" is that most of the companies in the world today are being run by men, former premier danseurs who have found a second life as choreographer, ballet master, and artistic director. Women, on the other hand, are relegated to the sidelines. The contribution former Balanchine ballerinas can make, ballerinas who worked directly with George and who created their roles, isn't being valued, not even in George's own company. Many of us are being excluded from the process of staging his ballets, and it's disappointing; worse, it is damaging to George's legacy.

[Osage Tribute after Washington Press Club "Woman of the Year" Award, 1953]
In the afternoon, Chief Pitts and the Osage Tribal Council held a special ceremony at my father's movie theater during which I was inducted into the tribe with the new title Princess Wa-Xthe-Thonba, Princess Two Standards. Grandma Tall Chief had selected the name. By choosing it she was saying that while I was a ballerina with an important career on the stage, I was also her grandchild, an Osage woman and a daughter of the tribe.

At the conclusion of the formalities, I was presented with the huge, beautiful tribal headdress encrusted with feathers, traditionally worn by men and Osage chiefs. I was also given moccasins, a ceremonial light blue Indian blanket fringed in red, and an official scroll testifying to my new status. As a further honor, I was named Fairfax's Honorary Mayor . . .

The day filled me with pride. I had always acknowledged my heritage. But I was living in a different world now, and it was inspiring to be reminded of my Indian roots. At the same time, proud as I was, it had always been important for me to have people understand that no concessions were ever made for me as a ballerina because of my ethnic background; the same rigorous standards that were applied to every Russian, French, English, or American dancer were equally applied to me.

Above all, I wanted to be appreciated as a prima ballerina who happened to be a Native American, never as someone who was an American Indian ballerina. . . .

[Controversy over Televised Dance Performance for American-Indian Children]
. . . When I walked onstage, the auditorium was empty. . . .

In the end we learned that someone had complained that classical ballet had nothing to do with Indian culture and had prevented the children from attending. . . . Whoever was in charge wanted no part in what he or she saw as Indian culture being infiltrated by a Western art form. It was a sensitive issue, and I understood it. . . .

Today, I see the Indian protest in Chicago as an early instance in the debate about multiculturalism, which is now part of our national discourse. . . .

A part of me sympathized with the point of view of the people who wanted to protect the glories of Native-American culture. I respect and value them too, but I was disappointed, . . . and sorry that the children didn't return for the telecast, because the beauty of ballet shouldn't be denied to anyone.

SUGGESTED READINGS

Literature

Beauvoir, Simone de. *Memoirs of a Dutiful Daughter.* Translated by James Kirkup. Cleveland: World
    Publishing Co., 1959.

Visual Art

Gardner, Margaret. *Barbara Hepworth: A Memoir.* London: Lund Humphries, 1994.
Goldberg, Vicki. *Margaret Bourke-White: A Biography.* New York: Harper & Row, 1986.
Rosenblum, Naomi. *A History of Women Photographers.* New York: Abbeville Press, 1994.

Dance

Aschenbrenner, Joyce. *Katherine Dunham: Dancing a Life.* Urbana: University of Illinois Press, 2002.
De Mille, Agnes. *Martha. The Life and Work of Martha Graham: A Biography.* New York: Random
    House, 1991.
Livingston, Lili Cockerille. *American Indian Ballerinas.* Norman: University of Oklahoma Press, 1997.

Audiovisual Sources

Free to Dance. v.1: "What Do You Dance?" v. 2: "Steps of the Gods." 2001. Produced and directed by
    Madison Davis Lacy. [Dunham and others]. 57 min. each. New York: National Black Program-
    ming Consortium, 2001. Videocassette.
Maria Tallchief: Her Complete Bell Telephone Hour Performances, 1959–1966. 2001. Production of
    Henry Jaffe Enterprises. 45 min. Pleasantville, NY: VAI, 2001. Videocassette.
Martha Graham Dance Company. 1976. Produced by Emile Ardolino. Directed by Merrill Brockway.
    90 min. New York: Nonesuch Records, 1998. Videocassette.

Chapter 13

Reclaiming Their Heritage: Women and Religion

Radical religious initiatives among women in Western Civilization during the nineteenth century constituted the foundation for unprecedented transitions and transformations in religions that ensued particularly in the latter half of the twentieth century and continue into the present. Catalysts for institutional change in the West were prompted by everything from the inestimable consequences of two world wars to an ensuing global awareness and a heightened awareness of racial/ethnic diversity that exists in the context of Euro-centric cultures of the West. The increasing impact of media and information technology on that awareness did not bypass religious institutions.

Despite the continued value placed upon political hegemony and male dominant social institutions in the West, voices that acknowledge human and ecological vulnerability and patterns of economic, social, and political oppression persisted. The need for legal, ethical, and economic accountability continued to be asserted with greater fervor. In the United States, as noted earlier in Part III of this text, the civil rights movement of the 1950s and 1960s created a climate for initiating alternative approaches to social inequities that eventually began to impact organized religion in the United States and abroad. Religious conservatives, in all traditions, who were determined to maintain the status quo resisted change. In the United States their resistance from the mid-1970s forward includes formal and informal initiatives in the political forum. As is true of selections in different disciplines throughout Part III, however, the women whose writings are included in the present chapter were sufficiently motivated to challenge religious and societal norms and to become visible and significant agents for institutional change in religion.

Increased access to higher education for women in the 1960s and 1970s and the advent of the study of religion as an academic discipline outside traditional seminaries were key to women's influence both within and outside religious institutions. Religious Studies emerged as an academic discipline in both private and public institutions of higher learning. This interdisciplinary discipline denotes the critical analytic approach to the study of the world's religious traditions from varieties of perspectives that include the sacred stories, rituals, art, symbol systems, doctrines, organizational structures, mystical traditions, and ethical systems that shape and define them. Feminist women's presence as graduate students, and then as professors, in seminaries, colleges, and universities have been significant in establishing and furthering scholarly inquiry that is increasingly inclusive of the rich diversity of religious expression among women and men in the human community. This diversity explicitly incorporates analyses of economic, political, environmental, and social/cultural influences in religious expression. Factors of social justice in areas of concern that include race/ethnicity, social class, gender, and sexual orientation, among other factors, are also addressed.

Several women-centered methodologies (ways of approaching and analyzing data) have emerged among scholars in Religious Studies since the 1970s that permit an intellectual climate for reclaiming women's history in the world's religious traditions. Women-centered spirituality permits options for women to explore different approaches to spirituality that are personally empowering. Feminist theologies explore various concepts of The Holy, as well as doctrinal and ethical positions that foster human wholeness. Some feminist theologies hearken back to Goddess traditions mentioned in Volume One; the majority, however, are directed to radical change within religious traditions and within all social institutions that legitimate themselves on the basis of patriarchal religious rhetoric.

Principal among changes that have occurred within religious traditions are the challenges posed by female seminary students and the subsequent ordination of these students as priests, ministers, bishops, teachers, rabbis, cantors, professors, and pastoral counselors. Some women ministers faithfully preach and teach from the point of view of accepted doctrines within established religious traditions. Some women ministers integrate a point of view that is more inclusive than traditional theologies envision or necessarily encourage.

Women's celebration of: solstices, bat mitzvahs, legal protection for the right to personal choices concerning their bodies, wilderness retreats, sweat lodges, and thousands of Circles of women who share women-centered spirituality are only a few of the newly appropriated spiritual practices among women. Greater agency and voice for women in matters personal, private, and political characterize the religious life of increasing numbers of women. Women's agency and initiative in staging global protests and interventions by women against war, environmental, human, and animal abuses, as well as personal, economic, and political inequities, are commonly rooted in spiritual, ethical, and religious convictions. These interventions are just a few of the ways that women have made and continue to make a positive difference in the world. By the beginning of the twenty-first century C.E. there exist literally thousands of women whose writings about religion and spirituality are published and disseminated worldwide. The extensive breadth of this literature makes it impossible to include any more than a representative sample in the present chapter. The three overarching and interrelated sections of this chapter pertain to women's history, women's spirituality, and women's theology and ethics.

FEMINIST THE(A)OLOGIES AND ETHICS

A maxim in feminist scholarship is that practice should inform theory, rather than the other way around. That means that feminist theologies are intentionally grounded in women's experience. Two additional areas of consideration in formulating feminist theologies and ethics include: (1) the dominance of Eurocentric theological and philosophical models that are grounded in a dualistic world-view; and (2) the implications for women of exclusively male god-language, imagery, and symbol systems.

The philosophical and political roots of dualistic world-views are discussed in some detail in Volume One (Chapters 7, 8, and 11). The principal issue for feminist thought occurs when dualistic world-views are presented and understood hierarchically. To say that spirit and matter co-exist is not a matter of consequence. However, when spirit and matter are posited as opposites and the higher value is attributed to spirit, seeds are sown that can, eventually, result in the mindless destruction of earth's ecosystems. In a hierarchically orchestrated dualism when the female is equated with nature and matter, and culture and spirit are equated with the male, the female is objectified (seen as object) as "less than." In Western Civilization this has been the case. The male-centered language, imagery, and symbol systems associated with God in the patriarchal, hierarchical religious systems in Western culture legitimate the objectifying and subjugating of women. Little formal resistance to this state of affairs has been voiced since its inception in Classical Greek culture some 2,500 years ago. Political systems, governance structures, practices, and policies in the West that legitimate themselves as consistent with religious principles reinforce women's subjugation and oppression in public and private spheres.

With a few notable exceptions, after the mid-twentieth century, the first women to formally address issues of women's subjugation in religion were themselves members of the privileged social hierarchy to whom higher education and advanced degrees were becoming more accessible. Within two decades, however, the situation gradually began to change and recognition of the vital importance of the voices of *all* women became increasingly central to women's movement. Today feminist theologies, ethics, and spiritualities address issues of social, political, and economic justice. Concerns of inequities incurred on the basis of race, ethnicity, gender, social class, age, sexual preference, or physical challenges are informed by perspectives rooted in the experience of an extensive and expanding diversity of women.

Rosemary Radford Ruether (1936–)

Rosemary Radford Ruether is foremost among Christian feminist theologians in the twentieth century. She is a Catholic feminist theologian and presently teaches in the Graduate Theological Union in Berkeley, California. Her advanced degrees in Philosophy (B.A.), Ancient History (M.A.), and Classics and Patristics (Ph.D.) are foundational for scholarship on the interrelation of Christian theology and history to social justice issues, including sexism, racism, poverty, militarism, ecology, and interfaith relations that are integral to her feminist theology.

A prolific author, Professor Ruether's publications are numerous and address such issues as feminist theology, religious nationalism, eco-feminism, and women in developing countries.

She has lectured at universities and church-related organizations around the world, and contributed regularly to religiously oriented journals such as the *National Catholic Reporter* and *Sojourners*. Principal among her interests is the expansion of global feminism.

Ruether is a supporter of and spokesperson for Women-Church. This feminist organization that began in the 1980s among Roman Catholic women has spread abroad and proliferated among women who seek spirituality that specifically addresses women's spiritual concerns, understanding that these concerns include personal, economic, social, and political issues. Women-Church gatherings use gender-inclusive language and develop ritual celebrations that represent the all-encompassing fullness of spiritual women's lives. The excerpt included here is from a sermon delivered by Professor Ruether to participants at the national conference of the Women of the Church Coalition in November of 1983 in Chicago.

THEOLOGICAL REFLECTION ON WOMEN-CHURCH*

> What does it mean theologically to be Women-Church? That is what I want us to think together about. How can women, the excluded half of the human race, the excluded gender from the tradition of the Church claim to *be* Church, claim to speak as Church? Is this not, in the most basic sense, schismatic, sectarian, breaking the whole into only one of its parts, tearing the "seamless robe of Catholic unity," as the fathers are wont to say? I would contend today that we as women can indeed speak as

*Excerpts from Rosemary Radford Ruether, *Women-Church: Theology and Practice of Feminist Liturgical Communities* (San Francisco: Harper and Row Publishers, 1988), pp. 69–70, 72–73.

Church, do speak as Church, not in exile from the Church, but rather that the Church is in exile with us, awaiting with us a wholeness that we are in process of revealing.

First of all, to speak as Women-Church means we speak to denounce, to cry out against the smothering of Church in the temples of patriarchy. We have a controversy with the representatives of patriarchy who claim to be the authentic spokesmen of the Church. We say that the temples of patriarchy have disfigured and hidden our true Mother and Teacher, and replaced her with a great mechanical idol with flashing eyes and smoking nostrils who spews out blasphemies and lies. What does this idol say? How speaks this monstrous robot of the temples of patriarchy? Let us recall the words that come from its mouth, the deeds that come from its hand.

This is the idol of masculinity, the idol of father-rule. And it claims all the earth as the creation and domain of father-rule. It monopolizes the image of God, claiming that God can only be spoken by the name of Patriarch, can only be imaged in the image of Father-rule. God is Sovereign, King, Warrior, God of Power and Might, who magnifies the rule of the powerful and abases the degradation of the lowly, who gives the scepter to the mighty and teaches the little ones of the earth to cower in fear and self-hatred. This God is not to be imaged as Mother, as Helper, as Friend, as Liberator. It cannot be imaged in the faces of women, or children, of the poor, of the timid and gentle creatures of the earth. . . .

As Women-Church we repudiate this idol of patriarchy. We repudiate it and denounce it in the name of God, in the name of Christ, in the name of Church, in the name of humanity, in the name of earth. Our God and Goddess, who is mother and father, friend, lover, and helper, did not create this idol and is not represented by this idol. Our brother Jesus did not come to this earth to manufacture this idol, and he is not represented by this idol. The message and mission of Jesus, the child of Mary, which is to put down the mighty from their thrones and uplift the lowly, is not served by this idol. Rather, this idol blasphemes by claiming to speak in the name of Jesus and to carry out his redemptive mission, while crushing and turning to its opposite all that he came to teach. In its hands, his transformative redemptive mission is overturned or, rather, turned back to the ways of Babylon. The *first* shall be first and *last* shall be last. This is the way God made the world, and this is the way it shall ever be. The powers and principalities of rape, genocide, and war achieve their greatest daring by claiming to be Christ, to represent Christ's mission. The Roman Empire clothes itself in the mantle of the crucified and seats itself anew upon its imperial throne.

As Women-Church we cry out: Horror, blasphemy, deceit, foul deed! This is not the voice of our God, the face of our Redeemer, the mission of our Church. Our humanity is not and cannot be represented here, but it is excluded in this dream, this nightmare, of salvation. As Women-Church we claim the authentic mission of Christ, the true mission of Church, the real agenda of our Mother-Father God who comes to restore and not to destroy our humanity, who comes to ransom the captives and to reclaim the earth as our Promised Land. We are not in exile, but the Church is in exodus with us. God's Shekinah, Holy Wisdom, the Mother-face of God has fled from the high thrones of patriarchy and has gone into exodus with us. She is with us as we flee from the smoking altars where women's bodies are sacrificed, as we cover our ears to blot out the inhuman voice that comes forth from the idol of patriarchy.

As Women-Church we are not left to starve for the words of wisdom, we are not left without the bread of life. Ministry too goes with us into exodus. We learn all over again what it means to minister, not to lord over, but to minister to and with each other, to teach each other to speak the words of life. Eucharist comes with us into exodus. The waters of baptism spring up in our midst as the waters of life, and the tree of life grows in our midst with fruits and flowers. We pluck grain and make bread; harvest grapes and make wine. And we pass them around as the body and blood of our new life, the life of the new humanity that has been purchased by the bloodly struggles of our martyrs, by the bloodly struggle of our brother Jesus, and of Perpetua and Felicitas, and of all the women who were burned and beaten and raped, and of Jean Donovan and Maura Clarke and Ita Ford and Dorothy Kazel, and of the women of Guatemala, Honduras, El Salvador, and Nicaragua who struggle against the leviathan of patriarchy and imperialism. This new humanity has been purchased by their blood, by their lives, and we dare to share the fruits of their victory together in hope and faith that they did not die in vain. But they have risen, they are rising from the dead. They are present with us as we share this sacrament of the new humanity, as we build together this new earth freed from the yoke of patriarchy.

Ada María Isasi-Díaz (1943–)

Professor Isasi-Díaz, a Christian ethicist, is widely known for her work in *mujerista* theology and for establishing the Hispanic Institute of Theology at the Graduate and Theological Schools of Drew University. Isasi-Díaz is recognized as an eminent scholar and is one of the most widely recognized Latina feminist theologians. Her interest to further the Latina perspective in Christian feminist theologies remains a principal objective and is furthered significantly by the initiatives and foundational principles of the Hispanic Institute of Theology.

In the following article Professor Isasi-Díaz addresses the question of biblical interpretation for the *mujerista*. She carefully distinguishes the vast variety of social and cultural perspectives that comprise the *mujerista* audiences for whom she writes. Cautioning the reader against facile assumptions, Isasi-Díaz outlines specific factors that must be taken into consideration in understanding how Scriptural texts might be appropriated among Hispanic women.

MUJERISTA BIBLICAL INTERPRETATION FROM *LA PALABRA DE DIOS NOSOTRAS—THE WORD OF GOD IN US**

Elsewhere we have begun to articulate the main elements of a critical *mujerista* interpretation of the Bible. We present them here briefly. First, there exists a Hispanic *mestizo* Christianity, heavily influenced by the Catholicism of the *conquistadores,* a religious practice with little biblical content. To this were added religious understandings and practices of African and Amerindian religions. As Protestant and evangelical traditions are now becoming part of the religious understandings and

---

*From Ada María Isasi-Díaz, "La Palabra de Dios Nosotras—The Word of God in Us," in *Searching the Scriptures,* ed. Elisabeth Schussler Fiorenza (New York: Crossroad, 1993), pp. 86, 87, 94.

practices of an increasing number of Latinas, we need to find a way to appropriate into our *mestizo* Christianity the central elements of these traditions as they are understood and practiced by Hispanic women. The centrality of the Bible in these faith traditions, the influence they have in the dominant culture, and the number of Latinas who are becoming members of Protestant and evangelical churches indicate the urgency of articulating a *mujerista* biblical interpretation.

Second, Hispanic women's experience and our struggle for survival, not the Bible, are the source of our theology and the starting point for how we should interpret, appropriate, and use the Bible. A great number of Latinas do not consult the Bible in our daily lives. The complexity of the biblical writings, the variety of messages, and the differences in socio-historical and political-economic context make it difficult for us to use the Bible. When we need help we find it not in the Bible but in praying to God, Mary, the saints—all part of the divine—to whom Hispanic women have the direct access they do not have to the Bible, which needs interpretation.

Third, the critical lens of *mujerista* theology is liberation. For us liberation is synonymous with survival, both physical and cultural. As *mujerista* theology struggles to discern how to appropriate and use the Bible, we must apply to it the same liberative lens that we use in all our theological work. Therefore, from the start we can say that *mujerista* biblical hermeneutics accepts the Bible as part of divine revelation and as authoritative only insofar as it contributes to Hispanic women's struggle for liberation.

Two caveats are in order here. For the great majority of Hispanic women, the marginal way they deal with the Bible is not intentional. We do not reject the Bible; we simply do not use it or we use it very sparingly and selectively. Second, since Hispanic women's lived experience is the source of *mujerista* theology, the task of *mujerista* theologians is to articulate the religious practice of Hispanic women. We do this to help our communities understand how their religious beliefs operate in our daily lives. Our task is to analyze those practices through a liberative lens and to evaluate them in view of the liberation of Hispanic women. Because *mujerista* theologians are an integral part of the Latina community, part of our task is to participate with the community in deciding how Hispanic women will relate to and use the Bible from now on. . . .

Mujerista biblical hermeneutics, our biblical interpretation, has as its goal the survival—the liberation—of Hispanic women. Therefore, our biblical interpretation, appropriation, and usage are tools in our struggle for survival. We have to be clear that for us Latinas, as members of a community engaged in a process of concientization, committed to enhancing our moral agency, and claiming our right to be agents of our own history, the final word on the interpretation, appropriation, and use of the Bible in our struggle for survival and liberation is ours. If not, the Bible can indeed become or continue to be a weapon in the hands of those who benefit from the oppression of Hispanic women.

Carter Heyward (1946–)

Most of Carter Heyward's life has been about embodying the equitable justice that she envisions for women everywhere. She is a lesbian, a feminist, and an Episcopal priest who has, in her very person, shattered many barriers to women's liberation. She presently spends half of each academic year at her retreat center in the North Carolina mountains near Asheville, and the other part of the year as the Howard Chandler Robbins Professor of Theology at the Episcopal Divinity School in Cambridge, Massachusetts.

She earned a B.A. in religion at Randolph-Macon Woman's College in 1967 and then studied at Columbia University/Union Theological Seminary, where she earned an M.A. in comparative religions (1971), a Masters of Divinity in religion and psychiatry (1973), and a Ph.D. in systematic theology (1980). In 1974 Heyward was among the first eleven women in the United States to be ordained an Episcopal priest, and in 1998 she received the Distinguished Alumni/ae Award from Union Theological Seminary.

The depth and breadth of Heyward's profound journey is represented in the autobiographical element that is vitally present in her writing. Her publications address such issues as feminist Christology, compassion and relationship, gender, justice, and images of power, sexuality, and liberation. Some of the core values that shape and inform Carter Heyward's quest for justice are represented in this brief selection from a publication in 1989.

POEM AND COMMENTARY FROM *TOUCHING OUR STRENGTH**

I had to prepare for this and
not just by reading Lorde and Weeks
    and Raymond
or my own stuff
I had to do more than think
about "sexuality" "theology" "ethics"

in order to come to this

I had to connect with you
through memories fantasies humor
and struggle
sometimes touching
often amazing
always worthy of respect

in order to come

I had to get myself some daffodils
and wait for them to open
and I had to lie down beside by old dog
    Teraph
and rub some comfort into his worn out
    legs
and make myself some Mocha Java decaf
with just enough milk to cut the acid

and then I had to sit for the longest time
and remember
Denise   ANC   Black Sash
South Africa
and I had to ask myself how
we are connected to these movements
for survival and joy
and I had to believe that we are

in order to come

I had to write a poem
about hiding some sisters and their cats
    from the fascists
a love poem it was
and then hold in my heart an image of
    my month-old niece
my namesake whom I love and have not
    seen
and spend some painstaking time with
    friends
and playful time as well
and I had to be alone for a good long
    while
for my roots to secure

*From Carter Heyward, *Touching Our Strength: The Erotic as Power and the Love of God* (San Francisco: Harper & Row, 1989), pp. 1–3, 17–18.

in order to come

I had to make love
and if I had not had a precious woman
to caress my lusty flesh
and bring me open not only to her
but to myself and you
I still would have had to find a way
to enter more fully

the warm   dark   moisture
of One in whose hunger
for survival and passion
for friends   and movement
for justice   and yearning
for touch and pleasure
we are becoming
ourselves.

This book is not about either sex or God as these terms have denoted particular traditional points of reference: to male and female reproductive/pleasure organs and their manipulation, or to an anthropomorphized deity to whom we ascribe absolute power. It is about sex and God as we are able to re-image both as empowering sparks of ourselves in relation. In the lexicon of these pages, *sexual* refers to our embodied relational response to erotic/sacred power, and *theology* to a critical reflection on the shape of the Sacred in our life together.

The presuppositions that we live in a relational matrix with one another in the world (regardless of what we may think about it or how we may feel about it), and that we have a common response/ability to live in mutual relation, provide the impetus for feminist/womanist liberation theology among jewish, christian, postchristian, and pagan women and men. Feminist liberation theologians are certainly diverse in our opinions on such issues as images and names of the divine; scriptural authority; the redemptive role and meaning of such figures as Jesus; and the viability of traditional patriarchal institutions as places within which women can remain healthy and creative. Nonetheless, we speak in unison of the primacy of justice, or right relation, as the goal and purpose of our life together on the earth.

Some of us identify this justice with the "righteousness" of the bond between Creator and creatures as well as between and among creatures. For all of us, friendship is a basic way to experience and envision justice. And many of us, feminist and womanist liberation theologians, understand right relation or justice to be a *mutual* relation that generates joy and justice and a desire for more of the relation. All feminist/womanist liberation theologians hold images of right relation as both impetus and goal of the various interrelated movements against oppression and unjust death and for justice and joy.

In this spirit, feminist/womanist liberation theologians experience and celebrate our connectedness to contemporary movements for justice for people of color in the United States and elsewhere; for a more fully socialized and humanizing economic order; for liberation of such countries as Nicaragua, Korea, and South Africa from the tyranny imposed by United States–backed interests; for women of all colors and cultures—our rights to ourbodies/ourselves and to decent, dignified conditions in which to bear and raise children free of filth and violence; for full access to life for differently abled men, women, and children; and for senior people among us (indeed, for ourselves as we age), that all of us may experience ourselves as worthy of respect, friendship, meaningful work, and good play; and for gaymen and lesbians who struggle not merely for tolerance or pity but for affirmation and celebration of our sensual, sexual, loving selves-in-relation.

Ten years ago I was preparing to write my doctoral thesis, and I had decided to try my hand at a constructive "relational theology." My interest had been stimulated by a series of questions that had emerged as I studied the experiences and questions of Elie Wiesel, a "survivor" of the Holocaust. I found myself wrestling with such questions as these: In a world in which evil continues to spread like wildfire over the earth, wreaking terror and abuse, what can we do? How do we know what is good and what is evil in the small, daily places of our lives? How can we liberate ourselves, with one another's help, from evil? What visions do we need to inspire our struggle?

Such questions haunted me then, and they still do. I suspect they always will. Their presence reminds me of a relational spark in myself that I know to be my soul—the core of myself in relation or, from a more traditional perspective, "the seat of God" within me.

In struggling to come to terms with the pervasiveness of evil in our life together—for example with anti-Semitism, racism, heterosexism, economic exploitation, and their violent interconnections—I have become increasingly interested in probing the character of that which is radically good in our commonlife: our power in mutual relation as the basis of our creative and liberating possibilities, literally the only basis of our hope for the world. This interest has produced this sexual theology. *For, at its core, this book is about nurturing and cultivating the goodness in our lives.*

And as we nurture our common goodness, are we better able to deal with evil? Are we wiser, more courageous, more patient with ourselves and others in this world as we learn to take seriously our power for touching the Sacred, our power for creating and sustaining right relation? Does this strengthen our desire, commitment, and ability to make no peace with oppression? Does the experience of mutuality teach us more fully what it means to live serenely—in quiet confidence that, regardless of the toll of violence, betrayal, and evil in our lives, nothing can separate us from the power of good, the power in right relation, which christians and other theists may choose to name "the love of God"?

This book is shaped in the matrix of such questions. I do not know the answers, and I cannot find them by myself. We work together, you and I. We help each other learn to risk, in gentle measure, a day at a time, involving ourselves more fully in healing the splits within, between, and among us. We call each other forth, daring to touch our strength: to participate, with confidence, with awe, and with one another, in the ongoing redemption of God.

Following my earlier academic effort to write personally rather than abstractly, the form of this book also is often more conversational, invitational, and imaginative than expository. Its intellectual roots are in a critical, reflective matrix of spiritual struggle; theological study; social analysis; political commitment; personal passions, fears, dreams, biases; and, of course, in the many relationships that continue to form and reform my capacities to love, learn, and work.

Rita M. Gross

Rita M. Gross is a professor of religion at the University of Wisconsin at Eau Claire and has been on the cutting edge of feminist scholarship since its inception. Among her most significant contributions is her scholarship on Buddhism, specifically as articulated concerning relationships between Buddhism and feminism. Professor Gross is widely published and has lectured extensively about feminism and religion. Her numerous publications reflect this emphasis and include: *Feminism and Religion: An Introduction; Soaring and Settling: Buddhist Perspectives on Contemporary Social and Religious Issues;* and *Religious Diversity: Some Implications for Monotheism.* The selection that follows is a short yet succinct introduction to some of the themes that Professor Gross addresses concerning a nexus between Buddhism and feminism.

EXCERPTS FROM *BUDDHISM AFTER PATRIARCHY**

BUDDHISM *IS* FEMINISM

Some women involved in both Buddhism and feminism simply say "Buddhism *is* feminism!" by which they express intuitively the conviction that when Buddhism is true to itself, it manifests the same vision as does feminism. Though the statement that Buddhism is feminism strikes deep chords in me, the opposite claim, that feminism is Buddhism, could not be made. First, feminism is a broad movement, and not all feminists end up with any spiritual orientation. Certainly they need not be or become Buddhists to be true to the vision of feminism, as Buddhism must, explicitly or implicitly, be "feminist" in order to be true to its vision. Secondly, some versions of feminism, the more militant or separatist versions of feminism would be difficult to reconcile with Buddhism. One could well sympathize with someone, unaware that such versions of feminism are not the feminist norm or vision, who balked at the claim than Buddhism is feminism.

Nevertheless, the intuition that Buddhism *is* feminism, when systematized, is a major resource for a Buddhist feminism. At least four profound similarities between the fundamental orientations of Buddhism and of feminism strengthen the claim the Buddhism is feminism.

First, contrary to most of the Western philosophical and theological heritage, both Buddhism and feminism begin with experience, stress experiential understanding enormously, and move from experience to theory, which becomes the expression of experience. Both share the approach that conventional views and dogmas are worthless if experience does not actually bear out theory. In other words, in a conflict between one's experience of one's world and what one has been taught by others about the world, both feminism and Buddhism agree that one cannot deny or repress experience.

*From Rita M. Gross, *Buddhism after Patriarchy: A Feminist History, Analysis, and Reconstruction of Buddhism* (Albany, NY: State University of New York Press, 1993), (Delhi, India: Sri Satguru Publications, 1993), pp. 130–131.

Allegiance to experience before theory leads to a second important similarity between Buddhism and feminism, the will and the courage to go against the grain at any cost, and to hold to insights of truth, no matter how bizarre they seem from a conventional point to view. In its core teachings about the lack of external salvation (non-theism), about the non-existence of a permanent abiding self (non-ego), and about the pervasiveness and richness of suffering, Buddhism goes against the grain of what religions generally promise. Yet Buddhists continue to see these unpopular religious insights as the only way to attain liberation "beyond hope and fear."* Feminism's equally unconventional and unpopular truths about gender arrangements lead many to ridicule, scorn, or misrepresent it as nothing but the emotional outbursts of a group of unbalanced women who can't conform gracefully to their "natural place." In a time of backlash, it becomes all the more common to read letters to the editor and columns proclaiming "the failure of feminism," or claiming that feminism is responsible for the woes of economic decline, drug abuse, and domestic violence. Such unreasoned attempts to dismiss feminism's prophetic proclamations against conventional gender privilege and hierarchy make the courage and humor displayed by battle-weary veterans of the first attempts to introduce feminist discourse all the more remarkable.

Thirdly, both perspectives use their willingness to hold to experience over convention and theory and their tenacious courage to explore how mental constructs operate to block or enhance liberation. For Buddhism, this exploration has involved the study of conventional ego, its painful habitual tendencies, and the underlying freedom of the basic egoless state. For feminism, this exploration involves looking into ways in which the social conditioning that produces gender stereotypes and conventional gender roles trap both women and men in half-humanity, encouraging mutual incompetence and threatening to destroy the planet. However, mingled with this fundamental similarity is a basic difference, to be explored more fully in later chapters. Buddhism has never looked deeply into gender conventions as an aspect of *samsaric,* pain-filled ego. Feminism, so caught up in immediate needs, often lacks an ability to convey the deep peace beyond ego. Nevertheless, beneath these important differences is the more profound similarity of outlook. Both Buddhism and feminism explore how habitual ego patterns block basic well-being.

Finally, both perspectives speak of liberation as the point of human existence, the aim toward which all existence strains. The language conceptualizing liberation is specifically different in the two perspectives. For Buddhism, the language wavers between seeing liberation as freedom from the world and freedom within the world—an important internal ambiguity within Buddhism. . . . For feminism the definition of liberation is clearer—freedom from gender roles and gender stereotypes. But to focus on these differences of language and conceptualization is to miss the point. Feminism, like Buddhism and like all other visions of the human spirit,

---

*The Buddhist insight that one needs to transcend not only fear but hope to attain spiritual maturity has long puzzled Christians, who have been taught that hope is a great virtue and saviour. But Buddhism claims that spiritual freedom is found only when we are able to accommodate what is happening, that so long as we hope that things could be different, we are enslaved to our hopes and fearful that they might not be realized. Thus hope and fear are seen as interdependent and interchangeable.

looks beyond the immediate and compelling entrapments of easy solutions and conventional perspectives to the radical freedom of transcending those entrapments.

WOMEN-CENTERED INTERPRETIVE FRAMEWORKS FOR RECLAIMING WOMEN'S HISTORY IN RELIGION

The following selections provide a representative illustration of methodological approaches to reclaiming women's history in religions. The traditions that are explored and the types of questions that are addressed to the historical record represent just a few of the many that constitute women's quest to know, understand, and re-appropriate for themselves positive, affirming, and empowering aspects of religious traditions. These methods also equip women and men to identify, critique, and seek ways to eradicate aspects of religious traditions that legitimize human oppression, subjugation, abuse/denial of personal freedoms, and a woman's positive understandings of herself in relation to The Holy.

Elisabeth Schüssler Fiorenza (1938–)

Elisabeth Schüssler Fiorenza is a pioneer in the area of feminist biblical scholarship. She is the Krister Stendahl Chair of Divinity at Harvard University in Cambridge, Massachusetts. She was born in Bavaria and earned degrees in Christian theology in Germany: Theologicum (Masters of Divinity), University of Würzburg, Lic Theol. at University of Würzburg, and Doctor of Theology at the University of Münst. Original scholarship in her formidable work, *In Memory of Her* (New York: Crossroad, 1984), established Schüssler Fiorenza as the foremost twentieth-century scholar of women in the New Testament world. She was the first female president of the Society of Biblical Literature (1987) and is co-founder and co-editor of the *Journal of Feminist Studies in Religion.* Her teaching and research focus on questions of biblical and theological epistemology, hermeneutics, rhetoric, and the politics of interpretation, as well as on issues of theological education, radical equality, and democracy.

In a brief article published in 1979, "Women in the Early Christian Movement" in *Womanspirit Rising* (Christ and Plaskow 1979, 84-92), Schüssler Fiorenza introduced, from a feminist-critical perspective, significant named and unnamed female figures in the biblical world from the first two centuries of the Common Era. Her article served as a catalyst for many burgeoning feminist scholars of religion.

Following Schüssler Fiorenza, and sometimes challenging her from the perspective of their own emerging methodologies and theology, numerous feminist historians of the Hebrew Testament and the Christian Testament are developing approaches to historical and theological analysis that are critical to retrieving women's history in religion.

We have highlighted the conclusion of her article for the Christian Century Foundation's *How My Mind Has Changed* Series that provides a sense of Schüssler Fiorenza's personal assessment of her journey as scholar and theologian from the 1960s through the 1980s.

EXCERPTS FROM *CHANGING THE PARADIGMS**

> *Ekklesia,* the Greek word for church, describes the democratic assembly of full citizens responsible for the welfare of the city-state. To link ekklesia or church with

*Excerpts from Elisabeth Schüssler Fiorenza, "Changing the Paradigms," in *How My Mind Has Changed* Series. Copyright by The Christian Century Foundation, December, 1990, pp. 799–800. Used by permission. This article was prepared for Religion Online by Ted and Winnie Brock.

women makes explicit that women are church and always have been church. It asserts that women have shaped biblical religion and have the authority to do so. It insists on the understanding and vision of church as the discipleship of equals. Thus women-church is not to be understood in exclusive, sectarian terms. Rather, it is a hermeneutical feminist perspective and linguistic consciousness-raising tool that seeks to define theologically what church is all about. . . . Women of color have always insisted that white feminist theory must relinquish its dualistic conceptualization of patriarchy as the supremacy of all men and the equal victimization of all women and develop a feminist analysis that could uncover the inter-structuring of sexism, racism, colonialism and class-exploitation in women's lives . . . Modern civil rights and liberation movements thus can be understood as struggles against patriarchal deformations of democracy. The feminist movement in society and biblical religion prevails at the center of these struggles. Such a political re-conceptualization of patriarchy allows one to distinguish between patriarchy and gender dualism, patriarchy and sexism. It helps one to conceptualize women's struggles for "civil rights" in the church and for our theological authority to shape Christian faith and community as an important part of women's liberation struggles around the globe.

This political re-conceptualization of patriarchy and women's struggle had three important implications for my work as a biblical scholar. It allowed me to re-conceptualize the study of "women in the Bible," by moving from what men have said about women to a feminist historical reconstruction of early Christian origins as well as by articulating a feminist critical process for reading and evaluating androcentric biblical texts. Such a critical feminist re-conceptualization challenges the androcentric frameworks of the discipline as a whole.

First: The historical-political analysis of patriarchy and the struggles for democracy provided a reconstructive model that could make the agency and struggles of women historically visible. . . . Such a feminist reconstruction of Christian origins requires a disciplined historical imagination that can make women visible not only as victims but also as agents.

Second: Insofar as the Bible encodes both the "democratic" vision of equality in the Spirit as well as the injunctions to patriarchal submission as the "Word of God," its interpretation must begin with a *hermeneutics of suspicion* that can unravel the patriarchal politics inscribed in the biblical text . . . feminist interpretation must develop a *hermeneutics of critical evaluation for proclamation* that is able to assess theologically whether scriptural texts function to inculcate patriarchal values, or whether they must be read against their linguistic "androcentric grain" in order to set free their liberating vision for today and for the future.

Third: The development of a feminist reconstructive-historical model as well as of a critical hermeneutics for liberation would not have been possible without the theoretical contributions of feminist historians, literary critics and political philosophers. . . . Only when religious and biblical studies decenter their stance of objectivist positivism and scientific value-detachment and become "engaged" scholarship can feminist and other liberation theologies participate in defining the center of the discipline. Not the posture of value-detachment and apolitical objectivism but the articulation of one's social location, interpretive strategies and theoretical frameworks are appropriate in such a rhetorical paradigm of theological studies.

> Whereas in the '70s my "public image" was marked by scholarly bifurcation . . . among scholars I was known as an "expert" on the Apocalypse and among women as an emerging feminist theologian—this perception has changed dramatically in the '80s. While some regret the "ideological deviation" tarnishing my scholarly reputation, many take pride in and draw courage from my theological work. As Dorothy L. Sayers puts it: "Time and trouble will tame an advanced young woman, but an advanced old woman is uncontrollable by any earthly force." It is gratifying not to have been tamed.

Feminist scholars of the New Testament world are indebted to Elisabeth Schüssler-Fiorenza not only for the legacy of her extensive research and numerous publications but also for her generosity that is indeed an embodiment of feminist spirituality. As the cofounder of *The Journal of Feminist Studies in Religion* and in numerous other initiatives, Schüssler-Fiorenza is an ardent supporter and creator of opportunities for burgeoning, and established female scholars alike. This is evident in the American Academy of Religion and the Society for Biblical Literature and in colleges, universities, and scholarly organizations globally. Elisabeth Schüssler-Fiorenza has furthered numerous initiatives that highlight scholarship in feminist studies of women in the biblical world and feminist theologies. She was also a founding figure in establishing the doctoral program in Feminist Liberation Theology at the Episcopal Divinity School in Cambridge Massachusetts in the early 1980s. The two-volume work, *Searching the Scriptures,* published by Crossroads in 1994 and 1995 again attests to Schüssler-Fiorenza's commitment to feminist scholars, feminist scholarship, and her devotion to articles that represent a rich variety of approaches to a feminist critical hermeneutic (interpretive framework) in research on women in the New Testament world. Schüssler-Fiorenza's introduction to that work articulates indebtedness to Elizabeth Cady Stanton and the publication of *The Woman's Bible* among present-day feminist scholars of the Bible. Volume 2 of *Searching the Scriptures* includes commentaries on canonical and extra-canonical texts from the New Testament world.

Riffat Hassan

Born into a Saiyyad Muslim family living in Lahore, Pakistan, Riffat Hassan is the granddaughter of a well-known playwright, poet, and scholar, Hakim Ahmad Shuja. She was educated in an Anglican missionary school in Lahore and pursued advanced studies at St. Mary's College, University of Durham, England. At St. Mary's she graduated with honors in English and philosophy from the University of Durham in 1964 and obtained her Ph.D. from the University of Durham in 1968 for a thesis on the philosophy of the outstanding modern Muslim poet-philosopher Muhammad Iqbal.

Riffat Hassan is a feminist scholar of Islam whose position as an advocate for female victims of violence in Pakistan has brought international acclaim. Dr. Hassan, a devout Muslim, has analyzed Quranic texts concerning women and has pointed out the distinctions between the texts as they are written and the manner in which they are interpreted within patriarchal cultures. She has lived in the United States since 1972 and teaches in the Department of Religious Studies at the University of Louisville in Kentucky. She has published widely and is sought as a speaker on women in Islam at international conferences on human rights. In 1999 she established the International Network for the Rights of Female Victims of Violence in Pakistan. Most recently, with the encouragement of supporters around the globe, she founded WEBB, Women Engaged in Bridge Building. Enhancing understanding and communication between the Muslim and non-Muslim world is the major focus adopted by this international organization. The following selection is from a series of three interviews with Dr. Hassan published by *Newsline* in 2001.

EXCERPTS FROM INTERVIEW WITH DR. RIFFAT HASSAN*

Q: There is a common perception that the status of women in Islam is a relationship of unequals. Will you comment?

A: I began my study on women in Islam in 1974. I realised very soon that there was a big gap in what the Quran was saying about women's rights and what was actually happening in Muslim culture. So one has to distinguish between Quranic text and the Islamic tradition. Quranic Arabic is like Chaucerian English and is in itself a specialised subject. The interpretation of the Quran from the earliest times till now has been done almost entirely by men. It was also done in a male-dominated patriarchal culture. So the Quran was interpreted through a male-centric cultural lens—which obviously has affected women's rights. What I have been trying to do for the past 25 years is to look at the text without a patriarchal bias and in terms of a linguistic and philosophical analysis. One of the most debated verses in the Quran, Chapter 4, Surah al Nissa verse 34, which says "men are appointed . . . " the crucial word here is "qawwamun." All the Urdu translations that I have read have translated that word as "hakim"—which means sovereign, which immediately has connotations of a master-slave relationship. But if you look at the root of the word, it is "qamma," which means to help something stand up, or to support. To the most accurate meaning of this word would be someone who gives economic support. So just that one word, depending on its translation, brings you to a different ending. And there are many such words that have been translated universally with a patriarchal slant. For instance even more basic is the creation of man. Again in Surah al Nissa it says, "And God created from her, her mate." Now there is no translation in the world that says that. All of them say "From him, his mate." There are many references in the Quran on creation and the term used is "*nafs-i-wahidatin*" meaning created from one being. *Nafs* in Arabic is a feminine noun, but has been mistranslated by most translators as masculine. So it is all about the politics of language. Surely all the great Arab scholars can differentiate between feminine and masculine in Arabic grammar?

Q: Are you saying all the great Arabic scholars have deliberately misinterpreted the Quran?

A: In the earlier centuries there was much more freedom in terms of interpretation. Imam Bokhari, the greatest collector of Hadith, for instance, translated "kavamool," as an economic support term, which is very interesting because later it was not translated like that. So even though there was chauvinism and a patriarchal bias, there was diversity of interpretation unlike the rigidity that prevails today. There is a consensus among the scholars of Hadith, beginning from Imam Bokhari to the present, that the vast majority of the Hadith is not authentic. Out of the six hundred thousand Hadith that Imam Bokhari examined, he authenticated less than 3000. So if the vast majority of the Hadith are not the words of the Prophet (PBUH), then what are they? They essentially reflect the Arab cultural ideas of the 7th and 8th centuries.

Q: The moot point in today's context seems to be to reinterpret the Quran through ijtihad and relate it to the modern world. This is not being implemented.

*Excerpts from Samina Ibraham, Interview with Dr. Riffat Hassan, *Newsline*. Karachi, Pakistan (April 2001), pp. 84–85, 87–88.

A: Ijma means collective so if a Muslim community is confronted by some problem, the community has to reach a consensus. Obviously this means knowledgeable people and whatever they come up with is binding on the community of that time. What has closed the doors for our legal system is that the early Islamic jurists proclaimed that the four schools of Islamic law were binding on Muslims for all times. This is what Allama Iqbal and others have been challenging for centuries that those people who formed these laws, were lawyers who were framing laws relevant to their own times. So who should implement ijtihad? The people of each era. They can take guidance from the past.

Q: Do you think Shariah should be enforced?
A: I am an academic, so again I will go back to the basics. What is Shariah? In Arabic the word means a path through running water for people and animals to be able to drink in safety. There can be nothing more fluid than running water and there is a connotation of safety. Shariah is really an umbrella concept. Shariah is not a term that has a rigid or fixed connotation or context. Pakistan follows the Hannafi School of Law. From that I understand the government will appoint a group of ulema who will then interpret the Shariah. That is a recipe for total destruction. The Hannafi school is one of four schools of law. As a Muslim I recognise the authority of the Quran. I believe the Quran is divine. However I do not consider the Hannafi school of law as divine. It is man-made. It is a system of law that can be challenged, it can be questioned. How can it be made the supreme law of the land? And then a group of ulema are given the authority to interpret . . . and given the political corruption in the country who are these maulanas going to be? It is just not doable. This is just a pointless discussion which is raised again and again. The constitution of Pakistan says that there can be no law or activity against the Quran or the Sunnah. So that's it. I think we should hold fast to the Quran. It is a great safeguard for us.

Q: In the field of women's rights in Islam, we have outspoken and often critical activists on the one hand, and Farhat Hashmi on the other. Where do you stand?
A: I feel that not only in Pakistan, but on the global level as well—I saw it in both Cairo and Beijing—there are two groups of women who are very vocal when it comes to women's rights. One is the extremely religious right, which could perhaps be represented by some one from the Jamaat-i-Islami or perhaps by Farhat Hashmi, and the human rights feminist activists. The position of the religious right is that Islam is a wonderful religion which gives us all our rights. We are treated like queens, we have no obligation to work, we are taken care of etc and what business is it of any secular organisation, like the UN, to interfere with us? Who are these western feminists anyway? Basically there are no problems for women in Islam. My disagreement with this school of thought is that though I agree that Islam is a wonderful religion, the first problem is that I don't see it practiced anywhere. The average Muslim woman is certainly not treated as she should be. She lives in sub-human conditions and is beaten and brutalised. So the extremist right wing view that all is well with Muslim women is nonsense. Now for the other side who call themselves human rights activists, the position that I see them representing is that religion and human rights are incompatible. This is also actually the position of the UN itself. So therefore when human rights are discussed, they do not want to introduce Islam as a category at all because they consider Islam as anti-humanistic.

My argument is that if anybody says that Islam and human rights are not compatible then they have not read the Quran. Secondly on a pragmatic level, I disagree because I have worked for years against violence against disadvantaged Muslim women. And when I want to reach the uneducated woman in rural Punjab or Turkey the UN Human Rights Declaration will be meaningless to her, it is outside her frame of reference. But if I relate her rights to her religion, which has always been a sustaining force for her, it can also be made into an empowering force. And believe me I have seen it happen myself across the Muslim world. What I feel is happening in Pakistan is that the religious right has hijacked Islam, while the human rights activists have hijacked human rights and the vast majority of women in between who also have an Islamic identity, who also want human rights, who also want to lead a modern life, be educated etc, have no representation in this discourse. And I personally feel that it is this important third option that has to be developed in Pakistan. That is where the future lies.

Q: Is there room for feminism in Islam, and do human rights issues come into conflict with the status of women in Islam?
A: What is feminism? For me feminism means women having the same rights as men. In that way I think it is perfectly compatible with Islam. When we talk about the status of women in Islam we normally mean what is their position in various situations. My argument is that all basic rights such as the right to live, to work, to marry, the right to freedom, to justice are all there in the Quran. Those laws are not gender specific, they are there for men and for women. Then there are special or "protective rights" for women, in the context of marriage, childbearing etc. So I would say that there is no conflict.

DIVERSE INTERPRETIVE FRAMEWORKS FOR PORTRAYING CONTEMPORARY WOMEN'S RELIGIOUS TRADITIONS

Selections in this section speak to women's religious traditions among contemporary women from two diverse cultures: Hinduism and Judaism. Savitri Bess speaks in her own voice to articulate her devotion to her Spiritual Mother, Ammachi. The selection from Susannah Heschel's *On Being a Jewish Feminist* is a short sketch about an experiential encounter with the tensions inherent in "pushing the envelope" to make progress in recognizing and claiming her religious heritage.

The readings in this section are about the importance of women's agency in their quest for authentic religious expression that celebrates their strength and advocates a positive, affirmative, self-understanding as a person. The women presented here are centered in the quest for spiritual freedom in the midst of their religious traditions whether those traditions were normative within their particular culture, or selected as answering a spiritual calling.

Savitri L. Bess

Savitri Bess, who holds M.F.A. and M.Ed. degrees, is a transpersonal therapist, workshop facilitator, fiber artist, and author. She has been a devotee of Mata Amritanandamayi (Ammachi) for many years and currently lives at the Amma Center of New Mexico ashram in Santa Fe. She also travels with Ammachi in the United States and India. The following excerpts have great value for the reader because they represent Ms. Bess' personal experience of Ammachi as a female spiritual avatar (incarnation of The Holy). First hand accounts of the powerful dynamics of relationship Ms. Bess experiences with a female incarnation of the Divine are yet another interpretive framework portraying women's spiritual experience in religion and reclaiming women's religious heritage.

Excerpts from The Path of the Mother*

...I did not comprehend fully that I had been on the Path of the Mother until ten years after my first spiritual teacher's death, when I met the Mother of Immortal Nectar, Mata Amritanandamayi, also known as "Ammachi," an Indian saint who considers all as her children. During one of her yearly visits to America, I watched thousands of people come to her one by one. For hours I sat spellbound, witnessing as she held them in her arms, listened to their tales of woe, and wiped tears from their eyes with her delicate brown hands.

After minutes in her lap, signs of transformation shone on all their faces as this small, round woman's boundless love caused children, the elderly, the infirm, and the able, to walk away smiling or weeping. That time I wasn't searching for a spiritual master and was taken entirely by surprise when something slipped into my heart and told me that my meeting with Ammachi had marked the end of my search. Not that I had reached spiritual enlightenment or the final liberation from birth and death—far from it. I had found the mother whale. I had found the sure way across the ocean. After twenty-two years, without even looking for it, the image I had received during Swami Satyananda's lecture in Denmark had become a reality. There was no doubt in my mind that my spiritual thread was attached firmly to this woman and, through her, to the Mother of the Universe.

[I] want you to meet the Mother, whom I will present to you in both a very personal way and an abstract, universal way. The purpose is for you to find your own unique relationship with her.

THE DIVINE GUIDE

To experience the warmth and wisdom of great souls or *mahatmas* is a blessing; they are the embodiment of divine love. Following the custom of many cultural traditions in ancient and modern times, I have chosen as a source for sage counsel throughout this book Ammachi, whose story is told in Part I. Many believe that mahatmas such as Ammachi are born into human bodies as a result of humanity's cries for help. (Amma means "Mother"; Ammachi means "Revered Mother.") *The Path of the Mother* would not be complete without including the age-old custom of seeking advice from a great soul.

THE SHADOW (FROM A SPIRITUAL PERSPECTIVE)

She who creates us, nurtures us, and protects us, she out of whose womb the whole universe is born, has been hidden in the unconscious shadow of our Western culture for thousands of years. Her warmth, her smile, her whisper in our ears, her gaze of a

*From Savitri L. Bess, *The Path of the Mother* (New York: Ballantine Wellspring, 2000), pp. xix–xxii.

million lifetimes, awaits our remembrance. She beckons us to uncover her multifaceted identity, summons us on a journey through the labyrinth of our own darkness, our own mystery, with the Mother herself as our guide.

Since she has been neglected for so many thousands of years in the West, many of us now long to know about her. Because of her incomprehensible nature, it is necessary to contemplate who she *might* be. Why is the feminine considered mysterious? Why is Goddess Kali black? Why is there so much secrecy around the Black Madonna? Why do we consider *black* scary? Why is dark associated with intrigue? You are likely to find many answers to these questions within the pages of this book.

The shadow refers to both the good and the bad aspects of ourselves, others, and the world of which we are unaware. The shadow is the unconscious mind, or that which is not seen, understood, or remembered. On many levels, both the divine and the demoniacal can reside there, until every detail about the entire universe is revealed. Because of its concealed nature, it is a complex subject and is dealt with at length in Part IV, The Shadow from a Spiritual Perspective.

THE STAGES

I have noticed six cyclical and nonlinear stages on the journey with the Mother. These will be addressed relative to each of the six parts. Stage one is getting to know the Mother; stage two, love and rapture; stage three, the Mother's discipline; stage four, the shadow; stage five, surrender; and stage six, contentment and yearning. The final liberation, a notion that will be discussed all the way through the book, is not included as a stage because, once attained, it is permanent.

The stages are cyclical; they happen over and over again in many different ways. Myths and personal accounts are used for illustrating each stage. Most of the stories contain elements of all of the stages, demonstrating a kind of microcosm of our entire spiritual journey.

The stages are nonlinear in the sense that one does not necessarily follow another. For instance, stage four can be followed by stage one, stage three by stage two, and on and on in innumerable patterns. Sometimes more than one stage will take place at the same time. Usually their motion resembles an ascending spiral. It can appear as though you have returned to the same spot. In reality, the same location could be a little higher up on the spiral. If you have been doing your practices regularly, you will notice a subtle, sometimes dramatic shift each time you return to the same stage. Sometimes your progress can appear to be unnoticeable, and you might think you are not getting anywhere. Ammachi likens this sensation to riding on a Boeing 707 to the other side of the world, to India or Australia; you don't notice that you are going anywhere until you land at your destination.

Evolution . . . is a slow process. It requires a lot of cutting, polishing, and remolding. It needs a lot of work and requires immense patience. It cannot be done in a hurry.

—Ammachi

Susannah Heschel

Susannah Heschel holds the Eli Black Chair in Jewish Studies at Dartmouth University and serves as associate professor in the Department of Religion. She received her Ph.D. from the University of Pennsylvania in 1989 and has taught at Southern Methodist University and Case Western Reserve University. Her research areas include modern Jewish thought, feminist theology, and German Protestantism. Professor Heschel served as the Martin Buber Visiting Professor of Jewish Religious Philosophy at the University of Frankfurt in 1992–93, and has lectured frequently in Germany on topics related to Jewish-Christian relations, and on feminism and religion. *On Being a Jewish Feminist,* which first appeared in 1983, was released in a second edition in 1995. The excerpt that follows is by a Jewish feminist Laura Geller from articles that appear in *On Being a Jewish Feminist.* Each article indicates some of the numerous tensions and issues addressed that can emerge in their everyday lives.

LAURA GELLER, *REACTIONS TO A WOMAN RABBI**

At the conclusion of High Holiday services during my first year as an ordained rabbi, two congregants rushed up to talk to me. The first, a middle-aged woman, blurted out, "Rabbi, I can't tell you how different I felt about services because you are a woman. I found myself feeling that if you can be a rabbi, then maybe I could be a rabbi too. For the first time in my life I felt as though I could learn those prayers, I could study Torah, I could lead this service, I could do anything you could do. Knowing that made me feel much more involved in the service—much more involved with Judaism! Also, the service made me think about God in a different way. I'm not sure why." The second congregant had something very similar to tell me, but with a slightly different emphasis. He was a man, in his late twenties. "Rabbi, I realized that if you could be a rabbi, then certainly I could be a rabbi. Knowing that made the service somehow more accessible for me. I didn't need you to 'do it' for me. I could 'do it,' be involved with Jewish tradition, without depending on you."

It has taken me five years to begin to understand the significance of what these people told me.

Throughout most of Jewish history the synagogue has primarily been the domain of men. It has also been a very important communal institution. Was the synagogue so important because it was the domain of men, or was it the domain of men because it was so important? Perhaps the question becomes more relevant if we ask it in another way. If women become leaders in the synagogue, will the synagogue become less important? This concern was clearly expressed in 1955 by Sanders Tofield of the Conservative Movement's Rabbinical Assembly, when he acknowledged that one reason women are encouraged to remain within the private sphere of religious life is the fear that if women were to be completely integrated into all aspects of Jewish ritual, then men might relegate religious life to women and cease being active in the synagogue. The fear connected with the "feminization" of Judaism is, largely, that once women achieve positions of power within the synagogue, men will feel that the synagogue is no longer sufficiently important to occupy their attention. The other side of the question is also being asked. Is the fact

*Laura Geller, "Reactions to a Woman Rabbi," in *On Being a Jewish Feminist: A Reader,* ed. Susannah Heschel (New York: Schocken Books, 1983), pp. 210–13.

that women are becoming leaders in synagogues a sign that the synagogue is no longer an important institution?

The fact that these questions are posed increasingly suggests to me that the synagogue is not very healthy. Are synagogues so marginal in the life of American Jews that men really would limit their involvement because women are active participants?

The participation of women as leaders and especially as rabbis raises another concern for synagogues. Those two congregants on Rosh Hashanah expressed a feeling that has been echoed many times since then. When women function as clergy, the traditional American division between clergy and lay people begins to break down. Let me give an example from another religious tradition. A woman who is an Episcopal priest told me that when she offers the Eucharist people take it from her differently from the way they would take it from a male priest, even though she follows the identical ritual. People experience her as less foreign, and so the experience is more natural, less mysterious.

People don't attribute to women the power and prestige that they often attribute to men. Therefore, when women become rabbis or priests, there is often less social distance between the congregant and the clergy. The lessening of social distance and the reduction of the attribution of power and status leads to the breakdown of hierarchy within a religious institution. "If you can be a rabbi, then certainly I can be a rabbi!"

Clearly some would argue that the breakdown of traditional religious hierarchy is bad. However, in my view this change could bring about a profound and welcome change in American Judaism. It could lead to synagogues that see their rabbi not as "priest" but as teacher, and that see the congregations not as passive consumers of the rabbi's wisdom but as active participants in their own Jewish lives.

The ordination of women will lead to change in another important area of Judaism: the way Jews think about God. On a basic, perhaps subconscious, level, many Jews project the image of their rabbi onto their image of God. As Dr. Mortimer Ostow has pointed out, "While it is true that no officiant in the service actually represents God, to the average congregant God is psychologically represented by the rabbi, since he is the leader and the teacher and preacher of God's word."

Most adult Jews know that it is inappropriate to envisage God as a male. But given the constant references in Jewish prayer to God as "Father" and "King," and given our childhood memories of imaging God as an old man with a long white beard, it is no surprise that to the extent Jews do conceptualize God in human terms, they often think of God as male or masculine.

Jewish tradition recognizes that God is not male. To limit God in this or any way is idolatrous; God is understood by tradition to encompass both masculinity and femininity and to transcend masculinity and femininity. Unfortunately, many Jews have never incorporated this complex image of God into their theology.

As long as the rabbi is a man, a Jew can project the image of the rabbi onto God. But when Jews encounter a rabbi who is a woman, it forces them to think about God as more than male or female. It provokes them to raise questions that most Jews don't like to confront: What or who is God? What do I believe about God? That primary religious question leads to others. How can we speak about God? What are the appropriate words, images, and symbols to describe our relationship to God? Does the English rendering of Hebrew prayers convey the complexity of God? How can we change language, images, and symbols so they can convey this complexity?

All of these questions could lead to a more authentic relationship to Jewish tradition and to God. Once Jews begin to explore their image of God, they will also reevaluate their image of themselves. Because all of us are created in God's image, how we think about God shapes how we think about ourselves. That thinking leads to a reevaluation of men's and women's roles within our tradition and our world.

The ordination of women has brought Judaism to the edge of an important religious revolution. I pray we have the faith to push it over the edge.

SUGGESTED READINGS

Brown, Karen McCarthy. *Mama Lola: A Vodou Priestess in Brooklyn.* Berkeley: University of California Press, 1991.

Detroit Ordination Conference, 1975. *Women and Catholic Priesthood: An Expanded Vision. Proceedings of the Detroit Ordination Conference.* Edited by Anne Marie Gardiner. New York: Paulist Press, 1976.

Isasi-Díaz, Ada María. *Mujerista Theology: A Theology for the Twenty-first Century.* Maryknoll, NY: Orbis Books, 1996.

Lehman, Edward C. *Women Clergy: Breaking through Gender Barriers.* New Brunswick, NJ: Transaction Books, 1985.

Ruether, Rosemary Radford. *Women and Redemption: A Theological History.* Minneapolis, MN: Fortress Press, 1998.

Schüssler-Fiorenza, Elisabeth. *Jesus and the Politics of Interpretation.* New York and London: Continuum, 2000.

Schüssler-Fiorenza, Elisabeth. *Jesus: Miriam's Child, Sophia's Prophet: Critical Issues in Feminist Christology.* New York: Continuum, 1995.

Sered, Susan Starr. *Priestess, Mother, Sacred Sister: Religions Dominated by Women.* New York: Oxford University Press, 1994.

Weidman, Judith L., ed. *Women Ministers.* San Francisco, CA: Harper & Row, Publishers, 1985.

Williams, Delores S. *Sisters in the Wilderness: The Challenge of Womanist God-Talk.* MaryKnoll, NY: Orbis Books, 1993.

Chapter 14

Feminism, Social Change, and Female Creativity

The lives and work of the women featured in this chapter reflect the wider educational and professional opportunities open to their sex after the late 1950s. Even more, they illustrate the impact of the new feminist movement as it built upon the strategies and successes of the American civil rights movement. The generation of women born in the late 1930s and after enjoyed unprecedented access to higher education, graduate and professional training in all fields, and access to previously all-male professions and occupations. By the 1990s, women had begun to move into the highest echelons of economic, political, and cultural institutions in parts of America and Europe, though their presence was still minimal in comparison with their credentials and percentage of the population.

In America, civil rights legislation and executive orders that prohibited race, religious, and ethnic discrimination in institutions and government agencies receiving public funding were gradually amended because of pressure from the organized women's movement to prohibit sex discrimination as well. These amendments opened doors to previously all-male institutions and fields from universities to the sciences and programs in architecture, law, and medicine. It also forced orchestras, professional journals, some art competitions, and educational institutions to institute "blind tryouts" and "anonymous" submissions and applications, in order to eliminate race and gender bias from the selection process.

Once women had gained access to education, professions, and cultural establishments, many began, as their predecessors had done, to ask new questions, challenge what they saw as arbitrary standards or values for scholarship or art, and bring their perspectives and experiences as women of differing backgrounds to their creative work. They also began a new search for a "useable past" and role models to counter persistent arguments that women were incapable of creating great literature, art, music, or performances. When they ran into opposition, or were silenced, they again created their own networks and institutions to ensure that their works and voices would be heard. They also engaged critics and naysayers in dialogue, openly challenging traditional values and assumptions with their own research and creative works.

ART

Judy Chicago (1939–): Artist, Author, Educator, and Feminist

Judy Chicago's career spans nearly four decades. Her art has been exhibited in the United States, Canada, Europe, Asia, Australia, and New Zealand. She is the author of seven books, including two autobiographies, *Through the Flower: My Struggle as a Woman Artist* (1975) and *Beyond the Flower: The Autobiography of a Feminist Artist* (1996), and she co-authored *Women and Art: Contested Territory* (1999) with British art writer Edward Lucie-Smith. As a statement against patriarchal naming conventions, she took her name from the city of her birth, Chicago, Illinois. She received B.A. and M.A. degrees in art from the University of California, Los Angeles, and began her art career in the 1960s. In 1970 she established the first feminist art program at Fresno State University in California, which she moved in 1971 to the California Institute of the Arts in Los Angeles. There she collaborated with artist Miriam Schapiro on their provocative project *Womanhouse*.

Chicago's work demonstrates why she is considered a leader in the feminist art movement. Between 1974 and 1979, she created her most famous work, *The Dinner Party*, aided by a team of hundreds of volunteers. This multimedia installation, which entailed extensive research, needleworkers, and ceramicists, introduced over a million viewers in six countries to women who were central to the history of Western Civilization. Between 1980 and 1985, Chicago brought the universal subject of birth to the forefront of art, again in a collaborative process with needleworkers. The *Birth Project* also introduced a gynocentric vision of creation missing from Western art. Her next project, *Powerplay*, examined the gender construct of masculinity and power. In 1993, she completed the *Holocaust Project: From Darkness into Light* in collaboration with Donald Woodman, and in 1994 began a new project with needleworkers. *Resolutions: A Stitch in Time* opened in June 2000 at the American Craft Museum, New York. Consisting of painting and needlework, the images re-interpret traditional sayings and proverbs. A retrospective of her work, *Judy Chicago: Trials and Tributes*, traveled from Tallahassee, Florida, to venues around the United States from 1999 to 2002, and the National Museum of Women in the Arts mounted an enlarged retrospective exhibition of her work in the fall of 2002, the same month *The Dinner Party* went on display at the Brooklyn Museum, its new permanent home.

Chicago's life and work reflect many of the themes evident in feminist intellectual and creative endeavors: recovering women's history, revisioning or retelling myths and stories from a woman's perspective, claiming women's life experiences as universal subjects worthy of attention, revaluing women's traditional forms of creative expression such as needlework which had been devalued as "crafts", using a collaborative approach to work, and believing that the arts can also be a means of social change.

A CONVERSATION WITH JUDY CHICAGO, 1997–1998*

> **Viki Wylder:** How do you react to the fact that now your work has been shown on several continents . . . and you are also studied in many art history classes?
>
> **Judy Chicago:** Well first of all, I think many people get impatient with me because they think . . . I'm not satisfied with the fact that this has happened. That's true, I'm not satisfied. The reason for that is because I'm a student of history and I know Elisabeth Vigée-LeBrun was unbelievably famous in her time. . . . I know Rosa

*Excerpts from Judy Chicago, transcripts of taped interviews, 1997–1998, by Viki D. Thompson Wylder, in conjunction with *Judy Chicago: Trials and Tributes*, a retrospective exhibition of Judy Chicago's works on paper, Viki D. Thompson Wylder, curator. Organized by the Florida State University Museum of Fine Arts, Allys Palladino-Craig, director, 1999. By permission of Viki D. Thompson Wylder.

Bonheur's work was widely esteemed during her lifetime. I know Mary Cassatt was commissioned to paint a sixty-five foot mural for the women's building. I know that was lost. I know when I went to art school I was told there were never any great women artists. I know the record . . . of their work was obscured, even though they achieved a level of fame probably far more than mine. . . . There is also this double thing, . . . that I have a very broad audience and yet at the top echelon of the art world there is total resistance to my work. . . . My work is not in the collections of the major museums that define taste and control the future in terms of what artists are seen. Even though I know it looks to a lot of women artists like I've achieved an enormous success, I think it's really important to understand my success is fragile, as fragile as the success of the women who preceded me.

VW: What did you think about the essay by Linda Nochlin, "Why Have There Been No Great Women Artists?"

JC: The question should be "Why have there been so many great women artists whom we know nothing about?" . . . I think one of the problems of not seeing women artists in the context of our own history, our own struggle, and our own experience is that our achievements can't be evaluated because they are evaluated against a false standard. What life is like for male artists is not at all what life is like for female artists. Because we do not have an understanding [of] the context in which women artists struggle to both express themselves or make a place for themselves, we can't evaluate either the achievements or see the consequences of the difficulties. . . . My youthful work was very free, very joyous, and very direct. Then I went to art school and I was told my forms were ugly and grotesque. Then I went through professionalizing and I was told that my ambition was unseemly for my gender. I was attacked constantly, mostly by other women, who were always telling me in one way or another . . . that I should be ashamed of my ambitions, ashamed of my accomplishments, and ashamed of my power. . . .

VW: What do you consider your most important contribution?

JC: . . . All I can talk about is what I wanted to try to contribute or what I thought I could contribute. . . . At first I just wanted to try to make a contribution to art because I didn't understand the issues of gender were going to be an obstacle to my being able to make the kind of contribution to art that I wanted to. . . . I wanted to make a contribution to younger women's educations so that young women artists wouldn't have to go through what I had to go through. . . . I didn't want them to have to go through the sense that there was something wrong with them because they were women, or not understanding that they had a history as women and that they could be proud of that. . . . Then I wanted to make a contribution to changing the way we saw history, and then I wanted to make a contribution to validating what it means to be a woman. After all, there is not much difference between men and women, except that women can give birth and men can't. If men had babies there would be thousands of images of the crowning, but what women do isn't important. So I wanted to validate what women do in the same way that men's experiences are validated. . . .

VW: There are authors in religious anthropology who have said that symbols affect us, and help to create who we are, that symbols create powerful, long lasting moods and motivations. . . .

JC: That's right, that's why the *Dinner Party* is not housed.

VW: Can you explain what you're talking about?

JC: . . . Because it's dangerous to have symbols that empower women. . . .

VW: I think the works you have created do empower.

JC: Well they can't do it unless they are seen. They don't do it from a page in a book. It's not the same to read about the *Book of the City of Ladies* by Christine Pisan as it is to read it. It's not the same to read about Mary Cassatt's *Modern Woman Mural* as it would be to see it. It's being in the presence of it, being able to see it and experience it and go back to it again and again [that] makes the symbol effective. To just read about it goes back to your question before, the reason I am not sanguine about the success of my work because if all that's left is the record of it, well now the record will be there because . . . my archives are in the Schlesinger Library in Radcliffe. As long as Harvard exists the record of my work will exist—and the *Birth Project,* significant pieces at your museum and the Albuquerque Museum. It's seeing the work, those are steps, but also it's just not enough steps yet.

 . . . People have laid a lot of stuff on me about . . . high and low [art]. . . . Why is oil paint on canvas inherently better than China paint on porcelain? Because somebody said so, that's the only reason and because that somebody had "power" to enforce what he thought. I don't agree with it. I just don't think like that. I try to pick the media that is most appropriate to my intent or my content. So, I don't care if it is high or low, male or female. I think those are all hindrances to the creative spirit. . . .

But . . . let's talk about the definition of art. The definition of artists, just like the role of art has narrowed. The definition of artists has narrowed since the Second World War. I have always looked at art in terms of the long, old, big historic picture and that's how I see myself. I don't think I'm that different from the traditional artists. Like Raphael designed for tapestry and worked in stucco and did oil paintings. . . . A lot of Renaissance artists did needle work designs . . . because there was this idea that a woman couldn't infuse a design with creative energy, only a man could do that. So even though women have done all these great needle works in the Middle Ages, right, suddenly that was forgotten. Women had to implement the designs that the great male artists came up with. . . . Then the other question is, is a woman allowed to take up that much space or is genius masculine? . . .

VW: . . . I want to know if there is any new feminist thinking infusing your work now, any new personal permutations.

JC: My thinking expanded dramatically during the *Holocaust Project.* . . . First of all I think feminist thinking has expanded tremendously, making links in terms of race, class, ethnicity, all that stuff. I think that's been a big advance in feminist thinking. In terms of my own development, the *Holocaust Project* gave me a much larger view of reality and of history. I would say I think much more globally now. I see woman's condition and experience in a larger context, in the overall context of the planet. . . . In terms of real change, it has to be global change or it will just sweep away. It would be momentary change for a small group of women. . . .

The other thing is . . . I'm completely tired of victim art. I am so tired of women portraying themselves as victims. I outgrew that at the end of the *Birth Project.* . . .

That's like not knowing their own history, just reinventing the wheel. I, myself, am not that interested in standing on the sidelines and critiquing patriarchy. I am much more interested in re-visioning and offering alternative ways of being, seeing and doing. I think that's more where I'm going.

VW: Offering the solution? . . .

JC: . . . I wouldn't say solutions, absolutely not. . . . I'm an artist and I think all an artist can do is envision . . . a different kind of a world, or . . . a different way of being. How to get there? I don't have a clue. All I can do is offer a vision, like *Rainbow Shabbat* [part of the *Holocaust Project*], a vision for the future.

National Museum of Women in the Arts, Washington, D.C.

The National Museum of Women in the Arts (NMWA) is the first museum in the world dedicated to acquiring, preserving, and exhibiting the work of women artists of all nationalities and all periods of history. It was incorporated in December 1981 as a private, nonprofit museum and operated for its first five years from temporary offices with docent-led tours of its art collection at the residence of the museum's founders, Wilhelmina Cole Holladay and Wallace F. Holladay. The Holladays' personal collection of art by women, acquired over a period of more than 20 years, comprised the core of the museum's permanent collection. In 1983 the museum purchased a run-down historic landmark near the White House, and painstakingly restored it as a museum. The NMWA opened in its permanent location in the spring of 1987 with an exhibition, *American Women Artists, 1830–1930,* curated by Eleanor Tufts, a leading feminist art historian. In addition to introducing the public to the first 100 years of art by American women, the NMWA highlighted the achievements of women musicians by sponsoring a concert as part of the dedication ceremonies. The concert featured two women pianists and the National Symphony Orchestra performing the Concerto for Two Pianos and Orchestra by Pulitzer Prize–winning composer Ellen Taaffe Zwilich.

In the first 16 years since its grand opening, NMWA presented over 150 exhibitions. Its permanent holdings have grown to over 3,000 works by more than 800 artists from the sixteenth century to the present. NMWA education efforts include the publication of books on women artists, an NMWA magazine, educational outreach programs each year for children, adults, and teachers, and the production of education materials for teachers the Girl Scouts, and families. The museum also sponsors literary, film, music, and lectures series featuring women and their work.

This remarkable story is largely a tribute to the work of one person, Wilhelmina Cole Holladay, with the support and collaboration of her husband Wallace F. Holladay. In the following excerpts from an interview, NMWA founder, Wilhelmina (Billie as she is known by her friends) Holladay tells how her dream came to fruition and shares her vision of the museum's future.

A CONVERSATION WITH WILHELMINA (BILLIE) HOLLADAY, NMWA FOUNDER, 2002*

Jean Bryant: Why did you start to collect art by women?

Wilhelmina Holladay: We were buying some paintings and a dear friend of ours said, "You know, you really must have a focus because it will be more interesting to

*From Wilhelmina Cole Holladay, telephone interview by Jean Gould Bryant, 22 March 2002. By permission of Wilhelmina Cole Holladay.

you and to others." We didn't want to specialize because we love all kinds of art, we didn't want to concentrate on one period, one artist, one anything. However, in an attempt to do research on a woman artist, Clara Peeters, we discovered that there was an absolute dearth of material on women artists. We had consulted our source books and found no woman in any of them. As a matter of fact, there was not a single woman in the leading text in our country, Janson's *History of Art,* used in every college and university in the country where you study history of art, until the year we opened—1987.

To show the contribution of women to the history of art seemed like a good focus in that we could buy whatever we really liked whether new or old, a sculpture or print, whatever pleased, so it proved a great choice for us. We are fortunate. We've traveled all over the world, so whereever we went we'd go into the top commercial gallery and say, "What do you have by a woman?" And they'd say, "Nothing." But then months later, remembering we were potential customers, they'd get in touch and say, "We've found a beautiful work from the seventeenth century Dutch Renaissance," or what have you. So collecting the works was great fun and very interesting. We have done it over a long period of time, starting about 1960, and we are still at it.

JB: How did you come up with the idea of creating the museum?

WH: The first exhibition of women artists was in the 1970s. It was curated by two feminist scholars, Dr. Ann Sullivan Harris and Linda Nochlin, and several of our paintings were in it. So I became acquainted with some of the feminist scholars. They invited me to a seminar one time and were talking about how less than two percent, I think it was, of all paintings in all museums were by women, and how shameful it was, etc. Then later, a friend, Nancy Hanks [chairperson of the National Endowment for the Arts], and I were having dinner, and I said, "You know, it is amazing these things that they've discovered." Ann and Linda corralled five other scholars and began to do research. If you could go back and translate from the Italian, French or German, you could discover the history of these women. I said to Nancy, "You know, there are literally only men's museums; there are no women artists in museums to speak of." And she said, "Well, maybe there should be . . . a woman's museum." So we chatted about that possibility. Excited, she called me up the next day and said, "Would you be willing to give your library and your collection?" It was just a joke the night before, and I said, "Well, maybe." Nancy had a lot of clout, so we were able to put together a very prestigious committee . . . and began to do a sort of museum without walls.

Then the Junior League throughout the country offered to identify works by women in private and public collections. They had docents all over the country so the material started rolling in and one thing led to another, and finally a *wonderful* thing happened. . . . There was a young girl on our committee. I had no idea she had any money. She was only in her twenties, and was a student at Georgetown University. . . . She said, "You know, we must have a building." I said, "Well, someday, my dear." This was all kind of light handed. At any rate, one thing led to another, and she said, "I want to help. I *really* want to help." The head of the National Trust for Historic Preservation was on our committee and he and my husband began searching, and they found the beautiful landmark building we have. At that time the area where it was located had become a terrible slum. The building was in a dreadful state of repair. I was horrified, but they said, "Oh, [the building's] got good bones, it's going to be beautiful." So two and a half years later it was! Our young patron gave a couple million and we were able to raise the rest. . . .

JB: At the time of the dedication, wasn't there a huge debate about the museum?

WH: Indeed, yes. We couldn't win! Thank goodness our detractors have all come around. It didn't occur to me anyone would be against what we were doing. I was so naive. . . . We were giving our art and our library, we were going mostly to New York and big corporations to raise the money. It just didn't occur to me that it would be attacked. Well, the feminists took us on, and they were furious because I wouldn't tackle the issues of homosexuality and abortion. I happen to have liberal views, but I said, no, no. Art is the one unifying thing. It rises above color and politics and religion, etc., and I want everyone to be comfortable in this museum. I don't want it to be divisive. I don't want it to offend anybody. Art is for the whole world. And then some of the old dowagers complained, "Oh, this is some feminist thing," and they had much to say. I finally just smiled sweetly and kept working hard.

I am amazed and grateful that they *all* love us now. We're in the top ten percent of museums when measured by membership. And all that controversy, . . . I think it was good, because it created a heightened awareness of the museum. . . .

I was never a fatalist before, but I am now. The museum was just meant to be. The weirdest things happen. We'll have a problem and all of a sudden out of the blue a solution is there. Like that young girl on the committee. . . . But this has happened over and over and over again. And of course the museum was timely. As women have become better educated they are assuming positions of greater importance and they're being recognized for their accomplishments.

There's still a long way to go, but it's exciting to me for another reason. Whenever a woman becomes prominent there's a transfer of dignity to all of us. I thought when Sandra O'Connor (she happens to be a good friend) went on the Court, every woman lawyer could walk a bit taller. They could at least aspire to the highest court of our land. And that sort of applies to women artists. Now that more are appearing in museums, it gives hope to all.

There is one thing I know, throughout our country, unless they are in the art world, even among very well educated people, they can't name five women artists. When I am asked to lecture I always throw that out and one can just see them counting on their fingers, trying to come up with five. They can't. They'll start out with Mary Cassatt, Grandma Moses or Georgia O'Keeffe, then they stumble, stumble, stumble, and maybe think of one more. We still have a long way to go! It's changing, but until we opened, I believe, the National Gallery had never had a show by a woman and the Metropolitan had not had a show by a woman in 138 years.

JB: You still believe then there's a place for your museum and other women-focused institutions?

WH: Oh, *absolutely*! There's still such a dearth of knowledge. The National Museum of Women in the Arts is the only institution in the world doing archival work on women artists. We have over 16,000 files from the Renaissance to the present. . . . So I would like to think that for a long time to come people are going to be doing research and writing papers and needing us.

My dream is to develop a presence in the whole world. And we're getting there. The queen of Denmark had a part of her state visit at our museum with an exhibition of Danish women artists, and the king and queen of Norway asked us to mount a show of their women. Their majesties opened it and brought their chamber orchestra led by a woman to play in our performance hall. We've also had an exhibition from Korea, two from Brazil, . . . etc. What I'm constantly impressed by is the ability of the arts to rise above differences and give understanding and friendship. We had an exhibition of women artists of the Arab countries. It was the first time ever that all thirteen Arab countries worked on something together culturally. . . . I was working with the ambassadors' wives, . . . it was during the Gulf War. The Jordanian ambassador's wife and the Kuwaiti ambassador's wife came to me and said, "Mrs. Holladay, you know because of the war and our countries are on different sides . . . , we can't attend public functions together. However, we are both *for* this exhibition and we'll do absolutely everything we can possibly do to make it a success." And they did. But to me it was so exciting that the women could all pull together because of art. . . .

MUSIC

Ellen Taaffe Zwilich (1939–): Pulitzer Prize–winning Composer

As the twenty-first century dawns and the musical offerings of the world are more varied than ever before, few composers have emerged with the unique personality of Ellen Zwilich. Her music is widely known because it is performed, recorded, broadcast, and above all, listened to and liked by all sorts of audiences the world over.

Ellen Zwilich is the recipient of numerous prizes and honors, including the 1983 Pulitzer Prize in Music (the first woman ever to receive this coveted award); the Elizabeth Sprague Coolidge Chamber Music Prize; the Arturo Toscanini Music Critics Award; the Ernst von Dohnanyi Citation; an Academy Award from the American Academy of Arts and Letters; a Guggenheim Fellowship; and four Grammy nominations. Among other distinctions, she has been elected to the Florida Artists Hall of Fame and the American Academy of Arts and Letters. In 1995, she was named to the first Composer's Chair in the history of Carnegie Hall, and she was designated *Musical America*'s Composer of the Year for 1999. She is also a Francis Eppes Distinguished Professor at her alma mater, Florida State University.

Ellen Taaffe Zwilich is a prolific composer, and her works have been performed by virtually all of the leading American orchestras and by major ensembles abroad. Her music first came to public attention when Pierre Boulez conducted her *Symposium for Orchestra* at Juilliard (1975), but it was the 1983 Pulitzer Prize for the Symphony No. 1 that brought her international attention. Commissions and major performances and recordings soon followed: Symphony No. 2 (*Cello Symphony*) premiered by the San Francisco Symphony; Symphony No. 3 written for the New York Philharmonic's one hundred and fiftieth anniversary; and Symphony No. 4 (*The Gardens*) (with chorus), commissioned by

Michigan State University. She is also the composer of a string of concertos for solo instruments and orchestra; and chamber works, commissioned and performed by top orchestras.

Baker's Biographical Dictionary of Musicians states: "There are not many composers in the modern world who possess the lucky combination of writing music of substance and at the same time exercising an immediate appeal to mixed audiences. . . . Zwilich offers this happy combination of purely technical excellence and a distinct power of communication . . . " (Baker 1992, 2115).

INTERVIEW WITH ELLEN TAAFFE ZWILICH, 2001*

Jean Bryant: How did you first get started in music and with what instruments?

Ellen Taaffe Zwilich: Well, when I was a toddler I discovered the piano in my living room and crawled up on the bench and found out what happens when you press down the keys. It excited me tremendously and I kind of still feel the same way. . . . When I was about in the sixth grade I began to play other instruments, first the violin and then the trumpet. . . . When I went to Coral Gables High School in the 10th grade, I auditioned for the band and I got one of the top chairs. . . .

JB: Did you ever get any flack for being a woman playing that "masculine" instrument? Since that was a time when there were very few girls in bands other than flutes and clarinets . . .

ETZ: That wasn't true in my high school band. As a matter of fact, my high school had behind-the-screen auditions. The purpose of that was to keep the seniors on their toes. But one of the results of it was the same thing that they have found when they have done this professionally. Suddenly, they find that females can play. And in my high school band, the first trombone was also a girl. I don't think it was taken into too much consideration. . . .

JB: In a 1984 interview, you were quoted as noting that women were apt to have fewer mentors than men. I was going to ask if you had any; . . . obviously your brass teacher was very important in your development.

ETZ: Oh yes, and so many of my teachers in college and beyond. Not only that, but when I moved to New York, after I had gotten a master's degree in composition, I had decided I really wanted to learn to play the violin better. . . . And shortly after I was there, I began to work as a violinist. This was around 1964, and this was a very peculiar time in a way because the major orchestras were still ninety-nine point something percent male. Every orchestra had only a couple of women here or there.

JB: Harp?

ETZ: Flute sections; a harpist perhaps, yes. There were women out there, but they were a tiny, tiny minority. [Leopold] Stokowski had started the American Symphony a couple of years before I got to New York and the American Symphony was the first orchestra that was a professional orchestra that looked like the rest of the country in that there was a large contingent of women. We were also quite unusual in that there were many Asians, which was something quite new at the time. There were also

*Excerpts from Ellen Taaffe Zwilich, telephone interview by Jean Gould Bryant, 6 December 2001. By permission of Ellen Taaffe Zwilich.

black people in the orchestra. It was just much more, much more open than the major orchestra world.

JB: That's interesting given his "Old World" background.

ETZ: Well, Stoki prided himself on being avant-garde. And I think he liked the idea of the thing being just sort of wide open and looking different. So that was an opportunity for me. I was there for seven years. . . . we had the most glittering array of guest conductors. So, I was exposed to all these different ways of thinking about music. It was quite a wonderful, wonderful part of my growth as a composer. . . . I was in the American Symphony when I went to Julliard and started my doctorate.

JB: And you were the first woman in Julliard with a Ph.D. in composition?

ETZ: It's a D.M.A. actually.

JB: Did they have the same breakthrough in conducting about the same time?

ETZ: Conducting, I think, is the last thing to fall. At this point there are people like JoAnn Falletta and Marin Alsop having real careers. . . . But the women conductors in the sixties tended to be very, very few and very, very far between. I remember doing a concert with Antonia Brico.

You know, sometimes people forget how social an art music is. After I had won the Pulitzer Prize, I got really annoyed at a certain point because I'd had so many people ask me, "how did it feel to be the first woman . . . " And I began to think: the piece that I won the Pulitzer Prize for (my first symphony) was commissioned by the American Composers Orchestra and the National Endowment for the Arts. It was conducted by Gunther Schuller. It was played by the American Composers Orchestra. An audience had to buy a ticket with that on the program. The critics had to write about it. At one point I made a list in my mind of all of the people who had to believe that I could do the work, who had to believe in me, for me to get my foot in the door. . . . And I think the music world was much further ahead than the rest of the world, perhaps, at that point. . . . I had a reputation as a composer, not as a woman.

. . . One of the things that occurred to me in thinking about all this is that writing music for people to perform is like being a playwright. It's not like being a poet. Because being a poet you can just write your poem in your room and that's it. But, being a playwright, you have to not only have your work performed you have to understand at the outset how it will work in performance. That is an essential part of your craft. If you have theater at a time in history when women are not even allowed to play female roles, then there is no mystery whatsoever why there are no female playwrights. And if women were shut out of most of the professional venues of music, people shouldn't have been so mystified by the fact that there have been few women composers. They should have been *amazed* that there were *any.*

. . . And I get back to the notion of universal schooling, where those opportunities are available for everybody; that they don't have to be born into a musical family; that they don't have to be someone who might know somebody in a court. They can be anybody who's got the gift and the desire. And I think that's the thing that's basically changed.

JB: . . . I know that you completed a commission for the opening of the National Museum of Women in the Arts. . . . I was curious about your thoughts about the strategy of separatism, then and now: women's museums, women's music and theater festivals . . .

ETZ: I think that museum is very interesting, beginning with the question why it is needed.

JB: Did the museum founder commission your work?

ETZ: Yes, yes. This grand lady, Billie Holladay, said, "Let everybody prove that it's not necessary. Let them put us out of business."

JB: They haven't yet. . . .

ETZ: No, they haven't. But you do find that there are more and more women recognized in the art world. When I was in college, the big art history text didn't have a single work of a woman. Women had been essentially erased from the history of art.

. . . I think people have wasted a lot of effort in trying to figure out how women's art and music is different from men's. I think everything we are enters into what we do. Our work is as different as we all are. I love to celebrate that. . . .

JB: Did you ever attend any of the women's music festivals?

ETZ: As a matter of fact, the first one I went to was one that Kitty Hoover had organized, and I remember thinking, "Good Lord, I'm hearing the premiere of a work that was written in the thirteenth century. The New York premiere." . . . these concerts, as long as it doesn't become a ghetto, I think they have served a very useful purpose. You know, in the past, in Europe, for instance, there were guilds. Artists helped one another along enormously. They knew who each other were. And we kind of have that as contemporary composers, but not too much of it. I think things that do form a kind of network—I think they are very helpful. . . . I think the main thing for women is for young women to know that they can get all the experience they need, they can get the education they need, they can have the opportunity, but there is no guarantee. . . .

Peanuts Gallery

In March 1997, cartoonist Charles Schulz, Ellen Zwilich, and Snoopy took a bow on the stage of Carnegie Hall, New York, to the cheers of children and their families. The occasion was the world premier of *Peanuts Gallery,* a six-part character study for piano and orchestra. When Zwilich accepted the newly created Composer's Chair at Carnegie Hall in 1995, she was particularly excited about the opportunity to inaugurate a family concert series to introduce music to young people. She and Carnegie Hall's director, Judith Aaron, agreed that the first of three Carnegie commissions she was to complete should be for a family concert. Zwilich immediately envisioned a piece based on Peanuts' characters. Schulz, she had discovered, was a fan of hers. In 1990, Zwilich had returned home from a trip to find her answer machine full of messages from friends calling to congratulate her she and her flute concerto were the subject of a Peanuts comic strip featuring Peppermint Patty and Lucy at a young people's concert. As she had hoped, Schulz agreed to her idea. The event brought a fun evening and a second Peanuts comic strip devoted to her music (see Figure 14–1).

Figure 14–1   *Peanuts Gallery,* **16 March 1997.** *PEANUTS reprinted by permission of United Feature Syndicate, Inc.*

CHALLENGING GENDER BARRIERS IN THE ARTS

Despite enormous gains in all fields, barriers persisted at all levels and in all areas of culture on the eve of the twenty-first century. The following selections provide additional glimpses of some forms discrimination has taken and strategies that have been used to combat it.

Anna Lelkes and the Vienna Philharmonic: Interview with Harpist Lelkes, 1997*

Harpist Anna Lelkes is the first woman to be given full membership in the Vienna Philharmonic in its 155-year history. Though she was admitted Thursday, her first chance to play as a full member will be tonight, when the orchestra performs . . . at the Orange County [California] Performing Arts Center.

Lelkes, 57, was born in Budapest, Hungary, and became an Austrian citizen in 1974. In 1971, she entered the Vienna State Opera orchestra, from which the philharmonic draws its members. She has played with the philharmonic since 1974.

Lelkes gave an exclusive interview to Heinz Roegle [on February 28]. . . .

*Excerpts from Heinz Roegle, "Notes on Twenty-six Years as Official Nonentity, Anna Lelkes and the Vienna Philharmonic," *Los Angeles Times,* 5 March 1997, Orange County ed., Pt. A, p. 3, metro desk. As reprinted with permission from the Saturday edition of *Salzburger Nachrichten,* transcribed by *Times* staff writer Jan Herman, trans. from the German by Mike Wiessner. By permission of the *Salzburger Nachrichten.*

Question: Ms. Lelkes, we congratulate you. How did you find out about your admission to the orchestra?
Answer: I've been attending its meetings for a long time.

Q: You've always been at the meetings?
A: I was hired Jan.1, 1971, by the state opera, and three years later, in 1974, I was admitted informally into the philharmonic as a regular without full membership. I didn't exist officially until yesterday. My name was never mentioned in any program . . . and they always claimed, even in my presence, right under my own nose, that they didn't have a woman in the orchestra.

Q: Did you have financial equality with the men?
A. I did since 1974. I just couldn't call myself a member of the philharmonic. My name wasn't allowed to appear anywhere. I couldn't vote. Originally, I shouldn't even have been allowed to attend the meetings. But it's at these meetings that we discuss the work schedule and general planning for the orchestra. I've often worked a lot more than my male colleagues. So they said, "All right, you can come to the meetings." As time went by, I was allowed to attend everything because otherwise I would not have found out if and when I would have to play and what the contracts would say. . . . I really couldn't say that I was treated badly. But it was the younger generation, especially, that fought it out for me. At the last meeting when they took the vote to admit women, it really wasn't nice. What I had to listen to there really hurt me. Someone said: "There are no women in the Vienna Choir Boys and no pigs at the Lippizaners, the Spanish Riding School in Vienna's famous dressage team of white horses." Everything was blocked at the meeting the week before when the vote had been scheduled but was postponed. They had mobilized all those pensioners retired members of the philharmonic. Quite a few younger players got together and even got organized and said this can't go on any longer. The younger generation stood up for me at the second meeting.

Q: Is there a conflict among the men in the orchestra that we've been hearing about?
A. Yes. I was not admitted unanimously, but with a big majority, as I heard. I had to leave the room before the vote. They were terribly frightened by the possibility of demonstrations by American women's rights activists. [The National Organization for Women (NOW) and other groups including the International Alliance for Women in Music (IAWM) had called for boycotts of all performances in the U.S.] I believe that this pressure was decisive. And that's why they said, "OK, we have to give some proof that we are not that bad. We must stand up for 'equal employment opportunity for both genders,'" as they formulated it officially for the press.

Q: Did you yourself ever express the desire to be admitted as a full member of the orchestra?
A: Again and again, almost every year. I've waited for this for 26 years. I also stated in writing that I wanted to be admitted at least as an "extra" or "special member."

The Guerrilla Girls (1985–): Conscience of the Art World

Since 1985, the Guerrilla Girls, the self-proclaimed "Conscience of the Art World," have shocked and amused the public and their targets as they have fought against barriers based on gender, race, and sexuality. At first, these "masked avengers" focused on those in the art world, from galleries and museums, to critics and artists, who clung to the notion that if women and people of color had created any truly good art, it would be shown. Soon they broadened their aim to include other arts, such as music, and then they expanded to critique virtually any institution, or prominent citizen who, in their eyes, ignored or perpetuated sexism, racism, or homophobia, or who sought to restrict freedom of expression. Typically, they created clever posters such as "The Advantage of Being a Woman Artist" (see Figure 14–2), which they and male allies posted in restrooms, on buses, buildings, or any available space, and placed in magazines. Groups of Guerrilla Girls carried their message to universities, galleries, and concert halls all over the United States, and they continue to attract enthusiastic audiences.

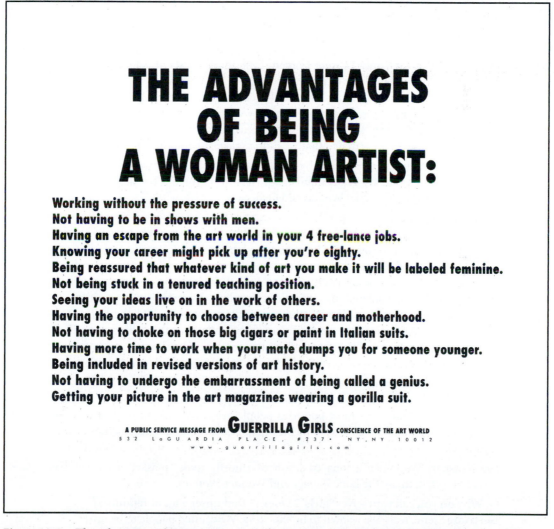

**Figure 14–2   *The Advantages of Being a Woman Artist.* From *Guerrilla Girls,* Confessions of the Guerrilla Girls. *(New York: HarperPerennial, 1995), p. 53. By permission of The Guerrilla Girls,* www.guerrillagirls.com.

*Guerrilla Girls Bare All**

Rosalba Carriera: When we first spoke to the press, it was clear we needed code names to distinguish between members of the group. The day we taped NPR's Fresh Air, Georgia O'Keeffe died. It was then that it came to us to use names of dead women artists and writers to reinforce their presence in history and to solve our interview problems. It was as though Georgia were speaking to us from the grave. So far, Frida Kahlo, Alma Thomas, Rosalba Carriera, Lee Krasner, Eva Hesse, Emily Carr, Paula Modersohn-Becker, Romaine Brooks, Alice Neel, and Ana Mendieta are but a few of the famous women from history who have joined us. We are actively recruiting Rosa Bonheur, Angelica Kauffmann and Sofonisba Anguissola. (Of course, one Girl didn't care for the idea and calls herself GG 1.)

Q: How did the Guerrilla Girls start?

Käthe Kollwitz: In 1985, the Museum of Modern Art in New York opened an exhibition titled "An International Survey of Painting and Sculpture." It was supposed to be an up-to-the-minute summary of the most significant contemporary art in the world. Of 169 artists, only 13 were women. Even fewer artists of color were chosen and none were women. That was bad enough, but the curator, Kynaston McShine, said any artist who wasn't in the show should rethink "his" career. And that really annoyed a lot of artists because obviously the guy was completely prejudiced. Women demonstrated in front of the museum with the usual placards and picket line. Some of us who attended were irritated that we didn't make any impression on passersby.

Meta Fuller: We began to ask ourselves some questions. Why did women and artists of color do better in the 1970s than in the '80s? Was there a backlash in the art world? Who was responsible? What could be done about it?

Q: What did you do?

Frida Kahlo: We decided to find out how bad it was. After about five minutes of research we found that it was worse than we thought: the most influential galleries and museums exhibited almost no women artists. When we showed the figures around, some said it was an issue of quality, not prejudice. Others admitted there was discrimination but considered the situation hopeless. Everyone in a position of power—curators, critics, collectors, the artists themselves—passed the buck. The artists blamed the dealers, the dealers blamed the collectors, the collectors blamed the critics and so on. We decided to embarrass each group by showing its records in public. Those were the first posters we put up in the streets of SoHo in New York.

Q: Why are you anonymous?

GG1: The art world is a very small place. Of course, we were afraid that if we blew the whistle on some of its most powerful people, we could kiss off our art careers. But mainly, we wanted the focus to be on the issues, not on our personalities or our own work.

Lee Krasner: We joined a long tradition of (mostly male) masked avengers like Robin Hood, Batman, the Lone Ranger and Wonder Woman.

Q: Why do you call yourselves "girls"? Doesn't that upset a lot of feminists?

Gertrude Stein: Yeah. We wanted to be shocking. We wanted people to be upset.

Frida Kahlo: Calling a grown woman a girl can imply she's not complete, mature, or grown up. But we decided to reclaim the word "girl," so it couldn't be used against us. Gay activists did the same thing with the epithet "queer."

Q: Why are you Guerrillas?
Georgia O'Keeffe: We wanted to play with the fear of guerrilla warfare, to make people afraid of who we might be and where we would strike next. Besides, "guerrilla" sounded so good with "girl."

Q: Isn't calling yourselves the Conscience of the Art World a little pretentious?
Eva Hasse: Of course. Everyone knows artists are pretentious!

GG1: Anyway, the art world needs to examine itself, to be more self-critical. Every profession needs a conscience!

Q: Why the gorilla masks?
Käthe Kollwitz: We were Guerrillas before we were Gorillas. From the beginning the press wanted publicity photos. We needed a disguise. No one remembers, for sure, how we got our fur, but one story is that at an early meeting, an original Girl, a bad speller, wrote "Gorilla" instead of "Guerrilla." It was an enlightened mistake. It gave us our "mask-ulinity."

Q: What about the short skirts, high heels and fishnet stockings?
Emily Carr: Wearing those clothes with a gorilla mask confounds the stereotype of female sexiness.

Meta Fuller: Actually, we wear mostly nondescript, bohemian black clothes—like everyone else in the art world. Sometimes we do wear high heels and short skirts. And that's what people remember.

Q: Why do you use humor? What does it do for your message?
Paula Modersohn-Becker: Our situation as women and artists of color in the art world was so pathetic, all we could do was make fun of it. It felt so good to ridicule and belittle a system that excluded us. There was also that stale idea that feminists don't have a sense of humor.

Eva Hesse: Actually, our first posters weren't funny at all, just smart-assed. But we found out quickly that humor gets people involved. It's an effective weapon.

Q: Do you allow men to join?
Frido Kahlo: We'd love to be inclusive, but it's not easy to find men willing to work without getting paid or getting credit for it.

LITERATURE AND THEATER

Christiane Rochefort (1917–1998): French Writer, Social Critic, and Feminist

Paris-born Christiane Rochefort studied psychology, ethnology, and medicine at the Sorbonne and then held various jobs as an actress, journalist, and model. For 15 years she was a press secretary at the Cannes Film Festival until her dismissal for radical ideas in 1968. She published 15 books, including 9 novels, short stories, fantasy works, and essays. Her 1958 novel *Le Repos du Guerrier* (*Warrior's Rest*) was runner-up for the *Prix Fémina* and won a new award, the *Prix de la Nouvelle Vague* (Prize of the New Wave). It was made into a film, *Love on a Pillow,* in 1962, directed by Roger Vadim and starring his ex-wife Brigitte Bardot. She received the *Prix du Roman Populiste* for her second novel, *Les Petits*

Enfants du Siècle, 1961 (*Children of Heaven/Josyane and the Welfare State*), a satire about France's post-war policy of family subsidies for babies to increase the nation's birth rate. Many of her works addressed issues of women in marriage and society, female sexuality, and the concerns of social and sexual minorities. In a book of essays, *Les Enfants d'Abord,* she wrote of children as another oppressed class. She received the *Prix Médicis* for *La Porte du Fond* (*The Far Door*), her 1988 novel about incest. In 1970, she and a few other radical feminists engaged in the first French protest action against patriarchy to gain wide publicity. They attempted to place a wreath inscribed with "to the unknown wife of the soldier" on the tomb of the unknown soldier at the Arc de Triomphe in Paris (Marks and de Courtivron 1981, 31). This act marked the birth of the French women's liberation movement.

In the following excerpt from her 1975 speech in the United States, she addresses the challenges that creative women (in her case, writers) often faced in the last quarter of the twentieth century.

ARE WOMEN WRITERS STILL MONSTERS? (1975)*

A man's book is a book. A woman's book is a woman's book. A crowd of fathers-husbands-big brothers-lovers are watching, not our capacities as writers, but our behavior. We are allowed to write, OK. But not anything. "I like your books very much, but why do you insist on using crude words?" "That's the way the character talks you know," I would say, "and besides it's the way you talk, yourself." "Yes, maybe, but is it necessary that you write it?" We have to be decent. Exceptions are tolerated if they are without ambiguity, part of the right erotic game. We have a body—university degrees don't obliterate the fact. When Kristeva got a prize not long ago, a critic wrote in a so-called liberal newspaper: "She has beautiful legs."

We have a psychology: I got some free analysis after my first book was published. One journalist wrote that I probably was ugly and frustrated till, meeting him at a cocktail party, I patted him on the shoulder saying: "Ho, sir, I'm the ugly, frustrated one." He ran away while the others laughed. He himself was a piece of fat.

We have a private life: dozens of times I was asked if I really went to bed with my hero. I didn't notice that such questions were asked of a normal writer (a man).

I'm perfectly sure that if my first book were written by a man, it would not have been a scandal, and, consequently, not a bestseller. There are sometimes good sides to oppression. But it took time for me to recover, and come up with the correct analysis: I was a woman, so emphasis was put on the smallest sexual issues appearing in my writings. If they see anything, this is all that they see. . . . In brief, we are read below the belt—men are at the glorious level of brain.

In spite of everything, I think creativity is a natural activity of humankind. All babies are born with a fantastic potential. But our present-day society doesn't need all that. It needs sheep, for production and consumption. In terms of potential, what is not necessary is not awakened, or it is stifled, or it is cut off: this is the enormous business of children's oppression, . . . This mutilating surgery which affects every child goes further for the poor, for the oppressed races, and for females. . . .

*Excerpts from Christiane Rochefort, "Are Women Writers Still Monsters?" a speech, written directly into English by Christiane Rochefort, given at the University of Wisconsin–Madison, February 1975, in Elaine Marks and Isabelle de Courtivron, eds. *New French Feminisms. An Anthology* (New York: Schocken Books, 1981), pp. 183–85. Published by arrangement with The University of Massachusetts Press. pp. 183–85. Copyright 1980 by The University of Massachusetts Press. By permission of The University of Massachusetts Press.

I know with certainty that my salvation as a creator (I mean as a person) is due to the fact that I was dumb enough, blind and deaf enough, not to understand that I was a female. Although it was obvious, and I received all the necessary information about it (don't do this, don't say that, don't, don't, a little girl does not), I remained deaf, blind, and reluctant: not me, not for me. "Me" was something else. Somewhere else. Since reality was a lie, I had a reality of my own: a secret life in dreams. . . .

I learned later on, in consciousness-raising groups, that it is a pretty common experience—female children are driven mad, schizophrenic because there is a total antagonism between what they are and what society wants them to be. Among them, a remarkable proportion is defeated in this combat. I almost was, between twelve and twenty: then I was rescued by a small light of political consciousness: I learned that I was an oppressed person. . . .

The husband of a friend of mine once read what his wife did write (when the housework was over). He said: "You know, you are so much better in helping me?" She stopped writing on the spot. Now she is pretty desperate, for she wants to work again but dares not. So I told her my own story: When I finished my first book . . . my first movement was to show it to the man I lived with at the moment. He said: "My poor girl, you better darn stockings." I stopped writing on the spot for three years—till I parted from my husband, swearing that never again in my life was I going to show anything to a man who loves me. . . .

Well. So, here you are now, sitting at your writing table, alone, not allowing anybody anymore to interfere. Are you free?

First, after this long quest, you are swimming in a terrible soup of values—for, to be safe, you had to refuse the so-called female values, which are not female but a social scheme, and to identify with male values, which are not male but an appropriation by men—or an attribution to men—of all human values, mixed up with the anti-values of domination-violence-oppression and the like. In this mixture, where is your real identity?

Second, you are supposed to write in certain forms, preferably: I mean you feel that in certain forms you are not too much seen as a usurper. Novels. Minor poetry, in which case you will be stigmatized in French by the name of "poetesse": not everybody can afford it. I must confess that, although I write poems, I couldn't afford showing them, except to close friends. They are in a drawer.

You are supposed, too, to write about certain things: house, children, love. . . .

Has literature a sex? With dignity, I, and most of my sisters, we would answer: No.

But. But. But, do we have the same experience? Do we have the same mental structures? The same obsessions? Death, for instance, is a specifically male obsession. As well as essential solitude.

After all, we don't belong to the same civilization.

Women's Experimental Theatre, New York (1976–1985)

Women's Experimental Theatre (WET) was one of numerous feminist and women's theater groups that emerged in the United States, Europe, Canada, and Latin America in the 1970s. Some disappeared within a couple of years, but WET, Lilith in San Francisco, and Rhode Island Feminist Theatre lasted into the mid-1980s. Their emergence reflected the barriers women still faced in mainstream theater—

from getting plays produced to obtaining positions as directors and technical crew. They also attested to feminists' determination to have women's experiences and perspectives portrayed on stage through the eyes and voices of women instead of from a male point of view. Some, such as the Lavendar Cellar Theatre of Minneapolis (1973–1975) were lesbian theater companies, formed to give voice to the lesbian community. Most were avowedly political groups that used art to protest oppression, discrimination, violence against women, and patriarchy in general. Some groups, such as Women's Interart Theatre (New York, 1969) sought to advance opportunities for women artists in all disciplines and to integrate music, dance, theater, and visual art in their productions. Isolating drama or music, they believed, limited appreciation of each form of art. (Chinoy and Jenkins 1987, ch. 6) The independent theater movement also gave rise to women's theater festivals. Although these theater groups disappeared in the 1980s, feminist theater activity continued and enjoyed a rebirth in the 1990s, particularly on college campuses and in cities such as Los Angeles, where a National Women's Theater Group organized a National Women's Theatre Festival in July 1992 (Breslauer 1992).

WET's *Electra Speaks* illustrates many of the features of the feminist theater movement and of works by women in other fields. This selection presents only two of the five women characters who appear in the full play. What is the purpose of WET's *Electra Speaks*? What is the significance of its authorship? What is the play saying through the depiction of Clytemnestra? Does Athena have any contemporary counterparts? The trilogy is derived from Aeschylus' *Orestia*.

The Daughters Cycle: Electra Speaks*

> The Daughters Cycle *is a trilogy of plays which centers on women within the family context. Every woman is a daughter. And the content of the trilogy springs from this reality. We look at the experience of mother, daughter, sister, the woman-self: the corridor of roles implicit in daughterhood.* . . .
>
> *. . . [Part III of the trilogy]* Electra Speaks *reaches back to the House of Atreus for the classic Western family. We call on Clytemnestra, Iphigenia and Electra in order to explore and challenge the myths of Mother/Daughter/Sister and the timeless assignment of women to vicious competition with one another and to victimization in relation to Men. In the characters of Clytemnestra and Electra we see the Mother and the Daughter as historical imperatives. But, they are also women and people. We see that, and it is here that possibility for transformation resides.*
>
> *Women have been silenced and recognize it. Across the globe, whatever the form, we recognize this silence. In* Electra Speaks *we attempt to name this universal silence and to give voice to women.* . . .
>
> THE OLD STORY. THESE ARE THE WORDS WE HAVE BEEN GIVEN. . . .
>
> *A recorded voiceover, ELECTRA's voice, tells "the old story" several times.*

The Old Story

> *The mother [Clytemnestra] has been at home with the children for the ten years that the father has been waging war. At the beginning of the war the father had sent for their*

---

*Excerpts from Clare Coss, Sondra Segal, Roberta Sklar (The Women's Experimental Theatre), "The Daughter's Cycle: Electra Speaks" (condensed), *Union Seminary Quarterly Review* 35, nos. 3 and 4 (spring-summer 1980), pp. 223–24, 226–27, 229–30, 237–39. By permission of *Union Seminary Quarterly Review*.

oldest daughter [Iphigenia], saying she was to be given in marriage to a war hero. But the marriage plan was a trick, and the daughter was killed at her father's command in order to make the winds favorable for his war voyage. The mother learns of the sacrifice of her daughter. The husband's betrayal leads her to take his life-long enemy as her lover and co-conspirator. She waits for his homecoming.

The father returns triumphant, bringing with him a woman as his mistress [Cassandra, the "other woman"], the spoils of war. In order to cleanse himself from the blood of those he has killed, he is prepared for the ritual bathing. As he stands naked at his bath, the wife raises her ax and slays him.

They say for years the younger daughter [Electra] obsesses on her father's death, longing to avenge his murder but unable to act. She waits motionless in her father's house, waits for her brother [Orestes] to return from exile. They say she persuades him it is his duty to avenge their father's death by murdering their mother and her lover. The son slays the lover first. Then he threatens his mother's life. She implores him to spare her. They say she bares her breast to him, reminding him that it was she who bore him, she who gave him sustenance. He stabs her with his blade.

The daughter disappears from the story here. Some say to marry her brother's best friend–some say to exile. She is not heard of nor spoken of again. The son is tried by the courts for mother murder. He is acquitted by the goddess Athena of the charge. She absolves him of all guilt and he ascends to his father's throne. . . .

CLYTEMNESTRA SPEAKS   ROLES: Mother, Daughter, Wife

WOMAN I: Clytemnestra speaks.

WOMAN II: I am Clytemnestra daughter of Leda some say my mother was the goddess of the night . . .

WOMAN I: I am Clytemnestra mother of Iphigenia, Electra and Orestes some say my daughters, Electra and Iphigenia loved their father best

WOMAN II: I am Clytemnestra daughter of Leda some say my father was King Tyndareus of Sparta

WOMAN I: some say my father was the god Zeus who changed himself into a swan and raped my mother at the side of the river Eurotas

WOMAN II: some say Zeus was a swan pretending to be an eagle took refuge with the goddess Nemesis, the protector of swans and ravished her

WOMAN I: they use that word ravished . . .

WOMAN II: some say the goddess Nemesis laid an egg of hyacinth hue which was tossed to earth and landed on my mother's lap while she was seated on a birth stool when the egg opened they say my sister Helen and I were born they say Zeus preferred birth from an egg because all of the blood of birth is contained cleanly inside an egg birth from inside a woman they say is impure

WOMAN I: I am Clytemnestra daughter of Leda who whispered to me out of her own mouth that I was born out of her own body

SHE states her case

I am Clytemnestra wife of Agamemnon, conqueror and king

Agamemnon who killed my first husband in battle

Agamemnon who tore my firstborn from my nursing breast and dashed my baby's head upon the rocks

Agamemnon who raped me I use that word rape and enslaved me as his wife . . .

ATHENA SPEAKS   ROLE: Daddy's Girl

ATHENA is *played by WOMAN III*

ATHENA *steps directly* [down center stage] *to the audience. SHE has a genuine investment in her point of view and argues it emphatically.*

ATHENA: Thank you. I'm glad I'm hearing this case. I've been waiting for this since I was in law school. I worked my way through law school. I had to work hard. Believe me, I know it's hard for a woman. But I did it. I know what it's like. I worked hard. I started out as an assistant in the D.A.'s office. I saw a lot of these cases there. I saw a lot of these women coming in with their sob stories. Now they're telling us, she got raped. Talking about how she got raped by Agamemnon. Frankly, I don't believe that. No woman—no woman is raped unless she wants to be. Look, I was followed home one night but I got out of it. I know it doesn't happen if you don't want it to happen. They say she was raped and then her first kid was killed. To me this is the first sign of her neglect. She abdicated responsibility for her children. Everybody is talking about how she was so upset about Iphigenia. I'm going to tell you who sent Iphigenia? If she felt so badly about it, why did she let her go? Why did she let her go? Agamemnon had to sacrifice her. Once she was there there was nothing else for him to do. He was motivated by the gods. But she didn't have to send her. It's really her fault. She sent her own daughter to be killed.

And here's this kid Orestes—her own son—he's been in exile for most of his life. She abandoned him, sent him away—threw him out of his own home. She sent him off to some stranger to take care of him—she didn't seem to care who was raising him. She had a new lover—that's all she cared about—took a lover. Brought him right into the house with her other daughter right there. . . .

This kid—this kid Orestes—have you seen him? He is an angel. He's got such a baby face. I feel so sorry for him. Where was this mother when he needed taking care of? I would like to know. Where was this mother. And you know in spite of everything— he had to be goaded into doing this. He didn't want to kill his mother. His sister egged him on. She was at him and at him to do it. It was not his idea. You know, the women in this family—they have pushed this boy. His mother got rid of him. His sister pushed him to murder.

And you're coming to me—telling me this court should take action against him— for murdering this woman. He did society a favor. Poor Clytemnestra. Poor Clytemnestra my ass! She let her daughter be killed. She took her own lover. She murdered her husband—the father of her children. She tried to take over his throne. This boy—this boy Orestes—he should be made king. He has saved us and the way we live. I tell you if that woman were alive today I'd haul her into family court.

She walks off self-righteously to be seated . . .

SUGGESTED READINGS

Art

Broude, Norma, and Mary D. Garrard, eds. *The Power of Feminist Art: The Movement of the 1970s, History and Impact.* New York: Harry N. Abrams, Inc., 1994, 1996.

Lucie-Smith, Edward. *Judy Chicago: An American Vision.* New York: Watson-Guptill, 2000.

Parker, Rozsika, and Griselda Pollock, eds. *Framing Feminism: Art and the Women's Movement, 1970–1985.* London and New York: Pandora, 1987.

Theater

Bassnett, Susan, ed. *Magdalena: International Women's Experimental Theatre.* Oxford, UK, and New York: Berg. Distributed in the U.S. and Canada by St. Martin's Press, 1989.

Canning, Charlotte. *Feminist Theaters in the U.S.A.: Staging Women's Experience.* London and New York: Routledge, 1996.

Music

Jill Halstead. *The Woman Composer: Creativity and the Gendered Politics of Musical Composition.* Aldershot, Hants, England; Brookfield, VT: Ashgate, 1997.

Osborne, William. "Art Is Just an Excuse: Gender Bias in International Orchestras." *IAWM Journal* (October 1996), pp. 6–14.

Audiovisual Sources

Zwilich, Ellen Taaffe. *Symphony No. 1: Three Movements for Orchestra; Prologue and Variations; Celebration.* New World Records, 1986. Compact Disc. NW336-2.

Women Artists: The Other Side of the Picture. 1999. Produced by Gillian Darling Kovanic. Directed by Teresa MacInnes. 54 min. Princeton, NJ: Films for the Humanities & Sciences, 1999. Videocassette.

Chapter 15

Contemporary Voices

This final chapter offers a tantalizing glimpse of the exciting work being done in diverse fields by creative women of various ethnic, racial, and cultural backgrounds. Again, we have included only a few examples from the vast array of accomplished contemporary women in the arts. Each of our examples has made distinctive contributions in her art form and has sought to express her own voice regardless of the pressures to conform to certain artistic, gender, ethnic, or cultural norms. In the process, each has continued to stretch the boundaries of her respective art form. Each woman has also sought through her particular art to facilitate social change, multicultural understanding, and a deeper awareness of the interconnectedness of the world and humankind. Note the importance of foremothers and/or family history to these women and how and why they draw upon the past. These women, like those we have met in previous chapters, illustrate the varied and significant ways in which women have shaped, and continue to shape, Western culture.

ART

Maya Lin (1959–): Sculptor, Architect, and Designer

Maya Lin is an innovative artist whose work defies the traditional boundaries that separate sculpture and architecture. She is best known for her public monuments and sculptures, especially her first work, the Vietnam Veterans Memorial in Washington, D.C. She was an unknown 21-year-old senior in architecture at Yale University when her design for the memorial was selected from the nearly 1,500 proposals submitted by artists in a nationwide competition. Soon after the design and its creator became known, a huge controversy erupted. Some veterans and prominent citizens attacked the wall design as a "black gash of shame" and demanded a more traditional marble sculpture. Soon after its completion, however, the Vietnam memorial became the most visited public monument in America and a place, as she had intended, with immense healing powers and the capacity to deeply move visitors.

Other commissions followed after she obtained her graduate degree in architecture in 1988, including the Civil Rights Memorial at the Southern Poverty Center in Montgomery, Alabama, and the Women's Table at Yale University. In the 1990s she designed private residences, renovated two floors of a building for New York City's Museum of African Art, and designed the interior of the Asian/Pacific/

American Studies Institute at New York University. She also does small-scale sculptures and has designed a collection of office furniture, based on African and Asian pillows and seats. Lin has created innovative sculptural landscape works: *Groundswell* at Ohio State University constructed of recycled glass poured into mounds that created a wave effect, and an earthwork and landscape sculpture called *Topo* on the approach to the Charlotte, North Carolina, Sports Coliseum.

Other commissions include a translucent clock sculpture, *Eclipsed Time* (Pennsylvania Station, New York City); a water wall installation with poetry, *Reading a Garden* (Cleveland Public Library); and a sculpture, *10 Degrees North* (Rockefeller Foundation, New York City). In *Timetable,* a sculpture at Stanford University, California, and *Wave Field,* a work based on turbulence studies of waves in flight at the University of Michigan's Aerospace Engineering Building, Lin explored connections between nature and science. She has also done sculptures and paintings (*Phases of Moon* and *Flatlands*) inspired by the National Aeronautics and Space Administration's topographical and satellite images of the earth and National Oceanic and Atmospheric Administration's images of the ocean depths.

She does extensive research for her projects, and collaborates with appropriate experts, from landscape architects, scientists, architects, and engineers to poets and historians. She develops her ideas by writing and then she models images (she shaped mashed potatoes while envisioning the Vietnam Memorial) (Lin 2000, 7:03). She seeks to make viewers aware of the world we live in.

Her work is shaped by her family and her Asian heritage as well as the environment. Both parents were born in China, but she grew up in Athens, Ohio. Her mother was a poet and professor of Asian and English literature, and her father was a ceramic artist and dean of the art school at Ohio University. Lin's art and designs were shaped by the art, furniture, and dishware he made for their home which reflected the Japanese and Chinese arts and crafts he had grown up with in his parent's home. At age 21, Lin learned that one of her aunts was an architect who, with her husband, designed Beijing's Tiananmen Square (Lamb 2000, 22).

SELECTIONS FROM MAYA LIN'S BOUNDARIES (2000)*

[Vietnam Veterans Memorial]

. . . I imagined taking a knife and cutting into the earth, opening it up, an initial violence and pain that in time would heal. . . . the initial cut would remain a pure flat surface in the earth with a polished, mirrored surface. . . . The need for the names to be on the memorial would become the memorial . . . .

It would be an interface, between our world and the quieter, darker, more peaceful world beyond. I chose black granite in order to make the surface reflective and peaceful. I never looked at the memorial as a wall, an object, but as an edge to the earth, an opened side. The mirrored effect would double the size of the park, creating two worlds, one we are a part of and one we cannot enter. The two walls were positioned so that one pointed to the Lincoln Memorial and the other pointed to the Washington Monument. By linking these two strong symbols for the country, I wanted to create a unity between the nation's past and present.

. . . until the memorial was built I don't think [the veterans] realized that the design was experiential and cathartic. . . . They didn't see that the chronology of the names allowed a returning veteran the ability to find his or her own time frame on the wall and created a psychological space for them that directly focused on human response and feeling. I remember one of the veterans asking me before the wall was built what I thought people's reaction would be to it. I realized then that these veterans were willing to defend a design they really didn't quite understand. I was too afraid to tell him what I was thinking, that I knew a returning veteran would cry.

[Civil Rights Memorial, Southern Poverty Law Center, Montgomery, Alabama]

I knew very little about the civil rights movement. I found it ironic that during my childhood I remembered there was more media attention on the war in Vietnam than on the battles for racial equality that were fought in our own country. . . .

. . . I spent months researching. . . . I was shocked by what I learned, but I was even more disturbed that the information I was learning about our history—events that were going on while I was growing up—was never taught to me in school. . . .

. . . I realized I had to give people an understanding of what that time period was about. . . . At the same time, I wanted to respond to the future and to the continuing struggle toward racial equality. . . . I came across a quote from Dr. Martin Luther King in his "I have a dream" speech: "We are not satisfied and we will not be satisfied until justice rolls down like waters and righteousness like a mighty stream." Immediately I knew that the memorial would be about water and that these words would connect the past with the future. . . .

What is inscribed across the top is a clockwise time line of the civil rights movement beginning in 1954 with *Brown* v. *Board of Education* and ending in 1968 with Martin Luther King Jr.'s assassination. The text forms a circle in time since a gap is left between 1954 and 1968, signifying that this time line is not closed and that we can only capture a part of that time.

Its design is inspired by a clock or a sun dial. . . . It intertwines events in the history of the civil rights movement with people's deaths. There are forty victims . . . whose deaths are listed here. . . .

In choosing to intertwine events with people's deaths, I was trying to illustrate the cause-and-effect relationship between them. The struggle for civil rights in this country was a people's movement, and a walk around the table reveals how often the act of a single person—often enough, a single death—was followed by a new and better law. . . .

The memorial was dedicated November 5, 1989. . . . Many participants in the movement were present as well as many of the victims' parents. . . . As they gathered around the circle, the circle closed and became more intimate, and as the tears that were shed fell onto the table and became a part of it, I realized we had all become a part of the shared experience of the memorial.

[Women's Table, Yale University, New Haven, Connecticut]

Initially I was asked to create a sculpture to commemorate the twentieth anniversary of Yale admitting women to its undergraduate class. . . .

[But] I found that there had been women at Yale from the very start; . . . even before they were technically allowed to enroll, women were allowed to sit in on classes, and they were called "silent listeners." I wanted to make them seen and heard.

My first sketch was of a circular table and a spiral of words. A spiral has a beginning yet has no end, which is how I saw what this piece had to accomplish: It had to mark a time when women started at Yale, but it had to incorporate infinity and growth. . . .

The use of numbers to count the women enrolled was very important. When women were first allowed into the undergraduate school, there was a strict quota on their enrollment numbers so that Yale could still graduate "a thousand Yale men"; the quota was bitterly disputed, and it took the administration seven years to drop the quota system. And it made the presence of women a battle over numbers.

The statistics department took more than a year to determine the total enroll-ment of women at Yale from when there were none to the present. At times it was quite difficult, since by the university's accounts certain graduate schools admitted women unofficially but listed them using their initials, and . . . records were simply hard to locate. The School of Art was the first department to admit women; thirteen were admitted in 1873.

The choice of the spiral allows the piece to display a set of historical facts, and these facts become a depiction of history. . . . The number of women at Yale grows ever larger, and though the spiral specifically traces Yale's enrollment figures, more generally it marks the emergence of women in modern society.

The Women's Table is also the only sculpture I know of with a footnote. The foot-note is for the date 1969: Yale admitted women into the undergraduate college. . . .

For once I was able to be a part of the piece; as a Yale undergraduate and gradu-ate student I am one of those numbers from 1977 to 1981 and from 1983 to 1986. . . .
[Personal Reflections]
Although I grew up almost completely oblivious to my Asian heritage, I have be-come increasingly conscious of how my work balances and combines aspects of my Eastern and Western heritages. I see my work as a voice that is of both cultures, pro-foundly tied to my Asian American identity. . . .

And I was naive about my racial identity . . . until after I had won the competi-tion to design the *Vietnam Veterans Memorial*. At my very first press conference a re-porter asked . . . "Isn't it ironic that the war in Vietnam was in Asia and you are of Asian descent?" I thought the question was completely racist . . . and completely irrelevant. . . .

[Then] an article came out in the *Washington Post* with the headline "An Asian Memorial for an Asian War." . . . it occurred to me to ask the veterans if my race mattered. They seemed embarrassed . . . and it was then that I realized that people were having problems with the fact that a "gook" had designed the memorial.

It left me chilled.

Sometimes a total stranger . . . will ask me where I am from. . . . I will respond, "Ohio," and the stranger will say, "No, no, where are you really from?" . . . [T]he question, however innocently it is asked, reveals an attitude in which I am left acutely aware of how, to some, . . . I am *not really an American*.

And I think it is that feeling of being other that has profoundly shaped my way of looking at the world—as if from a distance—a third-person observer. . . .

Amalia Mesa-Bains (1946–): Artist, Educator, and Activist

Amalia Mesa-Bains is a nationally renowned artist and speaker on Chicana/o art and culture, a curator, scholar, and community activist. She has received many distinguished awards including the Service to the Field Award (1992) from the Association of Hispanic Artists, New York. She was a 1992 MacArthur

Fellow, an honor referred to as the "Genius Grant," which includes a no-strings-attached grant from the John D. and Catherine T. MacArthur Foundation to support the recipient's creative endeavors.

Mesa-Bains was born in Santa Clara, California, and received a B.A. in painting at San Jose State University, and an M.A. and Ph.D. in clinical psychology from the Wright Institute in Berkeley, California. Her Ph.D. dissertation was on Chicana artists. Before assuming a position as director of the Institute for Visual and Public Art at California State University, Monterey Bay, she held a Regents professorship at the University of California, Irvine.

She has worked tirelessly to increase public appreciation of cultural diversity. Through scholarly articles, lectures, and her art, she has helped define an American and Latin American Chicano and Latino aesthetic and has delineated the cultural interconnections linking Indo-Hispanic, Afro-Hispanic, and Mexican traditions with contemporary Chicano life and art. To show the public how Chicano/a artists are exploring these links, she has curated exhibitions such as *Ceremony of Memory, Art of the Other Mexico,* and *Ceremony of Spirit.* She has also focused attention on issues of gender within the Chicano movement, delineating the ways in which Chicana artists (and non-artists) have struggled against patriarchal traditions for recognition, autonomy, and a share in leadership roles.

Mesa-Bains is also working to ensure opportunities for the next generation of Chicana/o artists and non-artists. She is involved with la Galaría de la Raza's Regeneracíon Project in which older artists work with young artists on community projects. With this approach she hopes to preserve her generation's method of combining art and social activism and to provide an antidote for the competitive individualistic training of most academic institutions. It is also a means of ensuring the inclusion of women, gays, and lesbians who have been excluded from or marginalized by the cultural establishment.

The following excerpts are from a video interview done in conjunction with her one-woman exhibition *Venus Envy Chapter III.* The show consisted of numerous three-dimensional installations that included paintings, sculptures, and objects comprised of a variety of materials.

VENUS ENVY CHAPTER III: CIHUATLAMPA, THE PLACE OF THE GIANT WOMEN (1997)*

> *Venus Envy* is in a sense an autobiography in a visual form; instead of chapters in a book, my chapters are related to exhibitions. I started it from early childhood by siting it in an event, my first holy communion, called *Chapter I: The First Holy Communion: Moments before the End.* It had to do with my relationships to the women in my family; my upbringing as a Catholic and that relationship to the feminine, to women, and to feminism. In a sense it was a kind of allegory, because it wasn't really about my first communion, but it was about the idea of young women raised in the church to think of themselves as brides of Christ; but from our earliest childhood we organize our lives around being married; belonging to someone, giving our selves, our bodies, our hearts to someone else. . . . Through a combination of objects, installations, and text I created a kind of discussion over the role of women in the church—what it was like to be brought up as a young Mexican girl—and personal

---

*Excerpts from Amalia Mesa-Bains, *Venus Envy Chapter III: Cihuatlampa, The Place of the Giant Women,* videocassette interview by Bernice Steinbaum for Exhibition at Steinbaum-Krauss Gallery, New York City, February 15–March 15, 1997. Video provided courtesy of Bernice Steinbaum Gallery, Miami, Florida. Transcribed and edited by Jean Gould Bryant. By permission of Amalia Mesa-Bains.

issues within women of my family historically, my grandmothers, and always siting it in the Ancient.

The second chapter was called *The Harem and Other Enclosures*. It was about life in the early years of my marriage. I visited the harem in Istanbul in 1997; it was a place that fascinated me for the same reason, domestic tension. It was a place of severe repression and ownership, but also a women's community, a place of relationships and solidarity. I had three areas in that too: the body sited in the harem; the spirit was the Virgin's garden . . . ; and the mind, sited in the library of Sor Juana de la Cruz, . . . a very famous colonial scholar in Mexico . . . who wrote . . . *La Respuesta* in a kind of dialogue with the church about the role of women as intellectuals. . . .

The third chapter, *Cihuatlampa, The Place of the Giant Women,* is the next part of my life; again a reference in the past. Cihautlampa was the place in Aztec cosmology that women were honored; [where] their spirits went to in afterlife when they died giving birth to children. That was considered an honorable death, comparable to a warrior. These very fierce women lived sort of suspended, like lost or mourning in the afterworld, but their job was to carry the sun to its setting. . . . I never had children. I wanted though to face up to that whole issue of why I wasn't able to have children. . . . So Cihuatlampa was a place that both attracted me and repelled me and I turned it into something else: I turned it into a place of giant women; women with really big spirits. . . . I wanted to refashion it, because I think that there are other things in the world that are of equal importance to having children for women, and so this idea that one has to give up one's life in that way in order to be a warrior was something I really wanted to put into question.

. . . Constantly in my work, there is a battle between very real critiques of class, and race, and gender, and sexuality, and politics, merged with my own faith and my own spiritual beliefs and practices which somehow don't always fit together; don't make sense, so I create these places in art works were they can kind of coincide.

I merged and blended the story of Cihautlampa and the women in the afterlife with . . . the story of the Amazons. . . . These women of Cihuatlampa were giant women like Amazons. They had a free country, a place where they could never be restricted and in which they could live on their own terms; they could live with men if they chose or without them. . . .

And part of [my art] is to investigate those situations in which women against their will are forced to live in conditions of oppression, but even in those conditions find a way amongst themselves to create community and to survive. These communities of women were similar to Sor Juana's who were intellectuals and scholars but were restricted in that period of time. I feel the same way about the harem as I did about the convent, and one would not see them as being parallel universes, yet in many ways they're similar in that they are at the service of a man—the sultan, pope, priest, or king—whatever you want to call them; they're women's communities who serve [men] on some level or another. . . . But these women—other than the twenty or so that would actually ever be on the level of having relations with the Sultan—the other 400 or so made up a community of women who wrote, who were librarians, who were dancers, singers, who lived a life.

I guess in a sense when I think of my own family I think about women who made choices in the only way they knew how in their generations. My grandmother came here during the revolution in 1916 as a twenty-year-old girl whose husband was executed in front of her. She had the responsibility of her three brothers, plus two infants under the age of three, and she came into this country speaking no English. She made her way, had more kids and survived. She lived in migrant camps and somehow through it all, she kept them together. And all the women in my grandmother's family were very strong and very connected to each other. . . .

So sometimes when I'm pursuing these issues in my own autobiography, which is just a form I'm using for speaking of a collective experience, I'm talking about a critique of patriarchy, but I'm also affirming the existence of women who somehow survive these difficult situations and make sense out of them for themselves and amongst themselves.

I feel that way about Chicanas that I've grown up with in the art community: [Judith] Baca, myself, and others. We've made our own community as artists, as activists; we've built community centers; our lives together have been part of a Cihautlampa to me. So in a sense, I begin with whatever the Aztec story is but that's really just a vehicle . . .

[Her Archaeology Table, 1997]

One of the devices I'm trying to use . . . is a concept of the archaeology of [my art]. So in the archeology room I'm creating these time lines that have to do with the objects in the show, but those objects in parallel to my own life and others who I site within that kind of time line reference. So my feathered cape is connected to an image of Ana Mendieta [a Cuban artist (1948–1985) who lived in the United States] covered in white feathers from a show that she did. I have Frida Kahlo's little deer sited with the Amazon's hunting dress. . . . I have these little time lines and all the archeology of my own installations on the shelves and all these little objects that I've been moving around from all the chapters of *Venus Envy*.

And that's the best part of this process: you're sifting through the remains of your own experience only it's not your own experience, because in fact it belongs to your peers, it belongs to your family, it belongs to women in your community, it belongs to intellectual mentors. . . . It makes most sense of course for me, because its my life, . . . but I also have hopes . . . that I'm making a line of thought, a body of knowledge, points in history, that have meaning for other people because I site them so frequently that sooner or later, even if you never studied colonial poetry of Mexico you would know who Sor Juana Cruz was and you would know that she had some relationship with Ana Mendieta, even if you never had reason to put them together; . . .

DANCE AND FILM

Jawole Willa Jo Zollar (1939–): Choreographer and Founder of Urban Bush Women

Jawole Willa Jo Zollar was born and raised in Kansas City, Missouri, where she was steeped from childhood in both sacred and secular aspects of popular African-American culture. She began her dance training with Joseph Stevenson, a student of Katherine Dunham. She received a B.A. degree in dance from the University of Missouri at Kansas City and an M.F.A. degree in dance from Florida State University. In 1980 she moved to New York City to study with Dianne McIntyre at Sounds in Motion.

In 1984, Zollar founded the award-winning Urban Bush Women (UBW), a dance company comprised of African-American, African-Caribbean, and African female dancers. Zollar and UBW received a 1992 New York Dance and Performance Award (BESSIE) for the company's collective work from *River Songs* (1984) through *Praise House* (1990). In 1994, UBW was the first dance company to receive the prestigious Capezio award for outstanding achievement in dance. In 1998, Zollar and UBW were awarded the Doris Duke Choreography Award for New Work by the American Dance Festival for *Hands Singing Song*. Zollar's work with the company has earned her three choreographer's fellowships and numerous other fellowships and grants, including two Inter-Arts grants from the National Endowment for the Arts. Zollar was featured in the PBS documentary *Free to Dance* which chronicles the African-American influence on modern dance. She and UBW have performed her works in leading American and international festivals and in venues across the United States. *Praise House,* which had its New York premiere in the 1991 Next Wave Festival at the Brooklyn Academy of Music, was also adapted for film, commissioned by CTCA-TV's series *Alive from OffCenter,* and directed by Julie Dash. She has created over 40 works for UBW, often in collaboration with artists from other disciplines. Her full-evening works include *Soul Deep* (2000); *Bones and Ash: A Gilda Story* (1995); *Praise House; Heat* (1989); and *Song of Lawino* (1988). Zollar's entertaining but thought-provoking works draw upon the music and dance of the African diaspora and African-American culture.

Zollar has received commissions to create works for the Alvin Ailey American Dance Theater, Ballet Arizona, Philadanco, and other institutions. She was also commissioned to design movement for Anna Deveare Smith's play *House Arrest,* produced by the Arena Stage (Washington, D.C.) and the Mark Taper Forum (Los Angeles) and to choreograph a revival of *St. Louis Woman,* produced at the Prince Theater (Philadelphia). She has been a resident artist/scholar at museums, art centers, and universities. Since 1996 she has spent part of each academic year at Florida State University where she is Nancy Smith Fichter Professor of Dance.

A Conversation with Jawole Willa Jo Zollar, 1999*

Jean Bryant: When did you discover you wanted to dance?

Jawole Zollar: Well, I started dancing very young because my mother was a dancer and so she got my sister and me in dance classes very young . . . I don't think that I understood that it was a possible career direction 'til I was in college, and there was a major in dance. That was just like, oh my goodness, you know, I'm majoring in dance. So the love of it was always there but I didn't even take seriously the love of it because I thought it was just something you kind of did for fun.

JB: What kind of training did you have?

Zollar: Well I think it was great because I got the training, from working within my community, of the dance forms that I think really gave me my character. Those were at the local dance school, what [the director] called Afro-Cuban dance, traditional jazz dance. . . . We learned the steps and the patterns but it was more about your expression as an individual, who you were . . . and what did you have that was unique. . . . It was really about developing that. But when I came to college, I studied modern

*From Jawole Willa Jo Zollar, interview by Jean Gould Bryant, tape recording, 1999; update 2002. By permission of Jawole Zollar.

and ballet. And it was in the studying of those forms that I started to embrace a professional career in dance, looking at not only what I was feeling, . . . but the technical facility I would need to be able to do that at its maximum.

JB: When did you found the Urban Bush Women and why?

Zollar: After I moved to New York. I think somewhere in the back of my head when I first took dance seriously as a career, I thought about having a company. But I think it's something that I just let be really, really far in the back. . . . I wanted to choreograph, but more than wanting to choreograph I was always interested in an ensemble that was training and thinking together. . . .

JB: You've talked about your training in Eurocentric forms and then seeking your own roots in African, Caribbean, African-American dance, but you said you came out of that tradition in your community. Did you have to return to that?

Zollar: I always carried it with me. I sought it out wherever I was. So that even when I was at Florida State University, I was part of the Black Players Guild. We did African dance, we did all, so I always made that a part of my experience wherever I was. I think I've always understood . . . that I was responsible for my own education, that the university had resources and was responsible for part of it, but I was not putting my education in the hands totally of the university and saying educate me. I picked a program that closest fit what my goals were and then I figured out what I needed to do to get the other part of my goals met that had nothing to do with university. . . .

JB: How did you select the first dancers for the Urban Bush Women?

Zollar: The first dancers were a pure group; two of them had gone to Florida State with me. We had gotten involved with Black Players Guild, started out in theater and so when we graduated we moved to New York, and we were all studying at the same place or around in some of the same circles. Then there were dancers that I'd met there. We were kind of these misfits and I just feel so fortunate because in looking at how I pick dancers, I pick dancers for who they were individually and their commitment to this exploration, to this journey. . . .

JB: Tell me about your creative process. How does a new dance happen?

Zollar: It varies, it is just not predictable. I just did a piece for a student and I started with the music. Sometimes it's an idea that's a nagging idea. My first piece, *River Songs,* was inspired by Jamaica Kincaid's work *At the Bottom of the River.* I just loved the idea of imagining if you lived in a river culture, what would women do at the river?

JB: When you did the piece with Jewelle Gomez, was that more of a collaborative effort?

Zollar: I had this idea for this piece called *Bones and Ash* for a couple of years before I found Jewelle's novel, and I knew it was about women moving through time. I didn't know what the mechanism was, [but] I knew it was about fairy tales or myth or mythology or something that was you know not quiet . . . I knew it was about black and Native American connection, and I had gotten a grant to explore the piece. I was just about to give the money back, and then I read Jewelle's book, and I thought this is the story I've been trying to figure out how to tell, so it came that way.

JB: We talked about art as a catalyst for social change, and certainly a lot of your pieces do that. Do you consciously start with that?

Zollar: I don't consciously start with it, it's just part of who I am. There are so many things that you see that disturb you but I don't think I could dance about all of those things that disturb me. The concert work of Urban Bush Women starts from creative chaos and wherever that lands. . . . The community projects start with a different objective and a different kind of creative process. . . .

JB: Do you see now that there perhaps is more of an emphasis or recognition of the value of the arts, for example in education?

Zollar: I think there's some degree of that emerging. . . . I think the definition of "at risk" needs examining because I think all of the kids are at risk. I challenge white dancers, "Okay, I know you may want to come and help us poor little kids in the inner city, but there's a lot of white kids who are at risk of being racists." And . . . I can't do that work as an African-American woman. It will take white people to do that work with white communities. . . . I can do work with women, it's going to take men to do that work with boys. And we've all got to step up to the plate of that challenge: . . . You don't do it in preparation to separate off. You do it so that we can come together, but it does need sometimes to be done separately. . . .

JB: If you could put together a group of people who you think would be most effective in addressing such community issues, who would you select?

Zollar: It's artists, it's scholars, it's community organizers, it's counselors, you know we need all of those voices for community projects, we need all those voices at the table. I think that we need each other's thinking. Unfortunately I think the artist has not been at the table, or when we have been it's in a dismissive way. Okay, so we're planning this conference and now you'll do the entertainment. We haven't been at the table in a real problem-solving sense. As people are meeting now all over the country trying to figure out [what to do], I'm not sure they're asking artists to be at the table. . . .

Deepa Mehta (1950–): Indian/Canadian Filmmaker

Deepa Mehta is an award-winning film director, producer, and screenwriter. She has produced educational films, documentaries, over 30 television specials, and 5 feature films. She was born in Amritsar, India, where her father was a film distributor and owner of several movie theaters. She received bachelor's and master's degrees in philosophy from the University of New Delhi. While a graduate student, she worked as an editor at Cinematic Workshop which made documentaries and educational films. She also met her husband, Canadian filmmaker and producer Paul Saltzman. At her suggestion, they moved to Canada and with her brother Dilip Mehta formed Sunrise Films.

Mehta's first film was a documentary, *At 99: A Portrait of Louise Tandy Murch,* that shattered myths about the elderly. The first feature film she produced and directed, *Sam and Me* (1990), won the critic's Honorable Mention at the Cannes Festival. The film, about a relationship between an aging Canadian Jewish man and a young East Indian immigrant, depicted prejudice based on age, class, culture, and color. She guest-directed an episode of George Lucas's *Young Indiana Jones Chronicles* in 1992 and directed the final episode in 1994. In the interim, she directed her second feature film, *Camilla,* reportedly the highest budget film ever directed by a woman in Canada.

Her most famous films consist of a trilogy, *Fire, Earth,* and *Water,* in which she examines aspects of Indian culture. *Fire,* about the politics of sexuality, tied for a Canadian award at the 1996 Toronto International Film Festival but generated angry protests and demands for censorship in India (Kirkland 1999). The film dealt with the realities of marriage for many women—silent domesticity. It also depicted a lesbian relationship between the wives of two brothers, in which the women found the intimacy and interpersonal connection missing in their marriages. *Earth* depicted the 1947 upheaval when India and Pakistan were partitioned and examined the dangers of nationalism, racism, class divisions, and religious intolerance that were the colonial legacy bequeathed the region by the British. *Water,* a story set in the 1930s about the tragic lives of Indian widows (some of whom were mere children), generated mass protests in the holy city of Varanasi in Benares when she began filming. She selected the location because it still had widow houses that women were forced to enter after their husband's death. She completed the film in 2000 in Bangladesh.

AN INTERVIEW WITH DEEPA MEHTA, 1993*

Q: Your films often reflect a sense of optimism within realism, for instance *Sam & Me,* and *At 99.* Is this a theme you've continued with *Camilla?*
A: Absolutely. The reason that I really liked *Camilla* when I read it was that it struck a chord in me. Other scripts I'd read hadn't done that to me. *Camilla* had. It was a story about two women, one older and one younger. One who hasn't given up on life and one who has. It was the young one who'd given up. So yes, I'd been sent several scripts and when I read *Camilla* I knew that I wanted to do it.

Q: How did you get involved with *Camilla?*
A: Christina [Jennings, producer] sent me the script. She had already approached Jessica Tandy who was very interested in playing one of the lead roles. She had told Christina that if she ever got the project together, she would do it. Of course when you get a star like that, the budget increases. I think the budget ended up being about eleven million. Once you start getting big stars like Jessica Tandy or Bridget Fonda, everything goes up. The insurance for Jessica alone put the budget way up, I believe. And she gets script approval, director approval, things like that. But I didn't feel any pressure by that. There was complete confidence from Christina and Simon [Relph, producer]. You hear rumors of there being back-up directors waiting to take over on these large budget films and things like that. But not once did they make me feel that there'd be someone standing there to take my job if I couldn't cut it. Not for a second.

Q: Were you nervous working with a big star like Jessica Tandy?
A: I was petrified. Are you kidding? And at first Jessica kept on saying, "Pardon me dear." And I thought that it must be my accent. I thought, "I've had it, I'm going to blow this because she can't understand a word I'm saying. It's going to be really intense." Then I discovered that she didn't have her hearing aid on. But yes, I was petrified. That goes away though. After about three days everything was fine.

*Excerpts from Janis Cole and Holly Dale. *Calling the Shots: Profiles of Women Filmmakers* (Kingston, Ontario: Quarry Press, 1993), pp. 138–42. © Janis Cole and Holly Dale, 1993. By permission of Quarry Press.

One thing that I really think helped, something I've learned from previous films, is to get rehearsal time. I'm sure it's obvious and that everyone does it, but I insisted on at least three weeks rehearsal. I find it very useful. I rehearsed with Jessica, Bridget [Fonda], Maury [Chaykin], and Elias [Koteas]. We discussed the arc of the characters, where they were going and why. Then by the time we started filming, nobody was coming up to me and asking, what's my motivation, or anything like that. So I found that very good.

Q: What was the jump like from a low budget independent film to an eleven million dollar picture?
A: On the first day of shooting, I get out there and it's petrifying. It really is. The crew was so big. There were so many people. I'd never seen that many people on a film set before. The first couple of days were difficult, but again, once we started working together it was just so smooth. Everyone that I was working with was so great, it went along smoothly. So it wasn't such a big jump really, not a noticeable one. The craft service was very good [laughs]. That impressed me. I thought, "This must be the big time, because the craft service is good and I can get cappuccino on set."

Q: Did it help that you had directed an episode of the *Young Indiana Jones* series between the two features?
A: Doing *Young Indi* helped prepare me in ways that I didn't even realize. Just the scope of it, it being a Lucas production. It was invaluable working on that show, and working with him. But it was also overwhelming. I mean there I am at his company, at Skywalker, cutting with George Lucas. And it was also funny at times. The phone would ring and I'd pick it up. One time a man asked me if George was there. I asked who he was, and he told me it was Steven. I handed the phone to George and I asked, "Is that Steven Speilberg?" George said, "Yes it is," and he just sort of looked at me like I'd arrived from the moon. It was very funny. And even when George first called me about the job it was very comical. I remember he called and right off the top he said, "Hello, this is George Lucas." I thought it was some kind of joke, and I said, "Ha, ha, very funny," and I put the phone down. I hung up on him because I didn't believe that it was really him. . . .

Q: Do you think that your films are distinctly Canadian?
A: Oh yes, I think they're really Canadian. They're idealistic. They're self-deprecating. I think they have a lot of suppressed anger.

Q: Do you think they reflect a woman's or East Indian's point of view?
A: They must. I am what I am. I am a woman. I am an East Indian. So my films must reflect that. Whether I'm making *Sam & Me,* which was a male cast, or *Camilla,* which is dominated by a female cast, I'll always bring my sensibilities with me. So I think that will always be there.

Q: How have things changed for women, especially women in visible minorities in the past twenty years?
A: I don't think it has. I really don't think it has. I think there are different problems. Things aren't any easier really. Maybe it will happen in the next ten years. Maybe it will change by the time my daughter grows up. But if you look at the number of women directing compared to men it's still so incredibly small. It's even the same for women working in Hollywood. I was reading an article in *Premiere Magazine* about

Nora Ephron. She really had to fight to get the opportunity to direct *Sleepless in Seattle,* and she's a highly respected screenwriter, and she's directed Meryl Streep and Jack Nicholson. But she really had to fight for it. So I don't think things have changed that much at all.

Q: Has anyone been influential in your career?
A: There aren't really any directors. As a person who has influenced me I would have to say that it has been Louise Tandy Murch from my film *At 99.* One day we were filming her in these yoga positions. She had done this head stand about three times. And I asked her what had made her take up yoga at her age. She told me that when she turned ninety, she had thought to herself that she really should take up something different, and that she thought it would do her some good. She was so eloquent. So strong. She really turned my head around. . . .

Q: What advice would you give to aspiring filmmakers?
A: Well, I guess I'd say don't take yourself too seriously. Patience. You have to have patience. Passion. Persevere. You must persevere and persevere and persevere. . . . What advice would I give? Nothing, probably nothing. You have to find it within yourself really.

LITERATURE

Sheila Ortiz Taylor (1939–): Poet and Novelist

Sheila Ortiz Taylor is professor of English at Florida State University, where she has taught women's literature, Chicana literature, the eighteenth-century novel, and fiction writing since receiving her Ph.D. from the University of California, Los Angeles, in 1973. Her first novel *Faultline* is considered the first Chicana lesbian novel. Her other publications include a volume of poetry, *Slow Dancing at Miss Polly's,* and novels, *Spring Forward/Fall Back, Southbound,* and *Coachella.* She has recently completed a new novel called *Extranjera.*

Her papers are in permanent repository at the California Ethnic and Multicultural Archives, Donald C. Davidson Library, University of California, Santa Barbara. She has been writer-in-residence at the Guadalupe Cultural Center, the Cottages at Hedgebrook, the Hambidge Center, the Dorland Mountain Arts Colony, and the Fundación Valparaíso. A former Fulbright Fellow, she is also the recipient of a Money for Women/Barbara Deming Memorial Fund Grant and a Florida Individual Artist Fellowship. The following excerpts are from her childhood memoir, *Imaginary Parents.*

IMAGINARY PARENTS. A FAMILY AUTOBIOGRAPHY (1996)*

Foreword

This book is made of bones. *La Huesera,* Bone Woman, crouching over the bones of the dead coyote, sings them back to life. I crouch over the bones of my parents, remembering and transforming. I strike attitudes, postures of innocence, reverence,

*Excerpts from Sheila Ortiz Taylor and Sandra Ortiz Taylor, *Imaginary Parents. A Family Autobiography* (Albuquerque: University of New Mexico Press, 1996), pp. xiii–xiv, 91–92. Text copyright 1996 by Sheila Ortiz Taylor; Art copyright 1996 by Sandra Ortiz Taylor. By permission of University of New Mexico Press.

amusement, anger, tenderness, mirth, fury. I accept what comes and the order in which it comes. All the ghosts that rise up are mine. I claim them. I am dancing with death.

Call this book autobiography. Or memoir. Call it poetry. Call it nonfiction. Or creative nonfiction. Call it the purest fiction. Call it a codex. Give it a call number.

I say it is an altar, an *ofrenda.* Small objects with big meaning set out in order. Food, photographs, flowers, toys, *recuerdos,* candles. *Pocadillas,* my grandmother would say. Scissors and paste, my father would say. *Bricolage,* my sister says. A miniaturist to the bone, Bone Woman insists on all the parts.

La Huesera. Who else am I, in this making?

A lawyer, like my father. I question, I return to the scene of the crime, search for weapons, motives, opportunities. I assemble the witnesses in the drawing room. And yet I cannot interrogate them; I can only heap up evidence.

I am a diver, too. Not in wet suit, mask, tank, knife. No, the kind of diver called from the village because she is known for her skill at swimming, because everybody knows this woman is running toward the river even before she has been told of the drownings. She is methodical. She swims back and forth across the river in an intricate pattern, her head disappearing below the surface, then reappearing. She is patient. Finding nothing, she begins a new pattern, one intersecting at different angles the old one. She is as committed to finding the drowned ones as if they were her own parents.

Call me Coyote too, driving my Selves too fast in weather too hot, through ambiguous zones of time, gender, and race with all the windows down. When you ask for my papers I hand you this book.

This book you hold, this *ofrenda,* like all altar art and most rescue work, was not realized in solitude. My sister and I have collaborated in this piece. She created the visual art and I wrote the text, . . . What remained constant and steadfast—in addition to a lifelong friendship—was our common vision of our parents as handsome, intriguing, perhaps unknowable people whose love affair with each other and with the strange southern California culture of the war years shaped them and us in ways we wanted to explore, critique, and celebrate with each other and with you.—*Sheila Ortiz Taylor*

Dinner 1947

My father is standing behind my chair, his hands on my hands as we allow the pressure of the steak knife to do its job. There is no need, my father explains, returning to his place at the head of the table, ever to exert pressure. Cutting meat is a question of control and weight, measure and balance. A person who knows the correct way to cut meat will never struggle.

I look at his mustache. There is a tiny crest of parsley resting just under his left nostril. I study my meat. If I lift my eyes from my plate, my sister's eyes will find mine. One of us will surely laugh.

My sister reaches for the milk pitcher. She is in dangerous territory. The pitcher may have been a little closer to Mother than to her. This miscalculation, together with the fact of the parsley just under my father's left nostril, has thrown her balance a little off. The milk brims up and over the rim of the glass, puddling onto the tablecloth. Mother and Daddy leap up at exactly the same moment and begin folding the tablecloth toward the center, like a flag. Nobody has said a word.

When they are settled back down in their places and our plates are resting on clean woven place mats, my father clears his throat and says in a calm tone, "Tomorrow, Hanny, I want you to take a glass and a pitcher of water outside and practice pouring." My sister does not look up. She hates to be called Hanny.

My mother is cutting her meat, exerting a little pressure, just on the verge of struggling. My father clears his throat. The parsley is still there. I try looking just past him, at the wall behind. The wall is painted blue up to my waist, then white, like a Mexican house. On the wall just to the side of my father's left ear hangs Pancho Villa's whip.

My mother has told me the story. Pancho Villa and his men riding up to the family's ranch house. Pancho Villa leaning down from his saddle. My mother scooped up in his right arm and held inside the sweet odor of sweat and trail. Pancho Villa arriving or leaving, she is not sure which. But amidst embracing and shouted greetings. And when Pancho Villa sets down my mother he lifts a long coiled whip of braided leather from his saddle horn and hands it to my grandfather, who accepts it in all honor. There it hangs on the wall just to the side of my father's left ear.

I cut my meat slowly and carefully, under my father's eye. The meat is tough. I chew, counting. Everything needs to be chewed a hundred times.

My sister raises her napkin as if to wipe her mouth and spits into it the impossible meat. Then she looks at the whip on the wall behind my father, lowers the napkin to her lap. She is remembering the other story of Pancho Villa's whip, the time when the whip still hung on the wall of my grandmother's house by the river and my Uncle Jimmy Doll came home from school, her youngest, beaten by the principal, crying.

My grandmother took that whip down from the wall, carried it coiled in her hand, walking all the way to Allesandro Street School, the school built on the land of her own people, carried that whip into the main office, called out the principal, whipped him as he had whipped her son.

My sister is feeling now my grandmother's brown hands on hers, the weight of her strong hands guiding her own, showing her the simple balance of justice.

Toni Morrison (1931–): Novelist and Nobel Prize Winner

Toni Morrison is recognized as one of the best writers of the twentieth century as well as one of the finest African-American writers. She is the first African American to win the Nobel Prize for Literature (1993). In the first 20 years of her career, she has published six novels and an important collection of essays, *Playing in the Dark: Whiteness and the Literary Imagination* (1992). She is also the author of an unpublished play, *Dreaming Emmet,* that was performed in 1996, and editor of *Racing Justice, Engendering Power: Essays on Anita Hill, Clarence Thomas and the Others on the Constructing of Social Reality* (1992). Her third novel, *Song of Solomon* (1977), won a National Book Critics Circle Award, and her sixth novel, *Beloved* (1984), brought her the Pulitzer Prize in 1988. She has been a member of the American Academy of Arts and Letters since 1981.

Morrison was born Chloe Anthony Wofford in Lorain, Ohio, where her parents had moved to escape the racism of the South. She was the second of four children in a working-class family, and the granddaughter of migrant sharecroppers. Her father transmitted his southern African-American cultural heritage to his children by telling them favorite folk tales. In 1949, she entered Howard University in Washington, D.C. After graduating with a humanities degree, she entered the graduate program at

Cornell University where she wrote a master's thesis on the theme of alienation in works of Virginia Woolf and William Faulkner. She was an English instructor at Texas Southern University (Houston) and Howard University from 1955 to 1957. Beginning in the mid-1960s, she was an editor for Random House, taught at several universities, cared for her children, and wrote her first novel. In 1984, she was appointed to a chair at the University of New York at Albany. Since 1989, she has been the Robert Goheen Professor of the Humanities at Princeton University. Throughout her career, Morrison has nurtured young writers, particularly African-American and fought to eliminate racism and sexism in academia, the publishing world, and in language. She helped shift the focus of literature about African Americans to women. Her works have also emphasized the diversity within African-American communities.

We have selected her Nobel Prize lecture as our final reading, because it offers a brilliant view of the meaning and power of language. Equally important, it brings together many of the themes we have followed throughout Volumes One and Two of *Creating Women*. Why is language important? What, to her, is the importance of foremothers? Of wise women? How does she envision the relationship between artists and their audiences? How does her story relate to female creativity in the past and in the future?

MORRISON'S NOBEL PRIZE LECTURE, 7 DECEMBER 1993*

"Once upon a time there was an old woman. Blind but wise." Or was it an old man? A guru, perhaps. Or a griot soothing restless children. I have heard this story, or one exactly like it, in the lore of several cultures.

"Once upon a time there was an old woman. Blind. Wise."

In the version I know the woman is the daughter of slaves, black, American, and lives alone in a small house outside of town. Her reputation for wisdom is without peer and without question. Among her people she is both the law and its transgression. The honor she is paid and the awe in which she is held reach beyond her neighborhood to places far away; to the city where the intelligence of rural prophets is the source of much amusement.

One day the woman is visited by some young people who seem to be bent on disproving her clairvoyance and showing her up for the fraud they believe she is. Their plan is simple: they enter her house and ask the one question the answer to which rides solely on her difference from them, a difference they regard as a profound disability: her blindness. They stand before her, and one of them says, "Old woman, I hold in my hand a bird. Tell me whether it is living or dead."

She does not answer, and the question is repeated. "Is the bird I am holding living or dead?"

Still she doesn't answer. She is blind and cannot see her visitors, let alone what is in their hands. She does not know their color, gender or homeland. She only knows their motive.

The old woman's silence is so long, the young people have trouble holding their laughter.

*Toni Morrison, NOBEL PRIZE LECTURE, 7 December 1993. Reprinted by permission of International Creative Management, Inc. Copyright © 1993 by Toni Morrison. Text from *www.nobel.se/literature/laureates/1993/morrison-lecture.*

Finally she speaks and her voice is soft but stern. "I don't know," she says. "I don't know whether the bird you are holding is dead or alive, but what I do know is that it is in your hands. It is in your hands."

Her answer can be taken to mean: if it is dead, you have either found it that way or you have killed it. If it is alive, you can still kill it. Whether it is to stay alive, it is your decision. Whatever the case, it is your responsibility.

For parading their power and her helplessness, the young visitors are reprimanded, told they are responsible not only for the act of mockery but also for the small bundle of life sacrificed to achieve its aims. The blind woman shifts attention away from assertions of power to the instrument through which that power is exercised.

Speculation on what (other than its own frail body) that bird-in-the-hand might signify has always been attractive to me, but especially so now thinking, as I have been, about the work I do that has brought me to this company. So I choose to read the bird as language and the woman as a practiced writer. She is worried about how the language she dreams in, given to her at birth, is handled, put into service, even withheld from her for certain nefarious purposes. Being a writer she thinks of language partly as a system, partly as a living thing over which one has control, but mostly as agency—as an act with consequences. So the question the children put to her: "Is it living or dead?" is not unreal because she thinks of language as susceptible to death, erasure; certainly imperiled and salvageable only by an effort of the will. She believes that if the bird in the hands of her visitors is dead the custodians are responsible for the corpse. For her a dead language is not only one no longer spoken or written, it is unyielding language content to admire its own paralysis. Like statist language, censored and censoring. Ruthless in its policing duties, it has no desire or purpose other than maintaining the free range of its own narcotic narcissism, its own exclusivity and dominance. However moribund, it is not without effect for it actively thwarts the intellect, stalls conscience, suppresses human potential. Unreceptive to interrogation, it cannot form or tolerate new ideas, shape other thoughts, tell another story, fill baffling silences. Official language smitheryed to sanction ignorance and preserve privilege is a suit of armor polished to shocking glitter, a husk from which the knight departed long ago. Yet there it is: dumb, predatory, sentimental. Exciting reverence in schoolchildren, providing shelter for despots, summoning false memories of stability, harmony among the public.

She is convinced that when language dies, out of carelessness, disuse, indifference and absence of esteem, or killed by fiat, not only she herself, but all users and makers are accountable for its demise. In her country children have bitten their tongues off and use bullets instead to iterate the voice of speechlessness, of disabled and disabling language, of language adults have abandoned altogether as a device for grappling with meaning, providing guidance, or expressing love. But she knows tongue-suicide is not only the choice of children. It is common among the infantile heads of state and power merchants whose evacuated language leaves them with no access to what is left of their human instincts for they speak only to those who obey, or in order to force obedience.

The systematic looting of language can be recognized by the tendency of its users to forgo its nuanced, complex, mid-wifery properties for menace and subjugation. Oppressive language does more than represent violence; it is violence; does more than represent the limits of knowledge; it limits knowledge. Whether it is obscuring state language or the faux-language of mindless media; whether it is the proud but calcified language of the academy or the commodity driven language of science; whether it is the malign language of law-without-ethics, or language designed for the estrangement of minorities, hiding its racist plunder in its literary cheek—it must be rejected, altered and exposed. It is the language that drinks blood, laps vulnerabilities, tucks its fascist boots under crinolines of respectability and patriotism as it moves relentlessly toward the bottom line and the bottomed-out mind. Sexist language, racist language, theistic language—all are typical of the policing languages of mastery, and cannot, do not permit new knowledge or encourage the mutual exchange of ideas.

The old woman is keenly aware that no intellectual mercenary, nor insatiable dictator, no paid-for politician or demagogue; no counterfeit journalist would be persuaded by her thoughts. There is and will be rousing language to keep citizens armed and arming; slaughtered and slaughtering in the malls, courthouses, post offices, playgrounds, bedrooms and boulevards; stirring, memorializing language to mask the pity and waste of needless death. There will be more diplomatic language to countenance rape, torture, assassination. There is and will be more seductive, mutant language designed to throttle women, to pack their throats like paté-producing geese with their own unsayable, transgressive words; there will be more of the language of surveillance disguised as research; of politics and history calculated to render the suffering of millions mute; language glamorized to thrill the dissatisfied and bereft into assaulting their neighbors; arrogant pseudo-empirical language crafted to lock creative people into cages of inferiority and hopelessness.

Underneath the eloquence, the glamor, the scholarly associations, however stirring or seductive, the heart of such language is languishing, or perhaps not beating at all—if the bird is already dead.

She has thought about what could have been the intellectual history of any discipline if it had not insisted upon, or been forced into, the waste of time and life that rationalizations for and representations of dominance required—lethal discourses of exclusion blocking access to cognition for both the excluder and the excluded.

The conventional wisdom of the Tower of Babel story is that the collapse was a misfortune. That it was the distraction, or the weight of many languages that precipitated the tower's failed architecture. That one monolithic language would have expedited the building and heaven would have been reached. Whose heaven, she wonders? And what kind? Perhaps the achievement of Paradise was premature, a little hasty if no one could take the time to understand other languages, other views, other narratives period. Had they, the heaven they imagined might have been found at their feet. Complicated, demanding, yes, but a view of heaven as life; not heaven as post-life.

She would not want to leave her young visitors with the impression that language should be forced to stay alive merely to be. The vitality of language lies in its ability to limn the actual, imagined and possible lives of its speakers, readers, writers. Although its poise is sometimes in displacing experience it is not a substitute for it. It arcs toward the place where meaning may lie. When a President of the United States thought about the graveyard his country had become, and said, "The world will little note nor long remember what we say here. But it will never forget what they did here," his simple words are exhilarating in their life-sustaining properties because they refused to encapsulate the reality of 600,000 dead men in a cataclysmic race war. Refusing to monumentalize, disdaining the "final word", the precise "summing up", acknowledging their "poor power to add or detract", his words signal deference to the uncapturability of the life it mourns. It is the deference that moves her, that recognition that language can never live up to life once and for all. Nor should it. Language can never "pin down" slavery, genocide, war. Nor should it yearn for the arrogance to be able to do so. Its force, its felicity is in its reach toward the ineffable.

Be it grand or slender, burrowing, blasting, or refusing to sanctify; whether it laughs out loud or is a cry without an alphabet, the choice word, the chosen silence, unmolested language surges toward knowledge, not its destruction. But who does not know of literature banned because it is interrogative; discredited because it is critical; erased because alternate? And how many are outraged by the thought of a self-ravaged tongue?

Word-work is sublime, she thinks, because it is generative; it makes meaning that secures our difference, our human difference—the way in which we are like no other life.

We die. That may be the meaning of life. But we do language. That may be the measure of our lives.

"Once upon a time, . . . " visitors ask an old woman a question. Who are they, these children? What did they make of that encounter? What did they hear in those final words: "The bird is in your hands"? A sentence that gestures towards possibility or one that drops a latch? Perhaps what the children heard was "It's not my problem. I am old, female, black, blind. What wisdom I have now is in knowing I cannot help you. The future of language is yours."

They stand there. Suppose nothing was in their hands? Suppose the visit was only a ruse, a trick to get to be spoken to, taken seriously as they have not been before? A chance to interrupt, to violate the adult world, its miasma of discourse about them, for them, but never to them? Urgent questions are at stake, including the one they have asked: "Is the bird we hold living or dead?" Perhaps the question meant: "Could someone tell us what is life? What is death?" No trick at all; no silliness. A straightforward question worthy of the attention of a wise one. An old one. And if the old and wise who have lived life and faced death cannot describe either, who can?

But she does not; she keeps her secret; her good opinion of herself; her gnomic pronouncements; her art without commitment. She keeps her distance, enforces it and retreats into the singularity of isolation, in sophisticated, privileged space.

Nothing, no word follows her declaration of transfer. That silence is deep, deeper than the meaning available in the words she has spoken. It shivers, this silence, and the children, annoyed, fill it with language invented on the spot.

"Is there no speech," they ask her, "no words you can give us that helps us break through your dossier of failures? Through the education you have just given us that is no education at all because we are paying close attention to what you have done as well as to what you have said? To the barrier you have erected between generosity and wisdom?

"We have no bird in our hands, living or dead. We have only you and our important question. Is the nothing in our hands something you could not bear to contemplate, to even guess? Don't you remember being young when language was magic without meaning? When what you could say, could not mean? When the invisible was what imagination strove to see? When questions and demands for answers burned so brightly you trembled with fury at not knowing?

"Do we have to begin consciousness with a battle heroines and heroes like you have already fought and lost leaving us with nothing in our hands except what you have imagined is there? Your answer is artful, but its artfulness embarrasses us and ought to embarrass you. Your answer is indecent in its self-congratulation. A made-for-television script that makes no sense if there is nothing in our hands.

"Why didn't you reach out, touch us with your soft fingers, delay the sound bite, the lesson, until you knew who we were? Did you so despise our trick, our modus operandi you could not see that we were baffled about how to get your attention? We are young. Unripe. We have heard all our short lives that we have to be responsible. What could that possibly mean in the catastrophe this world has become; where, as a poet said, 'nothing needs to be exposed since it is already barefaced.' Our inheritance is an affront. You want us to have your old, blank eyes and see only cruelty and mediocrity. Do you think we are stupid enough to perjure ourselves again and again with the fiction of nationhood? How dare you talk to us of duty when we stand waist deep in the toxin of your past?

"You trivialize us and trivialize the bird that is not in our hands. Is there no context for our lives? No song, no literature, no poem full of vitamins, no history connected to experience that you can pass along to help us start strong? You are an adult. The old one, the wise one. Stop thinking about saving your face. Think of our lives and tell us your particularized world. Make up a story. Narrative is radical, creating us at the very moment it is being created. We will not blame you if your reach exceeds your grasp; if love so ignites your words they go down in flames and nothing is left but their scald. Or if, with the reticence of a surgeon's hands, your words suture only the places where blood might flow. We know you can never do it properly—once and for all. Passion is never enough; neither is skill. But try. For our sake and yours forget your name in the street; tell us what the world has been to you in the dark places and in the light. Don't tell us what to believe, what to fear. Show us belief's wide skirt and the stitch that unravels fear's caul. You, old woman, blessed with blindness, can speak the language that tells us what only language can: how to see without pictures. Language alone protects us from the scariness of things with no names. Language alone is meditation.

"Tell us what it is to be a woman so that we may know what it is to be a man. What moves at the margin. What it is to have no home in this place. To be set adrift from the one you knew. What it is to live at the edge of towns that cannot bear your company.

"Tell us about ships turned away from shorelines at Easter, placenta in a field. Tell us about a wagonload of slaves, how they sang so softly their breath was indistinguishable from the falling snow. How they knew from the hunch of the nearest shoulder that the next stop would be their last. How, with hands prayered in their sex, they thought of heat, then sun. Lifting their faces as though it was there for the taking. Turning as though there for the taking. They stop at an inn. The driver and his mate go in with the lamp leaving them humming in the dark. The horse's void steams into the snow beneath its hooves and its hiss and melt are the envy of the freezing slaves.

"The inn door opens: a girl and a boy step away from its light. They climb into the wagon bed. The boy will have a gun in three years, but now he carries a lamp and a jug of warm cider. They pass it from mouth to mouth. The girl offers bread, pieces of meat and something more: a glance into the eyes of the one she serves. One helping for each man, two for each woman. And a look. They look back. The next stop will be their last. But not this one. This one is warmed."

It's quiet again when the children finish speaking, until the woman breaks into the silence.

"Finally," she says, "I trust you now. I trust you with the bird that is not in your hands because you have truly caught it. Look. How lovely it is, this thing we have done—together."

SUGGESTED READING

Art

Gumbo Ya Ya: Anthology of Contemporary African-American Artists. New York: Midmarch, 1995.

Hooks, Bell. *Art on My Mind: Visual Politics.* New York: The New Press, 1995.

LaDuke, Betty. *Women Artists: Multi-Cultural Visions.* Trenton, NJ: Red Sea Press, 1992.

Ringgold, Faith. *We Flew Over the Bridge: The Memoirs of Faith Ringgold.* Boston: Little, Brown, 1995.

Film

Juhasz, Alexandra, ed. *Women of Vision: Histories in Feminist Film and Video.* Minneapolis and London: University of Minnesota Press, 2001.

Unterburger, Amy L., ed. *Women Filmmakers and Their Films.* Detroit: St. James Press, 1998.

Literature

Anzáldua, Gloria, and AnaLousie Keating, eds. *This Bridge We Call Home: Radical Visions for Transformation.* New York: Routledge, 2002.

Minh-Ha, Trinh T. *Woman, Native, Other: Writing Postcoloniality and Feminism.* Bloomington: Indiana University Press, 1989.

Audiovisual Sources

Free to Dance, v. 3: "Go for What You Know." 2000. Produced and directed by Madison Davis Lacy. New York: National Black Programming Consortium, 2001. Videocassette.

Maya Lin: A Strong Clear Vision. 1994. Directed and produced by Freida Lee Mock. 98 min. American Film Foundation; Santa Monica, CA: Sanders and Mock Productions/Ocean Releasing, 1995. Videocassette.

Bibliography

Ady, Julia Cartwright. *Isabella d'Este, Marchioness of Mantua, 1747–1539*. Vol. I. London: J. Murray, 1903.

Alic, Margaret. *Hypatia's Heritage: A History of Women in Science from Antiquity through the Nineteenth Century*. Boston: Beacon Press, 1986.

Amore, Adelaide P., ed. *A Woman's Inner World. Selected Poetry and Prose of Anne Bradstreet*. Washington, D.C.: University Press of America, 1982.

Anderson, Bonnie S. and Judith P. Zinsser, eds. *A History of Their Own: Women in Europe from Prehistory to the Present*. Vol. II. New York: Harper & Row, 1988.

Andrews, Edward Deming. "Anna White." In *Notable American Women 1607–1950. A Biographical Dictionary*. Edited by Edward T. James, Janet Wilson James, and Paul S. Boyer. Cambridge, MA: Belknap Press of Harvard University Press, 1971. Vol. III P-Z, pp. 583–84.

Andrews, William L., ed. *Sisters of the Spirit: Three Black Women's Autobiographies of the Nineteenth Century*. Bloomington: Indiana University Press, 1986.

Arenal, Electa and Amanda Powell, eds. *The Answer/La Respuesta*, by Sor Juana Inés de la Cruz. New York: Feminist Press, 1994.

Bainton, Roland H. *Women of the Reformation in France and England*. Minneapolis: Augsburg Press, 1973

Bassanese, Fiora A. "Gaspara Stampa." In *Italian Women Writers. A Bio-Bibliographical Sourcebook*. Edited by Rinaldina Russell. Westport, CT; London: Greenwood Press, 1994.

Bell, Susan Groag and Karen M. Offen, eds. *Women, the Family, and Freedom: The Debate in Documents. Volume One, 1750–1880*. Stanford, CA: Stanford University Press, 1983.

Bernstein, Jane A. "'Shout, Shout, Up with Your Song!' Dame Ethel Smyth and the Changing Role of the British Woman Composer." In *Women Making Music: The Western Art Tradition, 1150–1950*. Edited by Jane Bowers and Judith Tick. Urbana and Chicago: University of Illinois Press, 1987.

Boroff, Edith. *An Introduction to Elisabeth-Claude Jacquet de la Guerre*. Brooklyn, New York: Institute of Mediaeval Music. 1966.

Bowers, Jane. "The Emergence of Women Composers in Italy, 1566–1700," In *Women Making Music*. Bowers and Tick, 1987.

Breslauer, Jan. "Sister Acts; A National Women's Theater Group, Formed to Put Feminist Issues in Center Stage, Finds a Second Home in Los Angeles." *Los Angeles Times*. 19 July 1992, Calendar section, p. 38.

Carter, Tim. "The Italian Baroque." In *Exploring Baroque Music*. Special Issue. *BBC Music Magazine*. 1997, 20–23.

Cerasano, S. P. and Marion Wynne-Davies, eds. *Renaissance Drama by Women: Texts and Documents*. London and New York: Routledge, 1996.

Chadwick, Whitney. *Women, Art, and Society*. London: Thames and Hudson, 1990.

Chinoy, Helen Krich and Linda Walsh Jenkins, eds. *Women in American Theatre*. New York: Theatre Communications Group, Inc., 1987.

Cook, James Wyatt and Barbara Collier Cook, eds. Antonia Pulci. *Florentine Drama for Convent and Festival. Seven Sacred Plays*. trans. James Wyatt Cook. The Other Voice in Early Modern Europe Series, Margaret L. King and Albert Rabil, Jr., eds. Chicago: University of Chicago Press, 1996.

Cott, Nancy F. *The Bonds of Womanhood: "Woman's Sphere" in New England, 1780–1835*. New Haven, CT and London: Yale University Press, 1977.

Criton, Marcia J. "Felix Mendelssohn's Influence on Fanny Hensel." *Current Musicology*. 37–38 (1984), 9–17.

Cropper, Elizabeth. "New Documents for Artemisia Gentileschi's Life in Florence." *Burlington Magazine*. 135 (November 1993), 760–61.

Current, Richard Nelson and Marcia Ewing Current. *Loïe Fuller, Goddess of Light*. Boston: Northeastern University Press, 1997.

De Baar, Mirjam and Brita Rang, "Historical Survey of Her Reception Since the Seventeenth Century." In *Choosing the Better Part: Anna Maria van Schurman (1607–1678)*. Edited by Mirjam De Baar, et. al. Dordrecht; Boston, London: Kluwer Academic Publishers, 1996.

Dersofi, Nancy. "Isabella Andreini (1562–1604)." In *Italian Women Writers: A Bio-Bibliographical Sourcebook*. Edited by Rinaldina Russell. Westport, CT: Greenwood Press, 1994.

Foster, Francis Smith. "Introduction." In Frances Ellen Watkins Harper. *Lola Leroy, or Shadows Uplifted* (1893). Schomburg Library of Nineteenth-Century Black Women Writers Series, Henry Louis Gates, Jr., gen. ed. New York: Oxford University Press, 1988.

Garrard, Mary D. "Artemisia Gentileschi: The Artist's Autograph in Letters and Paintings." In *The Female Autograph*. Edited by Domna C. Stanton. New York: New York Literary Forum, 1984.

Garrard, Mary D. *Artemisia Gentileschi. The Image of the Female Hero in Italian Baroque Art*. Princeton, NJ: Princeton University Press, 1989.

Gates, Joanne E. *Elizabeth Robins, 1862–1952: Actress, Novelist, Feminist*. Tuscaloosa and London: The University of Alabama Press, 1994.

Goen, C. C. "White, Ellen Gould Harmon." In *Notable American Women: A Biographical Dictionary*. Edited by Edward T. James, Janet Wilson James, and Paul S. Boyer. Cambridge, MA: Belknap Press of Harvard University Press, 1974. Vol. III, P-Z, pp. 585–88.

Haller, John S. and Robin M. Haller. *The Physician and Sexuality in Victorian America*. Norton Library. New York: W. W. Norton & Company, 1977.

Harriman, Helga H. *Women in the Western Heritage*. Sluice Dock, Guilford, CT: Dushkin Publishing Group, 1995.

Hayburn, Robert F. *Papal Legislation on Sacred Music: 95 A.D. to 1977 A.D.* Collegeville, MN: Liturgical Press, 1979.

Henderson, Katherine Usher and Barbara F. McManus, eds. *Half Humankind. Contexts and Texts of the Controversy about Women in England, 1540–1640*. Urbana and Chicago: University of Illinois Press, 1985.

Higginbotham, Evelyn Brooks. *Righteous Discontent: The Women's Movement in the Black Baptist Church, 1888–1920*. Cambridge, MA: University of Harvard Press, 1993.

Hill, Lorna. *La Sylphide. The Life of Marie Taglioni*. London: Evans Brothers, Ltd., 1967.

Johnson, Claudia. "Enter the Harlot." In *Women in American Theatre*. Edited by Helen Krich Chinoy and Linda Walsh Jenkins. New York: Theatre Communications Group, 1987.

Johnson, Rossiter and Dora Knowlton Ranous, eds. *An Anthology of Italian Authors from Cavalcanti to Fogazzaro, (1270–1907) with Biographical Sketches*. Literature of Italy, 1265–1907 Series. New York: The National Alumni, 1907.

Kearns, Martha. *Käthe Kollwitz: Woman and Artist.* Old Westbury, NY: Feminist Press, 1976.

Kelly-Gadol, Joan. "Did Women Have a Renaissance?" In *Becoming Visible: Women in European History.* Edited by Renate Bridenthal and Claudia Koonz. Boston: Houghton Mifflin, 1977.

Kelso, Ruth. *Doctrine for the Lady of the Renaissance.* Urbana: University of Illinois Press, 1956, 1978.

Kendall, Elizabeth. *Where She Danced.* New York: Alfred A. Knopf, Inc., 1979.

King, Margaret L. "Book-Lined Cells: Women and Humanism in the Early Italian Renaissance." In *Learned Women of the European Past.* Edited by Patricia H. Labalme. New York and London: New York University Press, 1984.

Kirkland, Bruce. "Will Earth Spark a Fire?" *Toronto Sun.* 7 August 1999. Reprinted, *www.canoe.ca/JamMoviesArtistsM/mehta_deepa.*

Lamb, Brian. "*Boundaries* by Maya Lin." C-Span Booknotes, 19 November 2000. *www.booknotes.org/Transcript/?ProgramID=1589.*

Lerner, Gerda. *The Creation of Feminist Consciousness: From the Middle Ages to Eighteen-seventy.* New York, Oxford: Oxford University Press, 1993.

Levinson, Andre. *Marie Taglioni (1804–1884).* Translated by Cyril W. Beaumont. London: Dance Books, 1977.

Lin, Maya. *Boundaries.* New York: Simon & Schuster, 2000.

Litzmann, Berthold *Clara Schumann; An Artist's Life, Based on Material Found in Diaries and Letters,* trans. and abridged from the 4th ed. by Grace E. Hadow with preface by W. H. Hadow. Vol. I (Reprint of the 1913 ed.) New York: Vienna House, 1972.

Manners, Victoria A. E. Dorothy. *Angelica Kauffmann, R.A., Her Life and Her Works, by Lady Victoria Manners and Dr. G. C. Williamson.* London: John Lane, 1924.

Marks, Elaine and Isabelle de Courtivron, eds. *New French Feminisms: An Anthology.* New York: Schocken Books, 1981.

McElrath, Joseph R. and Allan P. Robb. *The Complete Works of Anne Bradstreet.* Boston: Twayne Publishers, 1981.

Monson, Craig A. "The Making of Lucrezie Orsina Vizzana's *Componimenti Musicali,* (1623)," In *Creative Women in Medieval and Early Modern Italy.* Edited by Ann E. Matter and John Coakley. Philadelphia: University of Pennsylvania Press, 1994.

Neuls-Bates, Carol ed. *Women in Music. An Anthology of Source Readings from the Middle Ages to the Present.* Harper Torchbooks. New York: Harper & Row Publishers, 1982.

Numbers, Ronald L. *Prophetess of Health: Ellen G. White and the Origins of Seventh-Day Adventist Health Reform.* Knoxville: University of Tennessee Press, 1992.

Perlingieri, Ilya Sandra. *Sofonisba Anguissola: The First Great Woman Artist of the Renaissance.* New York: Rizzoli International Publications, 1992.

Prizer, William F. *Courtly Pastimes: The Frottole of Marchetto Cara.* Ann Arbor, MI: UMI Research Press, 1980.

Radycki, J. Diane. "The Life of Lady Art Students: Changing Art Education at the Turn of the Century." *Art Journal,* 41 (Spring 1982), 9–13.

Raney, Carolyn. "Francesca Caccini (1587-c.1630)." In *Historical Anthology of Music by Women.* Edited by James R. Briscoe. Bloomington and Indianapolis: Indiana University Press, 1987.

Raney, Carolyn. "Francesca Caccini's Primo Libro." *Music and Letters.* 48, no. 4 (October 1967), 350–57.

Raser, Harold E. *Phoebe Palmer, Her Life and Thought.* Lewiston, NY: E. Mellen Press, 1987.

Reich, Nancy B. *Clara Schumann. The Artist and the Woman.* Ithaca and London: Cornell University Press, 1985.

Rosand, Ellen. "Barbara Strozzi, *virtuosissima cantatrice:* The Composer's Voice." *Journal of the American Musicological Society* 31 (1978), 241–81.

Rossi, Alice S., ed. *The Feminist Papers from Adams to de Beauvoir.* New York and London: Columbia University Press, 1973.

Rubinstein, Charlotte Streifer. *American Women Sculptors: A History of Women Working in Three Dimensions.* Boston: G. K. Hall & Co., 1990.

Schwarzer, Alice. *After the Second Sex: Conversations with Simone De Beauvoir.* Translated by Marianne Howarth. New York: Pantheon Books, 1984.

Shelley, Mary. *The Journals of Mary Shelley, 1814–1844. Vol. II: 1822–1844.* Edited by Paula R. Feldman and Diana Scott-Kilvert. Oxford: Oxford University Press, 1987.

Silbert, Doris. "Francesca Caccini, Called La Cecchina." *Musical Quarterly* 32 (1946), 50–62.

Smyth, Ethel. *Impressions That Remained: Memoirs.* Vol. 2. London and New York: Longmans, Green, and Co., 1923.

Stewart, Andrew. "This Issue's CD." In *The Glory of Venice.* Special Issue. *BBC Music Magazine* (1999), 9–13.

Talbot, Michael. "Viva Vivaldi." In *The Glory of Venice.* Special Issue. *BBC Music Magazine* (1999), 49–52.

Thurman, Judith. "Louise Labe: Still Scandalous After 400 Years." *Ms.* 8 (March 1980).

Travitsky, B. S. and A. L. Prescott, eds. *Female and Male Voices in Early Modern England.* New York: Columbia University Press, 2000.

Trecker, Janice Law. "Sex, Science, and Education." *American Quarterly* 26 (1974), 352–366.

Washington, Mary Helen, "Forward." In *Their Eyes Were Watching God* by Zora Neale Hurston. Perennial Library. New York: Harper & Row, 1990.

Weaver, Elissa. "Spiritual Fun: A Study of Sixteenth-Century Tuscan Convent Theater." In *Women in the Middle Ages: Literary and Historical Perspectives.* Edited by Patricia H. Labalme. Syracuse, NY: Syracuse University Press, 1986.

Welter, Barbara. *Dimity Convictions: The American Woman in the Nineteenth Century.* Athens, OH: Ohio University Press, 1976.

White, Charles E. *The Beauty of Holiness: Phoebe Palmer as Theologian, Revivalist, Feminist, and Humanitarian.* Grand Rapids, MI: F. Asbury Press, 1986.

Wilson, Katharina M. and Frank J. Warnke, eds. *Women Writers of the Seventeenth Century.* Athens: University of Georgia Press, 1989.

Woolf, Virginia. *A Room of One's Own.* New York and London: Harcourt Brace Jovanovich, 1929.